in book not on card

1st ED
8.50
O.P. R4P
AMN2
J

D1207821

The Racial Attitudes of American Presidents

The Racial Attitudes of American Presidents

From Abraham Lincoln to Theodore Roosevelt

GEORGE SINKLER

Doubleday & Company, Inc., Garden City, New York

1971

Library of Congress Catalog Card Number 74-139061
Copyright © 1971 by George Sinkler
All Rights Reserved
Printed in the United States of America
First Edition

To my wife and my mother

ACKNOWLEDGMENTS

The writer wishes to express his sincere appreciation to the staffs of the Manuscripts Division of the Library of Congress, Washington, D.C., the Rutherford B. Hayes Memorial Library, Fremont, Ohio, and the W. R. Banks Library, Prairie View, Texas, for their assistance in the research for this book. He also wishes to thank Professors Erling M. Hunt and Alice W. Spieseke of Teachers College, Columbia University. He is especially grateful to Professor F. C. Kershner, Jr., also of Columbia, for his suggestions, criticisms, encouragement and assistance far above and beyond the call of duty. The Southern Fellowships Fund, the John Hay Whitney and Danforth Foundations generously supported the graduate study, the research and the writing necessary for this book. The late Parry Rout, Doris V. Hawkes and Friederike Dewitz performed invaluable typing services. The encouragement and technical services of my editors, Loretta Barrett and her staff, earned my gratitude. At every stage of these operations, Albertha Sinkler provided all of the necessary concern and understanding.

Baltimore, Maryland G. S.
January 1971

Contents

The Racial Attitudes of American Presidents

Preface

The chief objective of this investigation is to ascertain the racial views of American Presidents during a selected period of history. The major emphasis has been placed on the black American, the largest racial minority in America, but not to the exclusion of other racial groups. In 1944, a Swedish social scientist, Gunnar Myrdal, stated in an important study of the dilemma of race in America that the core of the black—or white—problem in the United States may be found in the Caucasian fear of amalgamation. A secondary purpose of this book is to determine the extent to which Myrdal's anti-amalgamation hypothesis was supported in the racial rhetoric of the Presidents covered in this study. A final and perhaps pervasive aim is to obtain additional insight into the dynamics of race adjustment, and to determine the extent to which ideas of race influenced the general thinking and political behavior of these Presidents.

Being under no illusion about the difficulties of relating thought to action, theory to practice, the author has limited the book primarily to what the Presidents *said* about race and is only secondarily concerned with what they *did*. Discerning accurately the relationship between thought and action may well be beyond the scope of the historical method. Yet, the two things can hardly be divorced, and so some attempt has been made to explain certain actions of the Presidents in terms of their ideas on race.

This book begins with the presidency of Abraham Lincoln and ends with the Administration of Theodore Roosevelt for a number of reasons. The election of Lincoln to the presidency in 1860 ushered in a critical era in American history. For matters of race the period from 1860 to the turn of the century proved to be very crucial. After the outbreak of the Civil War the black question, the Indian question, the Chinese question, the Japanese question, the Filipino question, and even the intraracial ethnic question, each had its turn upon the national stage. War, Reconstruction, reunion, reaction, all had racial overtones. If any question has been perennial in American history it is the race question. The freeing of more than 3,500,000 slaves as a result of the Civil War forced again upon Americans between 1860 and 1900, and in a most intense way, the long smoldering black question. The problem of race was certainly present and the period was a most fertile one for the expression of racial views.

Since the race question is such a persistent theme in American history, this study could well have extended itself to the present. On the other hand, Theodore Roosevelt provides a good terminating point. Chronologically he comes into the presidency at the end of an era and the beginning of another. He may be seen as a transitional figure between the nineteenth and twentieth centuries. Finally, the turn of the century marks the appearance of the more enlightened anthropology of Franz Boas, which provided the foundation for a potentially more positive racial thought.

For the sake of continuity the Presidents have been presented in chronological order. The assumption that "human thought arises and operates in a definite social milieu" becomes crucial in any investigation of the ideas of men.[1] For that reason this study includes a brief survey of racial thought in the United States from 1809, the birth of Lincoln, to 1909, the conclusion of the presidency of Theodore Roosevelt. The incoming cor-

[1] Karl Mannheim, *Ideology and Utopia: An Introduction to the Sociology of Knowledge* (New York: Harcourt, Brace and Co., 1936), p. 71.

respondence of the Presidents also provides additional illumination of the racial climate of opinion.

No historical study can be stronger than the sources upon which it rests. The published and manuscript papers of the Presidents represent the sources for this investigation. There are printed collections of the papers of all the Presidents treated here except Chester A. Arthur. Since published collections must of necessity be highly selective, liberal supplementary use was made of the manuscript collections of the papers of the Presidents in the Library of Congress. Books and periodicals contemporary to the period under study, as well as relevant secondary works, provided the materials for assessing the racial nature of the times in which these men lived. Again, the incoming mail of the Presidents was revealing and racially significant.

CHAPTER I

A Perspective on Race

The major portion of the problem of race relations in the United States has been the friction between black and white. While this proposition may seem sociological, it is easily documented historically. Men of the latter part of the nineteenth century, no less than their forebears, were well aware of the problem of race difference. As one contemporary writer of that period said, the race question in its utter simplicity was the problem of living with human beings who were not "like us."[1] Americans of this era, while they took for granted that Europeans would eventually become assimilated, did not as readily associate the melting-pot idea with the Afro-American. Instead, the Africans, and to a lesser extent Orientals, were put aside as unassimilable. Later, it was Myrdal's thesis that this predication of the Caucasian of no racial intermixture with colored peoples gave the black question its unique place among American minority problems.

Myrdal further felt that for the average white man, fear of amalgamation was the heart of the Negro problem. Racial crossing was thought undesirable. The anti-amalgamation doctrine posited the biological inferiority of the Afro-American stock and included strong social sanction against intermarriage. These beliefs were held in the North and the South but probably more tenaciously in the latter. "The boundary between

[1] Ray Stannard Baker, *Following the Color Line: An Account of Negro Citizenship in the American Democracy* (New York: Doubleday, Page and Co., 1908), p. 292.

Negro and white is not simply a class line. . . . [It] . . . is fixed. It is not simply a temporary expediency. . . . It is a bar created with the intention of permanency," Myrdal concluded, perhaps too strongly.[2]

The major purpose of the white man's theory of caste, according to Myrdal, was to guard the rampart of race purity. Social equality, particularly in the South, was rejected in order to lessen the chances of miscegenation and make intermarriage well-nigh impossible. The inner sanctum of race purity was carefully hedged about with myriad patterns of segregation and discrimination.[3]

Not all scholars believe that fear of intermarriage is the nucleus of the race problem. Nevertheless, it is true that unlike the whites in some other countries the American Caucasian, prior to the Civil War, consistently frowned upon absorption of the free mulatto into the white population. All known products of miscegenation were always relegated to the dark side of the union.[4] Myrdal saw the Negro problem as essentially a moral one involving a sometimes painful awareness of the discrepancy between America's code of values and social realities. This position has been criticized.[5] Yet, when it is observed that intermarriage and matters of social intimacy with blacks are regarded by much of white public opinion as somehow having to do with morality, Myrdal may not have gone too far afield.

Perhaps in no other area of Western thought are inherent

[2] Gunnar Myrdal, *An American Dilemma: The Negro Problem and Modern Democracy* (New York: Harper and Brothers, 1944), I, 54–58; Ulrich B. Phillips, "The Central Theme of Southern History," *The Course of the South to Secession: An Interpretation*, ed. by E. Merton Coulter (New York: D. Appleton-Century Co., 1939), p. 152. Phillips told the American Historical Association in 1928 that what gave unity to the South was ". . . a common resolve . . . that it shall be and remain a white man's country. . . . The consciousness of . . . these premises . . . is the cardinal test of a Southerner and the central theme of Southern history."

[3] Ibid.

[4] Abraham Harris and Sterling Spero, "The Negro Problem," *Encyclopedia of the Social Sciences*, XI, 335–36. New York: Macmillan Company, 1933.

[5] Merle Curti, *The Growth of American Thought* (New York: Harper and Brothers, 1943, 1951), p. 786.

contradictions and ambivalences more apparent than in the domain of race.[6] But the psychological self is not necessarily a unified and integrated whole. Instead, it is a host of complex attitudes learned in relation to persons, social institutions, things, groups, and norms with which one has been in contact. It is possible, then, for ambivalent attitudes and actions to be entirely consistent not only with one's own personality but even with the nature of the society in which he lives.[7]

With the exception of Theodore Roosevelt, the Presidents in this book paid little attention to the biology of race. Their racial ideas, then, cannot be properly understood solely in terms of scientific conceptions of biological difference, for it was the social conditions and historical experiences of the period that combined to give rise to their race rhetoric.[8] No other justification for the historical approach to the problem of race is necessary.

In approaching the literature of race, some attention to race terminology is necessary. In this book, the term *race* shall be interpreted to mean whatever the people of the particular period chose to call a race. The term was used loosely and broadly in this era to describe any group of people who were regarded and treated in actual life as a distinctive biological group with a common ancestry as well as psychological, cultural, social, and even national characteristics. The Presidents and their contemporaries thought in terms of this social conception of race and seldom with reference to scientific biological conceptions.

[6] Melvin Conant, *Race Issues on the World Scene: A Report on the Conference on Race Relations in a World Perspective* (Honolulu: University of Hawaii Press, 1955), p. 130. "These contradictions are represented in the belief in human equality of Christendom and the concept of political freedom and, in contrast, the undeniable expressions of racism and race superiority which have developed in so many areas over which Western man has extended his control."

[7] Muzafer Sherif, "The Problem of Inconsistency in Intergroup Relations," *Journal of Social Issues*, 5:36, No. 3 (1949).

[8] Andrew Lind (ed.), *Race Relations in a World Perspective: Papers Read at the Conference on Race Relations in World Perspective* (Honolulu: University of Hawaii Press, 1955), p. 7. E. Franklin Frazier, *Race and Cultural Contacts in the Modern World* (Durham: Duke University Press, 1940), p. 31.

Hence, a sociological conception of race was found to be more useful for this author.[9]

An ideology is a system of thought, a social belief or an idea that is strong enough to form the basis of negative or positive social thought or action. While none of the Presidents, except perhaps Roosevelt, had anything approaching a racial ideology, much of the racial thought of the times exhibited ideological characteristics. When the idea of race was used and put to some definite end in racial literature, it had become, according to Mannheim, an ideology.[10]

Racial ideology, carried to its logical or illogical extreme, became *racism.* Where racism was a strongly held creed it was also an emotional attitude. The racist believed that mankind was made up of genetically different races, relatively pure. He believed that mental and physical characteristics of people were determined biologically by the race to which they belonged; hence he was against intermarriage of races because he felt that the fruits of such unions were degenerate. He did not care for hybrids.[11] While the Presidents of this period were not racists (though a case might be made against Roosevelt) in the full sense of the word, the term was useful because much of the racial thought of the period took just such form.

The terms *race prejudice* and *race consciousness* were found to be useful in connection with the Presidents of this study. In

[9] Myrdal, *An American Dilemma,* I, 115. Lind, *Race Relations in World Perspective,* pp. 4, xi. "The evolution of the concept of race is social as well as biological," says Earl Count in "The Evolution of the Race Idea in Modern Western Culture During the Period of the Pre-Darwinian Nineteenth Century," *Transactions* of the New York Academy of Sciences, 8:163 (January 1946). Sir James A. H. Murry, *A New English Dictionary on Historical Principles* (Oxford: Clarendon Press, 1914), VIII, 87. Mitford M. Mathews (ed.), *A Dictionary of Americanisms on Historical Principles* (Chicago: University of Chicago Press, 1957), I, 1346.

[10] Karl Mannheim, *Ideology and Utopia,* pp. 67, 71. Hannah Arendt, "Race Thinkers Before Racism," *The Review of Politics,* 6:38 (January 1944). Ralph Bunche, "Conceptions and Ideologies of the Negro Problem," (New York: New York Public Library, Schomburg Collection, 1944), p. 12 (typewritten).

[11] G. P. Malalasekera, et al., *The Race Question and Modern Thought: Buddhism and the Race Question* (Paris: UNESCO, 1958), IV, 21–22; United Nations Educational, Scientific and Cultural Organization, *The Race Question in Modern Science: The Race Concept* (Paris: UNESCO, 1952), IX, 5; Ruth Benedict, *Race, Science and Politics* (New York: Modern Age Books, 1940), p. 122.

the past, as now, race prejudice involved a preferential dislike of various races based on assumptions of racial superiority from the standpoint of biology and culture.[12] Historically the term *race consciousness* for Americans implied an awareness of racial identity to the extent that it would keep one from too close an association with other races, at least not to the point of amalgamation.[13] In this sense, all of the Presidents considered here were race conscious, though not all of them shared completely the biases usually associated with race prejudice. Roosevelt was the only President of this group to express a belief in "race suicide," the gradual disappearance of race, especially through the voluntary failure of its members to produce offspring in sufficient numbers.[14]

Finally, a *stereotype* is a ready-made definition, a preconceived, fixed impression in one's mind which is stronger than the facts it pretends to observe. It is not difficult to see the close relationship between the "stereotype" and race prejudice. Since they permit economy of effort and attention in perception and expression, stereotypes are not necessarily bad things. However, their character and the perceptiveness with which they are employed are of crucial importance. Walter Lippmann, for a later day, warned against the failure to separate the "instinctive equipment" from the stereotype when discussing the mentality of a people. Such a failure had caused "oceans of loose talk about . . . race psychology." The race literature of the period under study was certainly overrun with "oceans of loose talk. . . ." A stereotype is seldom neutral when it represents a defense of tradition or position. When threatened it becomes highly charged with emotion. Much stereotyped racial thought, in defense of tradition and position, found its way

[12] Sir William A. Craigie and James R. Hulbert, A *Dictionary of American English on Historical Principles* (Chicago: University of Chicago Press, 1902), III, 1880. In America race prejudice meant bias against people of another race, especially against Negroes. Baker, *Following the Color Line*, p. 297, described race prejudice in 1908 as "repulsion of the unlike"; Eleanor E. MacCoby, et al., *Readings in Social Psychology* (New York: Henry Holt and Company, 3rd ed., 1958), p. 41. William Ogburn and Meyer Nimkoff, *Sociology* (Boston: Houghton Mifflin and Co., 1950), pp. 81–82.

[13] Mathews, A *Dictionary of Americanisms* . . . I, 1346.

[14] Ibid.

into the incoming correspondence of the Presidents of this study.[15] But what have American Presidents to do with race? one might ask.

Presidential Responsibility

Implicit in this study is the assumption that the Presidents had a role to play, a responsibility in race relations. In the nineteenth century as much as in the twentieth it was the unmistakable duty of the Presidents to use the moral prestige as well as the actual powers of their office to defend the Constitution and to execute the laws in letter and in spirit. How well the Presidents of this period discharged their responsibility for the enforcement of the Civil War amendments, for putting down domestic violence, and for leadership of public opinion in matters of race, would have to figure in any attempt to assay a judgment of their performance. A statement made in 1961 has relevance for much of the post-Civil War period in American history. ". . . Nowhere," says Professor Longaker, "has the distance between the Constitutional dream and social reality been more noticeable than in American race relations."[16]

The national government, through the President, has a constitutional responsibility to protect the states from domestic violence. There is evidence that in matters not involving race, the Presidents from Hayes through Roosevelt used troops effectively and successfully to put down civil disorder. However, they did this with great reluctance and, with the exception of Cleveland, not without a request from the governors of the states involved. After Reconstruction, it was highly unlikely that a Southern governor would make such a request in matters of race. It is possible to reason from the experience of the Presidents with labor troubles that under any circumstance the Chief

[15] Walter Lippmann, *Public Opinion* (New York: Harcourt, Brace and Company, 1922), pp. 90–104. This discussion of stereotype is based almost solely upon materials in this source; MacCoby, *Readings in Social Psychology*, p. 41.

[16] Richard P. Longaker, *The Presidency and Individual Liberties* (Ithaca, N.Y.: Cornell University Press, 1961), pp. 7, 31, 32.

Executives were reluctant to call out troops against the people. In matters of race, they were doubly hesitant.[17]

Leonard D. White has characterized the Republican era, 1869–1901, as one of progressive enfeeblement of the Executive in the face of a dominant Congress.[18] He concludes that not until McKinley and Roosevelt did the presidential prerogative return to the White House.[19] If the Presidents considered in this book were generally weak, then perhaps dynamic action from them in matters of race could not be expected. Rayford Logan concludes that the victory of white supremacy in the South and the alleged Northern acquiescence in that triumph were facilitated by "a succession of weak Presidents between 1877 and 1901."[20]

It does not necessarily follow that relatively weak Presidents failed to act because of personal prejudice or that they approved of what had been done in the South. Any talk about the absence of presidential vigor or prerogative in matters of race must be tempered by the realization that the Republican era was an age dominated by the concept of laissez faire in regard to federal-state relations as well as in economics. Direct action by the federal government in behalf of the people was not yet an established or accepted precedent. In regard to civil rights it must not be overlooked that a series of Supreme Court decisions beginning with the Slaughterhouse Cases had said that such matters were properly the prerogative of the states.[21] Nor did general public indifference to national affairs, noted by White, necessarily mean approval of the Southern subordination of black people, even though it was true that Roosevelt once asserted that this was indeed the case.[22]

[17] Bennet Milton Rich, *The Presidents and Civil Disorder* (Washington: Brookings Institution, 1941), pp. 72–109, 125, 135, 189, 219.

[18] Leonard D. White, *The Republican Era: 1869–1901: A Study in Administrative History* (New York: Macmillan Company, 1958), p. 46.

[19] Ibid., pp. 43, 395–96; ibid., pp. 20–28. White further contends that the Republican theory of the presidency was the subordination of the executive to the will of Congress.

[20] Rayford Logan, *The Negro in American Life and Thought: The Nadir, 1877–1901* (New York: Dial Press, 1954), p. 12.

[21] White, *The Republican Era: 1869–1901 . . .*, p. 3.

[22] Ibid., pp. 4–5.

It will be assumed here that "the President must lead public opinion. . . . To a much greater degree than we realize, ours is a government of public opinion, and we look to our chosen leader to sense our doubts, fears, hopes and aspirations and to be the nation's spokesman."[23] As Laski has put it, "a President so far ahead of his time as to voice aspirations the common man is not yet ready to understand is inevitably doomed to failure."[24] This seems to be the dilemma of the leader. He must lead but he must not lead too far ahead. "The obvious weakness of government by opinion," said Lord Bryce, "is the difficulty of ascertaining it."[25] In this regard, these Presidents, on matters of race, aptly fitted Bryce's description of the practical American statesman: ". . . Timid in advocacy . . . infertile in suggestion . . . always listening for the popular voice, always afraid to commit himself to a point of view which may turn out unpopular. . . ."[26] As the Presidents faced the race problem what seemed to matter most was not so much their own personal views on the subject but what they discerned as public opinion on the question. What mattered most to Lincoln, for example, was what he called the "universal feelings" of the white American majority on matters of race. Bryce labeled the tendency of Americans to acquiesce almost irrevocably in the will of the majority as the "fatalism of the multitude," a kind of helplessness before the will of the majority, which tends to discourage individual effort in the face of overwhelming numbers.[27]

Commenting further upon American politics Laski observed

[23] George Fort Milton, *The Uses of Presidential Power, 1789–1943* (Boston: Little, Brown and Company, 1944), pp. 4, 31; James Bryce, *The American Commonwealth* (New York: Macmillan Company, 1888), II, 209. "In no country," said Bryce, "is public opinion so powerful as in the United States." Longaker, *The Presidency and Individual Liberties*, pp. 194–95. John Brademas, "An Apology for Politics," *The American Scholar*, 30:559–62 (Autumn 1961). "This is what Presidential leadership largely means in an American Democracy—communication to the Citizenry of urgency of purpose and then of responsibility for action," stated Brademas.

[24] Harold J. Laski, *The American Presidency: An Interpretation* (New York: Harper and Brothers, 1940), pp. 269, 263.

[25] Bryce, op. cit., II, 315.

[26] Ibid.

[27] Bryce, *The American Commonwealth*, II, 302.

that "statesmanship in this nation consists not only in representing the special interests of the leader's own section but in finding a formula that will bring the different regions together in a common policy."[28] This assumption has tremendous implications relative to interpreting the racial utterances of the Presidents. The confusion, the hesitation, the ambivalence, and the caution displayed by the Presidents of the period and their colleagues in matters of race becomes intelligible to a greater degree when viewed in the context of sectional politics. The bane of the race question, as it concerned the blacks, was politics. None understood this better than the politicians and the Presidents. Though segregation has never rested easily on the American conscience, it has been the nature of democracy to move hesitantly when the interests involved are those of a politically impotent minority that could be served only by coercing an emotionally agitated, politically powerful and larger minority.[29]

With the exception of Lincoln there is no single work devoted to the racial ideas of any one of the ten Presidents. Where their views have been treated incidentally in biographies there is evidence of much disagreement and confusion.[30] This study

[28] Laski, *The American Presidency* . . . , p. 229.

[29] Harry P. Ashmore, "The Durable Issue," *The American Scholar*, 30: 555–58 (Autumn 1961).

[30] For example, there is much confusion on Lincoln's racial views. According to Professor David Donald, Lincoln was color-blind. See his *Lincoln Reconsidered: Essays on the Civil War Era* (New York: Alfred Knopf, 1956), p. 135. Another held that Lincoln could not escape the racial sensitivities characteristic of the average white American, and that his democracy was not broad enough to completely transcend the color line. See Richard Hofstadter, *The American Political Tradition and the Men Who Made It* (New York: Alfred Knopf, 1948), pp. 100, 116. Still another scholar who completed Randall's fourth volume on Lincoln stated: ". . . In the White House [Lincoln] outgrew his prejudices." See J. G. Randall and Richard N. Current, *Last Full Measure* (New York: Dodd, Mead and Company, 1955), IV, 298. Another said that Lincoln did not allow himself to get excited over such things as social equality and intermarriage and regarded them as emotionally toned "false issues." See Benjamin Quarles, *The Negro in the Civil War* (Boston: Little, Brown and Company, 1953), pp. 135–36. One of the most recent biographers of Andrew Johnson had little to say about his racial views (Eric McKitrick, *Andrew Johnson and Reconstruction* (Chicago: University of Chicago Press, 1960). Another said: "When Johnson's attitudes toward the Negro are examined, the first thing that strikes the eyes is that his views are not those of the Southern

impinges upon another historical controversy of the period: the abandonment of the blacks by the Republican party and the nation after Reconstruction and the almost simultaneous cessation of the bloody shirt technique in politics.[31] By implication, then, the Presidents of this Republican era abandoned the blacks too. There is evidence to warrant a reconsideration of the contention that the Republicans abandoned black people. There is evidence, too, that the technique of waving the bloody shirt was still being used when Theodore Roosevelt left office in 1909. The racial climate of opinion for the period covered by this book will be examined briefly.

---

poor whites from which he sprang. . . . Johnson's prejudice was not so much *against* the Southern Negroes as it was *for* the Southern whites. . . . He trusted the Southern whites and assumed that left alone they would deal fairly with the Negroes." See Milton Lomask, *Andrew Johnson: President on Trial* (New York: Farrar, Straus and Cudahy, 1960), p. 143. Said yet another Johnson scholar, "He felt that the Negro would fare better in the hands of the slave holding class than under Northerners and poor white loyalists." See Howard K. Beale, *The Critical Year: A Study of Andrew Johnson and Reconstruction* (New York: Frederick Ungar Publishing Company, 1930, 1958), p. 47. Finally, another said: "In the light of recent years and of racial conflicts the world over [1928] it must be recognized that racial instincts and antipathies are inescapable. Lincoln and Johnson appreciated that fact. Congress overlooked it." See Robert Winston, *Andrew Johnson: Plebian and Patriot* (New York: Henry Holt and Co., 1928), p. 517.

[31] Stanley Hirshon said that the bloody shirt technique and the blacks were discarded between 1891 and 1893. See the preface of Stanley Philip Hirshon, "Farewell to the Bloody Shirt: Northern Republicans and the Southern Negro, 1877–1893" (Ph.D. dissertation, Columbia University, New York, 1959). According to Paul Buck, "the defeat of the Lodge Bill [1890] marked the final passage of the sectional issue in its Civil War guise from politics. . . . The Republican Party tacitly accepted the fact of white supremacy in the South. It never again hoisted the Bloody Shirt to its masthead. . . . A strongly partisan Republican Congress had made its final surrender in obedience to the clearly expressed sentiment of the nation." See Paul H. Buck, *The Road to Reunion, 1865–1900* (Boston: Little, Brown and Company, 1937, 1938), p. 281. According to Rayford Logan, *The Negro in American Life and Thought* . . . , the Negro was abandoned in 1901. Beal, op. cit., p. 253, spoke of the "relegation of Reconstruction to unimportance after Hayes's removal of the troops in 1877. Of the Compromise of 1876, Vann Woodward said: "In the mood of reconciliation there were few who mourned the cause of the Negro or gave much thought to the Revolution in Northern sentiment on this." See C. Vann Woodward, *Reunion and Reaction: The Compromise of 1877 and the End of Reconstruction* (Boston: Little, Brown and Company, 1951), p. 214. There was one contemporary, Elihu Root, who thought that the bloody shirt was put away with the election of Cleveland in 1884.

The Racial Milieu for Presidential Racial Thought, 1809–1909

Historically there was a definite American race ideology with respect to Afro-Americans. But it should not be assumed that this ideology was completely Negrophobic. The black man had his champions as well as his detractors.

The coming of the African to the American continent in 1619 and his subsequent enslavement gave rise to the problem of conditioning a physical and culturally distinct people to the ways of the majority group as well as to slavery. Perhaps it was inevitable that in the process of making this adjustment there developed very early in American life and thought, racial philosophies of conduct some of which "have endured to this day."[32] Whenever blacks became an issue in local, state or national politics, stereotype rather than fact seemed to dominate the discussion. Race prejudice loomed large in the theoretical rationale of slavery in colonial days. ". . . The distinction in the states imposed upon the Negroes and Indians and their offspring in America was based upon the natural and ineradicable quality of race difference."[33]

The natural rights philosophy of the Enlightenment provided the rationale for the American Revolution and had a positive effect on racial ideology, but the results were not lasting and lost ground by 1800.[34] Much Negrophile thought accompanied the abolition movement. With the coming of Reconstruction, reunion and reaction, racial thought became difficult to weigh. For here again negative and positive racial thought existed side by side and an impressive case could always be made by stressing

[32] Gurion B. Johnson, "A History of Racial Ideologies in the United States with Reference to the Negro," Vol. 1. See Francis B. Simkins, A *History of the South* (New York: Alfred Knopf, 1957), Chap. 2, for a provocative discussion of race in early America. Merle Curti, *The Growth of American Thought*, pp. 22–24, 431, 168. Clement Eaton, *Freedom of Thought in the Old South* (Durham, N.C.: Duke University Press, 1940), p. 20.

[33] James Curtis Ballagh, A *History of Slavery in Virginia*, cited by Gurion B. Johnson, "A History of Racial Ideologies in the United States," I, 9 (1944).

[34] Gurion B. Johnson, "A History of Racial Ideologies in the United States," I, 39–48.

one side to the exclusion of the other. By World War I, the negative aspects of American racial thought on blacks was characterized by three popular stereotypes. The African was considered mentally inferior, immoral and criminal.[35] One scholar concluded that the concept of black inferiority had infested American social thought from the colonial period to the time of his writing in 1940. He found a "consistent and continuous effort . . ." to "present American Negroes as inferior beings and as a folk different from the normal American stock." He found this theme not only in the South but in the North as well and shared by well-known people.[36]

Another student of race ideology flatly stated that "the ideologies of the white world on the Negro problem have all been directed at reserving participation in the blessings of society exclusively for the white man."[37] Such a conclusion, however, in spite of its large measure of truth, does grave injustice to that persistent and significant Caucasian minority that had always, from the beginning of American history, pricked the American democratic conscience by saying that "the Negro too" was included in the Declaration of Independence. Yet it is difficult to disagree with Bunche's further conclusion in 1940 that the line between white and black was heavily drawn in America and that many whites felt that the black man had complicated American democracy, had created a nasty problem, and should go back where he came from since he could never be accepted as an equal because of his innate inferiority.[38] As we shall see, until the 1930s at least, anti-black thought was more widespread than positive racial thinking.

[35] Ibid., II, 400.

[36] Charles Wesley, "The Concept of Negro Inferiority in American Thought," *Journal of Negro History*, 25:541–46 (October 1940).

[37] Ralph Bunche, "Conceptions and Ideologies of the Negro Problem," (New York: New York Public Library, Schomburg Collection, 1944), pp. 7, 159.

[38] Ibid.; Merle Curti, *The Growth of American Thought*, pp. 486–91. Curti concluded that after the Civil War, "the great majority of Northerners looked on colored people as inferior and incapable of ever becoming the equal of the whites," and after Reconstruction, according to Curti, they believed it more strongly than ever.

THE NATIONAL SCENE: THE NEGATIVE AND THE POSITIVE CHARGE

With the exception of Roosevelt and McKinley, all of the Presidents in this study had reached the age of twenty-one when the Civil War began. What was the racial tone of the society into which they were born? Men are all born into social situations with *who* and *what* they are already established for them.[39] As these men grew into manhood between 1809 and 1865 they were not unaffected by the racial milieu of their day.

A number of studies have testified to a preponderance of negative racial thought for the period under study as well as to a corresponding lowly status for the black. In a chapter on the free black from 1830 to 1860, a scholar of the Victorian era concluded that though 10 per cent of the blacks in the South were free and though some of them, North and South, managed to make something of themselves, the triple disability of political, legal and social inferiority was a heavy burden to carry.[40] A study of black people in Pennsylvania from 1639 to 1869 revealed "none of the race equality . . . assumed by the Reconstruction statesmen in the solution of Southern problems after the Civil War."[41]

For a long time a study of race prejudice in the antebellum North did not exist. The saga of Reconstruction and the failure of the North to prevent the aborting of the Civil War amendments designed to secure the black man in his citizenship become more intelligible if it be admitted that much of

[39] J. Masuoko and R. Yokely, "Essential Structural Requisites in Race Relations," *Social Forces,* 33:30–35 (October 1954).

[40] A. B. Hart, *Slavery and Abolition* (*The American Nation:* A *History,* ed. A. B. Hart), (New York: Harper and Brothers, 1906), pp. 84, 79. Hart found a wide gulf between blacks and whites, the status of the free black inferior, imperfect and unstable, and "no legal distinctions . . . made between the quick Negro and the stupid, the coal black and the mulatto; the son of the planter and the son of a field hand."

[41] Edward R. Turner, *The Negro in Pennsylvania: Slavery, Servitude, Freedom, 1639–1869* (Washington, D.C.: American Historical Association, 1912), pp. 250–51, preface, viii. Turner found, too, that "along with dislike for the Negro developed a strong hostility to slavery which was manifested in opposition to the extension of Southern slavery. . . ."

Northern life and thought before the Civil War was rather Negrophobic. Such a study is now available. Litwack, in a heavily documented monograph for the period 1790–1860, makes it possible to say that the Presidents of this study were born into a society in which blacks were considered ". . . a depraved and inferior race which must be kept in its proper place in a white man's society."[42] Neither law nor court decree "could immediately erase from the public mind, North and South, that long and firmly held conviction that the African race was inferior and therefore incapable of being assimilated politically, socially, and most certainly physically with the dominant and superior white society."[43]

But while Litwack made a strong case for the universality of race prejudice in the North before the Civil War, he did not fail to point out important differences in the position of the black in the North and that of the slave in the South. "Above all, the Northern Negro was a free man. . . . Although a victim of racial proscription, he could—and on several occasions did—advance his political and economic position in the antebellum period," said Litwack.[44] And so it seemed that the Northern politicians of the post-Civil War period imposed a social revolution in race relations upon the South. They urged upon that section a revolution in racial social thought which had not yet taken place among their own constituencies!

Did all human beings originate from one biological species? This was a momentous scientific question from the eighteenth

[42] Leon F. Litwack, *North of Slavery: The Negro in the Free States, 1790–1860* (Chicago: University of Chicago Press, 1961), preface, viii.

[43] Ibid., p. 15, preface, vii. ". . . Discrimination against the Negro and a firmly held belief in the superiority of the white race was not restricted to one section but was shared by an overwhelming majority of white Americans in both the North and the South." J. B. Estlin, *A Brief Notice of American Slavery and the Abolitionist Movement* (London: Leeds Anti-Slavery Association, William Tweedie, 1846, 1853), pp. 17–19, passim. This contemporary discussed prejudice in Philadelphia, the abuse of Miss Prudence Grandall of Connecticut in 1833 because of her integrated school, the canceling of a lyceum lecture by Ralph Waldo Emerson and Charles Sumner because of discrimination against blacks. He quoted an outstanding New York clergyman, Reverend Doctor Dewey, to doubt the argument of an impossible physical barrier between the races every time he thought of "an almost white race of slaves at the South, the children of planters by Negro mothers."

[44] Leon F. Litwack, *North of Slavery* . . . preface, ix.

century of Thomas Jefferson until it was tentatively resolved in the affirmative by Darwin's theory of evolution of 1859.[45] Leading naturalists of the eighteenth century believed in the single rather than the multiple or plural origin of men.[46] The progress and nature of this battle (1815–1859) has been the subject of a recent study of scientific attitudes toward race in America. During those years the American school of anthropologists concluded that the races had separate origins and constituted separate species; that the Egyptians were Caucasians, and that of all the races of mankind the whites were at the top and the blacks at the bottom, a decided and hopeless inferior.[47] Though the conclusions of the pluralists bolstered the defenses of slavery and black subjugation, the scholar on this subject absolved those men of any studied ulterior motive to justify the political and social *status quo* in race relations. With perhaps the exception of J. C. Nott, if those men had any bone to pick it was to upset the dogmatic, theological and biblical underpinnings of the theory of the unity of the species.[48] In fact, Southerners rejected the plural origins theory because it attacked the Bible, even though it was a potential rationalization for slavery.[49]

Yet in researching this book I have been led to believe that while Southerners might not have accepted the unscriptural implications of the plural origins theory, laymen certainly used the findings in their writings to buttress their own ideas on

[45] John C. Green, "Some Early Speculations on the Origin of Human Races," *American Anthropologist*, 56:34 (February 1954).

[46] Ibid., p. 33. Some people felt that the original man was white and that yellow, black and brown were degenerations from that original color. Earl Count, "The Evolution of the Race Idea in Modern Western Culture During the Period of Pre-Darwinian Nineteenth Century," *Transactions* of the New York Academy of Sciences, 8:157 (January 1946). Dr. Prichard, a leading believer in the idea of single origin, thought that the original man was black and that various intensities of blending produced the fairer shades, ibid. In 1655, Lapeyrere published his Pro-Adamites, in an attempt to explain the origin of man as mentioned in the Bible and hence became the father of the polygenists, those who believed in the multiple or plural origin of man.

[47] William Ragan Stanton, *The Leopard's Spots: Scientific Attitudes Toward Race in America, 1815–1859* (Chicago: University of Chicago Press, 1960), p. 152.

[48] Ibid., pp. 192–93.

[49] Ibid., p. 194.

differences and peculiarities between black and whites. Just as Darwin's theories were prostituted by nonscientists for acknowledged social ends, so it was that the black man, an innocent bystander, suffered as the apologists for white supremacy "stood in the alleys of science beating the drums of race. . . ."[50] Indeed, some of the practitioners of the supposedly scientific American anthropology or ethnology sometimes referred to their studies as "niggerology," which in many cases might have been closer to the truth of the matter.[51]

After 1815, science deserted the democratic dream which it had found in eighteenth-century environmentalism. The weapons in its arsenal were not overlooked by those who favored the inequality of man and who believed more especially in the inferiority of the black man and the Indian. Unfortunately for the black man, he was found to have "seventeen cubic inches" less cranial capacity than his white brother. This was interpreted as a decisive sign of inferiority. In view of the black man's poor showing on the cephalic index, some people reasoned that education was powerless to elevate that race. The leopard could not change his spots. The black man could not add a cubit to his brain. The coming of the theory of evolution in 1859, while its doctrine of the survival of the fittest opened up new possibilities for the racial drum beaters, overthrew the American school of polygenists in favor of the monogenists and thus paved the way for equally significant possibilities for positive thought which would not break through until the turn of the century.[52]

When one turns to his own personal examination of some of the contemporary racial thought, the picture never seems quite as dark as painted by studies with some kind of thesis to propound. Yet the one dominant theme in the racial literature of the period was the idea of inherent racial differences. This was also the one racial belief held in common by all of the Presidents in this book. Was the black man inherently different

[50] Ibid., p. 72.
[51] Ibid., p. 161.
[52] Ibid., pp. 72, 182–83, 193.

from the white man? Most of the writers of antebellum America thought that he was.[53]

Many writers seemed to take it as a self-evident truth that the white man was the model for the human race. To the degree that other humans differed from that model, just so much were they judged as inferior. This was one reason why so much stress was placed on the differences between blacks and whites.[54] Much of the literature of the period peddled the idea that blacks had contributed nothing to civilization.

[53] Thomas Babington Macaulay, *Critical, Historical and Miscellaneous Essays* (New York: Hurd and Houghton, 1875), V–VI, 365, 368, describing the attempts of one Major Moody, in 1826, to show that there was a natural antipathy between the white and black races. To Macaulay this was absurd. P. A. Browne, *The Classification of Mankind by the Hair and Wool on Their Heads, with an Answer to Dr. Prichard's Assertion that the Covering on the Head of the Negro is Hair, Properly so Termed and not Wool* (Philadelphia: A. Hunt, 1850), p. 20. This paper was read before the American Ethnological Society in New York. Brown concluded after splitting hairs that the Negro had wool on his head while the white man had hair and so they belonged to "two distinct species." He was a polygenist and the English Prichard a monogenist. C. W. Jacobs, *The Free Negro Question in Maryland* (Baltimore: John W. Wood, Printer, 1859), pp. 2, 3, 5, 16, 15, passim. He called for the expulsion or enslavement of Maryland's ninety thousand free Negroes and was convinced that "freedom . . . equality and amalgamation of the Negro race with the Castilean race . . ." contributed to the decline and confusion of the Latin American countries.

[54] Julian Virey, *The Natural History of the Negro Race*, trans. from the French by J. H. Guenbault (Charleston, S.C.: D. Dowling, 1837), passim. The translator was a member of the Literary and Anthropological Society of South Carolina. The book quoted heavily from Jefferson's findings on blacks in his *Notes on Virginia*. The book tells about the inability of blacks and Chinese to pronounce the letter "R," the strong odor of Negro perspiration, the undeveloped intellect and the lasciviousness of black women, the keen sense of smell due to an overdeveloped olfactory sense, etc. John Campbell, *Negro Mania* (Philadelphia: Campbell and Power, 1851). Here is a treasury of Negrophobic thought. This book grew out of an interesting discussion of two months' duration on a loaded question: "Can the Colored Races of Men Be Made Mentally, Politically, and Socially Equal with the White?" Campbell used the entire book to answer the question in the negative. He was a member of the Philadelphia Social Improvement Society. He used twenty-five authors, including Thomas Jefferson, to buttress his arguments. Karl Hermann Burmeister, *The Black Man: The Comparative Anatomy and Psychology of the African Negro*, translated by Julian Freidlander and Robert Tomes (New York: W. C. Bryant and Co., 1853), passim. This book appeared serially in the New York *Evening Post* and was hailed by the editor as the most complete study of blacks to date, 1853. The book was based on a fourteen months' study of blacks in Brazil by a German professor of zoology at the University of Halle. Here is a treasury of detail on the alleged peculiarities of black physiology. The book approximated "The Negro both corporeally and mentally, to inferior animals," mainly the ape.

Louis Agassiz, described by one historian as one of the "most distinguished men of science in America," felt that way. He found little to redeem the black man.[55]

At least two studies testified to the hard core of pro-black thought that inhered in the abolitionist movement of the 1830s. One scholar concluded that the drive to give the black man equality before the law with the Fourteenth Amendment was but the culmination of this pro-black ideology.[56] On the same subject, a recent writer found a martyr complex in the zeal of the abolitionists to redeem American ideals of freedom and liberty by recognizing the slave as a person.[57] But Northern abolitionists were not without opposition. For "some saw in the movement the threat of northward migrating Negroes who would claim the white man's jobs, become his neighbor and social equal, even an aspirant for his daughter's hand in marriage." Many Northerners felt those who opposed the abolitionists were the defenders of law and order, battling contentious busybodies whose programs encouraged hatred, murder, amalgamation and rape.[58] At the same time many abolitionists flinched and drew back when the question of social intercourse with blacks came up.[59]

Granted the inadequacy of the sample, such was some of the racial thought before the Civil War. While pro-black thought

[55] James Ford Rhodes, *A History of the United States from the Compromise of 1850* (New York: Macmillan and Company, 1906), VI, 37–38. Agassiz said to Dr. Samuel Gridley Howe in 1863: ". . . Social Equality I deem at all times impracticable, a natural impossibility, from the very character of the Negro race." He then executed a favorite racial maneuver of that day. He turned to the inscriptions on the ancient Egyptian monuments for some indication of "the natural endowments of the Negro race" and found that "upon these monuments the Negroes are so represented as to show that in natural propensities and mental abilities they are pretty much what we find them at the present day—indolent, playful, sensual, imitative, subservient, good natured, versatile, unsteady in their purpose, devoted and affectionate."

[56] Jacobus Ten Broek, *The Anti-Slavery Origins of the Fourteenth Amendment* (Berkeley: University of California Press, 1951), preface.

[57] Hazel C. Wolf, *On Freedom's Altar: The Martyr Complex in the Abolitionist Movement* (Madison, Wis.: University of Wisconsin Press, 1957), preface.

[58] Ibid.

[59] Leon Litwack, *North of Slavery* . . . , pp. 214, 223–24. According to Litwack, many of the abolitionists failed to question the validity of the commonly accepted stereotypes of the black character.

other than abolitionism did exist, there reverberated through this thought, with sickening and monotonous regularity, the theme of the black man's natural inequality and inferiority.

The condition of the black man and his position in American life and thought during the post-Civil War era are subjects of controversy and extreme complexity. Rayford Logan concluded that for the African, 1877–1901 was the darkest period in American history.[60] However, a revision of this conclusion is already in the making.[61] Philip Hirshon thought that after the Civil War and certainly after Reconstruction "the great majority of Northerners looked on colored people as inferior and incapable of ever becoming the equal of the whites."[62] Still another study for the period 1860–1915 concluded that in post-Darwinian America not only was there strong race feeling but rank racism.[63] Yet, even before the end of the nineteenth century, science had slowly begun to cast doubt on the validity of the race superiority thesis as a scientific fact. No doubt the *positive* propensities of Darwinian thought had something to do with this. Studies such as those cited above tend to obscure the by no means inconsiderable fund of positive racial thought of the period.

Looking first at the negative aspects of post-Civil War racial thought, one finds a continuation of the antebellum idea of immutable differences between the races.[64] Perhaps the epitome

[60] Rayford Logan, *The Negro in American Life and Thought: The Nadir 1877–1901* (New York: Dial Press, 1954), p. 162. Logan found that the North was being fed on seven Negro stereotypes by Southern writers: the contented slave, the wretched freedman, the comic Negro, the brute Negro, the tragic mulatto, the local color Negro, and the exotic primitive.

[61] Philip Stanley Hirshon, "Farewell to the Bloody Shirt: Northern Republicans and the Southern Negro, 1877–1893" (Ph.D. thesis, Columbia University, New York, 1959). Both Hirshon and the present writer question the idea that there was a paucity of positive racial rhetoric in this period. This study has since been published.

[62] Merle Curti, *The Growth of American Thought*, 2nd ed. (New York: Harper and Brothers, 1945, 1951), pp. 486–91.

[63] Richard Hofstadter, *Social Darwinism in American Thought, 1860–1915* (Philadelphia: University of Pennsylvania Press, 1944), Chap. 9. Curti, op. cit., pp. 641–63, 670–72, 568.

[64] M. S., *The Adamic Race: Reply to Ariel, Drs. Young and Blackie on the Negro* (New York: Russell Brothers Publishers, 1868). On the eve of Reconstruction the preadamic theory was trotted out again to prove that

of alleged Northern disenchantment with the "Ethiopian" was an address by Charles Francis Adams at the University of South Carolina in 1913 on the subject "The Doctrine of Equal-

---

the Negro was a beast, not a man, because he was created before Adam (a white man) along with the animals. J. A. Hunt, "On the Negro's Place in Nature," *Anthropological Review*, 2:xv–xvi (November 3, 1863). W. H. Ruffner, "The Co-Education of the White and Colored Races," *Scribner's Monthly*, 8:86 (May 1864). Wallace Davies, "The Problem of Race Segregation in the Grand Army of the Republic," *Journal of Southern History*, 13:355–72 (August 1947). When this organization was extended to the Southern states, Northern whites resisted black membership and when blacks were included the whites insisted on social segregation. Equally significant was the reluctance of many ex-soldiers who had remained in the South to champion the black cause. *Abolition Is National Death or the Attempt to Equalize the Races the Destruction of Society* (New York: Van Evrie Horton and Co., 1868), 32 pp. Madame Clemence Royer, "The Mental Faculties of Monkeys," *Popular Science Monthly*, 30:17 (November 1886). The monkey mentality approximated those of the lower races of mankind, which consisted of the natives of Australia, Africa and New Zealand; James Bryce, *The American Commonwealth*, II, 278–79, 707–08. He contended that the North acquiesced in the political subjugation of the blacks because it was felt that the black man was safe in his person and poverty. Federal intervention was looked upon as a worse cure than the disease. James Bryce, "Thoughts on the Negro Problem," *North American Review*, 153–641, 643 (December 1891). Philip A. Bruce, *The Plantation Negro As a Freedman: Observations of His Character, Condition and Prospects in Virginia* (New York: G. P. Putnam's Sons, 1889), pp. 130, 139, 140. W. Y. Atkinson, "The Atlanta Exposition," *North American Review*, 161:392–93 (October 1895). Atkinson was governor of Georgia. G. Stanley Hall, "A Few Results of Recent Scientific Study of the Negro in America," Massachusetts Historical Society *Proceedings*, 2nd series, 19, 99, 102 (1905). Hall said that black mental development stopped at puberty because it was overpowered by an enormous sex drive. Ferdinand Blumentritte, "Race Questions in the Philippine Islands," *Popular Science Monthly*, 55:473 (August 1899). His contention was that blacks and Indians did not possess the same capacity for civilization as did the Filipinos; J. L. M. Curry, "The Negro Question," *Popular Science Monthly*, 55:178–79 (June 1899). Curry was general agent for the Peabody Fund. He supposedly wished blacks well but behind the history of the race he found "one dreary, unrelieved monotonous chapter of ignorance, nakedness, superstition, [and] savagery." W. S. McCurly [Seattle, Washington], "Impossibility of Race Amalgamation," *Arena*, 21:453 (April 1899). Black inferiority made race mixing impossible. Charles M. Harvey, "The Louisiana Exposition in World Perspective," *Atlantic Monthly*, 84:547–57 (1899). James Ford Rhodes, *A History of the United States* . . . , VI, 29. This famous work was published during the last decade of the nineteenth century. While Rhodes was antislavery in his earlier volumes he now claimed that what the North failed to understand after the Civil War was that "three and a half million persons of one of the most inferior races of mankind, had through the agency of their superiors been transferred from slavery to freedom. . . ." Ray Stannard Baker, *Following the Color Line* . . . (1908). He found the tendency toward racial (p. 300) separation increasing in 1908.

ity and the Race Problem." There was no doubt about his thesis. Ethnology had proved that the abolitionists were wrong about the black man. He was not the white man's equal, hence the doctrine of political equality implicit in the American idea of the melting pot was incompatible with race absorption.[65] It appeared at this point that racial theory had truly reached the lowest point.

But for a more balanced perspective one has to sample some of the more favorable racial thought. An American Missionary Association meeting in 1882, some National Educational Association meetings in 1886, 1890, the Lake Mohonk Conference on the Negro Question in 1890, articles by college professors, English and American anthropologists, Andrew Carnegie and others all represented a significant fund of positive postwar racial thinking.[66] This survey of race on the national scene

[65] Charles Francis Adams, "The Doctrine of Equality and the Race Problem," *Great Debates in American History*, ed. by Marian Miller (New York: Current History Publishers, 1913), IV, 4.

[66] *The American Missionary* 26 (December 1882). This entire volume contains the proceedings of the annual meeting of the American Missionary Association, October 24–26, 1882, at Plymouth Church, Cleveland, Ohio. W. H. Ashley, "Education of the Mexican," The Journal of the *Proceedings* and Addresses of the National Educational Association (1886), p. 222, ibid., p. 231. W. H. Bartholomew, "Educational Work Among the Colored Race," A. A. Gunby, "General Statement on the [Race] Problem," *National Education Association Journal of Proceedings and Addresses* (1890), pp. 255–66, 268–71. Isabel C. Barrows (ed.), *The First Mohonk Conference on the Negro Question* (Boston: George H. Ellis, Printer, 1890). N. S. Shaler, "Race Prejudice," *Atlantic Monthly*, 58:510–18 (July–December 1886). N. S. Shaler, "Scientific Aspects of the Negro," *Public Opinion*, 18:147 (1895). Willis Broughton, "The Negro's Place in History," *Arena*, 16:618 (September 1896). D. W. Culp, "The Past and Future of the American Negro," *Arena*, 17:791–92 (April 1897). J. Reade, "Intermingling of Races," *Popular Science Monthly*, 30:338 (January 1887). Franz Boas, "Human Faculty Determined by Race," American Association for the Advancement of Science *Proceedings*, 43:308, 317, 326, 327 (1894). Friedrich Ratze, *The History of Mankind* (New York: Macmillan and Company, 1896), I, 3, 5. Josiah Royce, "Race Questions and Prejudices" *International Journal of Ethics*, 16:283–85, passim (April 1906). Andrew Carnegie, *The Negro in America*, an address delivered before the Philosophical Institution of Edinburgh, 16th October (Cheyney, Pa.: Committee of Twelve, 1907), pp. 4, 8, 32. Sir Harry Johnston, *Views and Reviews: From the Outlook of an Anthropologist* (London: William and Newgate, 1912), pp. 211, 232. "We should indeed be living in a fool's paradise if we continued to assume that a Negro could never attain to the high mentality of a white man. . . ."

would not be complete without some attention to a few of America's other minority racial groups. The story can be quickly told because the same primacy of *difference* which caused the white man to shun the African also operated in his rejection of the Indian, the Oriental, and the "new" immigrant from Southern and Eastern Europe. The tale of "the poor Indian" is a well-told one. The big question here seems to be whether or not the post-Civil War Indian policy (the Dawes Act) was more for the benefit of the white man than the Indian. Since the Indian did not have the vote, he seemed to have had few spokesmen.[67]

Although the people of Southern and Eastern Europe belonged to the Caucasian race ". . . their physical characteristics were sufficiently different to set them apart. . . ."[68] The "factor of race" played a major role in congressional debates on immigration between 1882 and 1917.[69] Between 1865 and 1914, the South put on a drive to displace allegedly inefficient black labor with white immigrants from Europe. Xenophobia and ideas of

[67] H. L. Dawes, "Have We Failed with the Indians?" *Atlantic Monthly,* 84:280–85 (July–December 1899). Here the author of the highly touted Dawes Act of 1887 admitted that this new Indian policy was not so much for the good of the Indian as it was to make room for the white settlers who were overflowing from the frontier into lands previously reserved for the Indian. D'Arcy McNickle, "Indian and European Relations from Discovery Down to 1887," *The American Indian and American Life,* ed. by George E. Simpson and J. Milton Yinger, *Annals* of the American Academy of Political and Social Science, 311:1–11 (May 1957). This recent scholar of the American Indian, himself an Indian, called the Dawes Act "the unkindest cut" of all because between 1887 and 1930 it separated the Indian from some ninety million acres of land. Theodore Hass, "The Legal Aspects of Indian Affairs from 1887 to 1957," ibid., *Annals,* pp. 12–22.

[68] Henry Pratt Fairchild, "Public Opinion on Immigration," *Reappraising Our Immigrant Policy,* ed. by Hugh Carter, *Annals* of the American Academy of Political and Social Science, 262:187, 191 (March 1949). Fairchild put the problem of Oriental immigration into a "distinct field" not only for differences in culture and living standards but also because of "basic racial divergencies."

[69] Joseph Taylor, "The Restriction of European Immigration and the Concept of Race," *South Atlantic Quarterly,* 50:26–27, 29–30 (January 1951). James B. Clarke, "The Negro and the Immigrant in the Americas: An International Aspect of the Color Problem," *The Negro's Progress in Fifty Years, Annals* of the American Academy of Political and Social Science, 49:32–33 (September 1913). Negro sailors from Brazil wanted to know why they had to be separated from their white or white-Indian friends on the streetcars of Norfolk, Virginia, and a New York hotel. William Z. Ripley, "Race, Progress and Immigration," ibid., 34:130–38, 238–39 (July–December 1909).

race helped the plan to fail.[70] The states from which many of the Presidents came were not exempt from negative racial thought.

Conditions in Some of the Presidential States

Six of the Presidents in this book came from the Midwest, three from the East and one from the South. The legal racial status of the blacks in the states from which these Presidents came had few redeeming features. In Lincoln's Illinois before 1840 free blacks were ostracized, without citizenship, without social recognition, without the vote, without the right to own property, serve in the militia, sue for their liberty in court, be a witness, or attend the free public school. The free black had to have proof of his freedom certified by the county and he could not even remain in the state without posting a bond of one thousand dollars to insure that he would never become a charity case.

In 1835, an act was passed which permanently banned free black immigration to Illinois. As was true for Pennsylvania, antislavery and anti-Negroism in that state reached its peak in 1862 when a proposal for a new constitution failed while three anti-black amendments concerned with keeping blacks out of the state passed. That was one demonstration that the people of Abraham Lincoln's Illinois did not want blacks in the state and would deny the rights and privileges of citizenship to those already there.[71] More recently another scholar confirmed the preceding conclusions of Professor Harris, not only for Illinois but for the entire Northwest: ". . . White people of the Northwest were in fact not abolitionists, but actually, . . . Negrophobes. . . . They feared and detested the very thought of living side by side with large numbers of Negroes in their own states. . . ." Hofstadter also surmised that it was not slav-

[70] Rowland T. Berthoff, "Southern Attitudes Toward Immigration, 1865–1914," *Journal of Southern History*, 17:328–39 (August 1951).

[71] Norman D. Harris, *History of Negro Slavery in Illinois and the Slavery Agitation in that State* (Chicago: University of Chicago Press, 1904); see the chapter entitled "The Negro Question, 1840–1861," pp. 226–40, passim.

ery so much that troubled many people of the Northwest but ". . . the Negro, free or slave."[72] Perhaps it was in this regard that Abraham Lincoln transcended to some degree the limited outlook of his compeers in that both slavery *and* the black man troubled him.

Ohio was similar to Illinois. Though superseded later by the Fifteenth Amendment, the word "white" was not literally removed from the Ohio Constitution until 1923, one attempt having failed in 1912.[73] According to Woodson, Cincinnati blacks labored under the "black laws" of Ohio, which were not repealed until after the Civil War.[74] The story was the same for Harrison's Indiana and other states.[75] The constitution for California after 1879 abounded not in Negrophobia but Sinophobia, literally pushing the Chinese to the wall.[76] However, blacks could not vote in California until 1879. It seems almost fantastic that the North should have demanded from the South equality for blacks, in view of the fact that so many racial barriers in the North did not begin to crumble until well after the Civil War. On the other hand, the end of

[72] Richard Hofstadter, *The American Political Tradition and the Men Who Made It*, p. 11. Francis Thorpe (ed.), *The Federal and State Constitutions, Colonial Charters, and Other Organic Laws. . . .* (Washington: Government Printing Office, 1909), II, 975–87, 1001–43. Philip S. Foner (ed.), *The Life and Writings of Frederick Douglass* (New York: International Publishers, 1950–55), II, 385–87, 440–41. Robert Todd Lincoln Collection of the Papers of Abraham Lincoln (manuscript in the Library of Congress), Vol. 5, No. 805, ser. I. James G. Randall (ed.), *The Diary of Orville Hickman Browning*, 1865–1881, II, 259 (*Collections* of the Illinois State Historical Library, XXII, Lincoln Series, III), (Springfield, Illinois State Historical Library, 1933); ibid., II, 271.

[73] Charles Galbreath, *History of Ohio* (New York: A. H. Society, 1928), II, 112–15. *The Military Law of Ohio*, Being An Act to Organize the Militia and Volunteer Militia, passed March 28, 1857 (Columbus, Ohio: Richard Nevins, State Printers, 1857), p. 3. This law limited the membership in that body to whites.

[74] Carter G. Woodson, "The Negroes of Cincinnati Prior to the Civil War," *Journal of Negro History*, 1:2, 16, 17 (January 1916). "Documents," *Journal of Negro History*, 8:331 (July 1923). Leon Litwack, *North of Slavery*, p. 93, reported that Illinois, Ohio, Indiana, Iowa and California "prohibited Negro testimony in cases where a white man was a party. . . ."

[75] C. E. Fuller, *Reminiscences of James A. Garfield . . .* (Cincinnati: Stoddard Publishing Co., 1887), pp. 320–21; Thorpe, *The Federal and State Constitutions . . .*, II, 1867–86.

[76] Thorpe, op. cit., I, 393, 430–52. See Thorpe also for Iowa, Kansas, Missouri, California, New York and New Jersey.

the war *did* see some of the racial guardrails come down and the North could in truth boast that blacks, while socially and economically ostracized, were relatively safe in life and limb, a statement that could hardly be made for the South. A study of Southern racial thought from 1865 to 1914 revealed that while the general attitude toward blacks was one of paternalism, there were at least five variations on this theme, two of which did not posit black inferiority.[77]

In conclusion, then, the idea of race was certainly a live, important concern in the United States of the late nineteenth century. While much of this thought was hostile to blacks, a more positive leaven was never absent. How these conflicting racial attitudes manifested themselves in the lives and actions of the Chief Executives of our country from 1861 to 1909 is the main theme of this book.

[77] Gurion B. Johnson, "Southern Paternalism Towards Negroes After Emancipation, 1865–1914," *Journal of Southern History,* 23:486–501 (November 1957). C. Vann Woodward, *The Strange Career of Jim Crow* (New York: Oxford University Press, 1955). Professor Woodward found a conservative, a radical and a liberal racial philosophy in the post-Civil War South.

CHAPTER II

The Racial Attitudes of Abraham Lincoln (1861–1865)

Abraham Lincoln was born a Southerner. By the time he had reached manhood the slavery question had become meshed in national politics. During his entire life, the slavery issue slid from one crisis to another and culminated in the Civil War. By the end of the first decade of the nineteenth century a conservative reaction against positive ideas of race equality was evident in the North and the South. By the time Lincoln had become a man, this negative reaction to racial equality in the South had stiffened into an ideology.

The Pre-Presidential Perspective

Before he became President, Lincoln thought there was an immutable physical barrier of color and probably of mental and moral inferiority separating the black and the white races. The physical differences of race were real to him. In a political campaign against Stephen A. Douglas, he said that black men were certainly not his equal in color.[1] "There is a physical difference between the two which . . . will probably forever forbid their living together on the footing of perfect equality." He was obviously impressed with the visible difference of color

[1] Speech at Springfield, Ill., July 17, 1858. Paul Angle, *Created Equal? The Complete Lincoln-Douglas Debates* (Chicago: University of Chicago Press, 1958), pp. 81–82.

and thought, perhaps, the black man was not even his equal in "intellectual and moral endowments."[2]

Much of the racial thought in Lincoln's day depicted the black man as being more akin to the ape than to the human race. This may have been why Douglas, in the course of one of his debates with Lincoln, mockingly said: "The Negro is no brother of mine!" This might also explain why Southerners felt that if one could take a hog to Nebraska he should certainly be allowed to carry a slave there also. Lincoln would admit the logic of this argument only if there were no differences between hogs and black men. He insisted that the black man was human and believed that the South recognized this humanity: "But while you thus require me to deny the humanity of the Negro . . . [have] you of the South yourselves ever been willing to do as much?"[3] Having defended the humanity of the black man he faced yet another problem.

The Declaration of Independence, Slavery and the Democratic Conscience

Lincoln was a firm believer in the Declaration of Independence. However, certain practices that arose from the presence of the blacks in America were clearly in conflict with the spirit of that great document. Yet, Lincoln felt too strongly about the Declaration to abandon it, or even to see it impaired theoretically. On the other hand, racial "necessity" forbade him to embrace it unreservedly. He was in a quandary. While his acceptance of the "necessities" of race was inconsistent with his democratic proclivities, it was entirely consonant with his philosophy of race. In essence, his perplexity was also "America's dilemma." The Constitution, in espousing freedom while at the same time protecting slavery, was simply reflecting an incongruity already prevalent in American life and thought when that instrument was initially drafted.

Lincoln was against slavery. He seemed impressed with the

[2] Speech at Quincy, Ill., October 12, 1858. Ibid., p. 327.
[3] Roy Basler (ed.), *Collected Works of Abraham Lincoln* (New Brunswick, N.J.: Rutgers University Press, 1953), II, 263–65, 245–46, 329.

biblical injunction which read that a man should earn his bread by the sweat of his brow. Had not the "Almighty" said as much "to the first of our race"? The fact that some people enjoyed the fruits of the labor of others, Lincoln thought, was wrong and should not continue.[4] In 1849 he supported gradual, compensated emancipation for the District of Columbia, though only with the consent of the voters.[5] He thought it illogical to base slavery on color because ". . . the first man you meet with a fairer skin than your own" would be able to enslave you. Lincoln thought it equally fallacious to enslave on the fulcrum of a superior intellect. In such a case, one would have to become the bond servant of the first person he met who enjoyed a mentality greater than his own.[6]

Publicly and privately, Lincoln insisted that the Declaration of Independence included blacks. In so doing he was following Henry Clay as well as inheriting Clay's inconsistency. According to Lincoln, Clay, although he owned slaves, did not exclude blacks from the human race. Clay opposed extreme positions on slavery because he thought sudden abolition would do more harm than good. The moderation of Henry Clay was Lincoln's answer to the radical abolitionists who would rip the seams of Union asunder ". . . and even burn the last copy of the Bible, rather than slavery should continue a single hour. . . ." But neither would Lincoln have any truck with those ". . . few but increasing number of men who, for the sake of the perpetuation of slavery, are beginning to assail and to ridicule the white man's charter of freedom, the declaration that all men are created free and equal. . . ." This, said Lincoln, "sounds strangely in republican America."[7]

[4] John G. Nicolay and John Hay (eds.), *Abraham Lincoln's Complete Works Comprising His Speeches, Letters, State Papers and Miscellaneous Writings* (New York: Century Co., 1894), I, 92. A long fragment on labor (1846–47) which Lincoln used for slavery speeches. (Hereafter this work will be cited as Nicolay and Hay, *Complete Works*.)

[5] Ibid., I, 147–48. January 16, 1849. Lincoln moved that the bill be reported out of committee.

[6] *Speeches and Letters of Abraham Lincoln, 1832–1865* (New York: E. P. Dutton and Co., 1907), p. 27. A fragment for a speech, July 1854. See also pp. 45, 124, for similar sentiments.

[7] Nicolay and Hay, *Complete Works*, I, 174–75. Eulogy delivered by Lincoln upon the death of Henry Clay, 1852.

Lincoln could easily be mistaken for an abolitionist were it not for the fact that he was always careful to make crystal-clear the distinction between his disinclination to interfere with the "existing" institution of slavery and his opposition to its "extension." He feared the competition of slavery with free white labor in the Territories. The fact that the Northwest Territory was now ". . . the happy home of teeming millions of free, white prosperous people, and no slave among them," Lincoln attributed to the intention and forethought of Thomas Jefferson. He also hated slavery for the "monstrous injustice" of the institution itself. Finally, he hated slavery for its prostitution of the ideals of American democracy. He declared[8]:

> This . . . real zeal for the spread of slavery, I cannot but hate. . . . I hate it because it deprives our republican example of its just influence in the world—enabling the enemies of free institutions, with plausibility to taunt us as hypocrites—causes the real friends of freedom to doubt our sincerity, and especially because it forces so many good men amongst ourselves into an open war with the very fundamental principles of civil liberty. . . .[9]

But this rather strong indictment of slavery did not mean that Lincoln was unsympathetic toward the South. "If all earthly power was given to me, I should not know what to do, as to the existing institution," he said, taking some of the sting out of his rebuke to slaveholders. If the circumstances had been reversed, the North, Lincoln thought, would have reacted just as the South.[10]

Lincoln based his argument against the extension of slavery in the Territories upon the principle of the right of self-government. He deeply believed in the "proposition that each man should do precisely as he pleases with all that is exclusively his own. . . ." Perhaps this was why he wrestled boldly with the

[8] J. B. McClure (ed.), *Abraham Lincoln's Speeches Complete* . . . (Chicago: Rhodes and McClure Publishing Co., 1891), pp. 81, 83. Here is a very important speech for racial ideas, though specifically concerned with the Missouri Compromise, October 16, 1854, Peoria, Ill. This speech also reflects the Jeffersonian antecedents of Lincoln's ideas on race.

[9] Basler, *Collected Works,* II, 255. Speech at Peoria, Ill., October 16, 1854.

[10] Ibid.

dilemma presented by the blacks. Would not the question soon be asked: Should blacks have the right of self-government? Lincoln did ask the question and concluded: "If the Negro is a *man*, why then my ancient faith teaches me that 'all men are created equal,' and that there can be no more right in connection with a man's making a slave of another."[11] Is it any wonder that some people thought Lincoln smitten with abolitionism? He spoke in this humanitarian vein until political realities brought him back to earth. "Let it not be said," he cautioned quickly, "that I am contending for the establishment of political and social equality between the whites and the blacks." He assured his audience that he was in perfect harmony with "the argument of necessity," arising from the presence of blacks in this country. He simply would not use the rationalization that they were not included in the Declaration of Independence as an excuse to take slavery into the Territories.[12]

Racial reservations to the contrary, Lincoln felt that the love of liberty as a principle was regressing at mid-nineteenth century. "On the question of liberty . . . ," he lamented to a Kentucky judge, "we are not what we have been. That all men are created equal was once for Americans a self-evident truth . . . but now when we have grown fat, and have lost all dread of being slaves ourselves, we have become so greedy to be masters, that we call the same maxim 'a self-evident lie.' "[13] He told another friend that the Declaration of Independence now read, "*All men are created equal except* Negroes. When the know-nothings get control, it will read, *all men are created equal except Negroes and foreigners and Catholics*. When it comes to this," said Lincoln, "I shall prefer emigrating to some country where they make no pretense of loving liberty—to Russia. . . ."[14]

Stephen Douglas could not understand how Lincoln could include blacks in Jefferson's great treatise and at the same

[11] Ibid., II, 266.

[12] Basler, *Collected Works*, II, 240, 276. Speech at Peoria, Ill., October 16, 1854.

[13] Nicolay and Hay, *Complete Works*, I, 215–16. Letter to Hon. George Robertson, August 15, 1855.

[14] *Speeches and Letters of Abraham Lincoln, 1832–1865*. Letter to Joshua Speed, August 24, 1855. See also speech at Springfield, Ill., June 26, 1857.

time deny the social and political equality of the races. He seldom missed an opportunity to call this discrepancy to his adversary's attention.[15] As a candidate, Lincoln could both affirm and deny the equality of the Afro-American with great facility. He exercised this option on numerous occasions during his debates with Douglas. In 1858, for example, after telling his audience that race factors would prevent blacks and whites from getting along together, he said:

> . . . But I hold that, notwithstanding all this, there is no reason in the world why the Negro is not entitled to all the rights enumerated in the Declaration of Independence. . . . I hold that he is as much entitled to these as the white man. . . . In the right to eat the bread without leave of anybody else which his hand earns he is my equal . . . and the equal of every white man.[16]

Here, Lincoln was cutting the rights of blacks in America down to the bare subsistence level. A week or two later Lincoln, with obvious impatience, scribbled on a piece of paper:

> I do not perceive how I can more plainly express myself than I have done. . . . I have expressly disclaimed all intention to promote [?] social and political equality between the whites and blacks. I have made it equally plain that I believe the Nego [Negro?] is included in the word "men" used in the Declaration of Independence.[17]

Lincoln probably expressed the quintessence of his thoughts on the Declaration of Independence in the southern end of the state. With customary ambivalence he contended that there was no doubt that the Fathers "intended to include all men" in that document. But he also explained at some length that it was equally certain that "they did not mean to say all men

[15] Angle, *Debates*, pp. 291–93. Speech in Galesburg, Ill., October 7, 1858.

[16] Ibid., p. 327. Speech at Quincy, Ill., October 12, 1858. See also pp. 39–42 for similar sentiments in speech at Chicago, July 10, 1858. See also the Robert Todd Lincoln Collection of the Papers of Abraham Lincoln (MSS in the Library of Congress), Vol. 7, No. 1348, ser. I. (Hereafter this citation will be RTLC.) See letter of D. G. Hay, September 1, 1858, who tried to show Lincoln how social and political equality could be denied the Negro without violation of the Declaration of Independence.

[17] RTLC, op. cit., Vol. 7, No. 1404, ser. I. See fragment of uncertain date [September 16, 1858]. Here he gave Henry Clay as his authority for including the Negro in the Declaration.

were equal in *all respects* [italics added]. They did not mean to say all men were equal in color, size, intellect, moral development, or social capacity." The future President then took this position: The Declaration made all men equal in the right to life, liberty, and the pursuit of happiness. The Fathers, while they knew that all men were not actually enjoying these rights, "meant simply to declare the *right* so that the *enforcement* of it might follow as fast as circumstances should permit. They meant to set up a standard maxim for a free society which would be familiar to all . . . and even though never perfectly attained, continually approximated and thereby constantly spreading and deepening its influence and augmenting the happiness and value of life to all peoples, of all colors."[18] Here was an excellent exposition on the ultimate aspiration of American democracy. In this statement, Lincoln gave one of the most worthy interpretations of that famous document. The statement expresses clearly the "American Dilemma," as well as Lincoln's. For in spite of his desire not to jettison democratic principles, he believed that racial sensitivities were proper "circumstances" for delaying the complete implementation of that "Charter of American Liberties." Still, it is to Lincoln's credit that he did not sanction total repudiation of the principles of American democracy at a time when he was under great pressures to do so.

It may well be that Lincoln lost the senatorial race in 1858 because he insisted, in the face of popular Negrophobia, that black men were also included in the Declaration of Independence. He felt that Douglas and the Democratic party had succeeded in whipping up an increasing anti-black sentiment and he was alarmed:

> . . . Douglas . . . has got his entire party . . . saying that the Negro has no share in the Declaration of Independence. . . . The tendency is to bring the public mind to the conclusion that when . . . Negroes are spoken of, brutes alone are contemplated. That change in public sentiment has already degraded the black man . . . from the condition of a man of some sort, and assigned him to the condition of a brute.[19]

[18] Angle, *Debates,* p. 370. Speech at Alton, Ill., October 15, 1858.

[19] Nicolay and Hay, *Complete Works,* I, 262–63. Speech to Kentuckians in Cincinnati, Ohio, September 1859.

Rejecting the theory of inevitable race conflict, Lincoln said: "If there was a necessary conflict between the white man and the Negro, I would be for the white man as much as Judge Douglas; but I say there is no such necessary conflict. I say there is room enough for all to be free."[20] He was not to be so generous at a later date.

Why did Lincoln include blacks in the Declaration of Independence and at the same time refuse to support abolition? His political beliefs forced him into this position. To Lincoln, slavery was a local institution, falling entirely within the ken of state prerogative and therefore immune to congressional action. There is no reason to doubt the sincerity of Lincoln's conviction that "the Congress . . . has no power to interfere with the institution of slavery in the different states," and certainly not without the consent of the people.[21] With obvious reference to the Fugitive Slave Law, he told a friend: "I confess I hate to see the poor creatures hunted down and caught and carried back to their stripes and unrequited toil; but I bite my lips and keep quiet. . . . It is not fair for you to assume," he continued with evident feeling, "that I have no interest in a thing which has, and continually exercises, the power of making me miserable." Lincoln was not unaware that the North, while not necessarily pro-black, was, in a large measure, antislavery. "You ought to appreciate," he gently chided his correspondent, "how much the great body of the Northern people do crucify their feelings in order to maintain their loyalty to the Constitution and the Union. . . ."[22]

Lincoln remained loyal to the states' rights theory when he reached the presidency. During his first inaugural address, he recalled a previously proposed amendment which stipulated that "the Federal government shall never interfere with the domestic institutions of the states, including that of persons held to

[20] Ibid., p. 265.

[21] L. E. Chittenden (comp.), *Abraham Lincoln's Speeches* (New York: Dodd, Mead and Co., 1895), p. 25. This was the position taken by Lincoln and Dan Stone in the Illinois Legislature in March 1837 on the question of slavery in the District of Columbia.

[22] Nicolay and Hay, *Complete Works*, I, 216. Letter to Joshua Speed, August 24, 1855.

service." He felt that the Constitution *already* implied as much, so he said, "I have no objection to its being made express and irrevocable."[23] One of Lincoln's secretaries alleged that Lincoln's main objection to the Wade-Davis bill, the Reconstruction plan of the radicals in Congress, was its attempt to free the slaves without the benefit of a constitutional amendment.[24] It is not unlikely that Lincoln's awareness of the race problem inherent in the abolition of slavery contributed to his disposition to hide his ambivalence on this point behind constitutional scruples. On the other hand there was no question about his position on racial intermingling.

The Impropriety of Race Mixing

Because Lincoln included the black man in the Declaration of Independence, Douglas accused him of advocating race mixing. Lincoln did not think anyone really believed the charge.[25] He certainly did not believe in interracial procreation. He thought nearly all white people naturally loathed the "idea of an indiscriminate amalgamation of the white and black races."[26] Douglas was "especially horrified at the thought of the mixing of blood by the white and black races . . . ," and Lincoln agreed. "A thousand times agreed," he shouted. "There are white men enough to marry all the white women, and black men enough to marry all the black women, and so let them be married." The two men did not differ on this subject. They were at odds, it seems, only on the best method of preventing the admixture of the bloods.

Admitting that "a separation of the two races is the only perfect prevention of amalgamation," Lincoln thought that keeping blacks out of the Territories was a better way of

[23] James D. Richardson (comp.), A *Compilation of the Messages and Papers of the Presidents,* 1789–1897 (Washington: Government Printing Office, 1896–1900), VI, 5, 11 (March 4, 1861). (Hereafter this source will be cited as Messages.)

[24] Tyler Dennett (ed.), *Lincoln and the Civil War: In the Diaries and Letters of John Hay* (New York: Dodd, Mead and Co., 1939), pp. 204–05, entry made by Hay, July 4, 1964.

[25] Basler, *Collected Works,* II, 391. A fragment dated 1854.

[26] Ibid., p. 408.

preventing intermingling in Kansas, for example, than the squatter sovereignty principle of Douglas. In a not wholly serious vein he said, "If white and black people never get together in Kansas, they will never mix blood in Kansas. That is at least one self-evident truth." Slavery and the degeneration of free blacks were for Lincoln the twin seedbeds of race fusion.[27] His thesis was that the nearer blacks approached equality with the whites, the less amalgamation took place. Therefore, black slaves and white masters produced more mulattoes than did whites and free blacks. Small wonder that New Hampshire had only 184 mixed bloods while Virginia had over 70,000 of them, according to Lincoln.[28]

On another occasion Lincoln considered the hypothetical chances of Dred Scott's daughter having sexual relations with whites if the Supreme Court had declared her free. By Lincolnian logic if the High Tribunal had freed Scott and his daughters, "the chances of [those] black girls ever mixing their blood with that of white people, would have been diminished, at least to the extent that it could not occur without their consent." But if they remained slaves they would more likely be subjected to "the forced concubinage of their masters and liable to become mothers of mulattoes in spite of themselves." Had not nine-tenths of all the mulattoes in the country been produced that way? Lincoln thought the majority of the Republican party shared his view that the only effective preventative of amalgamation was racial separation.[29] Pressed by Douglas, Lincoln repeatedly asserted his anti-amalgamation sentiments. He protested against that "counterfeit logic which presumes that because I do not want a Negro woman for a slave, I do necessarily want her for a wife. I need not have her for either, but *as God has made us separate* [italics added] we can leave one another alone and do one another more good thereby. . . .[30] From the idea of natural separateness based on

[27] Ibid.
[28] Basler, *Collected Works*, II, 408.
[29] Ibid.
[30] Angle, *Debates*, pp. 39, 23. Speech at Charleston, Ill., September 18, 1858.

recognizable physical differences, Lincoln inferred the impropriety of mixing the races.

Facetiously Lincoln stated that he never had the slightest apprehension that he or any of his friends would marry blacks even if there were no law to keep them from it. This remark brought laughter from the crowd. He continued to poke fun at Douglas by giving him his "solemn pledge" that he would stand to the very last "by the law of the State [of Illinois] which forbids the marrying of white people with Negroes." He again bared his political creed when he said he knew of no place where the social and political relations of the races could be altered ". . . except in the state legislature—not in the Congress of the United States. . . ."[31] Here was an indication of the approach he would bring to the problem of race relations on the national level where action, as well as thought, was called for.

Theory versus Practice

Before he came to the White House Lincoln did not believe in social and political equality of the races, the Declaration of Independence to the contrary notwithstanding.

On Social and Political Equality

"I go for all sharing the privileges of the government who assist in bearing its burdens. Consequently I go for admitting *all* whites [italics added] to the right of suffrage, who pay taxes or bear arms . . . ," the twenty-seven-year-old candidate for the Illinois State Legislature informed the editor of the *Sagamo Journal* in 1836.[32] An Illinois black leader accused Lincoln of once having "refused to sign a legislative petition asking for the repeal of the state law barring Negro testimony

[31] Angle, *Debates*, p. 39.
[32] Basler, *Collected Works*, I, 48.

in cases involving whites."[33] Initially then, Lincoln was in harmony with the prevailing racial public opinion in his state.

Although he did not agree that blacks or abolitionists should be unjustly treated,[34] Lincoln was unwilling to grant blacks full equality. Sometimes he found the question rather irritating, and once he asked publicly, ". . . what next? Free them and make them politically and socially our equals? My own feelings will not admit of this; and if mine would we well know that those of the great mass of white people would not. Whether this feeling accords with justice and sound judgment, is not the sole question, if indeed, it is any part of it. A universal feeling, whether well or ill founded, cannot safely be disregarded. We cannot make them our equals."[35] Lincoln implied that public opinion was the great and final arbiter of all questions.

On the eve of the Civil War, the charge of Negrophilism could mean political death. Lincoln resisted the attempt of Douglas to smear him with the tarbrush of equality. ". . . What I would most desire would be the separation of the white and black races . . . ," Lincoln retorted on the defensive. "I will say then that I am not, nor ever have been in favor of bringing about in any way the social and political equality of the white and black races," Lincoln said in a debate with Douglas. The crowd applauded and Lincoln continued rather emphatically:

> . . . I am not or ever have been in favor of making voters, or jurors of Negroes nor of qualifying them to hold office, nor to marry with white people. . . . I will say . . . in addition . . . that there is a physical difference between the white and black races which I believe will forever forbid the two races living together on terms of social and political equality. And inasmuch as they cannot so live, while they do remain together there must be the position of superior and inferior, and I as much as any other

[33] Quoted in Leon F. Litwack, *North of Slavery: The Negro in the Free States, 1790–1860* (Chicago: University of Chicago Press, 1961), p. 275.

[34] Basler, *Collected Works*, I, 110–11. Speech on "The Perpetuation of Our Political Institutions," delivered to the Young Men's Lyceum, Springfield, Ill., 1838.

[35] McClure, *Abraham Lincoln's Speeches Complete . . .*, pp. 93–111. Speech in Peoria, Ill., October 16, 1854.

man am in favor of having the superior position assigned to the white race.[36]

Such was the core of Lincoln's racial creed in 1858. Significantly, he was quoting almost verbatim from the racial philosophy of the patron saint of democracy, Thomas Jefferson.[37] But Lincoln's sense of justice would not allow him to leave the issue there. He hastened to add that what he had just said should not be construed to mean "that the Negro should be denied everything." Taking refuge in public opinion he said that he had ". . . never seen . . . a man, woman, or child who was in favor of producing a perfect equality, social and political, between Negroes and white men."[38] But Douglas wanted an unequivocal answer from Lincoln on the question of blacks' citizenship. "I tell him very frankly that I am not in favor of Negro citizenship," Lincoln retorted.[39] Clearly Lincoln did not wish to get out of step with the *status quo* of racial thought in his own state. He never "manifested any impatience with the *necessities* [italics added] that spring from the actual presence of black people amongst us, and the actual existence of slavery amongst us where it already exist[s]," as he himself put it, perhaps a bit too strongly.[40] Social and political discriminations, fugitive slave laws, these were "racial necessities" which he would tolerate for the sake of Union.

[36] Angle, *Debates*, p. 235. Speech at Charleston, Ill., September 18, 1858; McClure, op. cit., pp. 211–14. Speech at Columbus, Ohio, September 1859. Nicolay and Hay, *Complete Works*, I, 272–73. Speech at Springfield, Ill., July 17, 1858; RTLC, Vol. 6, No. 1130–31, ser. I, letter to Judge David Davis, August 3, 1858, advising Lincoln on the "bugaboo of Negro equality"; ibid., No. 1155. Letter of Hiram Tremble, August 4, 1858, ibid., Vol. 7, No. 1404. See fragment dated September 16, 1858.

[37] Paul L. Ford (ed.), *The Works of Thomas Jefferson* . . . (New York: G. P. Putnam, 1904–05), I, 68. Jefferson, at the ripe old age of seventy-seven, was reflecting upon the failure of his emancipation plan of an earlier day: "It was found that the Public mind would not yet bear the proposition . . . nor will it bear it even today . . . nor is it less certain that the two races equally free, cannot live in the same government. Nature, habit, opinion, has drawn indelible lines of distinctions between them."

[38] Angle, *Debates*, p. 235.

[39] Angle, *Debates*, p. 266.

[40] Basler, *Collected Works*, III, 222. Speech at Galesburg, III., October 7, 1858.

Some newspapers were pleased with Lincoln's anti-black assertions.[41] But as far as one southern Illinois paper, the *Jacksonville Sentinel,* was concerned, Lincoln had failed to extricate himself altogether from the charge of belief in social equality. ". . . We are informed that he [Lincoln] took his text from the Declaration of Independence and labored for an hour to prove by that instrument that the Negro was born with rights equal with the whites, thus by implication assailing the Constitution . . . which supports slavery . . . ," ran the editorial.[42] Lincoln best stated his side of the case when he scribbled these words on a fragment of paper: "Negro equality! Fudge! How long, in the Government of a God great enough to make and rule the universe, shall there continue knaves to vend, and fools to quip, so low a piece of demagogism as this."[43] At the moment Lincoln was not for the equality of the races—at least not "unqualifiedly."[44] But at the same time he was by no means a Negrophobe.

At least once Lincoln referred to a black man as a "boy." He asked the Secretary of the Treasury to find a job for one ". . . William Johnson, a colored boy, who came from Illinois with me. . . ."[45] Yet no less a person than Frederick Douglass testified to the point that on an individual basis Lincoln surmounted the restrictive barrier of race. After an obviously dynamic encounter with the President at the White House, the black orator reported him "entirely free from popular prejudice against the colored people. He was the first great man that I talked with in the United States freely," continued Douglass, "who in no single instance, reminded me of the difference between himself and myself of the differences of color. . . ."[46]

[41] Ibid., I, 83. Editorial report on Lincoln's speech at Clinton, Ill., September 3, 1858, Bloomington, [Ill.]; pantograph, ibid., III, 96. Editorial in the *Greenville Advocate,* September 13, 1858.

[42] Basler, *Collected Works,* III, 328. Editorial in the *Jacksonville Sentinel,* October 22, 1858; ibid., III, 401. Editorial in the *Ohio Statesman;* ibid., IV, 56. See letter written December 18, 1860.

[43] Basler, *Collected Works,* III, 369 [1859].

[44] Ibid., IV, 56.

[45] RTLC, Vol. 204, No. 43447, ser. III (November 29, 1861).

[46] Quoted in Phillip S. Foner (ed.), *The Life and Writings of Frederick Douglass* (New York: International Publishers, 1950–55), III, 36–37. Douglass, disgusted with Lincoln's halting attitude toward blacks, had gone to the

In short, Douglass was not made aware of his race while in the presence of the President. Douglass was obviously overwhelmed by the racial demeanor of Lincoln when he was granted an interview at the White House. ". . . I have been down there to see the President," he later related to an antislavery group in Philadelphia. ". . . You may like to know how the President received a black man at the White House. I will tell you how he received me—just as you have seen one gentleman receive another," Douglass recounted amid great applause, "with a hand and a voice well balanced between a kind cordiality and a respectful reserve. I tell you I felt big there," said Douglass amidst more laughter from his audience. While Douglass did not see eye to eye with Lincoln on the conduct of the war he was convinced that the President would go down in history as "honest Abraham."[47] Douglass later claimed that he once had tea at the White House with the President.[48]

Another black man, claiming a "long acquaintance," wrote with great familiarity to the President, thanking him for a personal favor and for his general attitude toward the lowly. He called himself "Billy the Barber," and talked in a rather "folksy" way about Lincoln's children and home in Springfield as well as about his own children.[49] A few months later, when asked how he felt about ex-slaves working under contract on the plantations of their old masters, Lincoln answered, "I . . . should regard such cases with great favor and should, as the principle, treat them precisely as I would treat the same number of free white people in the same relation and condition. Whether

---

White House in July 1863. He came away a changed man, still in disagreement with the President but completely convinced of his sincerity.

[47] Foner, op. cit., III, 378–86. "I have just come from President Lincoln. He treated me as a man; he did not let me feel for a moment that there was any difference in the color of our skins." Douglass allegedly related this to John Eaton; see Eaton, *Grant, Lincoln and the Freedmen: Reminiscences of the Civil War* . . . (New York: Longmans, Green and Co., 1907), p. 75.

[48] Foner, op. cit., IV, 27–28. Douglass made this claim at the Republican Convention, Philadelphia, 1866, but he did not indicate when this supposed incident took place. The incident, if true, may be compared to the Booker T. Washington dinner at the White House with Theodore Roosevelt almost forty years later.

[49] RTLC, Vol. 136, No. 28923, ser. I. Letter of William [Fleurville?] the Barber, December 27, 1863.

white or black, reasonable effort should be made to give government protection."[50] Toward the end of the war, then, Lincoln's racial views were mellowing—but not before he had seriously toyed with the idea of black expatriation.

Colonization Advocated as the Solution to the Race Problem

Long before he reached the presidency, Lincoln accepted the idea of colonization as the best solution for the race problem in the South, if not in the nation. The reason behind this racial expatriation was the prevention of amalgamation. Lincoln advocated the measure on at least thirteen different occasions. Out of some thirty surviving pieces of mail that went to the White House on this subject, during the war years, at least twenty-four counseled the President to banish black people because of racial incompatibility. Only four letters were raised against this remedy.

As far as Lincoln was concerned, colonization should not be compulsory, but free blacks as well as slaves would be encouraged to accept the invitation. When praising the colonization imperative of Henry Clay, Lincoln quoted Jefferson as saying that the prospect of emancipation without the compulsion of expatriation was like having ". . . the wolf by the ears; we can neither hold him nor safely let him go. Justice is in one scale; and self-preservation in the other."[51] Lincoln was aware that for many people the factor of race complicated all questions of emancipation. He was sympathetic to the South for this reason. Hating both equality and inequality, his first impulse was to free the slaves and send them to Liberia, "to their own native land." Eventually insurmountable difficulties caused him to despair of colonization at times, forcing him to call simply for gradual emancipation.[52]

[50] RTLC, Vol. 139, No. 29765–66, ser. I. Letter of Abraham Lincoln to Alpheus Lewis, January 23, 1864.

[51] Basler, *Collected Works,* IV, 32. Eulogy on Henry Clay, delivered in Springfield, Ill., July 16, 1852; Nicolay and Hay, *Complete Works,* II, 173.

[52] McClure, *Abraham Lincoln's Speeches Complete . . . ,* pp. 93–111. Speech on the Missouri Compromise, at Peoria, Ill., October 16, 1854.

The mail brought the President many suggestions concerning the subject.[53] Orville H. Browning, a close friend of Lincoln's, claims that Lincoln told him blacks would be colonized after the War.[54] At any rate, Lincoln had not been long in the White House before the wheels started turning which were to move the Afro-American out of the country to some obscure place in South America.[55] In his first annual message to Congress, Lincoln implored them to consider the diplomatic recognition of Liberia and Haiti and requested an appropriation to colonize liberated slaves "in a climate congenial to them. . . ." "It might be well to consider too," he added significantly, "whether the free colored people already in the United States, could not, so far as individuals may desire, be included in such a colonization."[56] With an obvious appeal to the prejudices of the whites, Lincoln said: "If it be said that the only legitimate object of acquiring territory is to furnish homes for white men; this measure effects that object; for the emigration of colored men leaves additional room for whites remaining or coming here."[57]

The President's proposal for colonization brought him some interesting letters. John Latrobe, president of the American Colonization Society, was disturbed because Lincoln left the

[53] RTLC, Vol. 5, No. 882, ser. I. Letter of Kitchel Wickiffe [?], Hillsboro [Tenn.], June 14, 1858. He wanted to send the Negroes to Latin America immediately and halt the degeneration of the white race. RTLC, Vol. 61, No. 13003–05, ser. I. Letter of Francis P. Blair, November 16, 1861. He told the President that Guatemala was willing to take the Negroes. He told Lincoln that the time of which Jefferson had spoken had arrived. The African race either had to be deported or exterminated since "the prejudice of caste is [as] indelible as the love of liberty unconquerable. . . ."

[54] Theodore C. Pease and James G. Randall (eds.), *The Diary of Orville Hickman Browning, 1850–1864*, I, 478 (*Collections* of the Illinois State Historical Library, XX, Lincoln Series, II, Springfield: State Historical Library, 1927). Entry for July 8, 1861.

[55] RTLC, Vol. 59, No. 12770, ser. I. See an executive memorandum to the Secretary of the Interior, 1861; Paul J. Scheips, "Lincoln and the Chiriqui Colonization Project" (Reprint from the *Journal of Negro History*, 37:418–53, October 1952); Andrew N. Cleven, "Some Plans for Colonizing Liberated Negro Slaves in Hispanic America," *Journal of Negro History*, 11:35–50 (January 1926).

[56] Basler, *Collected Works*, V, 48. This suggestion was made necessary, in part, by the passage of the Confiscation Act, August 6, 1861, calling for the impounding of rebel property, including slaves.

[57] Ibid.

matter to Congress rather than relying upon his executive power to recognize Liberia.[58] "Who can read the message of the President," wrote the abolitionist Gerrit Smith to Thaddeus Stevens in disgust, "and see with what twaddle and trash the President has filled the space which should have been devoted to such great words on the great question. . . . Who, I say, can do so without feeling that the President is not the man for the hour?" According to Smith, the President wasted words "upon that utterly atheistic topic of 'homes for white men.'" Smith felt that Lincoln should have been talking about arming blacks rather than expelling them from the country. He felt that there was room enough in the country for both races. After soundly rebuking the President's position on colonization, emancipation, and on the arming and equal treatment of blacks, Smith concluded: "I am not disposed to underrate the President. . . . I admit [however] that he would have made a good President had he only not been trained to worship the Constitution."[59] On the other hand, a preacher from Indiana was very pleased with what the President had to say about colonization and was anxious to see black people on their way out of the country.[60]

When the President presented his plan for compensated emancipation to Congress in March of 1862 without calling for the removal of blacks, letters reached the White House urging upon him the imperative of colonization. Montgomery Blair, Postmaster General, encouraged the President, while the *New York Times* was impressed with the President's wisdom and awareness of the complexities of emancipation. The *Times* predicted that the country would refuse to pay the rebels for their slaves and that the country would not pay the cost of the Afro-Americans' transportation home.[61]

[58] RTLC, Vol. 62, No. 13255–56. Letter of John Latrobe to W. H. Seward, December 5, 1861.

[59] RTLC, Vol. 60, No. 12975, ser. I. Letter of Gerrit Smith to Thaddeus Stevens, December 6, 1861.

[60] RTLC, Vol. 62, No. 13389–95, ser. I. Letter of Reverend James Mitchell to Abraham Lincoln, December 6, 1861.

[61] RTLC, Vol. 105, No. 22217–18, ser. I. Letter of Montgomery Blair [March 6–14, 1862?]. Blair urged Lincoln to include free Negroes in his colonization plans; RTLC, Vol. 70, No. 14819, ser. I; Nos. 14820, 14822, for

"I have never doubted the constitutional authority of Congress to abolish slavery in the District . . . ," the President told Congress when slavery was abolished in the District of Columbia in April 1862. But then he added, "I am gratified that the two principles of compensation and colonization are both recognized; and practically applied in the Act."[62] The Congregational Church approved Lincoln's message on the measure and told the President that "future generations will rise up and call you blessed."[63] Caleb Smith suggested that in order to carry out the proposed "colonization of the blacks, the services of an efficient agent familiar with the subject would be very useful." Smith recommended the Right Reverend James Mitchell of Indiana.[64] His recommendation was followed and Mitchell became the new Commissioner of Emigration—black emigration. Mitchell then prepared a twenty-eight-page pamphlet setting forth the case for colonization, for the President's consideration. He was anxious to give blacks ". . . *separate* nationality," through expatriation.[65]

In view of what has been said up to this point it should not be difficult to understand the President's next move. On August

editorials from the *New York World* and *Evening Post*, March 7, 1862; RTLC, Vol. 75, No. 15840, ser. I. Letter of John B. Hepburn [May 7, 1862?], a colored expatriate living in Haiti, recommending Liberia over Haiti; RTLC, Vol. 76, No. 16031–34, ser. I. Letter to Thomas Corwin, Mexico, to Mr. A. C. Allen, May 18, 1862. The American minister to Mexico called for a treaty with Mexico to facilitate Negro colonization there; No. 16035. A printed broadside gave more arguments on the same subject. It said among other things: "It is well known that the Mexicans as a nation have no aversion to the African race." No. 16039. "The Leading Ideas of a Sermon Preached by one E. Kelly of the Second Baptist Church," New Bedford, [Mass.], was a rare voice calling in the wilderness for the affirmation of the melting-pot idea with the Negro included! RTLC, Vol. 82, No. 17427–34, ser. I. Letter of U. P. Usher, August 2, 1862, urging colonization as a means of "relieving the free states of the apprehension that they are to be overrun by Negroes made free by the War."

62 RTLC, Vol. 73, No. 15541, ser. I. Message to Congress, April 16, 1862, on the abolition of slavery in the District of Columbia.

63 Ibid., No. 15594. April 18, 1862. The church was in Cleveland.

64 Ibid., Vol. 75, No. 15829. Letter, May 5, 1862. Mr. Mitchell came from Jeffersonville, [southern] Ind.

65 RTLC, Vol. 76, No. 16044, ser. I. James Mitchell, "Letter on the Relation of the White and African Races in the United States Showing the Necessity of the Colonization of the Latter, Addressed to the President of the U. S." (Washington: Government Printing Office, 1862), 28 pp.; Vol. 98, No. 20758. Letter [n.d.] of Reverend Mitchell to an unidentified Negro preacher, sometime in 1861.

14, 1862, he called a group of blacks to the White House and told them about one of the hard realities of American life concerning the future of black men in the United States. What transpired must have been a bitter pill for the blacks to swallow. Lincoln told them that Congress had made an appropriation to colonize their kind outside the country, that he had long been in favor of the idea and that he wanted to tell them why this step was necessary. He began:

> You and we are different races. We have between us a broader difference than exists between any other two races. Whether it is right or wrong I need not discuss, but this physical difference is a great disadvantage to us both, as I think your race suffer very greatly, many of them by living among us, while ours suffer from your presence. . . . If this be admitted, it affords a reason at least why we should be separated. . . . Your race are suffering in my judgement, the greatest wrong inflicted on any people. But even when you cease to be slaves, you are yet far removed from being placed on an equality with the white race. You are cut off from many of the advantages which, the other race enjoy. . . . On this broad continent not a single man of your race is made the equal of a single man of ours. . . . Go where you are treated the best. . . .

For Lincoln the fact of physical difference made racial harmony impossible. He told the delegation of blacks that what he had just said was not a matter for discussion but "a fact with which we have to deal. I cannot alter it if I would. It is a fact about which we all think and feel alike, I and you." Again the President was prostrating himself helplessly before what Lord Bryce called the "fatalism of the multitude," before that great arbiter of issues in America, public opinion. Then Lincoln stated what probably was the great enigma of the Civil War: "But for your race among us, there could not be a war, although many men engaged on either side for you do not care one way or the other."[66] Lincoln had hoped to discover a group of in-

[66] Basler, *Collected Works*, V, 371.

telligent free blacks willing to be the first to emigrate to Central America, thus setting an example for the more timid freedmen to follow. He apologized for having to send them to such a wilderness, but gave his assurance that a warm welcome was awaiting them. Latin Americans, he declared, "are more generous than we are. To your colored race they have no objections. Besides, I would endeavor to have you made equals and have the best assurance that you will be the equal of the best."[67] How odd that the President promised to make blacks equal in Central America although he could not accomplish this in his own country.

Lincoln's proposal fell on deaf ears as far as the blacks were concerned. Furthermore, it soon developed that Latin Americans were not as receptive to the plan as Lincoln had supposed them to be. One report had it that the "Negroes in the District of Columbia received the colonization proposal with hostility. . . . The project was abandoned when first Honduras and later Nicaragua and Costa Rica protested the scheme and hinted that force might be used to prevent the settlement."[68] Frederick Douglass disagreed with Lincoln's proposal and rejected Lincoln's thesis that the "mere presence" of blacks caused the war and accused the President of being "a genuine representative of American prejudice and Negro hatred."[69]

Montgomery Blair tried to convince Douglass of the purity of the motives that impelled the Lincoln Administration to a policy of racial separation. He denied the imputation that black inferiority was the implicit assumption upon which the impulse to colonize rested. "The propriety of the removal," he tried to explain to Douglass, "arises . . . simply for the differences which the Creator Himself has made. . . ."[70] Douglass rejected this argument also and contended with unusual historical insight that considering the expansion of Europe into the waste

[67] Ibid.

[68] Ibid., V, 371–72. See editorial note.

[69] Foner, *Life and Writings of Frederick Douglass*, III, 266–70. Taken from an article in *Douglass Monthly*, September 1862.

[70] Foner, *The Life and Writings of Frederick Douglass*, III, 281. Letter of Montgomery Blair, September 11, 1862.

places of the world the black man could not escape the white man even if he wanted to.[71]

After Lincoln issued his preliminary emancipation plan on September 22, 1862, colonization was discussed frequently and fervently in Cabinet meetings. According to Attorney General Bates, the President asked all of the heads of departments to submit their ideas on the propriety of initiating plans to colonize free and freed blacks.[72] The essence of a much revised passage in Welles's diary stated that the President, at the encouragement of Blair and Smith, was "in earnest" to get the blacks started on their way. "The President keeps bringing it up," said Welles, who further declared that the President "thought it essential to provide an asylum for a race which we had emancipated, but which could never be recognized or admitted to be our equals." Blair, according to Welles, gave a long argument in a Cabinet meeting in favor of colonization. Welles reported that Bates favored compulsory deportation but Bates's own testimony contradicts this. Welles held that "the President objected unequivocally to compulsion." He would rather blacks go voluntarily, without expense to themselves and under the protection of a treaty.[73] It is ironic that while Lincoln and his Cabinet were hatching colonization plans, the Attorney General, Bates, who supposedly, according to Welles, disliked blacks, ruled two months later that qualification for citizenship depended not on color, race, condition, or the right to vote and hold office, and that blacks born free in the United States were citizens of the

[71] Foner, *The Life and Writings of Frederick Douglass*, III, 256. Letter from Frederick Douglass to Montgomery Blair, September 16, 1862. Douglass said: "But if we really wish to get away from this great Anglo-Saxon race; the plan now commenced to free the colored people would be unavailing. Indeed, no plan of separation can be permanently successful. The white man's face is seen; and the white man's hand is felt in every part of the habitable globe. Asia bows to the teutonic sway, Europe acknowledges no other than Caucasian power, Africa is invaded by the white race on all sides. . . . You may send us to Central America this year and the white man will be at our elbow the next year. . . ."

[72] *The Diary of Edward Bates*, pp. 262–64, September 25, 1862.

[73] Howard K. Beale (ed.), *The Diary of Gideon Welles: Secretary of the Navy Under Lincoln and Johnson* (New York: W. W. Norton and Co., 1960), I, 151–52. (To be hereafter cited as Welles, *Diary*.) Entry for Friday, September 26, 1862. Welles claimed that Lincoln had hopes that England, France or Denmark would take the Negroes. Bates stated in his diary that he was against compulsory emigration.

same.[74] Meanwhile, the *Philadelphia Press* noted that the President's preliminary emancipation plan had "directed renewed attention to all plans for the colonization of the colored people in America. . . ."[75]

With regard to the black question, the major theme in Lincoln's second annual message to Congress was colonization. He reported that many free blacks had approached him favorably on this subject but that Latin America had refused to receive them and blacks were not anxious to go to Haiti or Liberia.[76] He then presented his plan for gradual, compensated emancipation coupled with voluntary expatriation after freedom. This much is certain; colonization, however he intended to carry it out, was very close to Lincoln's heart. "I cannot," he told Congress, "make it better known than it already is, that I strongly favor colonization." Though he did not say so on this occasion, Lincoln's real reason for colonization was the fact of physical differences of race and the resulting antipathies. He went to some pains to make it clear that he was not advocating deportation on economic grounds. Obviously referring to his mail, he told Congress that the idea of colonization had been suggested to him by "other parties at home and abroad," but for mixed motives.[77] He felt compelled to refute what he called "the largely imaginary, if not malicious," opinion of some people who would welcome the removal of blacks on the strength of their fear that the blacks would replace white laborers. Evidently there were those who wanted the black man out of the country permanently for economic reasons. Despite Lincoln's disclaimer, historian Richard Hofstadter has attributed Lincoln's plan for a colonization emancipation package to his concern for the free white laborers and his fear of black competition.[78]

[74] Leon Litwack, *North of Slavery* (1961), p. 63, reports this incident.

[75] RTLC, Vol. 88, No. 18665, ser. I. Newspaper clipping, September 26, 1862. RTLC, Vol. 84, No. 17708–09, ser. I. Letter to M. T. Coswell, Baltimore [August 16, 1862], Md.

[76] Basler, *Collected Works*, V, 521, December 1, 1862.

[77] Richardson, *Messages*, VI, 128.

[78] Richard Hofstadter, *The American Political Tradition and the Men Who Made It* (New York: Alfred Knopf, 1948), pp. 129–30.

While Lincoln denied any economic motives, and while he failed in his message to cite his racial reasons for colonization, he did pause long enough to note that colonization would reduce the supply of black labor and increase the demand for, as well as the wages of, white labor.[79] But one is inclined to feel that Lincoln mentioned this mostly for political effect—to satisfy his Negrophobic constituency from the Midwest. Lincoln's admitted racial rationale for colonization was his primary justification. He was trying to solve the race problem. For many people the Afro-American was an undesirable element in the population.

Continuing his second annual message, Lincoln next attempted to calm the fears of those who might oppose emancipation because of visions of a black invasion. Hypothetically, he argued that even if slaves were distributed equally among the whites of the entire country, there would be only one black to every seven whites, a proposition that did not constitute a threat in Lincoln's estimation. ". . . If gradual emancipation and deportation be adopted," the blacks would labor in the South for wages ". . . till new homes can be found for them in congenial climes—and with people of their own blood and race."[80] As far as blacks were concerned, Lincoln would by colonizing end them!

The President's desire for colonization began to decrease in 1863. This particular year brought increased participation of blacks in the armed forces. In April of 1863, Lincoln withdrew his support of an ill-fated attempt to colonize blacks in Haiti.[81] The next month the Secretary of the Interior advised the President that due to recent activities of the War Department, there would be no further black emigration "for the present," and that the services of the Reverend Mr. Mitchell could probably

[79] Basler, *Collected Works*, V, 534–35.
[80] Ibid., V, 535–36.
[81] Richardson, *Messages*, VI, 167. Proclamation, April 16, 1863. RTLC, Vol. 200, No. 42620, ser. II. Letter of James Delong, U.S. consul, Haiti, to Henry Conard, acting consul general, June 25, 1863. John Eaton, see Eaton, *Grant, Lincoln and the Freedmen . . .*, pp. 91–92. Eaton claims that Lincoln told him in an interview that efforts to solve the Negro question by colonization had failed. Also, he was told that the black expatriates on Cow Island, Haiti, were suffering from "Jiggers."

be dispensed with.[82] Still, on November 5, 1865, the President, at the prompting of black Emigration Commissioner Mitchell, approved a request of a black group calling itself the African Civilization Society, for five thousand dollars to aid in the stated aim of civilizing Africa and the descendants of Africans.[83]

In his third annual message the President dropped all mention of colonization. Instead he encouraged Congress to foster immigration to meet the "great deficiency of labor in every field of industry."[84] While the racially incompatible black was being invited out of the country, the ethnologically acceptable foreigner was asked to come in. On February 1, 1864, Lincoln sent a ship to Haiti to pick up such colored colonists as desired to return.[85] A few months later, one of Lincoln's private secretaries, John Hay, wrote with apparent relief in his diary: "I am glad that the President has sloughed off that idea of colonization. . . . I have always thought it a hideous and barbarous humbug. . . ."[86] This ended, at least for the Lincoln Administration, the saga of colonization. One cannot fail to be impressed with the racial basis of this movement both in presidential and public thought. The failure of black removal only further complicated the problem of emancipation. Should blacks be freed if they have to remain in the country?

Emancipation and Racial Necessity

If Lincoln's racial sensitivities and his awareness of the "universal feeling" of the American people on the subject of race are admitted, then the caution and hesitancy with which he approached emancipation are more easily understood. An examination of more than thirty surviving pieces of presidential correspondence on the subject showed at least twenty-five in

[82] RTLC, Vol. 3, No. 23555, ser. I. Letter of U. P. Usher, May 18, 1863.
[83] RTLC, Vol. 200, Nos. 42664, 42662, ser. II. Newspaper clipping of letter of African Civilization Society to James Mitchell, September 12, 1863, note from James Mitchell to A. Lincoln, November 5, 1863, memorandum of the President to Secretary of Interior, November 5, 1863.
[84] Richardson, *Messages*, VI, 182, 246. December 8, 1863.
[85] Richardson, *Messages*, VI, 232. Memorandum of A. Lincoln.
[86] John Hay, *Diaries and Letters*, p. 203. July 1, 1864.

favor of freedom and ten against it for fear of race war.[87] Some of the letter writers were disgusted with the presidential "slows" on the emancipation question. The usual explanation is that Lincoln wanted primarily to save the Union and did not want to lose the border states. Seldom mentioned is the racial factor, which is now to be considered.

Frederick Douglass had grave doubts about the antislavery sentiments of the President-elect in 1860. While he never questioned the President's honesty and sincerity, he was thoroughly vexed with the racial hesitations of Lincoln during much of the war.[88] When Lincoln overruled General Frémont's premature emancipation proclamation in Missouri, one of the President's friends, O. H. Browning, Illinois politician, disapproved and thought Lincoln was too soft on the rebels: "Is a traitor's Negro more sacred than his life?" asked Browning. ". . . I am very sorry the order was made. It has produced a great deal of excitement and is really filling the hearts of our friends with despondency."[89] Lincoln seemed a little irritated with Browning: "Yours of the 17th is just received and, coming from you, I confess it astonishes me . . . ," said the President. He then proceeded to argue that Frémont's proclamation was dictatorial, political, unconstitutional and beyond the scope of military necessity. Lincoln thought it was not for Frémont to fix the "permanent future condition" of the slaves. Browning must understand that he took his course on the proclamation "be-

[87] RTLC, Vol. 43, No. 9448, ser. I. Letter of the anonymous "Count Johannes," against emancipation, April 28, 1861. RTLC, Vol. 196, No. 42024, ser. II. Letter of David Wilder, former Massachusetts state auditor [April 24–September 4?], asking for gradual emancipation. RTLC, Vol. 56, No. 11975, ser. II. Letter of John L. Scripps, September 23, 1861, for emancipation. RTLC, Vol. 55, No. 11831, ser. I. Letter of George Webb to W. H. Seward, September 19, 1861, asking for emancipation. Ibid., No. 11833–34. Letter of John L. Williams, Chillicothe, Ohio [September 14, 20?], for emancipation. RTLC, Vol. 60, No. 12975. Newspaper clipping of letter of Gerrit Smith to Thaddeus Stevens, for emancipation. RTLC, Vol. 70, Nos. 14818, 14819–22. Newspaper clipping from the New York *Herald Tribune*, Friday, March 7, 1862. RTLC, Vol. 73, No. 15462–63, ser. I. Letter of R. P. G. Baber, Louisville, Ky., to F. P. Blair, April 12, 1862. RTLC, Vol. 81, No. 17089, ser. I. Anti-emancipation petition from citizens of Kentucky, Virginia, Missouri and Maryland, July 14, 1862.

[88] "The Late Election," *The Douglass Monthly* (December 1860), in Foner, *The Life and Writings of Frederick Douglass*, II, 527, 484–86.

[89] RTLC, Vol. 55, No. 11724, ser. I. Letter, September 17, 1861.

cause of Kentucky."[90] Lincoln was always afraid that any abolition action on his part might lose border slave states still in the Union—especially Kentucky.

When, on March 6, 1862, Lincoln presented his plan for gradual compensated emancipation in border states, he did not defend it on humanitarian grounds. Nor did he mention colonization. Instead, he chose to offer the plan as an indispensable means of preserving the Union, as "one of the most efficient means of self-preservation."[91] Since it is known that Lincoln wished the abolition of slavery but not in violation of state sovereignty, he may have masked his humane motives in the guise of political and military necessity for tactical reasons.

After his emancipation message, the President tried to persuade a group of border state representatives of the sweet reasonableness of manumission. The President leaned over backward to avoid offense to Southern sensibilities, but nevertheless they gave his plan a chilly reception. One suggested that slavery would die of natural causes, making the plan unnecessary. Lincoln shrewdly observed that the propensity of slavery to die a natural death did not prevent border state slaveowners from complaining when their chattels absconded to the Union lines. A representative from Maryland said that his state would gladly give up the blacks provided compensation and deportation were a part of the plan.[92]

According to O. H. Browning, Lincoln would have preferred gradual emancipation for the District of Columbia because sudden freedom would cause a servant problem for many whites and deprive the slave of his white protector.[93] Fear of race conflict may have been one of the factors that drove Lincoln to nullify General David Hunter's attempt to free slaves in South Carolina. "The strong tendency to a total disruption of society in

90 RTLC, Vol. 56, No. 1192, ser. I. Letter, September 22, 1861.

91 Richardson, *Messages,* VI, 68–69.

92 Nicolay and Hay, *Complete Works,* II, 134. "Notes on an interview between Lincoln and the border state men, March 10, 1862, taken by the Hon. J. W. Crisfield."

93 Browning, *Diary,* I, Monday, April 14, 1863. Browning also claimed that Lincoln told him he was going to defer the signing of the District of Columbia emancipation bill long enough to allow old Governor Wickcliffe to get his two servants out of the city.

the South is apparent. *You* can stay it; . . . I cannot. You can stay it without harming a hair of white or black," Lincoln started to say. Apparently thinking it best not to spell out too plainly his inner fears, he scratched out the preceding lines and wrote instead: "You cannot if you would, be blind to the signs of the times—I beg of you a calm and enlarge [d?] consideration of them. . . ."[94] Carl Schurz then pleaded with Lincoln to read the handwriting on the wall, to accept the fact that "the arming of Negroes and the liberation of those slaves who offer us aid and assistance . . ." was inevitable.[95] But according to Browning, Lincoln would not be moved. While no escaped blacks would be rejected, neither would they be encouraged to seek Union lines and embarrass the government. Congress had no power over slavery in the states and, to quote Browning, ". . . so much of it as remains after the war is over will be in precisely the same condition as it was before the war began. . . ."[96]

On July 12, 1862, Lincoln tried again to get the border states to accept emancipation. He was surely, if ever so slowly and haltingly, moving toward emancipation. He reminded an invited group of border state politicians how he had always moved slowly on the slavery question, irrespective of his own feelings, because he did not want to lose their support. Things would now be easier had they accepted his proffered plan of last March. Then he repeated almost verbatim what Carl Schurz had told him two months earlier! While he knew they desired a Union restored with slavery unimpaired, such was not to be the case. The sheer weight of events was abolishing slavery. They had let compensated emancipation pass them by and now increasing pressures necessitated emancipation.[97] Gideon Welles did not fail to note this "new departure" of the President from a hands-off, slavery-is-a-states'-right affair, to the

[94] RTLC, Vol. 76, No. 16048A, ser. I. Altered draft of a letter of A. Lincoln to Hunter, May 19, 1862.

[95] RTLC, Vol. 76, No. 16012, ser. I. Letter of Carl Schurz, May 16, 1862.

[96] Browning, *Diary*, I, 555. July 1, 1862.

[97] McClure, *Abraham Lincoln's Speeches Complete* . . . , pp. 397–98. Speech by Abraham Lincoln, delivered before the senators and congressmen of the border Southern states, at the executive mansion, July 12, 1862.

themes of military and political necessity. After giving much thought and sober reflection "to a subject involving consequences so vast and momentous," Welles tells us, Lincoln became convinced that he either had to free the slaves or lose the war.[98]

The majority of the border state leaders rejected Lincoln's plan of compensated emancipation. A minority of seven later found his plan reasonable.[99] Oddly enough, at this time Lincoln vetoed a Confiscation Act of Congress on the grounds that he doubted the legality of any measures of the lawmakers that propounded to free slaves. Furthermore, the act did not give the rebels sufficient time to reclaim their property before it was liable to seizure.[100]

Opinions on Lincoln's latest move were varied.[101] Horace Greeley urged the President to move because the South was making great capital out of the anti-black riots in the North, telling their slaves that "they had nothing to hope from Union success. . . ."[102] It seems, however, that at the very time Lincoln was writing his famous answer to Greeley's equally famous "prayer of twenty millions," stating that what he did about "slavery and the colored race" would be dictated solely by the necessities involved in saving the country, he had definitely made up his mind to do the very thing Greeley asked—free the slaves.

Welles records that Lincoln came to one Cabinet meeting with his mind already made up to issue an emancipation proclamation. Montgomery Blair of Maryland, however, did not

[98] Welles, *Diary*, I, 71. July 13, 1862.

[99] RTLC, Vol. 81, No. 17132, ser. I. July 15, 1862.

[100] RTLC, Vol. 81, No. 17155–63, ser. I. July 15, 1862.

[101] Ibid., No. 17150. A sympathetic letter from Horace Maynard, a Tennessee Unionist, July 16, 1862. RTLC, Vol. 198, No. 423–09, ser. II. A pro-emancipation letter of Robert Dale Owen to Edwin M. Stanton, Secretary of War, July 23, 1862. RTLC, Vol. 82, No. 17316–18, ser. I. Letter of James Speed, July 28, 1862, questioned the utility of a mere paper emancipation, and doubted if the black could keep his freedom even if he were given it since he didn't have the gumption to fight for it. RTLC, 83, No. 17581, ser. I. Letter of Martin R. Ryerson to W. H. Seward, August 11, 1862, stating that "the President should lead public opinion instead of lagging behind."

[102] RTLC, Vol. 198, No. 42335, ser. II. Newspaper clipping of a letter of Horace Greeley, August 19, 1862.

think the time propitious, and by October the Cabinet was still hedging on the wisdom of proclamation. But Lincoln's mind was made up and no more was heard on the subject until the day before it was to be issued.[103] A month later, when a Union commander allegedly refused to return a slave boy to his owner, Judge Robertson, Lincoln offered to buy the boy from the judge for five hundred dollars or less and set him free.[104] After that can anyone doubt that the President was at last committed to emancipation?

The travail of emancipation continued unabated until Lincoln cut the Gordian knot by issuing his now immortal document on January 1, 1863. Once Lincoln had made up his mind, he was tenacious in holding to his position. "I have issued the emancipation proclamation and I cannot retract it," he said to one of his generals. Lincoln further explained the situation thus: "After the commencement of hostilities, I struggled nearly a year and a half to get along without touching the 'institution' and when finally I conditionally determined to touch it, I gave a hundred days fair notice of my purpose, to all the states and people within which time they could have turned it wholly aside. . . . They chose to disregard it. [The proclamation] . . . being made it must stand." He denied any desire on his part to enslave or liquidate the whites of the South. "It is too absurd," he said. That section had only to "adopt a system of apprenticeship for the colored people. . . ."[105]

In January, Lincoln told Union General John M. Schofield that gradual emancipation would be the best for both races in Missouri.[106] But by July there were clear indications that the President wished to see the pace of emancipation quickened. He wished gradual emancipation to begin at once in Missouri!

[103] Welles, *Diary*, I, 143. September 22, 1862, the day Lincoln issued his preliminary emancipation plan to the Cabinet. Ibid., 158–59. October 1, 1862.

[104] RTLC, Vol. 92, No. 19601, ser. I. Letter of Abraham Lincoln, November 20, 1862; for the rest of the story on this rather revealing incident see RTLC, Vol. 92, Nos. 19570–03, 19637; Vol. 94, No. 19856–59.

[105] RTLC, Vol. 100, No. 21082–84, ser. I. Letter of Abraham Lincoln to Major General McClernand, January 8, 1863.

[106] RTLC, Vol. 115, No. 24326, ser. I. Letter of Abraham Lincoln to J. M. Schofield, January 22, 1863. Ibid., No. 24325. Letter of J. M. Schofield to A. Lincoln, January 20, 1863.

That state had come up with a gradual emancipation plan that would not start until 1870. Now this was too slow even for a man who was himself usually slow on such questions. "I am sorry the *beginning* should have been postponed for seven years," Lincoln lamented, "leaving all that time to agitate the repeal of the whole thing. It should begin at once; giving at least to the newborn a vested interest in freedom which could not be taken away. . . ."[107] At last the President was talking like an emancipator! "I see you have declared in favor of emancipation . . . may God bless you," he told Andrew Johnson with obvious satisfaction. Most likely the President was advising Andrew Johnson of the political dividends in coming out for emancipation when he told the man from Tennessee: "Get emancipation into your new state government—Constitution—and there will be no such word as fail for your case."[108]

Lincoln was aware that on the question of slavery and Union there was a variety of opinion. "It is easy to conceive," he said to a Missourian, "that all these shades of opinion . . . may be sincerely entertained by honest and truthful men."[109] But Lincoln had not thrown caution to the winds. When Salmon P. Chase of Ohio urged him to make the Emancipation Proclamation universal in those states which contained regions excluded from that by no means catholic document, Lincoln made it known that in matters of race he still moved with great circumspection. He was not one to break the fetters of bondage with a single blow. There were too many "difficulties in the way of such a step." He still did not feel that he could afford to say that he would free the slaves on any ground other than "military necessity." That was why all regions failing to qualify as military imperatives were carefully exempted from the initial proclamation. If he were to make the proclamation universal as Chase was suggesting would he not have to do so

[107] RTLC, Vol. 118, No. 25203. Letter of A. Lincoln to General Hurlbrit, July 30, 1863.

[108] RTLC, Vol. 123, No. 26217, ser. I. Letter, September 11, 1863; also found in *War of the Rebellion: Official Records of the Union and Confederate Armies* (Washington: Government Printing Office, 1889), III, 789, ser. III.

[109] RTLC, Vol. 127, No. 26964, ser. I. Letter of A. Lincoln to Charles Brake, October 5, 1863.

"without the argument of military necessity. . . . And without any argument, except the one that I think the measure politically expedient, and morally right? Could this pass unnoticed and unresisted?" inquired the President. "Could it fail to be perceived that without any further stretch, I might do the same in Delaware, Maryland . . . and even change the law in any state? Would not many of our friends," he concluded, "shrink away appalled? Would it not lose us the election, and . . . the very cause we seek to advance?"[110]

The issue of emancipation ran unabated right down to the very end of the war. A look into Lincoln's Cabinet through the eyes of Gideon Welles discloses that as late as two months before he died, Lincoln had a plan to offer the rebels $400,-000,000 for their slave property. The Cabinet allegedly was cold to the proposal and the idea was dropped. Even Welles recoiled from it. "The earnest desire of the President to conciliate and effect peace was manifest, but there may be such a thing as . . . overdoing . . . ," he said.[111] And so died the one measure that might have removed some of the rebel bitterness for the loss of their property in slaves. As the final drive was made for the Thirteenth Amendment, William Lloyd Garrison sent Lincoln what was both an affirmation and an interrogation: ". . . I am sure you will consent to no compromise that will leave a slave in his fetters."[112]

Did emancipation make Lincoln or did Lincoln make emancipation? He was not anxious to take any special credit for emancipation. In explaining to a crowd the painful evolution of the emancipation policy, Lincoln said with perhaps too much modesty but not without a kernel of truth: ". . . In telling this tale I attempt no compliment to my own sagacity. I claim not to have controlled events, but confess plainly that events have controlled me."[113] On that momentous day of the Emancipa-

[110] RTLC, Vol. 122, No. 25983, ser. I. Letter of Abraham Lincoln to Salmon P. Chase, September 2, 1863.
[111] Welles, *Diary*, II, 237. February 6, 1865.
[112] RTLC, Vol. 203, No. 43254, ser. II. Letter, February 13, 1865.
[113] Chittenden, *Abraham Lincoln's Speeches*, p. 333. April 4, 1864.

tion Proclamation, in spite of its lack of catholicity, Frederick Douglass was jubilant and entirely willing to forgive everything: "In that happy hour we forgot all delay . . . all tardiness, forgot that the President had bribed the rebels to lay down their arms. . . ."[114]

One should not make too much of the point of view that Lincoln was impelled to emancipation by the demands of military necessity and steady pressure from the abolitionists. ". . . The necessity of emancipation cannot be proved," wrote Charles Beard. It may be contended with equal reason that the act sprang from the deep humanitarianism of the emancipator, who rose above circumstances in making use of them and expressing his will.[115] No doubt military necessity, humanitarianism, and public opinion each played its part in Lincoln's decision for liberation. It remained to be seen whether the President would be a national racial arbiter in the process of rebuilding the nation as he had been in the saga of emancipation.

Reconstruction and Lincoln

Had Lincoln lived, how would he have handled the business of Reconstruction in the South? He did do some reconstructing before his untimely death. When General Shepley prepared to reconstruct Louisiana under Lincoln's direction, he restricted voter registration to ". . . all free white male citizens. . . ."[116] In his third annual message Lincoln declared his willingness to agree to some kind of temporary apprenticeship for blacks in the South, in order to ease the transition from slavery to freedom. He also intimated that except for his insistence that the rebels give up slavery, "the cause of their afflictions," he

[114] Foner, *The Life and Writings of Frederick Douglass*, IV, 316. Speech, 1876.

[115] Charles Beard, *The Presidents in American History* (New York: Julian Messner, 1935 . . . 1961), pp. 2, 71.

[116] RTLC, Vol. 113, No. 24081, ser. I. Brigadier General Shepley to the state of Louisiana, General Order No. 24. RTLC, Vol. 93, No. 19651–52, ser. I. Letter of A. Lincoln to G. F. Shepley [November 25–30?].

would leave the remainder of "this vital matter . . . to themselves. . . . No power of the national government to prevent an abuse is abridged by the proposition."[117] The President would have allowed the Southerners to handle the black problem with the federal government standing by to prevent wrongdoing. Whether Lincoln, too, would have been seized with presidential paralysis in the face of rebel recalcitrance will never be known.

"I deem the sustaining of the emancipation proclamation, where it applies, as indispensable," Lincoln wrote to a correspondent from Louisiana.[118] However, he was not inflexible on the subject of the ultimate disposition of the black question, although slavery itself was no longer open for discussion. He had fallen away from his former position that slavery was a domestic matter for the states.

With obvious reference to the annual message, Salmon P. Chase sought to guide the President on that "document you are about to put forth." Chase suggested that the states be organized without any expression by the federal government about apprenticeship status or special legislation regarding the role to be played by the former slaves. Since there were differences of opinion on the question, Chase would "leave the whole subject, without any intimation from Washington, to the judgment of those immediately concerned."[119] In the annual message Lincoln did leave the subject of the blacks, slavery excepted, to the states. But he also volunteered the fact that he would be amenable to some kind of apprenticeship.

Frederick Douglass was uneasy over Lincoln's intentions for Reconstruction in the South: "I see no purpose on the part of

[117] Nicolay and Hay, *Complete Works*, II, 455. December 8, 1865.

[118] RTLC, Vol. 135, No. 28677, ser. I. Letter of A. Lincoln to Dr. Cottmen, December 15, 1963 [?]. Ibid., No. 28138, ser. I. Letter of Michael Hahn to A. Lincoln, November 20, 1863. Ibid., Vol. 131, No. 27837–38, ser. I. Letter of A. Lincoln to General N. P. Banks, November 5, 1863. Lincoln told Banks not to sustain any state government that repudiated the Emancipation Proclamation or re-established slavery. Ibid., Vol. 139, No. 29619–20, ser. I. Similar instructions went to General Steele, January 30, 1864.

[119] RTLC, Vol. 132, No. 28217. Letter of Salmon P. Chase to A. Lincoln, November 25, 1863.

Lincoln and his friends to extend the elective franchise to the colored people of the South. . . ."[120] Wiliam B. Hesseltine, a historian, has stated that Lincoln's program of Reconstruction "remained political with the interests of the Republican Party uppermost in his thoughts."[121] It is not difficult to infer that the President's failure to include the blacks in his plans for Reconstruction was due in part to his views on the race problem.

The President, willing as he was before the war to leave slavery untouched in the South, was equally disposed to put the postwar black question in Southern hands. His orders for Reconstruction beyond a timid suggestion or two did not envision political equality for the blacks. He merely let it be known that he would agree to a temporary apprenticeship only. One must agree with Francis B. Simkins who said of Lincoln's plan of Reconstruction: "His plans were almost entirely political in nature and not comprehensive enough to solve the revolutionary social and economic problems which the war forced upon the South."[122] In the midst of the black question another minority group claimed the President's attention, even if briefly—the Indians.

Lincoln and the Sioux

In the autumn of 1862, the Sioux Indians went on the warpath in Minnesota and killed more than four hundred whites. In retaliation, many whites demanded "the total extermination of the Sioux . . . ," while others would be satisfied with nothing less than the execution of the guilty and the banishment of the remainder beyond the wide Missouri.[123] According to

[120] Foner, *Life and Writings of Frederick Douglass,* III, 404. Newspaper clipping from the *Liberator,* September 16, 1864, containing a letter, June 1864.

[121] William B. Hesseltine, *Lincoln's Plan of Reconstruction,* No. 13 of Confederate Centennial Studies, ed. William Stanley Houle (Tuscaloosa, Alabama: Confederate Publishing Co., 1960), p. 19.

[122] Francis B. Simkins, *The South Old and New: A History,* 1820–1947 (New York: Alfred Knopf, 1947), pp. 179–80.

[123] RTLC, Vol. 89, No. 18902, ser. I. George A. S. Crooker to Abraham Lincoln, October 8, 1862.

Gideon Welles, one of the generals on the scene informed Stanton that the Indians had surrendered and that he was anxious to execute a number of them.[124]

On November 8, 1862, at a cost of $414.04, Major General John Pope of the Union army and the man to whom the Sioux had surrendered after being defeated by him, sent an unbelievable telegram to President Lincoln. "The following named Indians," the telegram began innocently enough, "have been condemned to be hung by the Military Commission . . . for the massacre of men and women and brutal violating of women and young girls in the late Indian outrages in Minn." The telegram then proceeded to list by name and tribe three hundred Indians and half-breeds! Oddly enough, an Afro-American headed the list.[125] At this point, one of the commissioners asked Lincoln, through the Secretary of the Interior, not to carry out such an indiscriminate punishment of the Indian, even though he was a member.[126]

In response to an apparent request from Lincoln for more information, Pope stood by his initial position. "It is certain," he told the President, "that the [three hundred] criminals condemned ought in every view to be at once executed without exception. . . ." Pope would not permit the Indians to hide behind the excuse that they were wild because they had been living with the Minnesotans for years, eating at their houses and enjoying government subsidies. He was holding fifteen hundred additional Indians as prisoners and was afraid that should the three hundred go unpunished the whites would take their revenge on these. He then suggested that if the federal government did not want to perform the executions the state government could handle such details.[127] Lincoln received ad-

124 Welles, *Diary*, I, 171. Tuesday, October 18, 1862.

125 RTLC, Vol. 92, No. 19428–46, ser. I. Telegram of Major General John Pope to A. Lincoln, November 8, 1862.

126 Ibid., No. 19477–78. William P. Dole to Caleb Smith, November 10, 1862. Ibid., No. 19500. A note from Smith to Lincoln saying that he concurred with Dole. November 11, 1862.

127 RTLC, Vol. 92, Nos. 19507, 19512. Telegram to A. Lincoln, November 12, 1862. The Indians had been tried by a military court and, according to Pope, used their existence in a state of nature in their defense.

monitions from the governor of Minnesota, from a doctor in St. Paul, and again from Pope urging the speedy execution of the Indians lest the whites take the situation into their own hands.[128] In his annual message Lincoln told Congress about the Indian attack. He gave the figure of eight hundred as the number of whites killed. For some reason he did not tell the lawmakers that three hundred Indians had already been condemned to hang subject to his approval.[129]

Lincoln may have tried to escape responsibility for the executions, but there is no proof of this. In any case, the Judge Advocate General expressed puzzlement over a memorandum from Lincoln on the subject. He said to the Chief Executive: "I am quite sure that the power cannot be delegated and that the designations of the individuals which its exercise involves must necessarily be made by yourself."[130] It seems that Lincoln wanted to know if the Indians could be pardoned "in whole or in part." Gideon Welles felt that to kill the "ignorant barbarians . . . wholesale, after they had surrendered themselves as prisoners," would in itself constitute barbarity. "The members of Congress from Minnesota are urging the President vehemently to give his assent to the execution of three hundred Indian captives," said Welles, "but they will not succeed. . . ."[131]

On December 6, 1862, the President signed an order that sent thirty-eight Indians to their deaths.[132] The President pardoned one condemned Indian because he had previously risked his

[128] Ibid., Vol. 93, No. 19805, ser. I. Telegram of Governor Alexander Ramsey, November 28, 1862, asking for speedy executions and offering to do it himself. Ibid., No. 19722–25. Letter of Thaddeus, M.D., to A. Lincoln, November 22, 1862, accusing the Indians of tearing out human entrails, cutting off heads and placing them either on poles or between the victim's "lifeless thighs," and contending that twenty-three red men raped one sixteen-year-old white girl. Ibid., No. 19746–47. Telegram of John Pope to A. Lincoln, November 24, 1862.

[129] Nicolay and Hay, *Complete Works*, II, 267. December 1, 1862.

[130] RTLC, op. cit., Vol. 94, No. 19852. Holt to Lincoln, December 1, 1862.

[131] Welles, *Diary*, I, 186. Thursday, December 4, 1862.

[132] Basler, *Collected Works*, V, 542–43. Telegram of A. Lincoln to H. H. Sibley, December 6, 1862. Ibid., VI, 6–7. RTLC, Vol. 95, No. 20210–11, ser. I. Telegram of H. H. Sibley to A. Lincoln, December 15, 1862, asking for a brief stay of execution.

life to save a white family.[133] In response to a Senate request, Lincoln explained how he arrived at the number thirty-eight rather than three hundred.

After Pope's request for the blood of three hundred, Lincoln sent for the records of the trials. He wanted to avoid either extreme harshness or softness in this matter. And then he let fall a most un-Lincolnian remark, with possible racial overtones: "I caused a careful examination of the records . . . to be made," he explained to the Senate, "in view of first ordering the execution of such as had been proved guilty of violating females." In this regard the President was doomed to disappointment. "Contrary to my expectation only two of this class were found." So Lincoln had the records combed again, this time for those Indians who had massacred as distinguished from killing legitimately in battle. This second search for candidates for the hangman's noose was more successful. Thirty-eight were now found guilty and an additional Indian, one "O-ta-kia Alias Godfrey, a black," was given ten years because he volunteered information.[134] Was the President more concerned with those women who had lost their chastity than with those who had lost their heads or their viscera? The reader as well as the historian must draw his own conclusion. And so was closed a most interesting case. Thirty-eight Indians were hanged, while after the Civil War not one rebel swung for rebellion. While the President expressed no attitude toward the Indian other than to remember that one sneaked up behind his grandfather and killed him while he was working in a field, a double standard of race value might have had something to do with his treatment of the Sioux.[135] But to return to the larger minority, it appears that the black man as a soldier rather profoundly affected Lincoln's racial views.

[133] RTLC, Vol. 198, No. 42426, ser. II. John G. Nicolay to H. H. Sibley, December 9, 1862.

[134] Basler, *Collected Works,* V, 551. Message of Lincoln to the Senate, December 11, 1862. RTLC, Vol. 100, No. 21071–77. Telegram of H. H. Sibley to A. Lincoln, January 7, 1863, which read in part, "Hung by order of the President 38. . . ."

[135] Nicolay and Hay, *Complete Works,* I, 596. Abraham Lincoln to J. W. Fell, December 20, 1859, for the Indian incident.

The Black Soldier Weakens the Racial Barrier

The evidence suggests that the use of black troops and their creditable performance breached the high wall of race prejudice and visibly affected Lincoln's attitude toward the blacks in America. William B. Hesseltine has suggested that "Lincoln's capacity for growth" must not be overlooked.[136] The story of that growth, though not without its moments of anxiety for the friends of freedom, is an exciting one for a student of race, and is the final subject of this chapter.

The black American was never an official part of the armed services of the United States until the Civil War. It is the thesis of Dudley Cornish that were it not for his participation and contribution to the Civil War effort, blacks "must have been excluded indefinitely from the rights and responsibilities of American citizenship."[137] Nothing affords more evidence of race prejudice against the black man in America than the sometimes painful story of his struggle to become a soldier. That he eventually succeeded, and effectively, was crucial for his own future as well as that of the Union. In view of the difficulty with which Lincoln's Administration brought the blacks into the army, one is surprised to learn that Gideon Welles in September of 1861 put them into the navy by a simple departmental order! The Secretary drew the color line however: "They will be allowed, however, no higher rating than 'boys' at a compensation of $10 per month and one ration per day," which was less than the whites received on each count.[138]

In initially refusing to use black troops, Lincoln was going against a considerable public opinion. According to his private secretary, "his daily correspondence was thickly interspersed by . . . suggestions" to use black soldiers. But Lincoln would not be stampeded: "Some of our Northerners seem bewildered and

[136] William Hesseltine, *Lincoln's Plan of Reconstruction*, p. 35.
[137] Dudley Cornish, *The Sable Arm: Negro Troops in the Union Army, 1861–1865*, New York: Longmans, Green and Company, 1956, p. 12.
[138] Ibid., pp. 17–18, 181.

dazzled by the excitement of the hour. . . . For my part, I consider the central idea pervading this struggle is the necessity that is upon us of proving that popular government is not an absurdity," said the President, in Hay's version.[139] Public opinion, however, was not unanimous.[140] Lincoln told Browning that no blacks were to be armed at present because to do so would create a dangerous and fatal dissatisfaction in the army and do more harm than good.[141] The President may have hesitated because of the implicit assumption that if the black man fought he might have to be given his freedom.

On July 17, 1862, Congress passed an act providing for the use of black soldiers at a pay rate of three dollars a month less than that bestowed upon white privates.[142] The responsibility for raising and deploying these troops was placed squarely upon the shoulders of the President. As things turned out, much time would elapse before Lincoln would execute the mandate with any enthusiasm. Meanwhile he would permit the use of blacks as laborers in the army and he had no objection to the recruiting of free blacks.[143]

Browning also kept his hand on the public pulse for the

[139] John Hay, *Diaries and Letters,* p. 19. May 7, 1861.

[140] RTLC, Vol. 60, No. 12975, ser. I. Newspaper clipping of a letter of Gerrit Smith to Thad Stevens, December 6, 1861, hoping that blacks would be used. Ibid., Vol. 65, No. 13917. Reverend Charles W. Denison to E. M. Bates, January 10, 1862. Ibid., Vol. 204, No. 43473, ser. II. A New England abolitionist, Elizur Wright, to A. Lincoln, May 23, 1862, in favor of black troops. Ibid., Vol. 78, No. 16554–55, ser. I. F. H. Pierpoint to A. Lincoln, June 20, 1862, asking that blacks be used to work. Ibid., Vol. 81, No. 17072. J. Stella Martin, "distinguished coloured orator and preacher . . . five years ago a slave," [No. 17076] offered the President his "services to the Union and the services of his people." Ibid., No. 17084–85. U. S. Marshal for Virginia, Edward M. Norton, July 4, 1862. Ibid., No. 17206. Newspaper clipping from the New York *Evening Post,* Saturday, July 10, 1862, providing Lincoln with precedents for use of black troops. Ibid., No. 17210. Newspaper clipping of letter of Dudley Field to A. Lincoln citing the testimony of Santo Domingo and the French to prove that blacks would fight. The article was entitled: "Will the Blacks Fight: Testimony of a French Soldier. . . ." Ibid., Vol. 83, No. 17650. Letter, August 13, 1862, from [S. H. Gay?] identified only as "our correspondent [New York *Tribune*]" in response to some queries from the President, cautioning the President that nonuse of blacks was a weakness. Ibid., Vol. 83, No. 17567. Newspaper clipping from the Hartford *Evening Press,* Friday, August 1, 1862, urging black troops.

[141] Browning, *Diary,* I, 555. July 1, 1862.

[142] Cornish, *The Sable Arm,* pp. 46–47.

[143] Basler, *Collected Works,* V, 338. [July 22, 1862.]

President, but advised his chief that the public approved of his policy of not enlisting blacks. Perhaps this was true of the "mid-Western public." "I have heard many say," related Browning, "if he [Lincoln] will accept one black regiment he will lose twenty white regiments by it." Browning concluded that "the time may come for arming the Negroes. It is not yet."[144] Lincoln was obviously dumfounded when confronted personally with a request from a delegation of ministers that blacks be freed and sent to battle. Lincoln at first expressed grave doubts about the capacity of the slave to fight: "But I am not so sure we could do much with the blacks. If we were to arm them, I fear that in a few weeks the arms would be in the hands of the rebels. . . ." Lincoln's next argument was that he didn't even have enough rifles for the white troops. He was probably closer to the truth when he told the clergymen that if he were to use black troops, "fifty thousand bayonets in the Union army from the border states . . ." would go over to rebeldom.[145]

Major General Dix of the Union army received with coolness an indirect suggestion by Lincoln that black troops be used for garrison duty at two Virginia forts. He was not impressed by the black's capacity or willingness to fight. Said Dix:

> It is a very grave question, therefore, independently of all other considerations, how far military positions, on the tenure of which the success of our arms in upholding the authority of the government and maintaining the integrity of the union depends, should be confided to any other class than the white people of the country. Prudence would, at least, dictate that the inferior element in the military organization should be incorporated in very small proportion, and employed in services of secondary importance.[146]

When it came to soldiers, Dix was not color-blind. His plea, however, apparently went unheeded because by 1863 Lincoln

[144] RTLC, Vol. 83, No. 17556–57. O. H. Browning to A. Lincoln, August 11, 1862.

[145] McClure, *Abraham Lincoln's Speeches Complete* . . . , p. 404. Lincoln's address to a delegation of religious men from Chicago, September 13, 1862.

[146] RTLC, Vol. 100, No. 21173, ser. I. A. Lincoln to Major General Dix [January 14, 1863?]. Ibid., No. 21194–97. Major General Dix to A. Lincoln, January 15, 1863.

had at last made up his mind that the time had come to utilize this "inferior element in the military organization." Over in Tennessee Andrew Johnson was wondering if a three-hundred-dollar bounty would encourage loyal masters to allow their slaves to enlist. By March of 1863, both Lincoln and Johnson had warmed to their tasks considerably. Lincoln believed that nothing could further the cause of black recruitment more than the spectacle of the ex-slaveholder, Johnson, participating in the process. Lincoln was now convinced that "the colored population" was the great untapped force for army recruitment. He wrote to Johnson: ". . . I am told that you at least thought of raising a Negro military force. . . . [The] bare sight of 50,000 armed and drilled black soldiers upon the banks of the Mississippi could end the rebellion at once. And who doubts that we can present that sight if we but take hold in earnest? If you have been thinking of it, please do not dismiss the thought."[147] While events were to prove that the rebels did not scare quite so easily, Lincoln's enthusiasm was by now unmistakable.

Next the President urged General Banks to cooperate with General Ullmann in trying to raise a "colored brigade. To now avail ourselves of this force is very important, if not indispensable . . . ," said Lincoln.[148] Nothing should be clearer by this time than the fact that he had made up his mind to use the black man in an armed capacity. Good relations were restored between himself and the general whose proclamation he had once rescinded. "I am glad to see the account of your colored force at Jacksonville, Florida," Lincoln wrote Hunter. "I see the enemy are driving at them fiercely, as is to be expected. Let the general be vigilant in preserving and increasing the Negroes since the rebels would surely make an 'extra effort to destroy them.'"[149] It is known that the Confederates felt rather insulted to have blacks hurled at them and it was a current rumor that

[147] RTLC, Vol. 107, No. 22638, ser. I. A. Lincoln to A. Johnson, March 26, 1863; the same letter is found also in *Official Records of the Rebellion*, III, 103, ser. III. RTLC, Vol. 125, No. 26513, ser. I. Andrew Johnson to A. Lincoln [February 23–September 28, 1863?].

[148] RTLC, Vol. 107, No. 22703, ser. I. Letter, March 29, 1863.

[149] RTLC, Vol. 107, No. 22767. A. Lincoln to Major General Hunter, April 1, 1863.

all captured black soldiers would be sold into slavery and their white officers hanged. There were those who urged the President to take a strong stand against this unequal treatment of the blacks by the rebels.[150]

Frederick Douglass did not feel that Lincoln was vigorous enough in insisting on equal treatment of black prisoners and in the matter of equal pay for blacks in the Union army. For a time he gave up his recruiting efforts in disgust. However, Lincoln told Douglass that he had felt constrained to wait for a few good performances by black troops before he would challenge the white prejudice that was preventing the blacks from getting their just due. True to his word, after black troops did well in battles at Port Hudson, Louisiana, May 27, 1863, and Fort Wagner, South Carolina, July 18, 1863, and obviously feeling that public opinion would now sustain him, the racially conscious President publicly declared that a rebel prisoner would be set at hard labor for every black soldier sold into slavery. He said it was his duty to protect citizens "of whatever class, color or condition" and contended that the law of nations and the uses of war permitted "no distinction as to color in the treatment of prisoners of war. . . ."[151] The issue was never satisfactorily resolved but at least the President had spoken, and the stature of the black man in America had improved.

Once he became convinced of the wisdom of this policy, Lincoln developed an almost unbounded optimism about the capacity of black troops to terminate the war. "I believe," he wrote Grant, "it [black troops] is a resource which, if vigorously applied now, will close the contest. . . . We were not fully ripe for it until the river [Mississippi] was opened. . . ."[152] General Banks told Lincoln that the assistance of black troops

[150] RTLC, Vol. 11, No. 23597, ser. I. Charles Sumner to A. Lincoln [May 6–26?]. Ibid., Vol. 112, No. 23703. Major General Hunter to A. Lincoln, May 27, 1863. Ibid., Vol. 118, No. 25222–23. Letter of the father of a heroic white commander of black troops who lost his life in a fatal charge of the black troops at Port Wagner, Frank George Shaw to A. Lincoln, July 31, 1863.

[151] *Official Records of the Rebellion,* VI, 163, ser. II. Abraham Lincoln's General Order No. 252. July 30, 1863. Foner, *The Life and Writings of Frederick Douglass,* III, 36, 383–85, 445.

[152] *Official Records of the Rebellion,* XXIV, 584, ser. I. Abraham Lincoln to U. S. Grant, August 9, 1863.

was decisive in the victory of Port Hudson.[153] By this time Lincoln was intensely engrossed in the performance of the black soldiers. John Eaton reported him anxious to know about their characteristics, capabilities and potentialities.[154] Perhaps it was this rising inquisitiveness about the black people that caused Lincoln to appoint in 1863 the American Freedmen Inquiry Commission "to consider," said Eaton, "the entire subject of our policy toward blacks in the present emergency." The report, though abolitionist in character, is illustrative of the ability of American nationalism to rise above the color line, especially when national preservation was at stake. The report clearly reflected that an improved image of the black race resulted from his direct participation in the fighting.[155]

When Lincoln visited the troops at the front, Grant asked the President if he wanted to see the black troops who had fought so well. Lincoln said that he had "read with the greatest delight . . . how gallantly they behaved. . . ." He recalled that when *he* first decided to use black troops he "was opposed on every side. But they have proved their efficiency; and I am glad they have kept pace with the white troops in the recent assault. . . . I used to tell them [those who opposed the use of black troops when every able-bodied man was needed at the front] that at some times it was just as well to be a little colorblind," Lincoln declared.[156]

When he could not attend a political rally in his home state, Lincoln wrote a letter aimed at those who were lukewarm in their support of the Union because of their racial sensitivities. "Some of you are dissatisfied with me about the colored man. . . . I certainly wish that all men . . . could be free, while I suppose some of you do not." Lincoln accused them of turning

[153] RTLC, Vol. 120, No. 25661–63, ser. I. N. P. Banks to A. Lncoln, August 17, 1863.

[154] John Eaton, *Grant, Lincoln and the Freedmen*, p. 88.

[155] *Official Records of the Rebellion*, III, 450–52, 430–51, Pt. 3, ser. 124, for the text of this not too well known report.

[156] Horace Porter, *Campaigning with Grant* (New York: Century Co., 1897), pp. 219–20. This is a secondhand report of a conversation between Lincoln and Grant. When the Negroes saw Lincoln allegedly "they cheered, laughed, cried, sang hymns of praise and shouted . . . 'God Bress Massa Linkum! De Lord save Fader Abraham. De day ob Jubilee am come. . . .'" The touching scene brought tears to Mr. Lincoln's eyes.

down compensated emancipation on grounds that they did not want to be taxed to buy blacks. The President again defended the Emancipation Proclamation.[157]

The aim of the war, Lincoln continued, was to prove that "among free men there can be no successful appeal from the ballot to the bullet. . . ." Once the war was successfully ended, argued Lincoln, "there will be some black men who can remember that with silent tongues, and clenched teeth, and steady eye and well poised bayonet, they have helped mankind on to the great consummation; while I fear that there will be some white ones, unable to forget that, with malignant hearts and deceitful speech, they have strove to hinder it."[158] After a few days Lincoln sent an additional paragraph to be inserted into what is now called the "Springfield Letter." He had forgotten to include the testimony of his field commanders, some of whom had no affinity for abolitionism or Republicanism, who felt that emancipation and the use of black troops constituted one of the heaviest blows yet dealt the Confederacy.[159] Lincoln also told his audience:

> You say you will not fight to free Negroes. Some of them are willing to fight for you. . . . But Negroes like other people act upon motives. Why should they do anything for us, if we will do nothing for them? If they stake their lives for us, they must be prompted by the strongest motives—even the promise of freedom. And the promise being made must be kept.[160]

Lincoln had changed his views. The Springfield letter affords an excellent review of Lincoln's position on the blacks and the war. It was well received and many felt, including Charles Sumner, that history would recognize that document as a landmark in the annals of American liberty.[161] In his third annual message

[157] RTLC, Vol. 121, Nos. 25840–41, 25845, ser. I. Rough draft copy of letter of Abraham Lincoln to James C. Conkling of Springfield, Ill. [August 26, 1863?].

[158] Ibid., No. 25846–53. A final draft.

[159] Ibid., No. 25933–34. A. Lincoln to James C. Conkling, August 31, 1863.

[160] Basler, *Collected Works*, VI, 406–09.

[161] RTLC, Vol. 122, No. 26040–41, ser. I. James C. Conkling to A. Lincoln, September 4, 1863. Ibid., No. 26108. Charles Sumner to A. Lincoln, September 7, 1863. Ibid., Vol. 123, No. 26119–20. Letter of one Bostonian, J. M. Forbes, to A. Lincoln, September 8, 1863. Ibid., Vol. 124, No. 26367. "No nobler

Lincoln announced that the policy of emancipating and arming blacks, while it involved both hopes and fears, had passed the test and the country could look confidently toward a successful end to the war. Of the blacks as soldiers he said: "So far as tested, it is difficult to say that they are not as good soldiers as any."[162] He emphatically stated that he would not retreat from the Emancipation Proclamation. He would leave the black question to the states, but under the scrutinizing eye of the national government. He again asked Congress to recall his earlier recommendation of compensated emancipation and colonization.[163]

As the war neared its close and the inevitable doom of slavery approached, Lincoln continually affirmed his determination not to put anyone back into bondage: "There have been men base enough to propose to me to return to slavery the black warriors of Port Hudson . . . and thus win the respect of the masters they fought. Should I do so, I should deserve to be damned in time and eternity."[164]

It seems likely that the black war effort may have been responsible for the slight change in Lincoln's position in regard to political equality for black folk. How to better the condition of the colored race had long engaged his most "serious and careful attention," said Lincoln. He was "clear and decided" as to what course to follow in the case of the black veterans—"these people who have so heroically vindicated their manhood on the battlefield, where in assisting to save the life of the republic, they have demonstrated in blood their right to the ballot, which is but the humane protection of the flag they have so fearlessly defended." The President seemed unequivocal in his next conclusion: "The restoration of the rebel states to the Union must rest upon the principle of civil and political equality of both races; and must be sealed by general amnesty."[165] However,

State paper was ever penned . . . ," said a newspaper clipping of an editorial from the London *Star*, September 17, 1863.

[162] Richardson, *Messages*, VI, 188, 189. December 1863.

[163] Ibid., V, 190–91.

[164] Nicolay and Hay, *Complete Works*, II, 562. Abraham Lincoln to John T. Mills [August 1864?].

[165] Basler, *Collected Works*, VII, 101–02.

when he wrote to the governor of one of his reconstructed states he put the proposition of giving the ballot to the most intelligent Afro-Americans and the black Civil War veterans as a *suggestion only*. Although he told Michael Hahn of Louisiana that the blacks might "probably help, in some trying time to come, to keep the jewel of liberty within the family of freedom,"[166] the President did not insist on political equality for blacks, either South or North.

The fact that Lincoln would only make a "suggestion" to Hahn on the ballot question was ominous. He soon encountered difficulty in carrying out his pledge (to Wadsworth) of political and civil equality of the races in the rebel states. In spite of his softened views on the subject, his political creed of state autonomy in domestic affairs, Southern recalcitrance, and the naturally complicated state-national-federal relations would all conspire to obstruct his obviously good intentions.

The Flexible Lincoln

On the evidence which this chapter presents, what can we conclude about Lincoln? A number of observations come to mind. Lincoln expressed prejudice toward the black race. At least until well into the middle of his presidency he felt that there was an impassable gulf between white and black men. He was sensitive to things ethnic, and the concept of race was a fairly well-defined element in his thinking. He was opposed to the mixing of the races. In his thoughts and his actions, however, he often betrayed a willingness and a capacity to bridge the racial gap. On occasion he demonstrated that democracy could be color-blind even if not completely.

There is no reason to doubt that his racial beliefs were matters of deep conviction. He demonstrated a capacity to grow, though by no means oblivious to political necessity. As

[166] Basler, *Collected Works*, VII, 243. Lincoln later publicly apologized for his failure to secure the vote for the blacks in reconstructed Louisiana. See McClure, *Abraham Lincoln's Speeches Complete . . .*, p. 458. Speech of Abraham Lincoln at the White House, Thursday evening, April 11, 1865.

President he had a decisive role to play in race relations. He played this role not so much according to his own racial views, but in response to what he honestly thought were the racial views of the majority of the American white people. The issue of emancipation, the use of the black man as a soldier, and the question of his status after the war, all of these were squarely upon the shoulders of President Lincoln. He could not escape the problem of race if he would.

Lincoln has been praised as a "chief of public opinion."[167] Upon closer examination, however, Lincoln was really being commended for discovering and following public opinion rather than leading it. It is true that Lincoln led some segments of public opinion in his early depiction of slavery as a moral evil which should not be allowed to spread. But even here it could be argued that he was following mid-Western thinking on the subject. The problem is that it is not possible to know with any degree of historical certitude just what the public opinion was at any particular time.

In regard to facets of the race question other than slavery, Lincoln also chose to follow rather than lead. He was, as Milton and Hofstadter noted, a master at sniffing out the "universal feeling" on the race question. He discovered that a significant number of white Americans did not like the black man and would not tolerate him. Yet, when military considerations forced him to make more use of the black man than the Negrophobic segment of the public probably desired, Lincoln skillfully, even if sometimes too cautiously for some, made certain that the public was prepared for every pro-black step he took. There is at least one question this chapter does not answer. How, in the face of the divergent and ambivalent views found in his correspondence, did Lincoln decide what the public's opinion was? One thing is certain. When Andrew Johnson came to the presidency he found the race question just where Lincoln had left it—unsolved and complex.

[167] George Fort Milton, *The Uses of Presidential Power, 1789–1943* (Boston: Little, Brown and Co., 1944), pp. 131–35; Richard Hofstadter, *The American Political Tradition and the Men Who Made It*, pp. 100, 116.

CHAPTER III

The Racial Attitudes of Andrew Johnson (1865–1869)

The successor of Abraham Lincoln was a Southerner and a Democrat. When the Civil War began he was a United States senator representing the state of Tennessee. Before the war was very old he was made war governor of Tennessee. He was chosen as Lincoln's running mate for the presidential election of 1864. Before the Civil War he had been a slaveholder and consequently reflected the proslavery proclivities of his region. According to the "mud-sill" theory of society, some kind of servitude was implicit in the very nature of things. Johnson accepted that doctrine and saw the blacks in that role. In his opinion the American ideal of equality did not apply to blacks.

The Pre-Presidential Perspective

Unlike Lincoln, Andrew Johnson did not believe that Jefferson had included the blacks in the Declaration of Independence. On the Senate floor in 1859 he had accused Illinois senator Lyman Trumbull of trying to "delude and deceive the . . . people by intimating that Mr. Jefferson meant Africans of the African race. . . . It is evident to my mind, as it must be to everybody else; that Mr. Jefferson meant the white race, and not the African race." Was Trumbull willing to give equality to free blacks emigrating into the Territories? If not, then he should cease his prattle about all men being equal, Johnson thought. Did not Trumbull know that when "our people speak of men being equal they do not mean the African race but regard them as an inferior race." Neither blacks, mulattoes nor Indians could vote, hold office, serve in the state militia, intermarry with whites or testify against them in court in Illinois, Johnson reminded Trumbull. "Your theory is one thing, and your practice is another," Johnson said.

Trumbull's response was more than a little ambiguous: "I do insist that all men are created equal, by which I do not mean that all men are equal in organized society. The fact is an abstract truth; but when we come to form government and organized society, all persons do not have equal rights. . . ." Under further questioning Trumbull admitted that he would not give the same political rights to blacks and women that he would extend to white males in the new Territories. Would the senator from Illinois be in favor of admitting Arizona into the Union on equal terms with the other states if she was populated with free blacks only? Trumbull's answer to Johnson's final question gave small comfort to the friends of freedom:

> In my judgement, as I said the other day when discussing this question, there is a distinction between the white and the black races, made by omnipotence himself. I do not believe that these two races can live happily and pleasantly together, or enjoying equal rights without one domineering over the other. And therefore I advocate the policy of separating these races by a system which shall rid the country of the black race, as it becomes free. I say I should not be prepared, in the existing state of things, to admit as a sovereign state of this union a community of Negroes or of Indians either.

"I thank the Senator for the admission he has made . . . ," said Johnson triumphantly.[1] Believing as he did in the inferiority of blacks, Johnson did not disapprove of their enslavement or their occupation of the bottom rung of the social ladder.

[1] Andrew Johnson's speech in the United States Senate, December 12, 1859. The Andrew Johnson Papers (Microfilm in the Library of Congress, Washington, D.C.), Reel 47, ser. V-E. [Hereafter cited as AJP (Microfilm).]

From Slavery to Antislavery

Andrew Johnson was always conscious of his plebeian past and rejected any insinuation that those who toiled for a living were necessarily slaves. Before the Civil War his definition of slavery was not predicated on race but on class. He disapproved of extreme agitation of the slavery question either South or North. Yet, before the war he agreed in principle that there should be a slave for every American family, should the people decide on such a plan. Ingeniously he argued that a homestead for every American would confirm his belief in the sanctity of property ". . . in whatever shape . . . elevate our race and make our institutions [including slavery] more permanent."[2]

On the eve of the Civil War, Andrew Johnson's position concerning slavery differed only slightly from that of Abraham Lincoln, though he voted against Lincoln for President. He, too, would enforce the Fugitive Slave Law and preserve slavery *and* the Union.[3] Three months after the war started he introduced a resolution in the Senate to the effect that the conflict should cease immediately after the Constitution had been defended and the Union preserved. He disclaimed any intention of "interfering with the rights of established institutions of the slave states."[4]

While Johnson was not against slavery he did oppose the counting of slaves for purposes of representation. He spoke against the "peculiar institution" because it was the cornerstone of the power of the slave aristocracy. What he resented as early as 1842 was the use of this alien race as a basis for political representation.[5] He was entirely willing to approve of slavery

[2] Andrew Johnson, speech in the Senate on the Homestead Bill, May 20, 1858; Frank Moore, *Speeches of Andrew Johnson* (Boston: Little, Brown and Company, 1865), pp. 66–67.

[3] Speech in the Senate on the Constitutionality and Rightfulness of Secession, December 18, 19, 1860. Moore, *Speeches of Andrew Johnson*, pp. 96–99, 171.

[4] Ibid., pp. xix, xvi (Appendix).

[5] He offered a resolution in the Tennessee Legislature to the effect that "the basis to be observed in laying the state off . . . shall be the voting population,

as long as the slaves were not used by the planter aristocracy to exert control over the Southern white masses. "It is upon the intelligent free white people of the country that all government should rest, and by them all government should be controlled," said the future President.[6] He once told a cheering Tennessee Legislature that he stood for a white man's government controlled by free, white voters, excluding blacks. In this speech he struck hard at the planters, accusing them of starting the war in order to establish "an aristocracy or Negro [-based] oligarchy.[7] As war governor of Tennessee, he decreed that one had to be "a free white man" in order to vote.[8] One of Johnson's correspondents recalled a conversation in the winter of 1865 in which Johnson had declared himself in favor of a white man's government.[9] After the beginning of the Civil War, Johnson began to take an increasingly antislavery position but not for humanitarian reasons.

He probably championed emancipation for political expediency in order to undermine the Bourbon aristocracy. At any rate, by 1863 he was decidedly for manumission. President Lincoln encouraged this stand with a "God bless you." Obviously pleased, Johnson wrote back to Lincoln: "I have taken

---

without any regard to the three fifths of the Negro population. . . ." John Savage, *The Life and Public Services of Andrew Johnson . . . including his State Papers, Speeches . . . Addresses . . .* (New York: Darby, 1865), p. 140.

[6] Speech in the Senate, July 27, 1861. Moore, *Speeches of Andrew Johnson*, p. 368. A newspaper reporter quoted Johnson in 1861: "Southern rights! Why a man in South Carolina is not eligible for a seat in the legislature unless he owns ten Negroes and is possessed of $500 freehold property." Savage, *Life . . . of Andew Johnson . . . including . . . Speeches*, p. 261.

[7] Speech of Governor Andrew Johnson on the Restoration of State Government at the meeting held in the Hall of the House of Representatives, Thursday evening, January 21, 1864, to take initial steps to restore civil government in Tennessee (Nashville: Dispatch Printing Company), p. 6. Johnson also revealed that he would be lenient to penitent rebels and that he was against executive amnesty and pardons. They implied, he said, that Southerners were criminals, p. 5.

[8] Draft of a message to the people of Tennessee in 1864; AJP (Microfilm), Reel 47, No. 27510, ser. I. A proclamation by Governor Johnson, January 28, 1864; RTLC, Vol. 140, No. 29980, ser. I.

[9] John W. Gorham, Clarksville, Tenn., to Andrew Johnston, June 3, 1865; AJP (Microfilm), Reel 15, No. 4154–55, ser. I. See also R. M. Brown, Nashville, to Andrew Johnson, September 30; ibid., Reel 18, No. 7155–58, ser. I.

decided ground for emancipation—for immediate emancipation. . . ."[10] If slavery was dead, he told a Nashville audience, he had not committed the murder nor was he going to "mourn over its dead body."[11] He thought that slavery should be abolished by constitutional amendment.[12] During the vice-presidential campaign Johnson explained his motives for emancipation thus: "I am for emancipation for two reasons: first because it is right in itself; second, because in the emancipation of the slaves we break down an odious and dangerous aristocracy. I think we are freeing more whites than blacks in Tennessee."[13]

In spite of opposition, the Republican vice-presidential candidate freed every slave in his home state by verbal fiat! "I . . . do hereby proclaim freedom, full, broad, and unconditional, to every man in Tennessee!"[14] Two months later Lincoln acknowledged the official receipt of Tennessee's ordinance of emancipation.[15] When Johnson became President he had to beg the constitutional conventions in the ex-rebel states to ratify the Thirteenth Amendment![16] In spite of his difficulty in getting some of them to approve, the President confidently stated in his 1865 annual message that ratification of the amendment provided a sufficient basis for the reunion of the nation.[17] In the face of congressional Reconstruction, Johnson lost his initial enthusiasm for emancipation. Abolition was not an object of the war but merely "an incident in the suppression of a great rebellion," he told a black delegation in 1866. While the black man had gained his freedom because of the war, the Southern

[10] Telegrams of Andrew Johnson to A. Lincoln, September 17, 1863; *Official Records of the Rebellion,* III, 819, ser. III. Found also in RTLC, Vol. 124, No. 26355, ser. I. (The latter carried the date of September 18, 1863.)

[11] Speech of Johnson as vice-presidential candidate, June 6, 1864. Moore, *Speeches of Andrew Johnson,* p. xxi (Appendix).

[12] Ibid., July 2, 1864, pp. xxxiv, xxxviii (Appendix).

[13] Moore, *Speeches of Andrew Johnson,* p. xxii (Appendix).

[14] The Negroes then went wild with rejoicing. October 24, 1864; ibid., p. xxxvii.

[15] January 14, 1865; AJP (Microfilm), Reel 12, No. 1884, ser. I.

[16] E. M. McPherson, *The Political History of the United States of America During the Period of Reconstruction* (Washington, D.C.: Solomons and Chapman, 1880); hereafter cited as McPherson, *Reconstruction.*

[17] First Annual Message, December 4, 1865; ibid., p. 65.

white and the slaveholder had gained nothing, in Johnson's opinion.[18] Before turning to an examination of Johnson's views on racial harmony, a word on his attitude on the black man as a soldier.

While the performance of black troops had a positive effect upon Lincoln's attitude toward blacks, Andrew Johnson's experience with the black soldier did not change his conviction that blacks and Southern whites were inherently opposed to one another. In 1863, Johnson was unopposed to black recruitment.[19] As governor of Tennessee during the war, he issued a proclamation calling for the enlistment of "all able bodied persons . . . white and colored. . . ." However, the directive specified the "enrolling of all colored persons upon a separate enlistment."[20]

As governor of Tennessee and as President of the United States, Johnson received unfavorable reports about black troops in the army of occupation.[21] Reports to the effect that black troops in Nashville had turned one of Johnson's own houses into a brothel did nothing to improve their image.[22] Although a commanding general on the spot denied these accusations, Johnson eventually ordered all black troops away from east

[18] Interview of Johnson with Frederick Douglass, George Downing, et al., February 7, 1866; ibid., p. 54.

[19] George L. Stearns to E. M. Stanton, September 16, 1863. *Official Records of the Rebellion,* III, 816, ser. III. Andrew Johnson to E. M. Stanton, September 17, 1863; ibid., p. 3.

[20] August 23, 1864; AJP (Microfilm), Reel 47, No. 307–08, ser. V-E.

[21] William Byrd, Nashville, to Andrew Johnson, August 24, 1864, accusing blacks of abusing white civilians; AJP (Microfilm), Reel 11, No. 331–02, ser. I. John O'Flanagan, Nashville, to Andrew Johnson, September 16, 1864; ibid., No. 573–78. H. M. Watterson to Andrew Johnson, July 18, 1865; ibid., Reel 16, No. 5263. William H. Boyce, Winnsboro, S.C., to Andrew Johnson, July 9, 1865; ibid., Reel 16, No. 5289–90. Captain E. Johnson, Provost Marshal, Atlanta, Ga., to Andrew Johnson; ibid., Reel 17, No. 5983, ser. I. Governor Sharkey, Mississippi, to Andrew Johnson, August 23, 1865. Andrew Johnson to Major General Steedman, Augusta, Ga., August 23, 1865, urging him to be on his guard against insurrection of blacks led by black troops. AJP (Microfilm), Reel 42, No. 269, ser. III-A. A New Jersey preacher and ex-Southerner to Andrew Johnson, August 31, 1865; AJP (Microfilm), Reel 17, No. 6458, ser. I-A. Governor Brownlow, of Tennessee, to Andrew Johnson, September 19, 1865; AJP (Microfilm), Reel 42, No. 390. Johnson to Brownlow; AJP (Microfilm), Reel 42 (Letter Press Book, Vol. 2), No. 390, ser. III-A.

[22] Andrew Johnson to Major General Thomas, Nashville, September 4, 1865; AJP (Microfilm), Reel 43, No. 4344, ser. III-B.

Tennessee for fear of insurrection.[23] Johnson had some difficulty in accepting the reality of a black man under arms. He seemed uneasy as he spoke to one group of black soldiers after he became President: "I repeat, I have little to say, it being unusual in this government and in most other governments to have colored troops in their service."[24]

Discord in Black and White: Racial Incompatibility

A persistent pre-Civil War racial theme of Andrew Johnson was that the blacks hated the poor whites of the South and looked upon them with contempt. Before the Civil War, Andrew Johnson did not think that America would become a permanent home for blacks. In 1845, he called for the annexation of Mexico as a gateway out of which blacks "would pass from bondage to freedom when they can become merged in a population congenial with themselves, who know and feel no distinction in consequence of the various hues of skin and crosses of blood."[25] Johnson was aware of the partiality of the Caucasian when complexion was involved. In 1847, he implied that the "various hues of skin and crosses of blood" were indicative of some kind of ethnological sin on the part of Mexico. He attributed America's successful war with Mexico to "the right . . . arm of an angry God [punishing the latter's racial infidelity and using] the Anglo-Saxon race . . . as the rods of her retribution."[26] In 1864, Johnson thought that the South could produce big cotton crops without the blacks. He still desired to see them sent to Mexico, Africa or some other place more suitable for

[23] Major General Thomas to Andrew Johnson, September 7, 1865; AJP (Microfilm), Reel 17, No. 6648, ser. I. Andrew Johnson to General Thomas, September 8, 1865; AJP (Microfilm), Reel 42 (Vol. 2, Letter Press Book), No. 345–47, ser. III-A. General Thomas to Andrew Johnson, September 9, 1865; AJP (Microfilm), Reel 14, No. 6702–04, ser. I.

[24] Speech to Negro soldiers, October 10, 1865, the First District of Columbia Colored Regiment reviewed and addressed by the President; Savage, *Life of Andrew Johnson* (Appendix). See also the militant petition of the Mississippi Colored Convention, November 24, 1865, claiming to represent 300,000 loyal Mississippi blacks. In AJP (Microfilm), Reel 19, No. 7973–76, ser. I.

[25] Savage, *Speeches*, p. 32.

[26] Savage, *Speeches*, p. 41.

them.[27] Even before the war, the perennial public discussion about blacks irritated Johnson. If the Lord's Prayer or the Ten Commandments were to be recited on the Senate floor, Johnson did not doubt that "somebody would find a Negro in there somewhere," Johnson once said.[28]

During the political campaign of 1864, Johnson decided to take up the subject before a black audience of interracial sexual promiscuity of the Southern slaveowners. He wondered how the planter aristocracy could dare accuse their opponents of black equality when they themselves, according to Johnson, were practicing it in a peculiarly intimate way: "Of all living men they should be the last to mouth that phrase. And even when uttered in their hearing, it should cause their cheeks to tinge and burn with shame," said Johnson. The blacks assembled may have received this appeal with mixed feelings. On one hand Johnson appealed to their race pride, asking them to shun illegitimate sexual relations with the masters of agriculture. But on the other hand he could well have been showing his disgust for any kind of race mixing: "Negro equality indeed!" He continued, "Why pass, any day, along the side walks of High Street where those aristocrats more particularly dwell . . . pass by their dwellings, I say, and you will see as many mulatto as Negro children, the former bearing an unmistakable resemblance of their aristocratic owners!" Reaching an apogee of moral indignation against interracial sex, the vice-presidential candidate then shouted: "Colored men of Tennessee, this too, shall cease! Your wives and daughters shall no longer be dragged into concubinage compared to which polygamy is a virtue, to satisfy the brutal lust of slave holders and overseers! Henceforth the sanctity of God's holy law of marriage shall be respected in your persons, and the great State of Tennessee shall no more give her sanction to your degradation and your shame!"

The black audience responded to this frank discussion of

27 A very significant speech delivered at a meeting held in the House of Representatives, Thursday evening, January 21, 1864, to take initial steps to restore civil government.

28 Speech in the Senate on the Homestead Bill, 1860, Savage, *Speeches*, p. 73.

illicit racial sex with a "Thank God! Thank God!" According to one reporter those words fell "from the lips of a thousand women who in their own persons had experienced the hellish iniquity of the man seller's code." With an almost unparalleled frankness, Johnson pleaded with the "sons of Ethiopia" to shun all interracial cohabitation: "And if the laws protect you in the possession of your wives and children, if the law shields those whom you hold dear from the unlawful grasp of lust, will you endeavor to be true to yourselves, and shun as if it were death itself, the path of lewdness, crime and vice?" "'We will!' cried the assembled thousand; and joining in a sublime and tearful enthusiasm, another mighty shout went up to heaven," or at least so one reporter thought.[29]

When Johnson became President much of his mail, coming largely but by no means solely from the South, reinforced and underscored his belief in racial incompatibility. The idea that blacks were an undesirable element in the body politic was constantly on the lips of many.[30] No small wonder then, after reading a quantity of Negrophobic mail, Johnson, as President, warned black soldiers to guard against forces which tended to pit the races against each other.[31] It is not surprising that he told a black audience that the big question to be

[29] Speech to Nashville blacks, October 24, 1864. Moore, *Speeches of Andrew Johnson* (Appendix).

[30] Isaac E. Morse, New Orleans, April 21, 1865; AJP (Microfilm), Reel 13, No. 2873, ser. I. D. H. Bingham, May 4, 1865; ibid., Reel 14, No. 3323, ser. I. A. G. Mackey, Charleston, S.C., to Carl Schurz (forwarded to Johnson). Mackey doubted that the South would grant a satisfactory social status to the Negro; ibid., Reel 16, No. 5333–34, ser. I. M. A. Richter, Jamaica, British West Indies, May 17, 1865; ibid., Reel 14, No. 3515–16, ser. I. Citizens of Chatham County, Ga., May 30, 1865; ibid., Reel 14, No. 4002. I. Y. McMasters, ex-Tennesseean from Minnesota, June 6, 1865; ibid., Reel 16, No. 4250, ser. I. Reverend James Mitchell, ex-commissioner of Negro immigration under Lincoln, July 13, 1865; ibid., Reel 16, No. 7947, ser. I. F. P. Blair, August 1, 1865. This letter was a classic example of Negrophobia; ibid., Reel 16, No. 5821–38, ser. I. James Russell, Cowetta County, Baltimore, Md., August 7, 1865; ibid., Reel 17, No. 6017, ser. I. C. W. Dudley, Bennettsville, S.C., August 12, 1865. This letter was twenty-one pages long; ibid., Reel 17, No. 6633–43. Mr. Beechcroft, No. 9173–75, ser. I. Memorandum from General Grant on the racial clashes in five Southern states, February 17, 1866; ibid., Reel 20, No. 9186.

[31] Speech to black soldiers, October 10, 1865. Savage, *Speeches*, p. 93 (Appendix).

settled was: Can America harmoniously and permanently absorb the black race? Could the government digest the blacks without indigestion? There can be no doubt of Johnson's awareness of race prejudice and its implications for race relations. In his third annual message the presidential tone began to sound like certain of his letter writers from the South and New England. He was more firm than ever in his conviction of the incompatibility of the races:

> The great difference between the two races in physical, mental and moral characteristics will prevent an amalgamation or fusion of them together in one homogeneous mass. If the inferior obtains the ascendency, it will govern with reference only to its own interests.[32]

In his last annual message Johnson showed himself solidly convinced that Reconstruction was a failure and that the two races were in powerful opposition to each other:

> The attempt to place the white population under the domination of persons of color in the South has impaired, if not destroyed the kindly relations that had previously existed between them; and mutual distrust has engendered feelings of animosity which leading in some instances to collision and bloodshed, has prevented that cooperation between the two races so essential to the success of industrial enterprise in the Southern States.[33]

The Racial Aberration: "Moses," and the Merit System of Race Relations

In 1864, Johnson verbally presented himself in the role of deliverer, a black Moses with a white skin. Was this merely a Johnsonian aberration? Or did he suppose that by posing in this most unlikely role, a Southern white champion of blacks, he could make political capital during an election year? The occasion for this momentary outburst of liberal racial thought was a speech Johnson made to blacks in November 1864.

"Looking at this vast crowd of colored people and reflecting

[32] December 13, 1867, Richardson, *Messages*, VI, 567.
[33] December 9, 1868, Richardson, *Messages*, VI, 673.

through what a storm of persecution and obloquy they are compelled to pass, I am almost induced to wish that . . . a Moses might rise who should lead them safely to their promised land of freedom and happiness," said the future President. Several voices shouted, "You are our Moses!" Johnson thought that somewhere in the wings of history God had prepared the instrument of the black man's deliverance. "Your Moses will be revealed to you," he told the crowd, only to hear them say: "We want no Moses but you!" Johnson could restrain himself no longer. "Well then," he answered, "humble and unworthy as I am, if no other better shall be found I will indeed be your Moses and lead you through the Red Sea of war and bondage to a fairer future of liberty and peace. I speak now as one who feels the world his country, and all who love equal rights his friends. . . ." Johnson said that when the heat of the Civil War was over, "loyal men whether white or black, shall alone control her [Tennessee's] destinies."[34]

Such pro-black sentiment on Johnson's part made the heart of at least one abolitionist happy.[35] To another the speech was the high-water mark in the great drama of freedom then unfolding before the country.[36] When he became President, Johnson was presented with a "Moses opportunity" when militant black Mississippians asked him to stand by them through the Red Sea of black codes which that state was about to pass.[37] Johnson received other appeals from many quarters to be Moses in the area of black political appointments.[38]

[34] Moore, *Speeches of Andrew Johnson*, pp. xi-xli (Appendix).

[35] E. W. Davis, Philadelphia, to Andrew Johnson, November 5, 1864; AJP (Microfilm), Reel 11, No. 1148, ser. I.

[36] Isaac Arnold to Andrew Johnson, November 9, 1864; ibid., No. 1185–86.

[37] Petition of the Mississippi Colored Convention to Andrew Johnson, November 24, 1865; AJP (Microfilm), Reel 19, No. 7976, ser. I.

[38] B. Shaw, Vermont, May 1, 1865; ibid., Reel 14, No. 3238–39, ser. I. James M. Thompson, Virginia Surgeon, May 5, 1865, asking that Frederick Douglass be made governor of South Carolina; ibid., No. 3344. A. D. Jones, a black Ohioan, May 23, 1865; ibid., No. 3832–33. W. B. Scott and Son [blacks] May 27, 1865; ibid., No. 3936. H. H. Hunter, colored Charlestonian, June 15, 1865; AJP (Microfilm), Reel 14, No. 4081–82, ser. I. J. H. Wilson, Macon, Georgia, June 15, 1865; ibid., Reel 15, No. 4490–94, ser. I. George L. Stearns (abolitionist), December 14, 1865; ibid., Reel 19, No. 8248–56, ser. I.

Although he was said by Gideon Welles to pride himself on treating blacks cordially when they came to the White House, Johnson showed some irritation and discomfort when confronted by the articulate Frederick Douglass and a black group that sought to lecture him on the black vote: "I am free to say to you that I do not like to be arraigned by some who can get up handsomely rounded periods and deal in rhetoric and talk about abstract ideas of liberty, who never periled life, liberty or property. . . ."[39] At another time Johnson boasted that he had done as much to bring about the freedom of the blacks as "any other living man," and not for the sake of gaining power.[40]

Toward the end of 1866, Johnson repudiated his Moses role completely. In this regard he suggested that he had been misunderstood. "But a shorttime since I heard some say in the crowd that we had a Moses," Johnson said to a white audience in St. Louis. "Yes there is a Moses; and I know sometimes, it has been said that I would be the Moses of the colored man." The audience shouted, "Never!" Johnson continued: ". . .While I have striven to emancipate the colored man, I have felt and now feel that we have a great many white men that want emancipation. There is a set amongst you that have got shackles on their limbs; and are as much under the heel . . . of their masters as the colored man that was emancipated."[41]

At this point Johnson was returning to his perennial hatred of the aristocracy. He implied that with emancipation his job with the blacks was finished. The next task was to free the Southern white from planter domination. The black as a free agent seemed to interfere with this white liberation, perhaps explaining this outburst of antipathy toward the freedmen. As it turned out, the promised land that Johnson had in mind for blacks was located beyond the continental limits of the United States. In 1867, Johnson toyed with the idea of placing Frederick Douglass at the head of the Freedmen's Bureau,

[39] Johnson's interview with a black delegation, February 7, 1866, McPherson, *Reconstruction*, p. 54. Welles, *Diary*, II, 410, Thursday, January 2, 1866.

[40] Speech to blacks in the District of Columbia, on the Third Anniversary of their Emancipation, April 19, 1866. McPherson, *Reconstruction*.

[41] Speech in St. Louis, September 8, 1866; ibid., pp. 137–38.

but the notion quickly passed.[42] One must agree with the contemporary satirist who remarked acidly: ". . . Andy Johnson is as much like Moses, as bramble bushes are like roses."[43]

One of the antebellum postulates was that blacks would not work without external compulsion.[44] Andrew Johnson missed no opportunity to instruct blacks that freedom meant simply the liberty to work.[45] At the same time he declared that he wanted to see "industrious, thrifty emigrants pouring in [to the South] from all parts of the country."[46] Three million slaves were about to be thrown on the labor market but Johnson was apparently looking for a more desirable population.

In the Tennessee Legislature of 1864, Johnson came out for equal opportunity for blacks and a merit system of race relations. He seemed willing to let the law of nature assign the black man a place in society. That place would be wherever his labor and the fruits of his labor and toil might take him. However, he was quick to add that this did not mean that the black man was equal to the Anglo-Saxon. The black would simply be given an equal chance in the race of life like any immigrant. Thus Johnson pleaded for the African in the Legislative Hall of Tennessee: ". . . And if he can rise by his own energy; in the name of God let him rise." Were not some white men inferior also in some ways? Yet this was not sufficient reason to enslave them.[47]

During the political campaign of 1864, Johnson said: "I desire that all men should have a fair start in the race of life . . . let him succeed who has the most merit. This I think is the

[42] Welles, *Diary*, III, 142–43, July 26, 1867.

[43] Oliver Star St. John, *Moses or the Man Who Supposes Himself to Be Moses, No Moses at All* (New York: American News Co., 1866), p. 4.

[44] Ben Shicklin to Andrew Johnson, October 22, 1864; AJP (Microfilm), Reel 11, No. 993–98, ser. I. Ann Fentress to Andrew Johnson, November 5, 1865; ibid., Reel 11, No. 1143. C. G. Memmenger to Andrew Johnson [no date]; ibid., Reel 17, No. 6249–52, ser. I. John W. Stone to Andrew Johnson, September 18, 1865; ibid., Reel 18, No. 6915, ser. I.

[45] Speech in Louisville, Ky., 1864. Savage, *Speeches.*

[46] Speech at Nashville, as vice-presidential candidate, June 6, 1864; Moore, *Speeches of Andrew Johnson*, p. xxx (Appendix).

[47] Speech, on the Restoration of State Government, January 21, 1864, pp. 7–8.

principle of heaven."[48] Later in the year Johnson expanded the point to a crowd in Louisville, Kentucky:

> This talk about "nigger equality" is all humbug. I have seen more of it in the South than I have in the North. If the Negro as a free man can compete with the white, he has a right to compete with him. If after a fair test he can't, he must give way to the white. In my opinion freedom will not make the Negroes any worse, and will result in their advancement. I am for an aristocracy of labor, of intelligent, stimulating, virtuous labor, of talent, of intellect, of merit, for the elevation of each and every man white or black, according to his talent and industry.[49]

Johnson continued his theme of merit as the standard for race relations in a lecture to black soldiers on October 10, 1865. With considerable racial acuity he told the soldiers that slavery was by no means the end of the black question. He also told them that they had to merit their place in American society by hard work, intelligence and morality. This was the only way that a black could become, as it were, a white man, according to Johnson. The black man's character and capacity were suspect; unlike other immigrants in American history, he was called upon to prove his fitness to be a citizen. In addition to the idea of merit, Johnson strove mightily in his speech to black veterans to convince them of the efficacy of puritan-like morality which, by implication, they lacked:

> It is for you to establish the great fact that you are fit and qualified to be free. . . . You must give evidence that you are competent for the rights that the government has guaranteed to you. Hence forth each and all of you must be measured according to your merit. If one man is more meritorious than the other, they cannot be equal; and he is the most exalted that is the most meritorious, without regard to color. And the idea of having a law passed in the morning that will make a white man a black man before night and a black man a white man before day is absurd. That is not the standard. It is your own conduct. It is your merit; it is the development of your own talents and your own intellectuality and moral qualities. Let this be your course,

[48] Speech in Nashville, July 6, 1864; Moore, *Speeches of Andrew Johnson*, p. xxii (Appendix).
[49] Savage, *Speeches*, p. 311 [September 8?], 1864.

> adopt a system of morality; abstain from all licentiousness. And let me say one more thing here, for I am going to talk plain. I have lived in a Southern State all my life, and I know what has too often been the case. There is one thing that you should esteem higher and more supreme than almost all others, and that is the solemn contract with all the penalties, in the association of married life. Men and women should abstain from those qualities and habits that too frequently follow war. Inculcate among your children and among your associations . . . that virtue, that merit, that intelligence are the standards to be observed, and those which you are determined to maintain during your lives. This is the way to make a white man black and a black man white.

At the conclusion of the last sentence the blacks cheered.[50] Just two months later, however, Johnson placed a narrow construction on the meaning of black freedom. In reality his merit system of race relations extended only to equality in the struggle to earn one's bread with the sweat of his brow. Like Lincoln, he thought that the black man had the right to labor and enjoy the fruits. He expressed his willingness to see the black man given every opportunity to *work* so that should he fail to make the grade on his own, the failure could not be imputed to the whites. But even as Johnson was defending the black's right to work, he spoke of peopling the South with an enterprising population "from the most cultivated nations of Europe."[51] Johnson also said that he would not advise the forced removal of blacks from the country and that hasty assumptions about the inability of the two races to get along should be avoided. He urged the country to "make the experiment in good faith . . . not to be easily disheartened," and to encourage the blacks to useful toil.[52]

In summary, Johnson approved of slavery before the Civil War. He also thought the black man was inferior and excluded from the Declaration of Independence. Johnson said that America was a white man's country and that the black and white races were incompatible. But when the war came, and for reasons not entirely evident, Johnson turned against slavery. Perhaps he

[50] Savage, *Speeches*, pp. 91–93 (Appendix).
[51] Savage, Annual Message, December 4, 1865.
[52] Ibid.

saw his opportunity to strike a blow at the white Bourbon aristocracy which he hated. Sometime during the war, Johnson underwent a racial change of heart. Perhaps it was the mesmerizing effect of black participation in the Civil War or a hint from Lincoln regarding the political utility of such a move, that caused Johnson to momentarily entertain hopes of being "Moses" to blacks and even to advocate a merit system of race relations, some forty years before Theodore Roosevelt. In advocating the merit system of race relations, Johnson apparently did not realize that if prejudice against the black man was not based on his condition but on his race, this very prejudice would remain to obstruct the operation of the merit principle.

And then the aberration ended. Johnson reverted to his pre-Civil War racial notions. Perhaps it was the rejection of his Reconstruction plans by the radical Republicans that soured him on blacks. Most of his racial statements after 1865 were of an extreme and intemperate nature. In 1866, he was denying his Moses role and implying that the promised land for the blacks was *beyond* the national limits of the United States. Lashing into the radicals, and admitting his role in emancipation, Johnson said: "And when they talk about Moses, and the colored man being led into the promised land, where is the land that this clan proposes to lead them into? When we talk about taking them out from among the white population and sending them to other climes, what is it they propose? . . . a Freedman's Bureau. . . ."[53] Johnson became convinced that Reconstruction was a failure and an attempt to put black over white. Johnson, as President, was rarely successful in making the successful transition from theory to practice in any real positive sense.

The Presidential Perspective on Civil and Social Equality: From Theory to Practice

As radical Republican opposition to Johnsonian Reconstruction loomed on the political horizon, old Gideon Welles con-

[53] Speech, September 8, 1866. McPherson, *Reconstruction*, p. 139.

tended that the people simply were not prepared for a political party based on racial equality.[54] George L. Stearns, the great New England champion of Afro-American rights, encouraged by Johnson's pro-black aberrations of 1864 and 1865, urged the President not to miss his big chance to implement the Declaration of Independence and secure equality before the law to all men.[55]

Johnson himself put his finger on the crux of the Reconstruction problem when he told delegates from nine Southern states that the demise of slavery had changed the status of blacks "and we as wise men, must recognize so potent a fact and adapt ourselves to the circumstances as they surround us." The delegates said that they were willing to do just that and Johnson answered that he believed them.[56]

Johnson encouraged the ex-Confederates to give at least a modicum of substantive equality to the blacks. Apparently he did this mainly to forestall a radical attack on his program. But the Southerners proved very recalcitrant, and very much in evidence was Johnson's disinclination to violate his states' rights scruples relative to domestic affairs. He would urge the ex-rebels to secure the blacks in their rights; if they refused, while this would be regrettable, there was nothing more he felt he could do.

On October 10, 1865, Johnson told some cheering black soldiers: "This is your country as well as anybody else's country. This is the country in which you expect to live and in which you should expect to do some thing by your example in civil life, as you have done in the field."[57] Three days after speaking to the black soldiers, Johnson urged a white delegation from the South to pass laws securing the black man in his personal and property rights. However, the newspaper reporter declared that he saw members of the delegation shrug their shoulders when

[54] Welles, *Diary*, II, 369. August 30, 1865.

[55] George L. Stearns, May 17, 1865; AJP (Microfilm), Reel 14, No. 3580–84, ser. I.

[56] Speech of Andrew Johnson . . . delivered September 13, 1865, at an interview accorded to the Representatives of nine Southern states; AJP (Microfilm), Reel 47, ser. V-D.

[57] Speech to black soldiers, October 10, 1865. Savage, *Speeches*, pp. 91–93 (Appendix).

General Grant suggested that a black man should be allowed to take the witness stand and his testimony taken for what it was worth.[58]

The passage of a black code in Mississippi—it was designated a civil rights bill for freedmen—denied blacks the right to testify in court against white people. This convinced one Freedmen's Bureau official that the only protection blacks would get in that state would have to come from the military arm of the federal government.[59] The President himself should have been uneasy over the fate of black rights in that state. Three days later, however, he penned a rather unconvincing note to the governor of Mississippi stating that he expected no concessions from the people of that state other than "loyal compliance with the laws and Constitution of the United States; and the adoption of such measures giving protection to all freedmen in person and property without regard to color as will entitle them to resume all their constitutional relations in the federal union."[60]

Indeed, it appears that in the crucial month of November 1865, Johnson did not make it at all clear that something more than freedom from slavery had to be accorded blacks. For example, the secretary of state for Tennessee wrote Johnson in obvious desperation:

> The bill to allow colored persons to testify in the courts will not pass the House unless they believe that its failure to pass may prevent the admission of our delegation to Congress [nor?] can any other legislation favorable to the Negro pass without a *reaction*.

The secretary closed with this significant statement:

> If it is your opinion that the defeat of the "negro testimony bill" will prevent our delegation from admittance, I would *be very glad if you will telegraph that opinion to me*.[61]

[58] Ibid., pp. 98–99.

[59] Lt. Col. R. S. Donaldson, Freedmen's Bureau Commissioner, Jackson, Mississippi, to Capt. J. H. Weler, Acting Asst. Adjutant General of Freedmen's Bureau, Vicksburg, Miss., November 17, 1865, including a newspaper clipping from the Jackson *Daily News*, November 14, 1865, gloating over the defeat of the black testimony bill; AJP (Microfilm), Reel 19, No. 7885, ser. I.

[60] Savage, *Speeches*, p. 107 (Appendix), November 17, 1865.

[61] A. J. Fletcher to Andrew Johnson, November 20, 1865; AJP (Microfilm), Reel 19, No. 7911, ser. I.

Whether or not Johnson replied has not been determined. Johnson later told the secretary of state for Tennessee that his annual message indicated his views on the subject: "Negro testimony in all cases where they are parties, would be conclusive." Apparently Johnson would let blacks testify only in cases which involved the freedmen. "It is to be regretted that our Legislature failed to make some advance at its present session upon this question, indicating that the public judgement was moving in the right direction," the President concluded hopelessly.[62] Obviously the Southerners were in no hurry to make black and white equal before the law. It was apparent too that Johnson was no more willing than Lincoln to insist upon anything more for blacks than the bare minimum of freedom of life, limb and property.

Johnson hoped that the South Carolina Legislature would "adopt a code in reference to the free persons of color that will be acceptable to the country, at the same time doing justice to the white and colored population."[63] Upon hearing that the Mississippi Legislature was going to disarm the blacks of that state, Johnson, through his Secretary of War, telegraphed instructions on the subject to General Thomas.[64] It is difficult to determine whether Johnson or Stanton spoke. Nevertheless, according to the directions General Thomas would be the judge of the necessity of disarming anybody in Mississippi. Should the occasion arise for black disarmament, the task should be executed by the military arm of the national government. "Under existing circumstances," continued the instructions, "any effort by one class of citizens to disarm another class under color of state authority might bring on a collision that would not otherwise occur, & should be carefully avoided." The duty of the military was to see that the public peace was kept by all citizens. And if it became necessary to disarm citizens to keep the peace

[62] Andrew Johnson to A. J. Fletcher [November 1865]; AJP (Microfilm), Reel 43, No. 112, ser. III-A (Letter Press Book, Vol. 5).

[63] Andrew Johnson to the provisional governor of South Carolina, November 27, 1865. McPherson, *Reconstruction*, p. 24.

[64] Andrew Johnson to Governor Humphreys, Mississippi, December 12, 1865; AJP (Microfilm), Reel 19, No. 8229, ser. I.

the national military would exercise this power without any discrimination of color or race.[65] The sentiments expressed by Johnson and Stanton in these instructions were admirable, if rather redundant.

There is one instance of a Tennessee legislator arguing that blacks should be allowed to testify in court because black testimony did not mean black equality.[66] Such champions of black rights were rarely encountered in the ex-rebel states during the later months of 1865. Some of the provisional governors seemed pleased with any slight concession they were able to wheedle out of their recalcitrant legislatures. For example, Governor Orr of South Carolina thought that ample provision had been made for the civil rights of the freedmen, and reported with obvious pride: "He is allowed to testify in court when the rights of a freedman are in any way involved. . . . The vagrancy laws are stringent but necessary. . . . They will only be enforced against the idle & dissolute and many of them you [know] will not work without the compulsion of law." Orr concluded that he was now looking forward to his state's admission to the Union, the removal of federal troops, and self-government.[67]

As the President and Congress prepared to engage in battle over the civil rights provisions for blacks in Southern states, Johnson was urged in one quarter to remain true to genuine democratic doctrine.[68] A New Yorker berated him gently: "While you announce to the colored people the proclamation of freedom, they are still groaning under the galling yoke of the black codes of the ex-rebel states. . . ."[69] On February 9, 1866, a friend informed Johnson of an interracial meeting in Philadelphia addressed by Frederick Douglass. According to this in-

[65] Edwin M. Stanton to General Thomas; AJP (Microfilm), Reel 19, No. 8220–21, ser. I.

[66] W. B. Lewis to Andrew Johnson, December 13, 1865; AJP (Microfilm), Reel 19, No. 8242, ser. I.

[67] James Orr to Andrew Johnson, December 23, 1865; ibid., No. 8361.

[68] Lorenzo Sherwood, Washington, D.C., to Andrew Johnson, December 23, 1865; AJP (Microfilm), Reel 19, No. 8365, ser. I.

[69] John Binny to Andrew Johnson, January 10, 1866; AJP (Microfilm), Reel 19, No. 8577, ser. I.

formant, Douglass spoke glowingly about Lincoln but disparagingly about Johnson: "Many of his utterances toward you were grossly insulting and abusive. . . . He gave loose rein to satire, anger, and slander. . . . He was particularly bitter in commenting upon your advice to the blacks, whenever you addressed them, to go to work and be quiet and orderly and prove by their conduct that they were capable of enjoying freedom. . . . He thinks you ought to have advised them to strike for the ballot & to assert their equality." Johnson's informant concluded his lamentations against the presumptuous Douglass by observing that in spite of a Supreme Court decision declaring that the black man was not a citizen, such a man in Philadelphia (Douglass) was allowed to "malign the Chief Magistrate of the Republic."[70]

Senator Heim of Kentucky expressed optimism about the way his legislature would treat the blacks, except on two points: "We will not consent," he told Johnson, "that a Negro shall be received as a witness between two white men as litigants. We think our laws allow him to be a witness in all other cases. Violence on the person of a white woman by a Negro is death, by a white man it is long confinement in the penitentiary. We could not & will not change that."[71]

Finally, Johnson wrote to another Southern governor, James W. Throckmorton of Texas, "I have nothing further to suggest than urging upon the Legislature to make all laws involving civil rights as complete as possible, so as to extend equal rights and exact justice to all persons, without regard to color, if it has not been done."[72] Thus after a brief excursion upon the sea of race liberality, Johnson came to himself, reset his sails and returned to the more familiar waters of Negrophobia, dropping his anchor in the muddy bottom of racial opposition to black aspiration.

[70] James H. Embrey to Andrew Johnson, February 9, 1866; ibid., Reel 20, No. 9001–04, ser. I.

[71] John L. Heim, state senator, Frankfort, Ky., to Andrew Johnson [n.d.], 1866; AJP (Microfilm), Reel 20, No. 9178, ser. I.

[72] Andrew Johnson to Governor Throckmorton, October 30, 1866. McPherson, *Reconstruction*, p. 315.

Civil Rights, Vetoes, and Racial Necessity

President Johnson vetoed the Civil Rights Bill of 1866 on racial and political grounds. And while there is some dispute concerning the authorship of the veto, Johnson must have agreed with the sentiments expressed there. Political arguments came foremost, but the document also sought to demonstrate the racial necessity of segregation and discrimination. The bill was branded an undue invasion of the rights of the states. Taking the position which the Supreme Court was later to take in disallowing another such act in 1883, the veto asserted that civil rights and citizenship were properly the concern of the states alone. The implication was that a state had the right to discriminate if it so desired: "Thus a perfect equality of the white and colored races is attempted to be fixed by a federal law in every state of the Union, over the vast field of state jurisdiction covered by these enumerated rights. In no one of them can any state exercise any power of discrimination between the races." In words reminiscent of Lincolnian racial necessity the veto message went on: "In the exercise of state policy over matters exclusively affecting the people of each state, it has frequently been thought expedient to discriminate between the two races."

The veto message next called attention to another possible consequence of federal power over civil rights: "May not Congress repeal, in the same way, all state laws discriminating between the two races, on the subject of suffrage and office." This was a strong point with Johnson, especially in view of his pre-Civil War theory about a white man's government. May not "Congress . . . also declare by law, who, without regard to race or color, shall have the right to act as juror or as judge, to hold office, and finally to vote in every state and territory of the United States?" In other words, political opposition to the bill was predicated on the racial principle that this was indeed a white man's country to be controlled by white men. The bill, charged the veto, might indiscriminately make citizens of gypsies, Indians, Chinese and blacks.

In the opinion of the veto message's author the black man was not a citizen but an alien incompetent to exercise the "privilege and immunities of citizenship of the United States. . . ." Citizenship was not needed to protect the black in his civil rights. Was he not already protected as much as other "domiciled aliens and foreigners"? The foreigner usually knows more about the government than the recently freed African. Why give the blacks citizenship all at once while the foreigner must wait five years? The black man is ignorant but can take care of himself without special class legislation—especially the kind that favored black over white. Discord between the races would surely result. "I will cheerfully cooperate with Congress in any measure that may be necessary for the preservation of civil rights of the freedmen . . . ," said Johnson, concluding his racial treatise.[73]

"I know I am right and I am damned if I do not adhere to it," Johnson allegedly said after vetoing the Civil Rights Bill.[74] Petroleum V. Nasby commented: "Moses lifted up the serpent in the wilderness that his . . . Hebrews might look and live. Trumbull tried to lift up just a serpent for Androo's Hebrews, but Andrew vetoed it."[75] But Gideon Welles agreed with Johnson.[76]

By the time the Congressional Reconstruction Act was passed in 1867, Johnson had become almost intemperate in his anti-black sentiments. When the veto of the supplementary Reconstruction bill was written the President or his ghost writer

[73] Veto Message on the Civil Rights Bill, March 27, 1866. Lillian Foster, *Andrew Johnson, President of the United States: His Life and Speeches* (New York: Richardson and Co., 1866), pp. 267–80. Hugh McCulloch, *Men and Measures of Half a Century* (New York: Charles Scribner's Sons, 1888), pp. 381, 406. McCulloch was Secretary of the Treasury under Lincoln, Johnson, and Arthur, and claimed that Johnson wrote all of his messages except his vetoes, which were probably written, he thought, by Stanbery. He also thought that the voiding of the Civil Rights Act of 1875 by the Supreme Court in 1883 was a vindication of Johnson's veto of such an act nine years earlier.

[74] William G. Moore, Private Secretary to the President (transcript of the "Small Diary"), p. 15, entry, 1866; AJP (Microfilm), Reel 50, ser. IX-A.

[75] Petroleum V. Nasby, *Swinging Round the Circle or Andy's Trip to the West* (New York: American News Co., 1866), pp. 25–27.

[76] April 19, 1866, Welles, *Diary*, II, 489–90.

seems to have drawn upon all the anti-black contents of the presidential mailbag for choice invectives to heap upon the blacks and the "ill-founded attempt" to put the ignorant and incompetent African over the Caucasian:

> The object of the bill . . . is to put the Southern states . . . in the hands of the Negroes. They are wholly incompetent to administer such a trust. Ninety-nine in a hundred of them have no idea what a constitution means. . . . It is vain to deny that they are an inferior race—very far inferior to the European variety. They have learned in slavery all that they know in civilization. When first brought from the country of their origin they were naked savages and where they have been left to their own devices or escaped the control of the white race they have relapsed, to a greater or less degree into barbarism.

Johnson conjured up blood-soaked visions of Santo Domingo as evidence of black degeneracy when away from the watchful eye of the white superior. Indeed, the government was doing for the helpless blacks "what no government ever did before for any class of its people except children, idiots, and lunatics. It has fed them, bought their clothes, superintended their labor, appointed officers to make their bargains and collected their wages." If the blacks could not manage "the most trifling concerns of their own . . . ," argued Johnson with some reason, how could they act as "lawgivers for a great nation"? Blacks simply had no "capacity for so high a function." They were satisfied to enjoy their own freedom and had no desire to seek control of public affairs, Johnson thought.[77]

Johnson next prepared, but did not submit, a veto for the District of Columbia Equal Rights Bill which was of exactly the same tenor. He continued to interpret every attempt to secure equal rights for blacks as another move to put blacks over whites. Here he objected to blacks serving on juries in cases where whites were involved, describing this as not only unconstitutional but insulting to the white mass of the American people. Milton Lomask has called this so-called turnabout of

[77] Veto of the Supplementary Reconstruction Bill; AJP (Microfilm), Reel 46, No. 28881–90, ser. III-A.

Johnson "the transubstantiation of a poor white."[78] It might be more nearly correct to call it a reversion to type. After all, Johnson was no Negrophile *before* the war. Johnson attacked the repeal of all limitations upon the rights of office holding or serving on juries in the District of Columbia as an unjust removal of initiative from the local people, by which was meant the white people: "I cannot believe that the American people are prepared to see . . . the government of the capital of the nation in the hands of negroes." Johnson resented the doctrine that "negroes are the peers and equals of white men" and hoped that it would not be sustained, lest it bring on a conflict between the races. A man had the right to be tried by his peers: "Does a white citizen of this District enjoy that right if negroes may be called to try him? I think not. . . . To put a citizen at the mercy of another class . . . which not only differs from his own in physical structure, in mental characteristics and moral sentiments, but which is besides hostile to his rights and liberties is to violate the Constitution. . . ." In another burst of Negrophobia, the hopelessly unreconstructed Johnson said: "We all know, all men know, that between the black and the white . . . on this continent there is socially and morally a great gulf completely dividing them and totally preventing all fusion or amalgamation of the two. . . ."[79]

In this connection Johnson approvingly noted that many Northern and Southern states had laws forbidding marriage of whites with blacks or mulattoes. Johnson quoted the great jurist, Chancellor Kent, to say: "Even [in] the states where intermarriage was not forbidden by law, they are revolting and regarded as an offense against public decorum." If the Civil Rights Bill of 1866 were passed what could prevent Congress from repealing all state laws regarding the "contract of marriage between the races"?[80] The only hope for blacks was the

[78] Milton Lomask, *Andrew Johnson: President on Trial* (New York: Farrar, Straus and Cudahy, 1960) Preface.

[79] Veto of the District of Columbia Equal Rights Bill, December 11, 1867; AJP (Microfilm), Reel 46, No. 29172–86; No. 29187–200, is a more detailed draft of this message which was never sent, ser. V-A.

[80] Veto of the Civil Rights Bill, March 27, 1866. Foster, *Andrew Johnson*, p. 269.

kindest feeling on the part of the superior toward the inferior.

According to Browning the ratification of the Fourteenth Amendment was "not a thing for discussion in [Johnson's] Cabinet. . . ." No one said a word when the news was announced in Cabinet meeting.[81] On the other hand Johnson vetoed a measure in the District of Columbia which would have given jurisdiction over "colored schools" to an all-white board where initially the board had some blacks on it.[82] But in the main, his opposition to blacks as a race caused the President to oppose nearly all civil rights for them, other than the right to work. He especially disliked the idea of a special mediator between blacks and white in the South as represented by the Freedmen's Bureau.

Race and the Freedmen's Bureau

The Freedmen's Bureau tried to supervise the contact between the black worker and his white employer. The fact that testimony by a black man was not admitted by the courts of most of the ex-rebel states complicated the job of the agents who were trying to secure justice for the freedmen. The President received letters from all over the South asking that the bureau be disbanded. Not one surviving letter was found in favor of the Freedmen's Bureau, except those coming from officials of that agency who told Johnson that employers were mistreating and cheating black people and that someone was needed to see that they were justly treated.[83] Even a poorly dressed black, carrying a few fowl which he had raised "from the hour they came from the shell," was subject to arrest on the streets of New Orleans.[84]

[81] Browning, *Diary*, II, 209. Entry Thursday, July 28, 1868.

[82] February 13, 1869; AJP (Microfilm), Reel 43, No. 346, ser. III-B.

[83] John Birchwell to Andrew Johnson, November 4, 1864; AJP (Microfilm), Reel 11, No. 1137–38, ser. I. R. D. Mussey, Office of the Chief Superintendent of Contrabands, February 20, 1865; ibid., Reel 13, No. 2309–19. T. W. Con-

[84] Thomas Conway to Mr. Kennedy, mayor of New Orleans, July 13, 1865. Ibid., Reel 16, No. 5397–98, ser. I; ibid., July 17, 1865, No. 5483.

way, Assistant Commissioner for the Freedmen's Bureau in Louisiana, to Major General Canby, April 30, 1865.

Brigadier General Fullerton of the War Department sent the President a twenty-page memorandum containing five major objections of the Freedmen's Bureau enlargement bill pending before Congress, reasons which, significantly enough, were almost identical to those the President used in his veto message on the bill.[85] Gideon Welles saw in the bill a diabolical plot of Northern philanthropy to create hatred between the races. He would advise the President not to sign it. The day before the veto Welles wrote: "I had an interview and pretty free exchange of opinion with the President on the Freedman's Bureau Bill. . . . I expressed myself without reserve. . . . The President acquiesced fully in my views. This being the case I conclude he will place upon it his veto. Indeed, he intimated as much."[86] Welles liked to picture himself as a power behind the throne. The President's theory of racial hostility between blacks and Southern whites probably made him disposed to agree with those correspondents who reported that the bureau was a catalyst for race conflicts.

The President vetoed the bill on the seventeenth of February, claiming that it gave too much power to the executive and perpetuated military rule in time of peace. The bill was welfare legislation which had not even been considered for "millions of the white race."[87] While the President was definitely raising the specter of race everywhere, the ghost of a black voting alarmed him uncontrollably.

The Presidential Perspective on Race and Black Voting

The political implications of emancipation were being considered even before the war was over. The contents of the President's mailbag for the year 1865 contained a decided sentiment in favor of some kind of voting privilege for blacks either as a matter of Christian charity and democracy or as a reward for

[85] February 9, 1866; AJP (Microfilm), Reel 20, No. 9018.
[86] Welles, *Diary*, II, 432–33. Entries for February 14, 1866, and Friday, February 16, 1866.
[87] Veto Message; Foster, *Andrew Johnson*, pp. 228–34.

the black war effort.[88] This is not to say that there were not those who thought that Johnson was right in leaving the question of the black vote to the states.[89]

S. P. Chase urged the President to order the registration of all loyal citizens in the South "without regard to complexion. . . ."[90] Gideon Welles was opposed to black suffrage and

[88] Joseph H. Glover [1864?]; AJP (Microfilm), Reel 12, No. 1736, ser. I. W. P. Hulbert, November 19, 1864, Cincinnati, Ohio; ibid., No. 1324. Mrs. C. C. Williams, February 15, 1865, Small Rock County, Iowa; ibid., Reel 13, No. 2279–80. Blacks were not voting in Iowa at this time. Jeremiah Clemens, April 2, 1865; ibid., Reel 13, No. 2841–42 (Alabama), ser. I. Joseph Hartley, Quaker, April 30, 1865; ibid., Reel 14, No. 3115. James E. Hamilton, New York: May 3, 1865; ibid., Reel 14, No. 3282. William D. Kelly, Philadelphia; ibid., Reel 14, No. 3435. White citizens of Charleston, S.C., May 16, 1865; ibid., Reel 14, No. 4589. I. S. Shailer, Roxbury, Mass., May 20, 1865; ibid., Reel 14, No. 3782–83. John D. Brown, Kansan, living in Norfolk, Va., May 23, 1865; ibid., Reel 14, No. 3834. Petition from the General Assembly of the Presbyterian Church, Brooklyn, N.Y., May 27, 1865; ibid., Reel 14, No. 5269. Petition from the General Assembly of the Congregational Church, Peoria, Ill., May 30, 1865; ibid., Reel 14, No. 3985. Petition of the Society of Friends [June 1865]; ibid., Reel 14, No. 39–79. Joseph Noxon; ibid., Reel 14, No. 3934–35. R. D. Goodwin, New York, June 2, 1865, asking that blacks be given the vote in ten years; ibid., Reel 15, No. 4095, ser. I. Richard Mitchell, Chicago, June 5, 1865; ibid., Reel 15, No. 4224–25. William Johnson, New York, June 6, 1865; ibid., Reel 15, No. 4247. Samuel H. Ortlip, New Jersey, June 7, 1865; ibid., Reel 15, No. 4274. Samuel Willets, New York, June 21, 1865 (Louisiana); ibid., Reel 15, No. 4690–95, ser. I. Petition from colored citizens of South Carolina, June 29, 1865; ibid., Reel 15, No. 4915–5010. Charles Sumner, June 30, 1865; enclosing a petition from three hundred colored Georgia citizens; ibid., Reel 16, No. 5021–30. Amos A. Lawrence, Boston, July 1, 1865; ibid., Reel 16, No. 4813. James M. Russell, Leeds, England, July 4, 1865; ibid., Reel 16, No. 5114–15, ser. I. H. B. Sherman, Titusville, Pa., July 4, 1865; ibid., Reel 16, No. 5117–18. T. A. White, letter of a black man on the suffrage question, newspaper clipping, May 29, 1865; ibid., Reel 16, No. 5115.

[89] Thomas Forney, January 7, 1865; ibid., Reel 12, No. 1825. Lewis D. Campbell, May 8, 1865, Hamilton, Ohio; ibid., Reel 14, No. 3403–04. R. Fuller, May 19, 1865; ibid., Reel 14, No. 3767. Thornton F. Marshall, Kentucky, June 14, 1865; ibid., Reel 15, No. 4477–78. Joseph H. Wright, Vermont, June 17, 1865; ibid., Reel 15, No. 4427–28. C. H. Lewis, secretary of state, Virginia, July 3, 1865; ibid., Reel 16, No. 5090, ser. I. R. P. L. Baber, Cincinnati, Ohio, July 4, 1865; ibid., Reel 16, No. 5130–32. H. M. Watterson, July 8, 1865, from N.C.; ibid., Reel 16, No. 5264. William Daily, Indiana, July 10, 1865; ibid., Reel 16, No. 5324–25, ser. I. I. S. Brock, Kentucky, to Montgomery Blair and forwarded to Johnson, July 15, 1865; ibid., Reel 16, No. 5451–55. Governor Holden, North Carolina, to the mayor and officials of Wilmington, July 20, 1865; ibid., Reel 16, No. 5456–59.

[90] His letter came from Beaufort Harbor, S.C., May 7, 1865; AJP (Microfilm), Reel 14, No. 3379–80. S. P. Chase, May 17, 1865, Hilton Head;

reported that Johnson's Cabinet was evenly divided on the matter.[91] After Johnson issued his proclamation for the reorganization of North Carolina and excluded the black as a qualified elector, letters poured in to him from several Northern states urging him to grant the black the ballot. While these letters contained a variety of reasons, the dominant concern was to prevent the ex-rebels from running the government they had so recently tried to destroy. Other reasons had to do with justice, equality before the law, protection of blacks, and the use of the black voter as a punishing insult to the hated rebels.[92]

Carl Schurz gave the President some astute political advice which went unheeded. He predicted a direct confrontation between the Administration and Congress over the issue of the black vote and urged the President not to oppose black suffrage in other Southern states as he had done in North Carolina.[93] How different the story of Reconstruction might have been had Johnson taken this advice. A future investigator might well conclude that for Andrew Johnson the last eight months of 1865 constituted his *critical* year rather than 1866.

Johnson did not ignore Schurz's advice completely. He did make an attempt to get at least a qualified vote for some blacks in the South. He asked Governor Sharkey of Mississippi to urge

---

ibid., Reel 14, No. 3585–86, ser. I. Chase to Johnson, May 21, 1865; ibid., Reel 14, No. 3797, ser. I. Chase to Johnson, May 23, 1865, Key West, Fla.; ibid., Reel 14.

[91] Welles, *Diary*, II, 301–04. Entries for Tuesday, May 9, and Wednesday, May 10, 1865. According to Welles, Stanton, Dennison and Speed favored black suffrage while McCulloch, Usher and himself were opposed. Welles was a rather angry old man, a conservative and a reactionary who often spoke as if he were a member of the Southern Confederacy rather than a Connecticut Yankee; ibid., III, 123–51.

[92] A. S. Willson to Andrew Johnson, May 31, 1865; AJP (Microfilm), Reel 14, No. 4050. See Footnote 88 above for additional citation of these letters.

[93] Carl Schurz to Andrew Johnson, June 6, 1865; ibid., Reel 15, No. 4243–44, ser. I. Frederick A. Sawyer to Carl Schurz, July 20, 1865; ibid., Reel 16, No. 5555–61, ser. I. Johnson rebuked Schurz for his stand on the black vote and said sharply: "The people must be trusted with their government, and if trusted my opinion is they will act in good faith. . . ." Andrew Johnson to Carl Schurz [August 1865?]; ibid., Reel 42, No. 298–300 (Letter Book, Vol. 2), ser. III-A.

his legislature to give the vote to all literate blacks holding $250 worth of property. Taking his cue from Schurz, perhaps, Johnson urged this course as a means of foiling the radicals in their attempt to keep the rebels out of the Union: "You will completely disarm the adversary . . . the radicals will be completely foiled . . . ," said Johnson.[94] Governor Sharkey reported that slavery had been abolished but that the subject of civil rights for blacks would be left to the next legislature.[95] Johnson was not pleased that the subject of black rights had been delayed. He was expecting Mississippi to set an example on qualified black suffrage which the other Southern states could emulate. With obvious reference to the radicals, he reminded Sharkey of the turn of events in the North: "Hence the importance of being prompt and circumspect in all that is being done."[96] On August 22, 1865, Johnson sent identical dispatches to the provisional governors of Mississippi, Alabama, Florida, Georgia, South Carolina, and Texas, cautioning them all against embarrassing his Reconstruction policies by favoring rebels in their governments.[97] They did not listen.

From Georgia the President learned that blacks would be allowed to testify in court but would not be given the right to vote. "On the question of suffrage there will be no debate in Georgia," said General Steedman who also helped to poison the President's mind against Schurz by saying: "I can see very plainly . . . that he is opposed to your policy. . . ."[98]

The provisional governor of Alabama, Lewis E. Parsons, reported the failure of the state legislature to give the blacks the constitutional right to testify in court. The South, Governor Parsons lamented, was not disposed to share political power with blacks. What was the indispensable minimum the state had to

[94] Andrew Johnson to Governor Sharkey, August 15, 1865; AJP (Microfilm), Reel 42 (Letter Book, Vol. 2), No. 230, ser. III-A.

[95] Governor Sharkey to Andrew Johnson, August 20, 1865; ibid., Reel 17, No. 6157–59, ser. I.

[96] Andrew Johnson to Governor Sharkey [August 21, 1865]; AJP (Microfilm), Reel 42 (Letter Book, Vol. 2), No. 230.

[97] Andrew Johnson to Governor Sharkey [August 21, 1865]; AJP (Microfilm), Reel 42 (Letter Book, Vol. 2), No. 260–61.

[98] General James Steedman to Andrew Johnson, August 15, 1865; ibid., Reel 17, No. 6035–41, ser. I.

do for blacks in order to return to the Union, Parsons asked Johnson. It was here that Johnson let a golden opportunity to be "Moses" pass by. He would insist on nothing. While Parsons personally could not see how 440,000 blacks could be governed without the right to testify in court, Johnson was not disposed to see the blacks cast a ballot. He wished that the "no distinction because of color" clause had been put into the Constitution which was about to be presented to the people so that *they* could decide "whether political power is to be retained by the white race or shared with the black. . . ." "But," said Parsons, "if we are compelled to share political power with the black race, it will result in a war of races of the most deadly character—one or both must go to destruction. . . ."[99]

Governor Parsons' next communication was instructive. While a large number of the Alabama Constitutional Convention was willing to admit black testimony into the courts, "the majority seemed to think that the people were not fully prepared for such a decided stand, and thought it best to wait for further developments. . . ."[100] In view of all of this travail over the mere right of the black man to testify in court, adamant resistance to his right to vote was a foregone conclusion. A few days later Parsons complained that Johnson had not yet answered his question regarding the indispensable minimum for the blacks. Perhaps the President was seriously reflecting upon the political as well as the racial implications of black voters in the South.

The Blacks and the Political Balance of Power in the South

What would the President do now? Most of his mail from April to October called for some kind of black suffrage. However, most of this favorable black opinion came from the North and was by no means unanimous. On the other hand, his Southern mail revealed an almost unanimous disinclination on the part

[99] Lewis E. Parsons to Andrew Johnson, September 23, 1865; AJP (Microfilm), Reel 18, No. 6980–84, ser. I.
[100] Ibid., September 28, 1865, No. 7068–70.

of the whites of that region to share political power with the former slave or to give him more than a modicum of anything even suggesting civil equality.

A full seven days before he made his famous speech to blacks expounding the merit system of race relations, President Johnson took a stand against them voting. He made the following points in an interview with George Stearns, a New England abolitionist: The South should be given more time to live down this new relation with blacks; giving blacks the ballot would produce a race war because of their antipathy toward the nonslaveholding Southern whites; the right to vote was not a natural but a political right resting in the people of the states and to take away this prerogative would be to unduly augment the power of the federal government; and if he were in Tennessee he would try to introduce black suffrage gradually: first the veterans, then the literates, and a property qualification of two hundred dollars for the rest. However, when Johnson was governor of Tennessee, all of his proclamations on the subject limited the franchise to whites and as far as is known by this writer did not advocate suffrage of any kind for blacks.

The idea that the blacks hated the white masses of the South played a large part in Johnson's thinking in matters of race. He claimed that in the antebellum days the slaves hated and looked askance at those whites who were too poor to own slaves and thus "hostility [grew] between the masses of the whites and the Negroes." For Johnson all of this had an important connection with politics. Politically active blacks in the South might determine the electoral balance of power. If the black man did have the vote, Johnson felt he would be more inclined to vote with the ex-slaveholding aristocracy rather than with the poorer whites. At this point Johnson reached back for what had been a pet scheme of his since 1843. In his attempt to undermine the political power of the slaveholding aristocracy he suggested that perhaps the entire country might change the basis of representation from that of population to the number of qualified voters. If this were done, then "in due course of time the states without regard to color, might extend the elective franchise to all who possessed certain mental, moral or such other qualifications, as might be determined by an enlightened public judgment."[101] It is not hard to imagine that probably few blacks would be found with the requisites which "enlightened public judgment" might require.

The racial rhetoric of the mailbag to the contrary, it does appear that Johnson objected to the black vote more for political reasons than for racial necessity. Considerations of race may have made him feel that political control should rest in the hands of the whites. But his experience with the political struggle between the Bourbon aristocracy and the "red-necked" democracy probably caused him to agree to black suffrage only if it were limited in a way to guarantee control by the poorer whites no matter how the blacks voted. He was concerned with the effect of the black vote on the political balance of power in each Southern state.

November found Johnson still pleading with Mississippi and South Carolina to secure the black man in his rights of person and property and thus facilitate re-entrance into the Union. "Justice and equality demand the admission of Negro testimony, they being all free . . . ," said Johnson to the governor of Mississippi.[102] In his first annual message the President seemed to give his answer to those who had urged him to give the blacks the vote. For the Chief Executive to take it upon himself to give the black man the vote would be an unwarranted usurpation of constitutional power. The suffrage question was more properly left to the states. If blacks would have patience until "the tumult of emotions that have been raised by the suddenness of the social change shall have subsided," counseled Johnson, "it may prove that they will receive the kindliest

[101] Interview between George L. Stearns and Andrew Johnson, October 3, 1865; McPherson, *Reconstruction*, pp. 47, 49. Savage, *Speeches*, p. 103 (Appendix).

[102] Andrew Johnson to Governor Sharkey, November 17, 1865; AJP (Microfilm), Reel 43 (Letter Book, Vol. 5), No. 76–78, ser. III-A. Andrew Johnson to Governor Perry, South Carolina, November 27, 1865; ibid., No. 99–101. George B[ancroft] to Andrew Johnson, December 1, 1865, telling him how to calm down Charles Sumner on the suffrage question. A little freedom of conversation on foreign affairs "would conciliate him amazingly," Bancroft thought; ibid., Reel 19, No. 8061–62.

usage from some of those [on] whom they have heretofore most closely depended."[103]

Florida ratified the Thirteenth Amendment on December 28, 1865, but not without a resolution stating that the step had been taken only "with the understanding that it does not confer upon Congress the power to legislate upon the political status of the freedmen in this state."[104] Many of the Southern states hesitated on the Thirteenth Amendment not because they wanted to keep slavery but because they feared that approval of the measure meant full equality for blacks above and beyond the minimum rights of person and property.

On February 7, 1866, a delegation of blacks representing more than ten states presented themselves at the White House to implore the President to let blacks vote. George T. Downing, a Northern independent politician and civil rights worker from Rhode Island, made a long speech followed by a shorter one by Frederick Douglass. The interview ended with an almost rude exchange between Douglass and the President. The President floundered in his opening remarks and may have been a little unnerved and taken aback, if not outright vexed, by this sudden confrontation with articulate blacks. Obviously annoyed, he said: "I am free to say to you that I do not like to be arraigned by some who can get up handsomely rounded periods and deal in rhetoric, and talk about abstract ideas on liberty, who never periled life, liberty or property. . . ." Johnson had not changed his mind. Black voting would bring about a war of races. Johnson suggested colonization or at least black emigration from the South.

At one point in the interview Johnson said that ours was a government of the people and that nothing should be done without the consent of the majority. Douglass seized this opening to ask the President to apply his concept of majority rule to South Carolina where the blacks were in the majority. But the President preferred to use Ohio for *his* example. For in that state blacks were in the minority.[105]

[103] Savage, *Speeches*, pp. 11–13.
[104] McPherson, *Reconstruction*, pp. 24–25.
[105] Foner, *Life and Writings of Frederick Douglass*, IV, 182–91.

Since Johnson terminated the interview before the blacks could rebut him, they took their case to the newspapers: "Be lieving as we do that the views and opinions you expressed in that address are entirely unsound and prejudicial to the highest interest of our race as well as the country at large, we cannot do other than expose the same, and, in as far as may be in our power arrest their dangerous influence." The blacks admitted the prevalence of racial antagonism in the antebellum South but contended that this was indigenous to the slave system. Now that the "peculiar institution" was gone, they reasoned, there was no longer any need for this antipathy. Furthermore, if antipathy still existed, what better excuse was needed to give the blacks the ballot in self-defense.[106] Some of those who also did not believe in racial equality wrote to thank the President for his remarks to "the colored men who visited you yesterday. . . ."[107] Seven months later, the President told a Cleveland heckler: "Let the Negro vote in Ohio before you talk about their voting in Louisiana."[108] To the very last Johnson stood at the gate blocking congressional legislative relief for blacks.

More Vetoes: Johnson the Racial Gatekeeper

The passage of the District of Columbia Voting Bill in the House of Representatives was upsetting to President Johnson, more than 150 citizens of Hamilton, Ohio, and at least one Philadelphian. Johnson thought that Congress had many more important things to consider than the black vote.[109] Henry D. Lewis of Ohio did "a job of *first class cursing*" alone in his office when he heard the news.[110] Meanwhile, Gideon

[106] Ibid., IV, 191–93. McPherson, *Reconstruction*, pp. 53–55.

[107] R. R. French, Washington, to Andrew Johnson, February 8, 1866; AJP (Microfilm), Reel 20, No. 8973–74, ser. I. French recommended to the President "a most forceful article on the races of men . . . ," from the pen of the Negrophobic Doctor Josiah Nott. William S. Hodge to Andrew Johnson, February 8, 1866; ibid., No. 9585–86.

[108] September 3, 1866. McPherson, *Reconstruction*, p. 136.

[109] Interview with Senator Dixon of Connecticut. Ibid., p. 52.

[110] January 22, 1866; AJP (Microfilm), Reel 20, No. 8671–72, ser. I. Petition of 150 names from Hamilton, Ohio, against the Negro vote; ibid., No. 8733.

Welles reported the entire Cabinet solidly in agreement with the President's anti-black vote position. Seward, according to Welles, in favor of black suffrage in New York, opposed it in the District because blacks were too numerous there. Secretary of the Treasury Hugh McCulloch of Indiana and Attorney General Henry Stanbery of Ohio opposed the proposition in their own states as well as in the District of Columbia. Welles, Browning, Stanton, and Randall all nodded agreement as the President read the veto message in the Cabinet.[111]

The message was long and rather thorough. In essence the veto said: Since only 35 out of 6556 white voters favored having black voters, Congress had obviously disregarded the will of the people and violated the sacred principle of self-government. Northern states with much, much smaller black populations had refused to give blacks the ballot; the black man was not competent to pass on important questions because he had no property and would not have the interest of the District at heart. Why force blacks upon an unwilling white people and engender race hatred? Blacks had not yet been on probation long enough to successfully take up the duties of citizenship. But more important, there were so many blacks in the District that they could, with an unlimited vote, control the elections of the city. Finally, Johnson conjured up visions of a mass invasion of the District by blacks from adjacent Southern states: "It is within their power in one year to come here in such numbers as to have the supreme control of the white race and to govern them by their own officers and by the exercise of all municipal authority. . . ."[112] When Congress overrode the President's veto, Gideon Welles said: "The ignorant, vicious, stupid negroes who have flocked hither cannot vote intelligently."[113]

On January 28, 1867, the President vetoed a bill admitting Colorado to the Union. He did so on the grounds that the

[111] Welles, *Diary*, III, 4–5. Entry for Friday, January 4, 1867.

[112] Veto Message on the District of Columbia Vote Bill; AJP (Microfilm), Reel 45 (Messages), No. 28486–537, ser. V-A.

[113] Welles, *Diary*, III, 8; January 7, 1867. McPherson, *Reconstruction*, pp. 154–55.

enabling clause gave the vote to blacks and mulattoes against the expressed will of the people.[114] Two days later Johnson vetoed the admission of Nebraska for the same reason.[115] He also vetoed the First Reconstruction Bill of March 2, 1867. "The Negroes," he said (though his mail does not confirm this), "have not asked for the privilege of voting—the vast majority of them have no idea what it means. . . ."[116] Gideon Welles, meantime, thought that making the black man a political entity by giving him the ballot was but the first step toward tainting the Anglo-Saxon "blood" and institutions.[117]

The tone of President Johnson's annual message of December 3, 1867, was enough to convince anyone that he was beyond all hope of recovery from the malady of acute Negrophobia. He was willing to do what he could to improve the situation of the blacks, but to turn the government over to them was most unwise. Unless the whites despaired of their own competence, the job of organizing the Southern states should not be given to blacks. To propose that blacks should rule the white race and shape the destiny of the country was to Johnson ludicrous. He had grave doubts about the capacity of the black man to govern himself. "It must be acknowledged that in the progress of nations Negroes have shown less capacity for government than any other race of people. . . . It is the glory of white men to know that they have these qualities." The ballot being the very epitome of democracy, the very safety of our form of government required that the franchise be ensconced in the bosom of none but the most highly qualified electors, "those who are fitted morally and mentally to administer it well."[118]

[114] AJP (Microfilm), Reel 45 (Messages), No. 28538–45, ser. V-A. Johnson had previously vetoed the bill on May 15, 1866, on the ground that the population was too small and that the people had not asked for admission. The first constitution drawn up by the state denied the vote to blacks but directed that the question be submitted to the people, who promply turned it down 4192 to 476. They also refused to let blacks sit on juries; ibid., No. 28153. See also ibid., January 12, 1866, Reel 27, No. 30–33, ser. V-A.

[115] McPherson, *Reconstruction*, p. 164.

[116] AJP (Microfilm), Reel 45 (Messages), No. 28664, ser. V-A. McPherson, op. cit., p. 171.

[117] Welles, *Diary*, III, 136–37, entry July 16, 1867.

[118] Richardson, *Messages*, VI, 264–66.

Such were the ideas on race expressed in Johnson's third annual message to Congress.

On June 20, 1868, Johnson, the racial gatekeeper, pronounced anathema upon an attempt to bring Arkansas into the Union. The Arkansas Constitution, in addition to stating that all males over twenty-one could vote, contained a clause reminiscent of the egalitarian fervor of the French Revolution. Every voter had to make the following declaration: "I accept the civil and political equality of all men, and agree not to attempt to deprive any person or persons, on account of race, color or previous condition, of any political or civil right, privilege or immunity enjoyed by any other class of men." Johnson had his doubts about the validity of such a sweeping injunction. "It is well known," he countered, "that a very large portion of the electors in all the states, if not a large majority of them, do not believe in or accept the political equality of Indians, Mongolians, or Negroes with the white race to which they belong." The whites of the North would refuse to vote "rather than comply" with the "degrading conditions" of such a declaration, said Johnson.[119] For similar reasons the President vetoed bills to readmit other rebel states.[120] After he left office he and Gideon Welles reflected upon Lincoln's intentions for blacks and concluded that the emancipator did not intend to give them the vote.[121]

Race and Andrew Johnson: A Summing Up

After an examination of the expressed racial ideas of Andrew Johnson it is difficult to agree with the contention of one scholar that the President's racial views were "not those of the Southern poor whites from which he sprang."[122] The idea that America was a white man's country seemed basic to Johnson's

119 AJP (Microfilm), Reel 46, No. 29265–73, ser. V-A.

120 McPherson, *Reconstruction*, pp. 650–51.

121 Welles, *Diary*, III, 719 (Appendix 5), containing a letter of Gideon Welles to Andrew Johnson, July 27, 1869.

122 Milton Lomask, *Andrew Johnson: President on Trial* (New York: Farrar, Straus and Cudahy, 1960), p. 143.

racial thought. This idea, evident enough in his pre-Civil War speeches, was subordinated during the Civil War and even for a brief time after that struggle as Johnson allowed himself, apparently for political expediency, to be swept momentarily into the prevailing mood of Negrophilism.

But when faced with the implementation of his admirable merit system of race relations he easily retreated into his initial cocoon of Negrophobia. While he accused blacks of hating the class of Southern whites below the planters, he seemed oblivious to the possibility that the seeds of Negrophobia might thrive mightily in the loam of white supremacy. Considering his own predilection for the idea of white supremacy and in view of the steady influx of anti-black letters from the South, it is difficult to understand Johnson's optimistic view that Southern whites would deal with the blacks without prejudice. And in view of Johnson's often repeated belief in a natural affinity between the black man and his aristocratic master, it would seem the President feared a political alliance between the freedman and his former masters which would prolong the domination of the Southern white masses by the Bourbons.

One finds more intemperate racial utterances and Negrophobic epithets expressed in the speeches of Andrew Johnson than in the writings of the other nine Presidents combined. As the contest between the executive and Congress grew in intensity, the anti-black expressions of the President became more bitter. Gideon Welles called him the great defender of the Constitution. Yet he seemed more like a great racial champion, defending the ramparts of white supremacy against the real or imagined dangers of black domination.

Before the Civil War, Johnson favored slavery, excluded blacks from the Declaration of Independence, preferred white supremacy, and even looked hopefully toward the ultimate exodus of "the sable sons of Africa" to Mexico and points beyond the boundaries of the United States. When the war came, Johnson turned against slavery and secession. The genuinely strong humanitarian and moral disapproval of slavery so easily recognized in the sentiments of Abraham Lincoln is conspicuously absent in

Johnsonian racial thought. More prominent was his undisguised antipathy for the planters and his happy anticipation that at last slavery, the source of their power, was being smashed on the anvil of civil strife.

While the evidence is not conclusive, it does seem that Johnson's brief masquerade as a black Moses, and his momentary flirtation with the idea of equal opportunity for blacks, were pursued for their political advantages. Even Lincoln at one time advised Johnson of the political utility of advocating emancipation in Tennessee. Further investigation might well reveal that such emancipation proclivities figured in his nomination for the vice-presidency in 1864.

Somehow Johnson's attempts to induce the Southerners to give civil rights to blacks lacked the sincerity and conviction of a Lincoln, who was obviously moved by black's participation in the war effort and urged that the ballot be given to those blacks who had fought to keep the "jewel of liberty in the family of freedom." The role of the blacks in the war seemed almost wholly lost upon Johnson. His expressed motivation for advocating a modicum of equality for blacks was the desire to confound the radicals and pilot the former rebel states safely back into the harbor of Union.

The President then was race conscious and expressed prejudice against the black race. He frowned upon legal and illegal race mixing and appeared ill at ease when confronted by black audiences. Transcending the color line seemed more difficult for Andrew Johnson than for any other President. He could not escape the problem of race and he failed to exercise a positive leadership role in the racial questions of Reconstruction. Although he was aware of the great social revolution precipitated by black freedom he could not bring himself to in any way force the ever militant, ever recalcitrant South to implement his merit theory of race relations. Perhaps it was not in his power to do so. Yet he did not appear to have seriously tried.

Though public opinion from the North was divided on the race question, the President was disposed to stand with that segment of thought which contended that the races were incompatible and that equality was either undesirable or impossible without race conflict. Johnson seemed unaware of the fact that while the North was to some degree prejudiced against blacks, a considerable amount of good will had been built up by the feats of blacks on the battlefield. Johnson chose to follow the opinion of his section, which seemed to be against political equality of the races. Like Lincoln, Johnson felt that this was the universal feeling of the country. His associations with Northerners such as Gideon Welles of Connecticut gave him little reason to think otherwise. It would seem that the racial ideas of Andrew Johnson only aided and abetted a region already recalcitrant on the question of race and a region which needed no encouragement, and that in this critical period of racial adjustment it was most unfortunate that Andrew Johnson was President.

CHAPTER IV

The Racial Attitudes of U. S. Grant (1869–1877)

Ulysses S. Grant came to the presidency destined to bear the brunt of Reconstruction. The task had not been made any easier by the preceding tenure of Andrew Johnson. But the story must begin at the beginning.

The Pre-Presidential Perspective

Grant was a Midwesterner but his marriage to Julia Dent of St. Louis, Missouri, put him in touch with Southern culture even to the extent of having a slave of his own.[1] Toward the end of his life he reflected that in 1856 many educated and otherwise sensible people of the Southern and border states feared that emancipation meant social equality. While not disclosing his personal feelings on the subject, he recalled his fears that a Republican victory in 1856 would bring about secession. For this reason he cast the first vote of his political life for Buchanan in the hope of averting the impending crisis. He did not vote in 1860 but he further reflected that had he done so his vote would have gone to Douglas for the same reason he had given it to Buchanan.[2]

In 1858, Grant had this to say about his wife's small slave boy:

[1] Jessie Root Grant, *In the Days of My Father, General Grant* (New York: Harper and Brothers, 1925), pp. 59, 211.

[2] U. S. Grant, *Personal Memoirs of U. S. Grant* (New York: C. L. Webster Co., 1885–86), I, 214, 218. (Hereafter cited as Grant, *Memoirs.*)

"He is a very smart, active boy, capable of making anything."[3] According to his own testimony, Grant read the Lincoln-Douglas debates; while not a Lincoln man, he recognized the man's ability.[4] On March 29, 1859, when in need of funds but for no stated reason, Grant freed his "negro man, William, sometimes called Williams Jones, of mulatto complexion, aged about thirty-five years. . . ."[5]

Like his contemporaries, Grant expected a rapid conclusion of the Civil War with a minimum of bloodshed. He also thought that slavery would soon die a natural death and with it the black question. The worst that the country had to fear was a black revolt. He told both his father and his "Dear Julia" that "a Northern army may be required in the next ninety days to go South to suppress a negro insurrection." And would the North go to the aid of its "kith and kin" in such an instance? "As much as the South have vilified the North," said Grant, "that army would go on such a mission and with the purest motives."[6]

Grant's early position on the slavery question was similar to that of Lincoln. He would put down rebellion while "preserving Constitutional rights," but "if it be necessary, that slavery should fall that the Republic may continue its existence, let slavery go." Early in the war, Grant felt that those newspapers that advocated making the war a contest for emancipation were doing a disservice to their country.[7] When the war

[3] U. S. Grant to his father, Covington, Ky., October 1, 1858, Jessie Grant Cramer (ed.), *Letters of Ulysses S. Grant to His Father and Youngest Sister, 1857–1878* (New York: George P. Putnam's Sons, 1912), p. 2. There was a possibility of taking the boy to Galena to learn the farrier's trade. Grant left the matter to his father-in-law and said, "I can leave him here and get about three dollars per month for him now, and more when he gets older"; see also Grant's letter to his sister, March 21, 1858, disclosing his efforts to farm with two hired blacks and a slave of the Dents'.

[4] Grant, *Memoirs*, II, 121–22.

[5] Lloyd Lewis, *Captain Sam Grant* (Boston: Little, Brown and Company, 1950), p. 365, as cited by that author, who also claimed that Grant knew the Blows of Dred Scott fame as well as John Brown.

[6] U. S. Grant to his father, May 6, 1861, Cramer, op. cit., pp. 36, 37; U. S. Grant to "Dear Julia," May 6, 1861, U. S. Grant Papers (Manuscript, Library of Congress), ser. 1A. Box labeled "Letters to Julia." (Hereinafter cited as USGP.)

[7] U. S. Grant, Cairo, Ill., to his father, November 1861, Cramer (ed.), *Letters of Ulysses S. Grant to His Father and Youngest Sister*, p. 69.

began, Grant was accused of being too disposed to protect the slave property of the rebels, that is, of giving up slaves seeking refuge within the Federal lines. But Grant took the position that it was his duty to obey orders—even those that he did not like. "I have no views of my own to carry out," he told an Illinois friend and ardent supporter, Elihu Washburne, "so long as I hold a commission in the army." When Congress passed a law too objectionable for him to execute he would resign.[8] As a military man it was his contention that one's personal views should not interfere with the obligation to do one's duty. Grant told his father, "I have no hobby of my own with regard to the negro, either to effect his freedom or to continue his bondage. . . ."[9]

However, Adam Badeau, Grant's military secretary and aide-de-camp, reported that after the Battle of Shiloh in 1862, Grant committed himself unconditionally to crush the rebels, their property not excepted. Said Badeau of Grant, "He abandoned all desire to protect the institution of slavery, although he himself had been a slave holder, and had no sympathy with the merely political idea of abolition."[10] In August of 1863, Grant told a friend that slavery was dead beyond resurrection. The baptism of blood had obviously steeled him against the "peculiar institution": "I never was an abolitionist, not even what could be called anti-slavery . . . ," he explained. Early in the rebellion it had become clear to him that there could be no united nation with slavery. "I would not . . . be willing to see any settlement until this question is forever settled," he concluded.[11]

[8] U. S. Grant to Elihu Washburne, March 22, 1862, U. S. Grant, *General Grant's Letters to a Friend* (New York: Crowell, 1897), p. 7; John Russell Young, *Around the World with General Grant. . . .* (New York: American News Co., 1879), II, 447.

[9] U. S. Grant, Corinth, Miss., to his father, August 3, 1862, Cramer, op. cit., p. 85. Grant did not believe in fighting his superiors. "One enemy at a time is enough . . . ," he said.

[10] Adam Badeau, *A Military History of U. S. Grant from April 1861 to 1865* (New York: Appleton and Co., 1881), I, 96. Badeau was Grant's military secretary and aide-de-camp.

[11] U. S. Grant to E. B. Washburne, August 30, 1863, McPherson, *Reconstruction*, pp. 294–95; same letter also in U. S. Grant, *General Grant's Letters to a Friend*, p. 28.

From Contraband to Soldier

Blacks who came into his lines were readily put to work at housekeeping tasks by Grant, "thus saving soldiers to carry the musket." He did not know what would be the ultimate fate of these men but felt that to have them run away from their masters was a boon to the Union. "Their *institutions,*" he remarked about the South, "are beginning to have ideas of their own."[12] Grant later thought that his method of putting Southern black refugees to work under the supervision of an army chaplain was the forerunner of the Freedmen's Bureau. He apparently did not share the Southern conviction that blacks would not work.[13] Grant assigned Chaplain John Eaton the job of overseeing that unknown quantity, the freedman. Certainly not anxious to take on the job, Eaton went to Grant's headquarters to talk himself out of the assignment but was a little taken aback by the way the general greeted him with, "Oh, you are the man who has all these darkies on his shoulders."[14] According to Eaton, Grant took the step to care for the freedmen on the grounds of military necessity and humanity. Eaton claimed that Grant felt that if it could be proved that the black man could work it would be easier to put a musket in his hand and make him a soldier. Should he perform well as a soldier, eventually he could be given the ballot and made a citizen.[15]

According to Eaton, officers and men objected to waiting on blacks in any way. Grant on the other hand was always solicitous of the freedmen's comfort in spite of his preoccupation with the fighting.[16] Grant himself told Lincoln that he

[12] U. S. Grant, Corinth, Miss., to his sister, August 19, 1862, Cramer (ed.), *Letters of Ulysses S. Grant to His Father and Youngest Sister*, p. 88.

[13] Grant, *Memoirs*, I, 424–26.

[14] John Eaton, *Grant, Lincoln and the Freedmen: Reminiscences of the Civil War With Special Reference to the War for the Contraband Freedmen of the Mississippi Valley. . . .* (New York: Longmans, Green and Co., 1907), p. 519.

[15] Ibid., pp. 13–15.

[16] Ibid., pp. 20, 22, 44, 114–19.

selected Eaton to do what he could not attend to personally, and with his customary objectivity informed Lincoln of the ambivalent nature of the white reception of the blacks. The blacks received "kind or abusive treatment according to the peculiar views of the troops they first come in contact with. . . ."[17] This is not to say that the freedmen did not present problems even for the patient Grant. "In regard to the contrabands," he told his colleague, "the question is a troublesome one."[18] However, other than being anxious about the tendency of some of the freedmen not to want to provide for future needs, Grant seemed to have no doubt that the Afro-American would work and make progress in freedom.[19] It only remained to be seen if the "contraband" would fight.

Today, little notice is given to the fact that though the black man was allowed to fight in the Civil War he did so in separate units. Since there were already Indian and Irish regiments and brigades of other nationalities, the point is perhaps of no special moment. In a rare mention of the topic, Eaton notes that he recommended a separate troop policy to Grant. The army chaplain claimed that his awareness of the friction and disturbance that ensued with any "enforced relationship between the Negro and the Union soldier convinced" him of "the importance of drafting the Negro into regiments composed of his own race."[20]

Grant made it clear to his men in General Order Number 15 that the policy of the Administration in respect to black troops was to be obeyed. Not only were the blacks to be trained efficiently, but the men were to aid "in removing prejudices against them. . . ."[21] After the battle of Milliken's Bend, Mississippi, June 6, 1863, Grant said to General Thomas: "In this battle most of the troops engaged were Africans; who

[17] U. S. Grant to Abraham Lincoln, June 11, 1863, RTLC, Vol. 113, No. 23990, ser. 1.

[18] U. S. Grant to [General] McPherson, March 13, 1863, *Official Records of the Rebellion*, XXIV, 105, Pt. 3, ser. 1.

[19] U. S. Grant's Report on his Trip South, December 18, 1865, McPherson, *Reconstruction*, p. 68. First Annual Message, December 6, 1869, Richardson, *Messages*, VII, 28.

[20] Eaton, *Grant, Lincoln and the Freedman . . .*, p. 67.

[21] April 22, 1863, McPherson, *Reconstruction*, pp. 293–94.

had but little experience in the use of firearms. Their conduct is said, however, to have been most gallant, and I doubt not but with good officers they will make good troops."[22]

Not long after Milliken's Bend, there were rumors that Southerners had hanged captured black troops with their white officers. Grant sent a letter to the Confederate General Richard Taylor and told him that he would not hesitate to retaliate, though he would regret it, if the rebels were going to treat black troops differently from other prisoners of war. Taylor responded with a denial of the charges, which was accepted by Grant.[23] Meanwhile Grant was looking forward eagerly to more extensive use of black troops. "I am anxious to get as many of these negro regiments as possible and to have them fully and completely equipped . . . ," he told his adjutant general.[24] ". . . The negro troops are easier to preserve discipline among than our white troops, and I doubt not will prove equally good for garrison duty. All that have been tried have fought bravely," Grant wrote enthusiastically to Halleck.[25]

Grant was unusually articulate in his reports to Lincoln on the behavior of black soldiers. The President must have been impressed because he later used this evidence to confront his detractors. "I have given the subject of arming the negroes my hearty support," Grant wrote to Lincoln. He then stated what Lincoln was so often to repeat in his speeches, letters and messages, that the arming of the blacks and their emancipation was "the heavyest [*sic*] blow yet given the Confederacy." He assured the President that he would give the great recruiter of blacks, General Thomas, "all the aid in my power. . . ." Then he paused to state his philosophy of duty before personal feeling. "I would do this," he continued, "whether arming the negro seemed to me a wise policy or not because it is an order. . . . In this particular instance," Grant went on, "there is no objection however to my expressing an honest conviction.

[22] General Grant to General Thomas, June 16, 1863, *Official Records of the Rebellion*, XXXV, 466, Pt. 2, ser. 1.

[23] U. S. Grant to General Taylor, June 22, 1863, *Official Records of the Rebellion*, XXIV, 426, Pt. 3; see p. 469 for Taylor's answer.

[24] July 11, 1863, Badeau, *A Military History of U. S. Grant*, I, 408.

[25] *Official Records of the Rebellion*, op. cit., p. 547, Pt. 3.

That is, by arming the negro we have added a powerful ally. They will make good soldiers and taking them from the enemy weakens him in the same proportion as they strengthen us. I am therefore more decidedly in favor of pushing this policy."[26]

According to his aide, Badeau, Grant did not arrive overnight at his conclusion that the "troublesome property" could fight. True, he was ready to cooperate once the government decided to use the blacks. But Badeau contended that Grant felt at first that the blacks would be more effective for defense rather than in the open field. Badeau could not resist the temptation to give his own opinion of the blacks, even if not too clearly. "The influences," said Badeau, "whether of race or of their recent condition, seemed to cling to them in some degree; and, apparently, they fought better behind bulwarks." But on second thought Badeau observed, "It has often happened that white men did the same."[27]

Grant gave his chief of staff, General Henry Halleck, an account of a clash between the rebels and the black troops under General James G. Birney of the Union army. Grant reported Birney saying, "The enemy attacked my line in heavy force last night and were repulsed with great loss. In front of our colored regiment 82 dead bodies of the enemy are counted. The colored troops behaved handsomely and are in fine spirits. . . . The enemy's loss was at least 1000."[28] "Sherman," one of Lincoln's private secretaries wrote, "does not think so hopefully of Negro troops as does many other Generals. Grant himself says they are admirable soldiers in many respects; quick and docile in instruction and very subordinate; good in a charge; excellent in fatigue duty." However, according to Hay, the private secretary, Grant did not think that the black troops could have stood up under the weeks of pounding at the Battle of the Wilderness and Spotsylvania as the white troops did.[29]

[26] U. S. Grant to Abraham Lincoln, August 23, 1863, RTLC, Vol. 121, No. 25799–800; Horace Porter, *Campaigning with Grant* (New York: Century Co., 1897), p. 218.

[27] Badeau, *A Military History of U. S. Grant*, I, 408.

[28] General U. S. Grant to General Halleck, August 19, 1864, USGP, No. 32 (Accession No. 3187), subseries IC.

[29] Entry November 16, [1864], Hay, *Civil War Diaries*, p. 242.

Having used the freedman as a soldier, Grant, like Lincoln, was determined to stand by him when the rebels put black prisoners of war at work in trenches. Grant had rebel prisoners so employed and refused to discontinue the practice until the Confederates also stopped this practice. He discussed all of this in a letter to General Lee. "I shall always regret the necessity of retaliating for wrongs done our soldiers," Grant said, "but regard it my duty to protect all persons recruited in the Army of the United States, regardless of color or nationality. . . . I have nothing to do with the discussion of the slavery question. . . ."[30]

Grant, as General-in-Chief of the Union Armies, overruled General Ambrose Burnside in deference to the ranking officer George Meade when the decision was made as to who would lead the charge at the Petersburg crater. Burnside, according to Badeau, felt that fresh troops should lead the assault, his white troops having been in trenches for forty days. Burnside wanted to use black troops but Meade insisted on white ones. Badeau defended Meade. The black troops had been under fire only once, their activities having been limited to guard duty. Anyway, the white troops led the charge which failed. Badeau reported that a congressional investigating committee concluded that the mission failed because of the failure to use the black troops in the vanguard.[31]

In apparent deference to the racial sensitivities of the rebels, General Sherman rejected a suggestion to garrison Savannah with black troops thus releasing the white ones to continue the march to the sea. Grant understood Sherman to say, "No matter how good colored troops were there is a prejudice against them in Savannah and . . . the best kind of feeling exists now and had better be kept that way." Grant was about to send Sherman's reasons to Stanton when he apparently thought better because he scratched them out and instead simply directed Stanton to tell Sherman to use black troops to garrison the forts and is-

[30] General Grant to General Lee, October 29, 1864, McPherson, *Reconstruction*, pp. 295–96.

[31] Horace Porter, *Campaigning with Grant*, II, 477, 481, 490.

lands, "leaving all of his white troops for Savannah. . . ."[32] Grant was not in the habit of overruling his field commanders. So strong was the idea of race that apparently for some generals not even a war could make them wholly oblivious to racial sensitivities—not even those of the enemy.

Grant must have still been thinking about Sherman's observation later in the year, when after his famous fact-finding trip south for President Johnson he advised the use of white troops for occupation duty in the South. "White troops generally excite no opposition," Grant said. He also felt that black occupation troops had a demoralizing effect on the colored populace, making them indisposed to labor. Why this would be true, he did not elaborate. He also suggested that perhaps the ex-slave turned soldier might not make a good protector of property since he often felt that the property of his ex-master should be his![33] At this time, Grant was General of the Army—in peacetime. Later events were to show the black fully capable of loyalty. In 1873, when Spanish authorities executed two American prisoners in Cuba, one hundred colored national guardsmen of Pennsylvania offered their services to the President to avenge the national honor.[34] And from Savannah, the place where Sherman was afraid to use black troops for occupation duty, five hundred black citizens were "ready to enlist for Cuba to teach the Spanish authorities respect for the American flag."[35]

Equality before the Law

In his report of his trip south, Grant revealed an awareness of prejudice on the part of the whites. "It can not be expected,"

[32] U. S. Grant to E. M. Stanton, January 6, 1865, USGP, No. 447–48 (Accession No. 3187), subseries 1C.

[33] Grant's Report on Conditions in the South, December 18, 1865, *Pamphlets on Reconstruction*, pp. 106–07.

[34] Telegram of the Taylor Guards, Captain John White, Commander, Williamsport, Pa., November 17, 1873, USGP, Box I, subseries 1B.

[35] Telegram from Black Citizens of Savannah, Ga., November 25, 1873, USGP, Box I, subseries 1B.

he said, "that the opinions held by men at the South for years, can be changed in a day." Unlike some observers Grant regarded existing prejudice not as an excuse to delay the exercise of civil rights by blacks, but as a reason for granting additional protection. He felt that for a few years at least the freedmen would need "not only laws to protect them but the fostering care of those who will give them good counsel, and in whom we can rely."[36] Perhaps that was why he told Johnson, "In some form the Freedmen's Bureau is an absolute necessity until civil law is established and enforced securing to the freedmen their rights and full protection."[37] Those who like to single out Grant's report as the one upon which Johnson chose to rely rather than the allegedly biased document of Schurz, usually fail to quote these lines which showed that Grant was in favor of temporary supervisory administration for the freedmen, a position which Johnson spurned.

According to Gideon Welles, Secretary of the Navy under Andrew Johnson, Grant advised Arkansas to accept the Fourteenth Amendment before Congress imposed more difficult terms.[38] Grant, while still in his capacity as General of the Army under Johnson, also reinstated the integrated New Orleans City Council after he decided that the initial removal by General Hancock was unwarranted.[39] Governor Hamilton of Texas sent Grant, who had by this time been elected President of the United States, a copy of the state constitution which, he said, "makes all equal before the law."[40] Upon the readmission of Virginia to the Union in 1869, Grant hoped that the state was now ready to give "to all its people those equal rights under the law which were asserted in the Declara-

[36] Grant's Report on Conditions in the South, December 18, 1865, copy in McPherson, *Reconstruction*, p. 68.

[37] Grant on Conditions in the South, *Pamphlets on Reconstruction*, p. 107.

[38] Entry January 5, 1867, Welles, *Diary*, III, 8.

[39] Correspondence between General Grant and Major General Hancock, Relative to the Removal of Members of the City Council, New Orleans, February 27 to March 5, 1868, a pamphlet in the Library of Congress, Washington, D.C.

[40] Letter, March 16, 1869, USGP (manuscript, Rutherford B. Hayes Library, Fremont, Ohio).

tion of Independence."[41] When the Georgia Redeemers expelled the black members of the state legislature, Grant asked Congress for a law to authorize the governor to reconvene the original legislature.[42] Also in his first annual message he called for the securing of all citizens in their rights "without reference to original nationality, religion, color, or politics." Given "time and a firm but humane administration of existing laws . . ." this could be achieved.[43] Grant also noted that the jury system had broken down in Virginia in part because of "the prejudice between white and black," the resultant "strong prejudice of class and of caste" making unanimous verdicts almost impossible.[44]

The problem of equality made an early appearance at the White House gates in the dispute over how Grant should receive white and black audiences. It appears that ". . . the usual custom of dividing the time between the colored and the white people . . . ," whites apparently coming first, backfired one day when blacks allegedly rushed the gates in order to be first. What happened after that was not exactly clear. George T. Downing, a prominent black politician and civil rights worker from Rhode Island, apparently accused the President of discrimination in his reception of whites and blacks; Babcock, the President's private secretary, in his reply asserted that when the blacks rushed the gates they were allowed to come in. As for the President, "he gave no other order of instructions in the matter."[45] Downing later left the Republican party because he was disenchanted with it on matters of race.

In a message to Congress on Latin American relations Grant said, "We have constitutionally fixed the equality of all races and of all men before the law."[46] But by December he regretted

[41] Message to House and Senate, April 7, 1869, Richardson, *Messages*, VII, 12.

[42] First Annual Message, December 6, 1869, Richardson, *Messages*, VII, 28.

[43] Ibid., pp. 37–38.

[44] U. S. Grant's Report on the First Military District, Virginia, 1869, Howland, Appendix, p. 592.

[45] O. F. Babcock to George T. Downing (January 2, 1870?), USGP (Letter and Telegram Book), Vol. I, ser. 2.

[46] July 14, 1870, Richardson, *Messages*, VII, 71.

the need to report in his second annual message that "a free exercise of the elective franchise has by violence and intimidation been denied to citizens in exceptional cases in several of the states lately in rebellion, and the verdict of the people has thus been reversed." It should be recalled that by the time Grant left office only two of the ex-Confederate states, South Carolina and Louisiana, were still "unredeemed" by the whites. This was in the face of numerous declarations by the President that the laws would and must be enforced. "I would sum up the policy of the Administration to be a thorough enforcement of every law . . . honest and fair dealing with all other peoples . . . a reform in the treatment of the Indians . . . a pure ballot . . . without fear of molestation or proscription on account of . . . color."[47] Though he seldom committed himself on paper about racial issues, as President, Grant seemed more than willing to have the civil rights of blacks protected by law. When the Klansmen rode uninhibited through the counties of South Carolina he asked for an extra session of Congress to deal with the subject. "There is a deplorable state of affairs existing in some portions of the South demanding the immediate attention of Congress," he wrote to James G. Blaine.[48] He was accused of favoring the extra session for reasons other than civil disorder in South Carolina. He denied it.[49] Meanwhile, upon the request of a Reconstruction governor of South Carolina, Congress not being in session, Grant issued a proclamation asking the insurgents to disperse within twenty days.[50] When Congress passed the Ku-Klux Act of 1871 in an attempt to enforce the Fourteenth Amendment, Grant called it a law of "extraordinary public importance" and urged the public to give it full support. He told the South that despite his reluctance to do so he would "not hesitate to exhaust the powers vested in the executive whenever it should become necessary to do so . . ." to protect citizens in their rights under the law. He

[47] Richardson, *Messages*, VIII, 96, 112.

[48] U. S. Grant to James G. Blaine, March 9, 1871, USGP (Letter and Telegram Book), Vol. I, No. 302, ser. II.

[49] U. S. Grant to A. G. Cattell, March 21, 1871, ibid., No. 312.

[50] March 24, 1871, Richardson, *Messages*, VII, 132–33.

then stated what was destined to become a constant theme on the lips of all Presidents and Republican politicians of this period: reunion could be achieved only if the South would acquiesce in the results of the war, namely the amendments, and agree to their enforcement. Grant concluded that the necessity for national intervention resulted from the failure of local communities to provide for the just and impartial enforcement of the law.[51] In that statement Grant had gotten to the heart of the real problem of Reconstruction.

In spite of all this positive racial rhetoric and the Ku-Klux Act of 1871, all but two Reconstruction governments in the South were in the hands of white Redeemers when Grant completed his second term. George Frisby Hoar, United States senator from Massachusetts during most of this period, reflecting many years later upon the events surrounding the Ku-Klux Act, said that Grant told him he had been asked to request power from Congress to suppress violence in the South but that he hesitated for fear of public disapproval of too vigorous a show of force by a military man. Hoar took for himself a large share of the credit for getting Grant to make the move which led to the passage of the bill. Hoar claimed that he told the President it would be good strategy to ask Congress for power even though that power might already be lodged in the executive. Such a procedure would help the people to understand his unwillingness to act without Congress and there would be no criticism.[52] This story, though unconfirmed, is highly plausible. Public men hate criticism. It appears that many decisions involving blacks were made on the basis of political considerations exclusive of race, though the matter of race may have been the occasion requiring a decision in the first place.

Whatever the circumstances or motives which brought about the enforcement of the law in South Carolina, this show of

[51] Grant's Message on the Ku-Klux Act, May 3, 1871, Richardson, *Messages*, VII, 132–33; on October 12, Grant issued another proclamation giving the insurgents five days to disperse, and on October 17 he used the Enforcement Act and suspended the writ of habeas corpus, ibid., VII, 135–40.

[52] George F. Hoar, *Autobiography of Seventy Years* (New York: Charles Scribner's Sons, 1903), I, 206.

force in behalf of the black man did not go entirely unapplauded. "Sir, allow me to thank you for the proclamation of the 12th inst. in behalf of an outraged and oppressed people of my race and also in behalf of the interest of a common humanity and the brotherhood of man," a colored preacher wrote from Charleston, South Carolina. ". . . Are you our Joshua?" he asked, obviously at home with biblical comparisons. He also informed the President that the black race was not without its quota of rascallions. ". . . Heed not the voice of traitors among my race; for we have those who will write and speak for the Ku Klux for money or other considerations as against protection. . . . We have traitors in this city:—Heed not those of your race and mine who are trying to serve two masters: —who are on both sides of every question."[53] Even Frederick Douglass was impressed by Grant's disposition to use force against the whites to put down violence in the South.[54]

The third annual message found Grant dwelling, as usual, on his duty to enforce the law. "The policy has been," he said, "not to inquire into the wisdom of laws already enacted but to learn their spirit and intent and to enforce them accordingly."[55] When Grant turned down an invitation by Frederick Douglass and George T. Downing "to attend a mass meeting to be held for the purpose of aiding in securing civil rights for colored citizens of our country," he said, "I beg to assure [you] however that I sympathize most cordially in every effort to secure to all our people of whatever race, nativity . . . or color the exercise of those rights to which every citizen should be entitled."[56] In his letter of acceptance for the nomination of 1872 the President made known his desire to see the end of sectional bitterness and to see all citizens secure their rights.[57] But by December he was wishing that certain citizens would cease to deprive

[53] Reverend H. H. Hunter to U. S. Grant, October 13, 1871, USGP (manuscript, Rutherford B. Hayes Library, Fremont, Ohio).

[54] Foner, *The Life and Writings of Frederick Douglass,* IV, 62, 72, 83.

[55] December 4, 1871, Richardson, *Messages,* VII, 142.

[56] U. S. Grant to Frederick Douglass et al., May 9, 1872, USGP (Letter and Telegram Book), Vol. I, No. 455, ser. II.

[57] Grant's Letter of Acceptance for a second term, to the National Republican Convention, June 10, 1872, USGP (Letter and Telegram Book), Vol. I, No. 465, ser. II.

other citizens of their rights, and thus make it unnecessary for him to resort to the Enforcement Act. He was prepared, he said, however reluctantly, to enforce the law.[58]

The President knew that blacks were being deprived of their rights in the South. In his second inaugural address he expressed regret that while the war had made the slave a citizen ". . . yet he is not possessed of the civil rights which citizenship should carry with it. This is wrong and should be corrected. To this correction I stand committed so far as executive influence can avail."[59] He then asked Congress to consider a law to "better secure the civil rights . . ." of blacks.[60] Congress apparently obliged him with the Civil Rights Act of 1875. But even before the law was passed he was advised by an ex-Union soldier and friend of Carl Schurz in the following manner: "If possible for God's sake and the welfare of our country please veto the Civil Rights Bill."[61] Grant did not veto the bill but the United States Supreme Court declared it unconstitutional in 1883.

A prominent black Reconstructionist, C. C. Antoine, lieutenant governor of Louisiana, thanked the President for opposing congressional interference in Louisiana affairs. "Permit me," he said, "in behalf of the colored population of this State to thank you for this renewed evidence of friendship for and care of my race. . . ."[62]

At a veteran reunion gathering in Des Moines, Iowa, Grant called for "equal rights and privileges to all men, irrespective of nationality, color or religion."[63] Meanwhile, the return of all-white governments in the South went on unabated. A report

[58] Fourth Annual Message, December 2, 1872, Richardson, *Messages*, VII, 199–200.

[59] March 4, 1873, ibid., VII, 221.

[60] Ibid., VII, 255.

[61] Jacob Manthe, to U. S. Grant, January 15, 1874, USGP, Box I, subseries I.

[62] Telegram from New Orleans, January 24, 1874, USGP, Box I, subseries I.

[63] Speech made at the Reunion of the Army of the Tennessee, September 29, 1875. Copies of this speech are found in the following places: Grenville Dodge, *Personal Recollections of President Abraham Lincoln, General Ulysses S. Grant and General William T. Sherman* (Council Bluffs, Iowa: Monarch Printing Co., 1914), p. 106; USGP (facsimile, Rutherford B. Hayes Library, Fremont, Ohio); original in USGP (manuscript, Library of Congress), Box 9, ser. 5; *Grant, Lincoln and the Freedmen*, p. 271.

came from Tennessee to the effect that one thousand blacks were ready to emigrate from Coahoma County, Mississippi, because of abusive treatment.[64] The President was thoroughly disgusted and taken aback by lawlessness in South Carolina, Mississippi and Louisiana. He said that the atrocities of the whites of Mississippi could "scarcely be accredited to savages, much less to a civilized and Christian people." Like all Chief Executives after him, Grant did not know what to do. How does the head of a democratic state combat wholesale violence on the part of the multitude? "How long these things are to continue," Grant wrote to Governor D. H. Chamberlain of South Carolina, "or what is to be the final remedy the Great Ruler of the Universe only knows." Confrontation with the race problem seems to have brought forth in these Presidents a burst of piety and a sudden penchant to leave the blacks in the lap of the Almighty.

But Grant had "an abiding faith that the remedy" would come, and speedily too. He also hoped that it would come peacefully. The refusal of the South to be pacified puzzled the President. The North had asked nothing of the South except that it forgo the "right to kill Negroes and Republicans without fear of punishment, and without loss of caste or reputation." Grant promised Governor Chamberlain of South Carolina every aid for which he could find precedent in law and the Constitution. He felt that a government which could not protect its citizens in their constitutional rights was a failure. ". . . Too long a denial of guaranteed rights is sure to lead to revolution. . . ." Grant closed his letter to Chamberlain with the hope that lawbreakers in South Carolina could be fairly tried and punished if convicted—"without aid from the federal government—but with the promise of such aid . . . ," under certain conditions.[65] On the other side of the question the secretary of a Democratic club in Florence, South Carolina, told the President that "armed men all black [,] with muskets & bay-

[64] Telegram from O. W. Cole [n.d.], Memphis, Tenn., to U. S. Grant, USGP, Box 1, subseries IB.

[65] U. S. Grant to D. H. Chamberlain [July 31, 1875?], USGP (Letter Book), Vol. 3, No. 105, ser. II; Grant also sent the preceding little dissertation to the Senate.

onetts under officers are parading here in the Republican procession intimidating white voters."[66]

Having come out for law enforcement and equality before the law, how did Grant stand on things social? At the risk of too broad a construction of the meaning of things social, it may be said that Grant characterized John M. Langston, the black lawyer and politician, as "a gentleman of liberal education and of high standing. . . ." He also added that Langston was influential "with the people of his own race. . . ."[67] Black employment at the Executive Mansion sometimes took a curious twist. For example, a black man, Charles H. Lewis, was not only Grant's barber but a "clerk in the 3d. Auditor's office." More than that, Grant asked that Lewis be detailed to the White House to bring up to date the presidential newspaper files. This at least showed a small disposition to give blacks work above the menial level.[68]

Like most of the Presidents, Grant was anxious to see the ex-slave educated. Did he favor mixed schools? The evidence on the point is scanty and inconclusive. As interim Secretary of War under Andrew Johnson, Grant said in a report that Howard University was "designed to be national and free to all."[69] The ex-army chaplain John Eaton was against mixed schools. He said that while mixed schools were right in theory they were impractical because the whites would either burn or close the schools. There was a clause in an early version of the Civil Rights Bill of 1875 which would have compelled school integration. Eaton and the agent of the Peabody Fund, Dr. Sears, went to sound Grant out on the matter. According to Eaton, Grant allegedly said, "I have read the bill to which you refer, and have made up my mind that if it comes to me I shall veto it."[70]

[66] Willie Quirk to U. S. Grant, October 25, 1876, USGP, Box 1, subseries 1B.

[67] December 13, 1870, Grant wrote an introductory letter for Langston. He also agreed with General O. O. Howard that it would be all right to send Langston to visit the colored schools.

[68] Horace Porter to George Boutwell, Secretary of the Treasury, March 16, 1872, USGP (Letter and Telegram Book), Vol. I, No. 437, ser. II.

[69] Edward Howland, *Grant as a Soldier and Statesman: Being a Succinct War History of his Military and Civil Career* (Hartford: Burr, 1868), p. 569. To be hereafter cited as Howland, *Grant.*

[70] Eaton, *Grant, Lincoln and the Freedmen,* pp. 262–64.

During the election of 1872, and due to the discontent of some blacks, Frederick Douglass spoke in behalf of Grant's racial record. He pointed to some 249 black appointments, including two foreign ministers, blacks to West Point, customs collectors, postmasters and tax assessors, to name the major ones. But Douglass devoted most of his remarks to his personal relations with Grant. "I affirm," said the black orator, not wholly oblivious to the political stakes involved, "that after our martyred President, Abraham Lincoln, and Senator Charles Sumner, no man in high position has manifested in his entire course with me upon all occasions and in all places more entire freedom from vulgar prejudice of race and color than Ulysses Grant." For the benefit of his black critics Douglass had to reconcile this high rating with his failure to be invited to the White House for dinner with the Santo Domingo Commission, of which he was secretary, although he had accompanied them to that island in the Caribbean. Whatever the reasons Douglass believed that color was not one of them. "The failure of the President to invite me could not have been because my personal presence on account of color would have been disagreeable to him. . . ." Had not the President given every social courtesy to the minister from the Republic of Haiti? And did not the Haitian minister have the same complexion as Douglass? Had not Grant shown himself free from not only prejudice against blacks, but also Indian bias by having the Indian General Ely Parker on his staff? Douglass answered all of the preceding questions in the affirmative. Did one of the commissioners object to the black man's presence? Douglass ruled out that possibility also. Had he not dined with those distinguished gentlemen for ten weeks aboard an American ship, and with the press present? Furthermore, Douglass argued, there were others who went on the trip but were not invited to the dinner.

Douglass' explanation of the matter was that only the four officials appointed by Congress to the Santo Domingo Commission called in a body to see the President, and he invited them to dinner. Douglass was confident that had he been present when the invitation was given he would have been included. Douglass concluded his defense by holding that his loyalty to the President was based on higher and broader grounds than mere personal favor. "I see in him," said Douglass, "the vigilant, firm, impartial, and wise protector of my race from all the malign, reactionary, social, and political elements that would [over]whelm them in destruction."[71] While this was a campaign document, the subject treated has its special significance to the student of race.

How did the President really feel about social equality? He was not indifferent to that subject. In his second annual message of 1873, he said to Congress, "Social equality is not a subject to be legislated upon, nor shall I ask that anything be done to advance the social status of the colored man, except to give him a fair chance to develop what there is good in him, give him access to the schools, and when he travels let him feel assured that his conduct will regulate the treatment and fare he will receive."[72] It would appear from this statement that Grant approved of integrated transportation, if not mixed schools. What caused the President to make this public denial of any intention to advance social equality? The answer probably lies buried in the missing Grant papers or in Grant's own reticence. Yet it is not unlikely that because of his disposition to enforce the laws he was accused of pushing social equality. Twelve years later Grant reflected that in spite of the fact that the nation had given the black man his freedom, the ballot, and public schools, "the nation still lives, and the people are just as free to avoid social intimacy with the blacks as ever they were, or as they are with white people."[73] If whites were free to avoid blacks socially, avoiding them politically was quite another matter.

[71] Frederick Douglass, *U. S. Grant and the Colored People: His Wise, Just, Practical and Effective Friendship Thoroughly Vindicated by Incontestable Facts in His Record From 1862 to 1872 . . .* (Washington, D.C., 1872), p. 7; a memorandum in USGP listed 203 blacks employed "in general service" of the government (Letter and Telegram Book), Vol. I, ser. II.

[72] Richardson, *Messages*, VII, 221.

[73] Grant, *Memoirs*, I, 215. According to William McKinley, on a trip south blacks swarmed to Grant's hotel to shake hands with the President but were about to be ejected when Grant said, "in his quiet way, full of earnest feelings, 'Where I am they shall come also.'" J. S. Ogilvie (ed.), *Life and Speeches of William McKinley* (New York: Ogilvie Publishing Co., 1896), p. 254.

Race and the Right to Vote

"The extension of the suffrage to freedmen has evidently aroused a sentiment of hostility to the colored race . . . which did not exist before," Grant noted, as Secretary of War under Johnson. He had been told by General Ord that more troops would be needed if the freedmen were to exercise their franchise safely. Ord also told Grant that though the colored people desired to support loyal men for office "their intelligence is not now sufficient to enable them to combine for the execution of their will." More than that, white politicians could lead them only under protection of troops.[74] It does not appear that Grant was always in favor of giving blacks the ballot. Both Browning and Gideon Welles, although neither were unprejudiced witnesses, testified that Grant agreed with Johnson's veto of the District of Columbia Voting Bill.[75]

But by the time he became President, however, Grant was committed to the black vote. A Michigan politician, at the suggestion of Governor Hayes of Ohio, sought to have Grant formally recommend ratification of the Fifteenth Amendment. "It is not necessary for you to say a word on that subject," Grant allegedly replied, "I will certainly do it. I fully agree with you as to the importance of my doing so in view of the elections this summer."[76] As good as his word, Grant stated in his inaugural address that so long as a portion of the citizens of the nation were excluded from its privileges in any state, the ballot would remain an issue for public agitation. He expressed his desire to see the question settled by the ratification of the

[74] (1867), Howland, *Grant*, p. 597.

[75] "General Grant was very emphatic against the bill, not because it disfranchised rebels, for he rather liked that, but he thought it very contemptible business for members of Congress whose own states excluded blacks to give them suffrage in the District . . . ," said Welles, who had no love for Grant. Entry for Friday, January 4, 1867, Welles, *Diary*, III, 5–7, 15; Browning, *Diary*, II, 122.

[76] R. E. Trowbridge to Rutherford B. Hayes, February 15, 1869, Rutherford B. Hayes Papers (manuscript, Rutherford B. Hayes Library, Fremont, Ohio).

Fifteenth Amendment.[77] Grant urged the governor of Nebraska to call a special session of the legislature to consider ratification. The stated reason for this plea was his desire to see "a question of such great national importance brought to an early settlement, in order that it might no longer remain an open issue and a subject of agitation before the people."[78]

The evidence suggests that Grant was well aware of the historical importance of the Fifteenth Amendment. When that document was finally ratified, he took the unusual step of sending Congress a special message of congratulations. In his memoirs, Senator George F. Hoar of Massachusetts claimed that the message was his suggestion, and was written by Grant in his presence with the help of quotations from the writings of George Washington, provided by Hoar.[79] Grant, in the message, felt that the enfranchisement of four million blacks was the most important act since the making of the Constitution. More especially was this true when it was remembered that the Supreme Court once held, according to Grant: "At the time of the Declaration of Independence the opinion was fixed and universal in the civilized portion of the white race regarded as an axiom in morals as well as in politics that black men had no rights which the white man was bound to respect." Grant appeared to be in earnest as he called upon the "newly enfranchised race . . . to make themselves worthy of their new privilege." Grant also revealed a knowledge of the racial discrepancies of American law. "To the race more favored heretofore by our laws," he said, "I would say, withhold no legal privilege of advancement to the new citizen," It was significant that Grant implied that a man was not a citizen in fact until he had the unquestioned right to vote. Strange that he should have felt compelled to say this even after the passage of the Fourteenth Amendment. Just as Hoar had stated, Grant quoted Washington on the importance of education to successful American citizenship and urged Congress to support public education

[77] March 4, 1869, Richardson, *Messages*, VII, 8.

[78] U. S. Grant, to David Butler, governor of Nebraska, December 23, 1869, USGP (Letter and Telegram Book), Vol. I, ser. II.

[79] Hoar, *Autobiography*, I, 204.

throughout the country so that the ballot would be a blessing and not a curse.[80] In his desire for actual political and legal integration the President was way ahead of the country.

Events that followed the ratification of the Fifteenth Amendment must have dampened the initial optimistic spirit of the President considerably. In connection with subsequent troubles in Louisiana Grant told Congress that he was executing the Enforcement Act of May 31, 1870, implementing the Fifteenth Amendment. Yet he still expressed his reluctance to interfere in state politics and asked Congress to help him solve the problem.[81] The next year as the process of regaining complete white control in the South moved into high gear, the President deplored the intimidation and violence perpetrated by whites upon blacks in their campaign to drive the freedmen from the ballot box. Grant could not understand it. He thought that the Fifteenth Amendment was designed to prevent just such occurrences. He said that since he had been sworn to execute the laws he decided he must send troops to apprehend the offenders. To the critics of this show of force Grant said, "Complaints are made of this interference by federal authority; but if said Amendment and Act [Enforcement Act of 1870] do not provide for such interference under the circumstances as above stated, then they are without meaning, force, and effect, and the whole scheme of colored enfranchisement is worse than mockery and a little better than a crime."[82] Here was no political hedging; here was plain speaking.

While the President felt that the better part of the Southern population was law-abiding, and while he sympathized with "their prostrate condition," he asked if they were "right in ignoring the existence of violence and bloodshed in resistance to constituted authority. . . ."

> The theory is even raised that there is to be no further interference on the part of the federal government to protect citizens within a state when the state authorities fail to give protection—

[80] U. S. Grant's Special Message to Congress, March 30, 1870, Richardson, *Messages*, VII, 55–56.
[81] February 25, 1873, Richardson, *Messages*, VII, 212–13.
[82] Sixth Annual Message, December 7, 1874, Richardson, *Messages*, VII, 297.

> This is a great mistake. While I remain executive all the laws of Congress and the provisions of the Constitution, including the recent amendments added thereto, will be enforced with vigor, but with regret that they should have added one jot or tittle to executive duties or powers.[83]

Given the history of the tyranny of kings and monarchs in ancient and even modern times, it is not difficult to see that in a democracy the executive will always be reluctant to use force against the population. This would be doubly true in matters of race wherever it was felt that the white majority had "universal feelings" on the subject.

As for the politics of the question, Grant said that the black man voted with the Republicans because he felt they were his friends. To those whites who voted with the Democrats solely because of opposition to black rule, Grant suggested "this is a most delusive cry." Then Grant gave his solution to a major political problem that occupied the attention of Republican Presidents and politicians from Grant to Theodore Roosevelt, namely, how to divide the white and the black vote in the South on significant issues thus creating a two-party system and removing forever the racial basis of party formation. "Treat the Negro as a citizen and a voter, as he is and must remain, and soon parties will be divided, not on the color line, but on principle."[84] What Grant and the politicians after him who suggested similar solutions never really faced squarely was that the very race prejudice which they were trying to remove would prevent their theory of fair treatment from being tried.

In a special message to the Senate on the state of Louisiana affairs, Grant reminded the gentlemen that while the right of the United States courts to intervene in state elections to insure political equality "irrespective of race or color" may be "comparatively a new, and to some . . . a startling idea," such authority was clearly implied in the constitutional amendments and in the Enforcement Acts.[85] When fifty-nine blacks fell mortally wounded in the Colfax, Louisiana, massacre on April

[83] Ibid., VII, 299.
[84] Richardson, *Messages*, VII, 299.
[85] January 13, 1875, Richardson, *Messages*, VII, 306.

13, 1873, Grant pointed out the fact that while everybody was denouncing federal intervention in Louisiana politics, "everyone of the Colfax miscreants goes unwhipped of justice, and no way can be found in this boasted land of civilization and Christianity to punish the perpetrators of this bloody and monstrous crime."[86]

In 1876, Grant requested the resignation of a United States marshal for Maryland because it was necessary "to draw out the Republican vote. . . . Many of the colored men," Grant explained, "after their former experience, declare that they can not risk themselves out on the day of election without a change. I have therefore concluded to ask your resignation. . . ."[87]

After leaving the White House, Grant said that it was too late to discuss the wisdom or unwisdom of having given the black man the ballot. He had the ballot, "and no one could look on satisfied to see it taken away from him."[88] Grant freely admitted he did not think the majority of the people in the North were in favor of giving blacks the ballot immediately after the war. They were thinking in terms of a probationary period in which the freedmen could be better prepared for citizenship. But if Northerners were against immediate suffrage, why did they grant it? Grant, in these later reflections, attributed black suffrage to Johnson's championship of the rebel cause. Those who had fought the war were not prepared to reward the rebels for rebellion. "Finally . . . it became necessary," Grant said, "to enfranchise the Negro, in all his ignorance." It was the result of the "foolhardiness of the President [Johnson] and the blindness of the Southern people to their own interests." And what about Grant's personal opinion? "As to myself, while strongly favoring the course that would be the least humiliating to the people who had been in rebellion, I had gradually worked up to the point where, with the majority of the people, I favored immediate enfranchisement."[89]

[86] July 1875, Richardson, *Messages*, VII, 308.

[87] Letter, August 11, 1876, USGP, Vol. 3, No. 112, ser. 2.

[88] John Russell Young, *Around the World with General Grant* . . . (New York: American News Co., 1879), II, 301.

[89] Grant, *Memoirs*, II, 511–12.

The President, content to let social equality alone, was certainly in favor of political equality for blacks. He faced the problem of law enforcement in this critical juncture of history with a certain diffidence and surprising objectivity.[90]

Federal Troops and Disputed State Elections

Though he must have been concerned about what party held power in the South, in his instructions to the occupying troops Grant showed greater interest in keeping the public peace. Commanders were told to take no part in political controversies but to prevent bloodshed and armed clashes.[91] The troop role was highlighted during the disputed presidential election of 1876. On November 25, Governor Chamberlain of South Carolina asked to have federal troops so deployed as to prevent armed Redeemers from interfering with the assembling of the legislature.[92] Meanwhile, Wade Hampton, a leading Redeemer of the South and member of a rival political faction, got wind of Chamberlain's request. Hampton's group jumped to the conclusion that the governor had asked for the troops to be placed under his personal command. To this they were utterly opposed. In a five-page telegram to Grant, the Hampton faction explained its peaceful intentions, claiming that both white and black votes had defeated Chamberlain.[93] Next, General Ruger, the military commander on the scene, reported that a rival legislature had been certified by the state supreme court but was not recognized by Chamberlain. He revealed that Chamberlain planned to use a small force in an attempt to eject the rival group from the statehouse and wanted United States

[90] This opinion was also by a contemporary, George F. Hoar. See his *Autobiography*, II, 161.

[91] U. S. Grant's Instructions to Belknap and Babcock, 1873, 1877, USGP (Letter and Telegram Book), Vol. 1, No. 549, 317, ser. II.

[92] Coded telegram of Governor D. H. Chamberlain to U. S. Grant, November 25, 1876, USGP (manuscript, Rutherford B. Hayes Library, Fremont, Ohio).

[93] Telegram from J. B. Gordon, Wade Hampton et al., to U. S. Grant, November 27, 1876, USGP (manuscript, Rutherford B. Hayes Library, Fremont, Ohio).

troops to stand by in case the Redeemers put up a fight. "I have no doubt resistance will be made . . . ," Ruger said, and suggested that the federal troops be authorized to move at the first sign of resistance, or better yet, let the troops themselves do the ejecting and so prevent bloodshed.[94] But this suggestion was rejected by Grant who telegraphed back, "I do not think you would be justified in taking U. S. troops into the legislative hall to resist opposition made by persons claiming to have a right to be there. . . . Unless further advised you will confine your action to preventing unauthorized outside parties from resisting the action of the legal governor of the state."[95]

The same day Grant elaborated upon the preceding telegram. He wanted it understood that Chamberlain was the legitimate governor "and he is entitled as such to your support and protection." Grant made it equally clear that the business of organizing the legislature was a state function. "It is not your duty to purge the legislature," he told Ruger. The President did not relish a strong executive role in the "unhappy state of affairs" in South Carolina. "The question of recognition of a legislature may become incumbent upon me," said Grant. "I hope it will not, but if it does I shall not shirk the responsibility. . . ." It seems clear that both the President and President-elect Hayes hoped to stay out of state politics. "To be plain," Grant continued, "I want to avoid anything like an unlawful use of the military and I believe it would be regarded with disfavor if they were used in taking men claiming seats out of the legislative hall."[96]

Ruger wired back the next day to say that the troops were still occupying the lower part of the statehouse in South Carolina. More significantly he felt that the presence of the troops was preventing compromise between the two rival groups. While the Republican members expected the troops to expel the Democrats, the latter felt that they could remain unless coerced by

[94] Telegram of General Ruger to U. S. Grant, December 3, 1876, 11:22 P.M., ibid.

[95] Telegram of U. S. Grant to General Ruger, December 3, 1876, ibid.

[96] Telegram of U. S. Grant to General Ruger, December 3, 1876, USGP (manuscript, Rutherford B. Hayes Library, Fremont, Ohio).

the troops.[97] On the morning of December 5, Chamberlain mistakenly thought that his position was "impregnable."[98] Later that day he wired to say that the legislature had declared him to be the properly elected governor.[99] But twenty-four hours later General Ruger reported rifle club members on the streets of Columbia, supposedly headed for the State Fair, and engaging in threatening talk on the streets.[100] The next day Grant cautioned Ruger not to recognize anyone but Chamberlain until further notice. Before he closed he inquired of the general, "Are there armed men in Columbia? I have heard as much."[101] Ruger replied that the South Carolina State Supreme Court had declared the rival faction to be the legitimate legislature. So now there were two legislatures again.[102] Ruger next sent a letter in which he stated that there were some non-resident men in town. "Most of the men had pistols, which," Ruger added, ". . . is a common custom in the South. . . ."[103]

Meanwhile a man who called himself "the only white Republican in Edgefield County," South Carolina, praised Grant for responding to Chamberlain's call for troops. He felt that were it not for two companies of troops in Edgefield the Democrats would "kick up hell generally. . . . Please excuse me for using the word Hades, for I know of no more appropriate term to use."[104]

Matters were similarly disturbed in the delta state of Louisiana, where not only state but also national election returns of the presidential contest of 1876 between Rutherford B. Hayes and Samuel J. Tilden were in dispute. James Longstreet, Re-

97 Telegram of General Thomas H. Ruger to U. S. Grant, December 4, 1876, USGP (manuscript, Rutherford B. Hayes Library, Fremont, Ohio).

98 Telegram of D. H. Chamberlain to U. S. Grant, December 5, 1876, 6:21 P.M., USGP (manuscript, Rutherford B. Hayes Library, Fremont, Ohio).

99 Chamberlain to Grant, December 5, 1876, 8:20 P.M., ibid.

100 Telegram of General Ruger to U. S. Grant, December 6, 1876, 12:05 A.M., ibid.

101 Telegram of U. S. Grant to General Ruger, December 7, 1876, ibid.

102 Telegram of General Ruger to U. S. Grant, December 7, 1876, ibid.

103 General Ruger to U. S. Grant, December 7, 1876, ibid.

104 W. M. Heath to U. S. Grant, January 16, 1877, USGP (manuscript, Rutherford B. Hayes Library, Fremont, Ohio).

publican and ex-rebel, in a letter that probably carried weight, tried to convince Grant of the logic of recognizing the Hayes electors in Louisiana for the presidency and the Democratic Nichols ticket for the state contest. He claimed that many Republicans voted freely for the Democrats. He thought it would be better for the Republican party if the Democrats were approved. Longstreet felt that the Republicans in Louisiana would abandon the party should the incumbent Governor S. B. Packard again be "forced upon this state. . . ." His major contention was that Packard was not strong enough to maintain himself and the party successfully. More significantly, Longstreet also felt that when Hayes became President the Republican party in the South could "be so organized as to divide the white and colored vote, not only in Louisiana but throughout the South, and make the party strong. . . ." Oddly enough all of this could be facilitated by allowing the state Democratic ticket to triumph during the election of 1876. On the other hand, a Republican Administration would only reawaken white opposition.[105] Longstreet sent an identical letter to Governor Hayes of Ohio. Grant had already arrived at much the same conclusions relative to dividing the vote. Hayes and Republicans after him were destined to struggle long and unsuccessfully with the theme of how to rejuvenate the party and split the Solid South. But then there was another minority group in the country that did not have a vote but who, desperately, needed attention.

The New Indian Policy

The settlement of the last frontier in the Western United States and the arrival of the railroads upon the Great Plains "precluded any inertia or indifference on the part of the government toward the ultimate solution of the Indian problem" at the inception of the Grant Administration.[106] The Indian prob-

[105] James Longstreet to U. S. Grant, February 17, 1877, USGP (manuscript, Rutherford B. Hayes Library, Fremont, Ohio).

[106] Elsie Mitchell Rushmore, *The Indian Policy During Grant's Administration* (New York: Marion Press, 1914), p. 74.

lem was twofold. What should be done with the red man as an obstacle in the way of civilization? What should be done with him as a ward of the nation?[107] One student believes that race prejudice did not affect the Indian problem to the degree that it complicated black-white relations, though antagonism from centuries of frontier conflict was by no means negligible.[108] The new Indian peace policy individualizing the Indian problem and putting an end to treaty making with the Indians, was the signal for twenty years of Indian reform which began in the Grant Administration.[109] The solution to the Indian problem involved at least three possibilities: extermination, compulsory location on reservations with government aid until self-supporting, and eventually full absorption into white American culture. People on the frontier leaned toward extermination of the Indian. The peace policy of Grant involved the second alternative with a gradual addition of the third possibility with the Dawes Act of 1884.[110] Of course the Indian had little to say in the matter. In practice his only choice was between reservations and extermination.

During the Mexican War, Grant told his "Dear Julia" of the difference between Mexicans and Americans. He said, "the inhabitants are generally more like Indians, in looks and habits than white men."[111] In 1853, Mrs. Grant cautioned her husband, who was then stationed in the Oregon country, about going out alone lest the Indians kill him. Grant, himself, found the Indians in this region rather docile. "It is really my opinion that the whole race would be harmless and peaceable if they were not put upon by the whites."[112] He described the condition of the Chickitat tribe in this manner: "This poor remnant

[107] Ibid., p. 56. Originally a Ph.D. dissertation completed at Columbia University.

[108] Ibid., p. 14.

[109] Ibid., p. 74.

[110] Leonard D. White, *The Republican Era: 1869–1901: A Study in Administrative History* (New York: Macmillan Co., 1958), pp. 181–83.

[111] U. S. Grant to Julia Dent, May 24, 1846, from Matamoras, Mexico, USGP, Box of "Letters to Julia," ser. 1A.

[112] U. S. Grant to "Dear Julia," March 19, 1853, ibid.

of a once powerful tribe is fast wasting away before those blessings of civilization 'whisky and small pox.' "[113]

However, after the Civil War, Grant felt that there was no alternative course with the hostile Apaches but "active and vigorous war till they are completely destroyed; or forced to surrender as prisoners of war."[114] Grant even wanted the Indian Bureau transferred from the Interior to the War Department and the Indian Agencies abolished. The result, he thought, would be greater economy and "diminution of conflict between the Indian and the white races."[115] Browning, as Secretary of the Interior, reported a Cabinet meeting in which Grant was against sending a peace commission to the Indians, preferring that they be left to General Sherman to handle as he pleased.[116] Also, Welles felt that Grant and Stanton were determined to have an Indian war. "It is evident that the military intends to control Indian affairs to the annihilation of the whole race." Grant's sympathies, according to Welles, were with the military.[117] If Welles is to be believed, Grant's view on the Indians underwent some change.

When he became President he seems to have personally favored the policy of putting the Indians on reservations as the alternative to a cruel war of extermination. In his inaugural address he said: "The proper treatment of the original inhabitants of the land—the Indian—is one deserving careful study. I will favor any course toward them which tends to their civilization and ultimate citizenship."[118] In the face of negative public opinion, said John Eaton, Grant "strongly maintained the right of the native American to represent himself, his interests, and his racial culture" at the Centennial Exposition

[113] U. S. Grant to Major O. Cross, Pacific Division, San Francisco, July 25, 1853, ibid., Box 1, No. 39–42, subseries 1C; Grant, *Memoirs*, I, 204.

[114] Howland, *Grant*, p. 603.

[115] U. S. Grant, General of the Armies, to Edwin M. Stanton, November 21, [1866], ibid., Box 9, ser. 4; Eaton, *Grant, Lincoln and the Freedmen . . .* , p. 274.

[116] Entries for January 25, 1867, and February 5, 1867, Browning, *Diary*, II, 126, 128.

[117] Welles, *Diary*, III, 98–100.

[118] March 4, 1869, Richardson, *Messages*, VII, 8; Eaton, *Grant, Lincoln and the Freedmen . . .* , p. 277.

at Philadelphia in 1876.[119] In his first annual message of 1869 Grant stated the hard facts of Indian-white relations on the frontier as the railroad brought settlers closer to the Indian on the Plains. "No matter what ought to be the relations between such settlements and the aborigines, the fact is they do not harmonize well, and one or the other has to give way in the end. A system which looks to the extinction of a race is too horrible for a nation to adopt without entailing upon itself the wrath of all Christendom and engendering in the citizens a disregard for human life and the rights of others, dangerous to society." So Grant arrived at the idea of placing all Indians on reservations under government protection, eventual individual land ownership, and territorial government.[120] It would not be true to say that Grant had no ideas of his own about the Indians. He told Congress that the management of the "original inhabitants of the Continent . . ." had always been a source of embarrassment and expense to the government. He knew these things, he said, from his "own experience upon the frontier and in Indian countries." While both ill-conceived regulations and white mistakes had to share in the blame, the past could not be undone, said Grant, and the question had to be faced as it presently was. "I have attempted a new policy towards these wards of the nation. (They can not be regarded in any other light than wards) with fair results so far as tried. . . ."[121]

It may have been a historic moment when Grant decided to appoint an Indian as Commissioner of Indian Affairs. The Indian, General Ely Parker, Seneca by tribe, engineer by trade, had served on Grant's personal staff in the adjutant general's office during the Civil War. Because of his excellent handwriting he was later made into a military secretary and it was he who prepared the draft for peace negotiations at Appomattox.[122] Parker's admiring biographer, himself an Indian, con-

[119] Eaton, op. cit., pp. 277–78.

[120] December 1869, Richardson, *Messages*, VII, 39.

[121] Ibid., VII, 38–39. The good record of the Quakers in getting along with the Indians caused Grant to turn a few of the reservations over to them.

[122] Arthur C. Parker, *The Life of General Ely S. Parker, Last Grand Sachem of the Iroquois and General Grant's Military Secretary* (New York: Buffalo Historical Society, 1919), pp. 141, 150.

tended that the Board of Indian Commissioners and its peace policy were initiated under Parker's tenure in office. Parker, it was said, urged the need for legal definition of the status of the Indian, which was not forthcoming until 1924.[123]

The career of the first Indian Commissioner of Indian Affairs ended rather strangely and not without its racial innuendo. One of the commissioners, William Welsh, resigned and promptly accused Parker of trying to defraud the Indians and the government. In addition Welsh rebuked the President for having appointed as Indian commissioner a man who himself, according to Welsh, was but one step removed from the barbarian. In February of 1871, Parker was tried before a committee of the House but the charges were not sustained. Even after this vindication, pressure continued for his removal. According to his biographer the cry went up, "The Indian must be put out!" Six months later Parker resigned.[124]

In January of 1871, Grant recommended to the Senate, the organization of a territorial government for the Indians. One impetus for this was the adoption of a constitution and a declaration of rights by the Ocmulgee Indians in the new territory if all went well. He wanted authority to appoint only "native citizens of the territory" as territorial officers with perhaps the exception of the judiciary. The President was really ready, it seemed, to give the Indian self-government and eventually statehood. "It is confidently hoped," he said, "that the policy now being pursued toward the Indian will fit him for self-government and make him desire to settle among people of his own race where he can enjoy the full privileges of civil and enlightened government."[125] In his third annual message, Grant again recommended territorial status, with all Indians to be placed in the region which is today Oklahoma, and with the expectation of eventual statehood.[126]

123 Ibid, pp. 152–53.

124 Ibid., pp. 150–61. The episode concerning the Indian commissioner is discussed, without any reference to the racial angle in the case, by Rushmore, *Indian Policy During Grant's Administration*, p. 72.

125 Richardson, *Messages*, VII, 119, 200. Here was the old familiar theme that an alien race could not enjoy equality except among their own people.

126 Ibid., p. 152.

The Indian peace policy was probably intended as much for the benefit of the white people as for the Indian. To reiterate, the Indian had little choice in the matter: "Indians who will not put themselves under the restraint required will have to be forced, even to the extent of making war upon them," Grant told General J. M. Schofield, "to submit to measures that will insure security to the white settlers of the territories. It is not proposed that all protection should be to the Indian. . . ."[127] Grant next directed that Sheridan be allowed to use his troops ". . . to compel Indians in Utah to go upon reservations."[128] In his second inaugural address the President again called attention to the Indian alternative of civilization or extermination. He also cautioned against white rapacity. "Our superiority of strength and advantages of civilization should make us lenient toward the Indian," he said. He was confident that with proper teaching and treatment the Indian could be made a "useful member of society." The nation's reputation and conscience would rest more easily were this program attempted in good faith.[129]

At the end of his first Administration, members of the Utes and Crow tribes called upon the Grants at the White House and were given presents by the President and his wife. Grant thanked the chief of the Crows for a coat and "the scalp."[130] Meanwhile, peace did not seem to be resulting from the peace policy. The whites were encroaching upon reservations and hunting grounds. Grant warned in his annual message of 1873 that troble would continue "until every race appreciates that the other has rights which must be respected." He again reminded Congress that all of America's Indians could and should be collected into the Indian territory ". . . except a few who may elect to make their homes among white people. . . ." He also asked that the Indian be prohibited from selling

[127] U. S. Grant to J. M. Schofield, Division of the Pacific, March 6, 1872, USGP (Letter and Telegram Book), Vol. 1, No. 432, ser. 2.

[128] O. E. Babcock to W. W. Belknap, Secretary of War [1872], ibid., No. 477.

[129] March 4, 1873, Richardson, *Messages*, VII, 223.

[130] U. S. Grant to Utes and Crows, November 5, 1873, ibid. (Letter Book), Vol. 2, No. 209, ser. 2.

his land for twenty years.[131] This feature was later put into the Dawes Act of 1887, though the idea of a separate Indian state never materialized. The issue of race would not restrict itself to domestic minority problems but sometimes became a factor in our foreign relations.

Race in International Perspective

Though Grant's apparent mania for the annexation of Santo Domingo is well known, the connection between the acquisition of that Caribbean island and a possible solution to the race problem is not.

Santo Domingo

Grant once wrote a long paper on the attractions of Santo Domingo. Among other things, the place was capable, Grant thought, of "supporting the entire colored population of the United States, should it choose to emigrate." Grant then made one of his rare references to the existence of race prejudice: "The present difficulty in bringing all parts of the United States into a happy unity and love of country grows out of the prejudice to color. The prejudice," he continued, "is a senseless one, but it does exist. The colored man cannot be spared until his place is supplied, but with a refuge like Santo Domingo his worth here would be soon discovered and he would soon receive such recognition as to induce him to stay: or if Providence designed that the two races should not live together he would find a home in the antiliase [*sic*]."[132] Grant, unlike Lincoln, but similar to Johnson, would leave the colonization imperative to the Almighty. With a haven for the red man in the Oklahoma Territory and a refuge for the black man in Santo Domingo the President, if successful, would have perfected two racial safety valves, thus taking some of the pressure off the explosive racial boiler.

131 Richardson, *Messages*, VII, 252.

132 U. S. Grant, "Reasons Why Santo Domingo Should be Annexed to the United States" [1869], USGP Box 9, ser. 4.

On January 12, 1870, Senator Willard Warner urged Grant to appoint "Frederick Douglass as one of the Santo Domingo Commissioners designated to visit the island. I understand him not to be committed on the question of annexation. His race are deeply interested, and a strong effort is being made to prejudice them against annexation. . . ."[133] Very significantly Grant did not mention the utility of Santo Domingo as a safety valve for the race problem, other than to say that the island could support ten million more people than it then possessed.[134] On January 11, 1871, Douglass was called to the White House and for a moment it appeared that he would be chosen a commissioner as Warner had suggested.[135] However, Douglass was not so named. Instead, he traveled with the commissioners as assistant secretary. One writer claimed that sending Douglass on the mission was a move to foil Sumner who was against the entire scheme.[136] On the trip Douglass was treated on terms of equality almost to the very end. As the *Potomac Mail Packet* steamed from Charleston to Washington and dinnertime came, the captain would not let Douglass into the dining room, whereupon Commissioners Andrew D. White and Samuel G. Howe got up and left. The source did not say what were the actions of Benjamin F. Wade, another commissioner.[137] It has already been shown how the failure of Douglass to receive an invitation to dine at the White House with the commissioners became an issue in the election of 1872, in the black community. In this case, Douglass was chided because he did not get an invitation to dinner. Almost thirty years later Booker T. Washington would be scolded because he did get an invitation to dine at the White House—and accepted it.

In his second inaugural address, Grant asked for a broader perspective on the subject of annexing territory with the mutual approbation of the people involved. He suggested that rapid

[133] Letter, USGP (manuscript, Rutherford B. Hayes Library, Fremont, Ohio).
[134] Message to the Senate, May 31, 1870, Richardson, *Messages*, VII, 61–62.
[135] Horace Porter to Frederick Douglass, USGP (Letter and Telegram Book), Vol. 1, Nos. 254, 262, ser. 2.
[136] Foner, *Life and Writings of Frederick Douglass*, IV, 67.
[137] Ibid., pp. 67–72.

developments in trade, commerce and communications presaged a cosmopolitan world! "Rather do I believe," he said, "that our Great Maker is preparing the world, in His own good time, to become one nation, speaking one language, and when armies and navies will no longer be required."[138] In his eighth and final annual message the President was still pleading for the annexation of Santo Domingo. It was in this message that Grant revealed his hopes for Santo Domingo as a "congenial home" for the "emancipated race in the South . . . where their civil rights would not be disputed and where their labor would be so much sought after that the poorest among them would have found the means to go." Grant felt that if such a place as Santo Domingo had been available during the past eleven years of "great oppression and cruelty . . . practiced upon . . ." the freedmen, "whole communities" would have sought refuge in that island. "I do not suppose that the whole race would have gone," said Grant, "nor is it yet desirable that they should go. Their labor is desirable—indispensable almost—where they are now. But the possession of this territory would have left the black man 'master of the situation,' by enabling him to demand his rights at home on pain of finding them elsewhere." Why would the President wait until his last annual message to present a paper which appeared to have been in readiness since 1869? "I do not present these views now as recommendation for a renewal of the subject of annexation but I do refer to it to vindicate my previous action in regard to it,"[139] the President concluded. It is not known whether the President was giving a racial reason to cover up his imperialism or if the fresh eruption of racial conflict during the recent election of 1876 caused him to resurrect the subject. Whatever the reason, Grant's plan seemed to have been given in a different spirit than Lincoln's. It was significant that Grant saw Santo Domingo not solely as a means of ridding the country of the African, but also as a lever or club which the Afro-American could hold over the head of his oppressor in

[138] Richardson, *Messages*, VII, 222.
[139] Eighth Annual Message, December 5, 1876, in Richardson, *Messages*, VII, 412–13.

the hope of getting equal rights. That the "oppressor" might have welcomed the opportunity to put the blacks on the high road to Santo Domingo did not seem to worry the President.

Grant made only a few comments on Santo Domingo after leaving office in 1877. When only months away from death and working feverishly on his memoirs, Grant commented briefly on the durability of the race question. "It is possible that the question of a conflict between races may come up in the future," Grant said in 1885, "as did that between freedom and slavery before." But while the ex-President showed anxiety for the condition of the black man in America, he had this to say also about the Afro-African: "But he was brought to our shores by compulsion, and he now should be considered as having as good a right to remain here as any other class of our citizens. It was looking to a settlement of this question that led me to urge the annexation of Santo Domingo during the time I was President of the United States. . . . I took it that the colored people would go there in great numbers so as to have independent states governed by their own race. They would still be states of the Union, and under the protection of the American government; but the citizens would be almost wholly colored."[140] Grant seemed unaffected by the very popular theme in his day that the black man could not govern himself. But what is more significant here is that after grappling for eight years with the race problem, Grant was hard put for a solution and turned in desperation, as it were, to racial separation. The blacks would still be under the protection of the American Eagle, under a separate but equal wing. But the difficulties of blacks in America did not adversely affect Grant's rather cosmopolitan attitude toward people from other lands wanting to make their home here.

IMMIGRATION

Grant felt that a native citizen should have at least as many privileges as an immigrant. He confessed in 1885 that for a

[140] Grant, *Memoirs*, II, 550.

week in the 1850s he did belong to the Know-Nothing party but was repelled by its secrecy and oath taking.[141] In his first inaugural address and on other occasions he said that he would protect all law-abiding citizens, whether of native or foreign birth.[142] In 1873, he reported approvingly the desire of a large colony of Russians to settle in America.[143] The liberal Chinese immigration policy that was to cause so much trouble later, was initiated during the Grant Administration. In his first annual message Grant called the Burlingame Treaty an "enlightened policy. . . ." He then endorsed the improvement of our commercial relations with China and Japan, upgrading the American embassy in China to first-class status, and took steps to put an end to the coolie trade.[144] In 1871, he asked that at least four American youths be assigned to the Japanese and Chinese embassies to learn the language, thus making it unnecessary to continue the use of Chinese nationals as interpreters.[145] Grant accepted the stories that coolies were being brought in as slaves and Chinese women for immoral purposes.[146]

During his world tour Grant found "the Chinese . . . enduring, patient to the last degree, [and] industrious. . . ." He found them weak militarily. However, Grant felt that the Chinese were destined to become great provided they could maintain a sovereign state.[147]

He urged the Chinese and the Japanese to settle their differences without the aid of a foreign power. The ex-President again evidenced a global perspective when he said, "In the

141 Grant, *Memoirs*, I, 213.

142 March 4, 1869, Richardson, *Messages*, VII, 8; First Annual Message, December 1869, ibid., VII, 36; Third Annual Message, December 1871, ibid., 154.

143 Fifth Annual Message, December 1873, Richardson, *Messages*, VII, 253.

144 December 1869, Richardson, op. cit., VII, 371; December 1, 1873, ibid., VII, 236.

145 Ibid., VII, 147.

146 December 7, 1874, ibid., VII, 288; see his conversation with the king of Siam on the subject, newspaper clipping, New York *Herald*, June 22, 1879, USGP, Box 2, subseries IB.

147 John Russell Young, *Around the World with General Grant* . . . , II, 442–43; U. S. Grant to General E. F. Beale, June 7, 1879, USGP, Box 2, subseries 1C.

vast east, embracing more than two thirds of the human population of the world—there are but two nations, even partially free from the domination and dictation of some one or other of the European powers with intelligence and strength enough to maintain their independence—Japan and China. . . ." Grant then went on to describe the people of the two countries as "brave, intelligent, frugal and industrious." He felt that "with a little more advancement in modern civilization, mechanics, engineering, they could throw off offensive treaties which now cripple and humiliate them, and could enter into competition for the world's commerce."[148] He expressed doubt about the sincerity of some European powers' solicitude for China's independence. He told the Japanese he felt that many foreigners in China were interested in keeping her depressed and in bleeding her. He hoped that these efforts would not succeed.

Grant, like Theodore Roosevelt, was more impressed with Japan than he was with China. After a stay of seven weeks in the former he said to a friend, "The country and people are exceedingly interesting. . . . They have school facilities for every child in the empire male and female, equal to the Northern states of the Union. Their naval and military academies, their colleges and their schools of science are equal to the best of ours. . . ."[149]

When Grant arrived in San Francisco from his world tour, one story had it that a question came up about the propriety of his receiving a delegation from the Chinese community. The Chinese were not loved in California, the complaint ran, and there would be objections. When Grant was approached on the subject, he allegedly said that in view of the hospitality he had just received from the Chinese on his trip he would "only be too happy to return it in any courtesy he could show Chinamen in America." However, one racial expedient was exercised. It was thought safer to receive the Chinese delegation at General McDowell's residence, which was govern-

[148] U. S. Grant to H. Ili, prince king, and H. E. Twakwara Tomonri, prince minister of Japan, August 13, 1879, on the LooChoo Question, USGP, Box 2, No. 6312, subseries IB.

[149] U. S. Grant to E. F. Beale, August 10, 1879, USGP, Box 2, subseries IC.

ment property.[150] Not only did Grant appear to be tolerant of Asiatics but he seemed to reject the idea of territorial expansion by force.

Imperialism

With reference to Spain's troubles in Cuba and the Caribbean, Grant disclaimed any imperialistic intentions. While the United States sympathized with all who struggled for liberty and self-government, "we should abstain from enforcing our views upon unwilling nations and from taking an interested part, *without invitation*, in the quarrels between different nations or between governments and their subjects. . . ."[151] On June 18, 1870, the President urged neutrality in regard to the contest between Cuba and Spain.[152] In his third annual message he asked Congress for legislation prohibiting American citizens from holding or having interest in slave property in foreign lands.[153] Though he eschewed imperialism for America, on his world tour he approved of British imperialism in India. He said that before his trip, he had thought English imperialism purely selfish with no benefits for the subject peoples. Now that he had seen it and although his suspicions were partly justified, he was now convinced that were the English to leave India the Indians would start raping, murdering and fighting among themselves again.[154] "It would be a sad day for the people of India and for the commerce of the world if the English would withdraw," he told his nephew.[155] He was impressed with the idea of 250,000,000 people living at peace with each other under English tutelage.

That Grant was a true imperialist, however, is doubtful. On his world tour he said that he was interested in Mexico and

[150] John Russell Young, *Around the World with General Grant*, II, 629–30.
[151] First Annual Message, December 1869, Richardson, *Messages*, VII, 31.
[152] First Annual Message, December 1869, Richardson, *Messages*, VII, 64–68.
[153] December 1871, ibid., VII, 146–47. This had particular reference to slavery in the West Indies.
[154] U. S. Grant to Jessie Grant Cramer, March 20, 1879, p. 152.
[155] U. S. Grant to Elihu Washburne, *General Grant's Letters to a Friend*, p. 89.

the Mexican people and always wished them well. He felt that Mexico would be wise to become a part of the United States, now that the slavery question was settled. "But," he added, "it would have to come, as Santo Domingo tried to come, by the free will of the people. I would not fire a gun to acquire territory. I consider it too great a privilege to belong to the United States for us to go around gunning for new territories." Grant had still another reason for opposing annexation; it would inevitably bring up the question of suffrage which he thought was becoming more serious daily and would be a major problem in the future.[156] Grant, still looking backward, was ashamed of America's role in the Mexican War. "I do not think," he said, "there was ever a more wicked war than that waged by the United States on Mexico." He still berated himself for not having had the moral courage to resign from the army when that war began.[157] However, there seemed to be no lack of nerve on his part when he ordered a certain group of businessmen out of his area of command.

The Jews

"I am now reading the Wandering Jew," Grant wrote to his future wife in 1845.[158] This may well have been Grant's first introduction to the subject. However, his major controversy with the Jews was centered around his famous General Order Number Eleven, issued on December 17, 1862. This read in part: The Jews as a class, violating every regulation of trade established by the Treasury Department orders, *are hereby expelled from the Department within twenty-four hours from receipt of this order by Post Commanders. . . .*[159] The order created quite a stir. The Board of Delegates of American Israelites held a special meeting of its executive committee in New York City, on January 8, 1863, to discuss Grant's order, which had just been revoked by General Halleck under orders

[156] Young, *Around the World with General Grant*, II, 448–49.
[157] Ibid., pp. 447–48; Grant, *Memoirs*, I, 53–56, 169.
[158] U. S. Grant to Julia Dent [October 23, 1845?], USGP (Box labeled "Letters to Julia"), ser. IA.
[159] Cited in P. H. Von Bort, *General Grant and the Jews* (New York: National News Co., 1868), p. 16.

from Lincoln himself. The committee proceeded to condemn the order, likening it to the Jewish persecutions of the Middle Ages. They reasoned that merchants who had been guilty of malpractices in trading should have been punished individually rather than having an entire "religious community" proscribed. The committee concluded the meeting with a vote of thanks to Halleck "for the promptitude with which he revoked General Grant's unjust and outrageous order, as soon as it was brought to his attention."[160] On January 2, 1863, Halleck said to Grant, "It may be proper to give you some explanation of the revoking of your order expelling all Jews from your Department. The President has no objections to your expelling traitors, and Jew peddlers, which I suppose was the object of your order; but as it . . . proscribed an entire religious class, some of whom are fighting in our ranks, the President deemed it necessary to revoke it."[161]

During the campaign of 1868, Francis Lieber identified certain politicians for Grant as being Jewish. "Dr. Jacobi is a Jew and I believe Dr. Schurtz [*sic*] . . . is also one. Whether he is a Jew or not, he is a most exceptional man and ardent Republican. . . ."[162] Grant's anti-Jewish order was reprinted in the *New York World* on March 24, 1868, as campaign ammunition for the opposition.

Whether Grant's order was racially or religiously inspired has not been determined. However, it did arouse Jewish defenders to ask why Jews were pointed out while Protestant and Catholic merchants were ignored: "The country to which we are proud to belong, where every citizen holds the great principle that equality before the law is the inalienable right of every man; where as a consequence of our great war, the half brutish Negro now participates in this great blessing, for whose sake the law has actually been made to act backwards . . ." was betraying its principles, asserted P. H. Von Bort. Grant had

[160] A copy of the Proceedings found in RTLC, Vol. 100, No. 21089–90, ser. I.

[161] Halleck to Grant, January 2, 1863, *Official Records of the Rebellion*, XXIV, 9, Pt. 1, ser. I.

[162] Francis Lieber to U. S. Grant, June 23, 1868, USGP (manuscript, Rutherford B. Hayes Library, Fremont, Ohio), Accession No. 141.

insulted the Jews; both as a "religious brotherhood and as a class . . . you have stigmatized and expelled us! As a *class* we rise up and vote against you, like one man!"[163] Grant won the election, yet this incident is not without significance as an illustration of the variety of problems in a multiracial and religiously plural society.

Certain generalizations can be made concerning Grant. He was indeed conscious of the race factor, although it does not appear to have been an overriding consideration with him. He spoke little on racial matters and when he did so it was with exceptional objectivity. His outlook on the world and its problems, at least after his global tour, was rather cosmopolitan. However, the reality of racial conflict during the Reconstruction period, and continuing antipathy on the frontier between white man and Indian caused him to consider seriously the propriety of separate, self-governing territories for blacks and Indians as solutions to the race problem.

Grant made it clear that he would not insist that anything be done to advance social equality. This, he felt, was not a subject for legislation but a matter of choice. According to the evidence examined for this study he said nothing at all on the matter of race mixing. Like other politicians of his day he felt impelled to deny any inclination toward social equality. In freeing his slave, in using the black man as a soldier, in federal appointments, in law enforcement, in the matter of the ballot and for a variety of reasons Grant demonstrated that democracy could break through the racial barrier. His beliefs seemed sincere enough. But in the matter of black voting, political considerations also affected his thinking. Given Reconstruction, it was impossible for him to escape the problem of race. He played a decisive role in law enforcement and in encouraging political legislation. Though little given to talk, Grant attempted to lead public opinion to support federal intervention for the protection of basic civil rights. His experience as a military man caused him to dislike the use of force and to employ it only with great reluctance.

[163] Von Bort, *General Grant and the Jews*, p. 16.

CHAPTER V

The Racial Attitudes of Rutherford B. Hayes (1877–1881)

When Rutherford B. Hayes came to the presidency in 1876 from Ohio, the race problem was waiting in all its urgency. The subject was by no means new to him. At the very beginning of his political career in 1865, he had endorsed the radical program of Reconstruction. In unemotional terms this meant having a penchant for the rights of blacks and the preservation of the political power of the Republican party, though not necessarily in that order.[1]

The Racial Focus

A college classmate and lifelong friend, Guy M. Bryan of Texas, was a little uneasy about the radical proclivities of Hayes. When the Reconstruction Acts were passed in 1867 while Hayes was a congressional representative from Ohio, the two men began a correspondence that continued long after Hayes retired from politics. Bryan turned out to be the con-

[1] R. B. Hayes to Murat Halstead, February 2, 1886, Charles R. Williams (ed.), *Diary and Letters of Rutherford B. Hayes* (Columbus, Ohio: Ohio State Archaeological and Historical Society, 1925–26), III, 16 (to be hereafter cited as Hayes, *Diary*). Rutherford B. Hayes to Manning F. Force, March 17, 1866, Rutherford B. Hayes Papers (manuscripts and typescripts in the Rutherford B. Hayes Memorial Library, Fremont, Ohio), to be hereafter cited as RBHP. Speech of RBH at Town Hall, 17th Ward, Cincinnati, Ohio, September 7, 1866, RBHP (typescript).

science of the South continually working on Hayes when the latter returned to the White House, a kind of Southern Rasputin of the Hayes Administration. To Hayes he sang but one monotonous, though effective, song: The South wanted peace and reunion above everything. Only unscrupulous persons who stirred up trouble between the superior whites and the inferior blacks prevented the healing of the wounds of war. The freedman would be better off if left to his former master. Bryan skillfully applied the argument of "kith and kin":

> Hayes let me appeal to you as one with whom I have so often broken bread, whose associations so long were identical with my own, whose blood and skin are from the same tree, . . . I beg of you to aid us in resisting the reckless manner with which the question of race is dealt with by the agitators at the South. . . .[2] I here say that Southern and Northern people are of the same blood and people and that they and the Negro are not from the same stock. . . . The South is worth cultivating by the American statesman.[3]

Bryan was attempting to reach this Northerner by constantly referring to "ethnological kinship" based upon race. At first Hayes seemed unaffected by his pleas, at least as far as official politics were concerned. On August 5, 1867, he defied the anti-black sentiment in Ohio with a radical speech, radical in the sense that he called for equality for blacks and firmness toward the South if necessary. He ran for governor of that state on an extremely unpopular platform of suffrage. He saw great merit in the radical Reconstruction plans of 1867, and he declared that the war was fought for equal rights for all people as well as for Union. He agreed that troops were necessary in the South to protect white and black Union men. Lashing out at states' rights and the rebels, Hayes said: "They wish to return to the old state of things—*an oligarchy of race and the sovereignty of states*. . . ." He rebuked the peace Democrats for opposing "every measure tending to the enfranchisement and elevation of the African race . . . laboring to keep alive

[2] Guy M. Bryan to RBH, May 18, 1867, RBHP.
[3] Guy M. Bryan to RBH, June 24, 1867, RBHP.

and inflame the prejudice of race and color, on which slavery was based."[4] The Hayes of 1867 was a far cry from what was going to be the Hayes in 1877.

Hayes challenged the alleged concept of the Democrats that ours was a white man's government and the conferral of "suffrage on the colored races—the African or Chinaman . . ." would destroy our government.[5] During his radical flirtation Hayes would also wave the bloody shirt. In response to a speech by Senator John Sherman of Ohio on the "Ku-Klux outrages" Hayes approvingly said: "It will do us a great good. You have hit the nail on the head. Nothing unites and harmonizes the Republican Party like the conviction that Democratic victories strengthen the reactionary and brutal tendencies of the rebel states."[6] But by March of 1875 the country's reaction against Radical Reconstruction had begun to set in and Hayes wrote: "I doubt the ultra measures relating to the South."[7]

Hayes had a long history of contact with and concern for Afro-Americans. As a young lawyer in Cincinnati, Ohio, he defended fugitive slaves.[8] His home was run by a large staff of black servants.[9] His staff of domestics may have been integrated because he spoke of "our German girl, Anna." Anna found a naked black infant on the steps of the Hayes residence in Cincinnati and "after a deal of trouble [Hayes] got the little thing into the Negro orphan's asylum."[10] Hayes was always aware of the presence of black people.[11]

While still in the throes of so-called radicalism, he verbally

[4] Speech of RBH at Lebanon, Ohio, August 5, 1867, as the Republican gubernatorial candidate of that state, James Quay Howard, *The Life, Public Services and Selected Speeches of Rutherford B. Hayes* (Cincinnati: R. Clark and Co., 1876), pp. 167–202.

[5] Speech of RBH at Zanesville, Ohio, August 24, 1871, RBHP (transcribed speeches).

[6] Letter, April 1, 1871, RBHP (transcript).

[7] Hayes, *Diary*, III, 269.

[8] Ibid., I, 505. Entry for December 20, 1856.

[9] Ibid., p. 541. Entry for July 19, 1859.

[10] Ibid., p. 470. Entry for October 15, 1854.

[11] RBH to Sardis Birchard, December 26, 1866, RBHP. Hayes, *Diary*, II, 247, entry in 1862. RBH to Lucy Webb Hayes, April 19, 1866, Hayes, *Diary*, III, 24. RBH to Andrew J. Chambers, September 13, 1876, RBHP. See also Hayes, *Diary*, IV, 303, 466–67, 342; III, 488, 573, 371. RBH to Lucy Webb Hayes, August 7, 1867, ibid., III, 289.

assigned the black man a very high place in American life. As Hayes saw it, the black man was not an alien, for not only had black men voted and defended the flag since colonial days, but also this was not a white man's country. Speaking as a gubernatorial candidate in Ohio in 1867 he said,

> Whether we prefer it or not, they are our countrymen, and will remain so forever. They are more than countrymen—they are citizens. . . . Our government has been called the white man's government. Not so. It is not the government of any class, or sect, or nationality, or race. It is a government founded on the consent of the governed. . . . It is not the government of the native born, or the foreign born, or the rich man, or of the poor man, or of the white man, or of the colored man—It is the government of the free man. . . .[12]

At one point, while he was President, the activities of the Southern Redeemers were causing some Florida blacks to consider emigration to Santo Domingo. Hayes, in a letter to a black preacher, disapproved: "My impression is that your people should not be hasty in deciding to leave this country. The mere difference in climate is a very serious objection to removal. . . . It is my opinion also that the evils which now affect you are likely steadily, and I hope, rapidly to demish [*sic*]. My advice is . . . against the proposed emigration."[13] While blacks should not leave the country, their current exodus from the South, Hayes felt, was a good thing in that the "better class of Southern people" would be forced to suppress the violence of the ruffian class and protect the blacks in their rights. Significantly, Hayes seemed undisturbed by the black invasion of the North: "Let the emigrants be scattered throughout the Northwest. Let them be encouraged to get homes and settled employment."[14]

Even after he left the presidency, Hayes was no less convinced that blacks should have an equal place in American life. At the Lake Mohonk, New York, Conference on blacks in

[12] Speech at Lebanon, Ohio, August 5, 1867, Howard, *The Life . . . of Rutherford B. Hayes,* p. 97.

[13] RBH to Reverend Mr. Sturks, January 14, 1878, RBHP (transcript).

[14] Hayes, *Diary,* III, 553–54.

1890, Hayes said whites were responsible for the black man's presence and his condition in America, and were "the keepers of 'our brother in black.'" At this time Hayes, personally, found the character and personal conduct of the freedmen "unpromising and deplorable. It is perhaps safe to conclude that half of the colored people of the South still lack the thrift, the education, the morality, and the religion required to make prosperous and intelligent citizenship." At the same time, Hayes was encouraged "in respect to the future of this race" and concluded that after just twenty-five years of freedom, "one third of them [could] read and write. Not a few of them are scholars of fair attainments and ability, and in the learned professions and in conspicuous employments are vindicating their title to the consideration and respect of the best of their fellowman." A personal experience which deepened Hayes's faith in the Afro-Americans' potential was his experience with black pilots, the grandsons of slaves, taking ships in and out of Bermuda's reef-studded harbor in situations where "the most solid qualities that are supposed to belong peculiarly to our Anglo-Saxon race are needed. . . ."[15]

Hayes was keenly aware of the presence of race prejudice in American life and he accused the Democrats of taking political advantage of this prejudice against blacks. Yet he was optimistic: "The Negro prejudice is rapidly wearing away, but is still strong among the Irish, and people of Irish parentage, and the ignorant and unthinking generally."[16] Hayes did not think that racial antagonism was the chief cause of conflict among men. He found differences of class, nationality, language and religion equally divisive. History taught him that "unjust and partial laws" increased and created antagonism.[17] As Presi-

[15] Isable C. Barrows (ed.), *The First Mohonk Conference on the Negro Question* (Boston: George H. Ellis, Printer, 1890), pp. 8–12, 138. Hayes was the chairman of this conference and the materials above came from his opening and closing addresses, including the story he told about being guided by black pilots when he went to Bermuda.

[16] RBH to his uncle Sardis Birchard, October 6, 1866, Hayes, *Diary*, III, 34. See also a letter to his mother, October 7, 1866, RBHP.

[17] Speech of RBH at Lebanon, Ohio, August 5, 1867, Howard, *Speeches*, p. 200.

dent, Hayes often warned of the dangers of race prejudice.[18] On his tour of the South in 1877 he suggested that "State Governments as well as the National Government should regard alike equally the rights and interests of all races of men."[19]

With great regularity, Hayes stated his belief in the equality of all men before the law.[20] He deprecated attempts to place a racial hedge around Jefferson's immortal dictum, "all men are created equal." The founding fathers did not declare all men equally beautiful, strong, or intellectual, but equal in their rights. It was foolish to limit the phrase "all men, to the men of a single race." Hayes thought that Jefferson *did* include the African in his definition of "men." Slavery was founded upon the denial of the Declaration of Independence and was the ultimate cause of the Civil War.[21]

In 1871, as he thought about retiring from the political arena, Hayes expressed a belief that after the settlement of the slavery question there were no more struggles worthy of full political commitment. He believed it impossible for any political or party revolution to unsettle the fact that all men in this country were to have equal civil and political rights.[22] It was his view that "the administration of Grant has been faithful on the great question of the rights of the colored people. . . ."[23] So frequently did the theme of equal rights appear in the speeches of Hayes that one would suspect that he thought talking would make it so. He viewed his country as "a nation composed of . . . different races . . . all of which have equal rights. . . ."[24] He told himself that he must "insist

18 Speech of RBH in Vermont, August 26, 1877, Hayes, *Diary*, III, 442, 622; ibid., IV, 295, November 28, 1886. Speech at Tilton, N.H., August 22, 1877, RBHP (transcribed speeches).

19 Speech of RBH at Lamar House, Knoxville, Tenn., RBHP (transcribed speeches).

20 RBH to Lucy Webb Hayes, April 8, 1866, in connection with the passage of the Civil Rights Bill, Hayes, *Diary*, III, 22.

21 Speech of RBH at Lebanon, Ohio, August 5, 1867, Howard, *Speeches*, pp. 168–70.

22 November 16, 1871, Hayes, *Diary*, III, 135.

23 Speech of RBH at Glendale, Ohio, September 4, 1872, Howard, *Speeches*, p. 128.

24 Speech of RBH at Nashua, N.H., August 24, 1877, RBHP (transcribed speeches). Ibid., Speeches of RBH at Manchester, N.H., August 23, 1877;

that the laws shall be enforced . . . insist that every citizen, however humble . . . be secure in his right. . . ."[25] Two months later when he wrote his first annual message he tried to convince the South of "the wisdom and justice of humane local legislation" for the education and general welfare of the freedmen, "objects . . . dear to my heart."[26] In his second message to Congress he accused the South of failing to live up to its promise to secure to all the equal protection of the laws "without distinction of color." He noted that blacks were being mistreated in South Carolina and Louisiana and asked Congress for funds to allow the Justice Department to better execute the Enforcement Act of 1871.[27]

In contrast to the patient, gentle, and mild remonstrances of the annual messages, the President's public speeches to Northern audiences, especially soldiers, condemned lawlessness in parts of the South, vigorously, righteously and indignantly. He called for public support of all civil servants who believed in sustaining black rights. Since the war had been fought for equal rights as well as union, the equal rights amendments "ought to stand."[28]

As he prepared to leave the White House Hayes knew that the race question had persisted to plague all of his efforts for reunion: "The disposition to refuse a prompt and hearty obedience to the equal rights amendments to the Constitution is all that now stands in the way of a complete obliteration of sectional lines and political contests."[29] Hayes hoped that Congress would seat no one whose election was due to the violation

---

at Jeffersonville, Ind., September 18, 1877; and at the Hall, Chattanooga, Tenn., September 20, 1877.

[25] Hayes, *Diary*, III, 499, October 21, 1877.

[26] First Annual Message, December 3, 1877, *Letters and Messages of Rutherford B. Hayes* (Washington, D.C., 1881), pp. 76–77.

[27] Ibid., pp. 120–22. Second Annual Message.

[28] Remarks of RBH at the annual reunion of the 23rd Regiment, Ohio Veterans, Youngstown, Ohio, September 17, 1879 (pamphlet in Columbia University, Butler Library, Box 846), pp. 9–11. Ibid., remarks of RBH at the Ohio Soldiers Reunion at Columbus, Ohio, August 11, 1880.

[29] Last Annual Message, December 6, 1880, *Letters and Messages of Rutherford B. Hayes*, p. 314.

of the Fifteenth Amendment. His executive duty, he said, was to prosecute the guilty.[30]

How did Hayes stand on social equality? The evidence on this point is scanty. When Hayes appointed a black, Frederick Douglass, marshal of the District of Columbia, it created something of a social crisis. According to one anonymous letter writer, some people found the selection of Douglass distasteful because the marshal acted as master of ceremonies at certain White House functions. This correspondent congratulated Hayes for serving in that capacity himself at a recent function and hoped he would continue.[31] Whether or not Hayes did act as his correspondent suggests and for what reason cannot be ascertained. But the very fact that such a letter was written illustrates the working of the idea of race in the mind of one Northerner, the very least.

In 1880, nearly fifteen years before the famed Atlanta Exposition, President Hayes made a remark that anticipated Booker T. Washington's historic pronouncement on social equality. The occasion was the twelfth anniversary of Hampton Institute where Hayes was one of the speakers. He cited the problem of a multiracial society as the most difficult facing the nation and then cast his lot with the anti-amalgamationists:

> We would not undertake to violate the laws of nature, we do not wish to change the purpose of God in making these differences of nature. We are willing to have these elements of our population *separate as the fingers are, but we require to see them united for every good work, for national defense, one, as the hand.* [Italics added.] And that good work Hampton is doing.[32]

Evidently Hayes was not one to advocate putting together what God so markedly had put asunder. He could not escape

[30] Last Annual Message, December 6, 1880, *Letters and Messages of Rutherford B. Hayes,* p. 314.

[31] This unsigned letter with the bottom part torn off, came to Hayes from Greensburg, Pa., March 19, 1877, RBHP (MSS).

[32] Speech of RBH, delivered at Virginia Hall, Hampton, Va., May 20, 1880, RBHP (transcribed speeches). Did Booker Washington ever see or hear this speech? In his own speech he said: "In all things that are purely social we can be as separate as the finger; yet one as the hand in all things essential to mutual progress. . . ." Basil Mathews, *Booker T. Washington: Educator as Interracial Interpreter* (Cambridge: Harvard University Press, 1948), Chap. 6.

the customary ambivalence in assigning the black his place in American life: biological separation but political and civil integration. As presiding officer at the first Mohonk Conference on the black question in 1890, Hayes tried to rule out any discussion of the controversial subject of social equality. He preferred to defer this question until both blacks and whites were more disposed to live by the golden rule. He said:

> What is sometimes called the social question, with its bitterness, irritations, and the ill-will which it often breeds between the children of a common father, may well be left out of associations like this until the Golden Rule, with its enlightenment and precious tendencies, has obtained a more perfect sway than it has yet found either in our own hearts or in the lives of those we are seeking to lift up.[33]

Race and Politics: Equality and the Ballot

As Congress prepared in December of 1865 to override President Johnson's plan of Reconstruction with one of its own, Congressman Hayes advocated suffrage with an educational qualification.[34] But by January 10, 1866, he was saying: "Universal suffrage is sound in principle, the radical element is right." At the same time he was not very enthusiastic about black suffrage in the District of Columbia. He thought Congress had more important business to attend to.[35] He gave no clue as to what that more important business would be. On the other hand he was preoccupied with the voting clause of the Fourteenth Amendment and told a friend: "I care nothing about the other amendments but we cannot admit the South until this Amendment is safe."[36] The voting clause, here referred to, called for the reduction of the congressional representation of any state guilty of denying any male citizen over

[33] Opening remarks of Hayes at the First Mohonk Conference on the Negro Question, Lake Mohonk, 1890. Barrows, *The First Mohonk Conference on the Negro Question*, pp. 8–12.

[34] Hayes, *Diary*, III, 7.

[35] Hayes, *Diary*, III, 13. Entry, January 10, 1866.

[36] RBH to Warner M. Bateman, January 31, 1866, RBHP (transcribed).

twenty-one years of age the right to vote. The clause did not require that blacks be given the vote but would penalize any state not allowing blacks to vote. However, at this point, Hayes may have been thinking more about the political utility of a black vote for the Republican party than he was about the blacks as such.[37] But there is no way of knowing for certain what his motives were. He seemed prepared at this point to have the South deprive the blacks of the vote as long as blacks were not counted for purposes of representation.

Congressman Hayes was not initially committed to forcing black suffrage on the South. When the Committee on Reconstruction reported, Hayes said that suffrage for blacks would not be insisted upon and a difference of opinion would be allowed.[38] He told a friend that the policy of the Republicans would be to leave the question of the ballot to the states.[39] While still a congressman, Hayes was nominated by his party to run for the governorship of his state. He resigned his seat and went home to endorse enfranchisement of blacks in the state of Ohio.

The Ballot in Ohio

Hayes displayed great courage when he ran the gauntlet of Negrophobia and campaigned for the governorship of Ohio on the platform of voting rights for blacks. An amendment to strike the word "white" from the Ohio Constitution was before the people. The Democrats declared that their purpose was to nominate "men of noble hearts, determined to release the state from the thraldom of niggerism." Hayes, on the other hand, ran on the platform of "impartial manhood suffrage," which included blacks.[40] As a matter of fact, he refused to run for governor unless an opportunity was provided for an

[37] RBH to Murat Halstead, editor of the *Cincinnati Commercial*, February 2, 1866, RBHP (photostat), Accession No. 772.

[38] RBH to Warner M. Bateman, May 15, 1866, RBHP (photostat). Found also in Hayes, *Diary*, III, 16.

[39] Hayes, *Diary*, III, 25.

[40] Howard, *Speeches*, p. 65.

honest vote on the suffrage issue.[41] While the future President was at first in favor of qualified black suffrage, whatever reservations he had about universal suffrage were not based upon race, for he wanted the ballot given to the black man in Ohio on the same basis that it was given to the white man.[42]

Hayes won the governor's chair but the black suffrage clause was defeated. In his inaugural address, he touched on the subject of civil and political equality in Ohio. He gave a summation of the battle for the elimination of race distinctions in Ohio, beginning in 1849. He said he was encouraged by the fact that though black suffrage was lately defeated, 45 per cent of the vote was cast in favor of the proposition. He also disapproved of the attempt which was afoot to repeal Ohio's initial consent to the ratification of the Fourteenth Amendment. Significantly, he defended the amendment not on the basis of the equal protection of the laws clause but on the article that limited representation to the actual voting population.[43]

In his second annual message of 1869, Governor Hayes was still pleading not only for the repeal of the voting restrictions on "citizens having a visible admixture of African blood," but also for approval of the Fifteenth Amendment. He repeated the plea in 1870.[44] While he was sincerely hoping to see the Afro-American cast his ballot, he was no less joyful when that ballot went to the Republicans. "They vote Republican almost solid," he said of Cincinnati blacks casting ballots for the first time under the new amendment.[45]

Hayes, like Grant, sincerely thought that a political millennium had come with the Fifteenth Amendment. Triumphantly he asked: "The war of races, which was so confidently predicted

[41] The secretary of state of Ohio, May 23, 1867, Hayes, *Diary*, III.

[42] Speech of RBH in Sidney, Ohio, September 4, 1867, Howard, *Speeches*, pp. 219–22.

[43] *Inaugural Address of the Governor of Ohio to the General Assembly* (Columbus: L. D. Myers and Brothers, State Printers, 1868).

[44] Howard, *Speeches*, p. 89. *Annual Message of the Governor of Ohio to the Fifty-Ninth General Assembly Session Commencing January 3, 1870* (Columbus: Columbus Printing Co., State Printers, 1870), p. 10. This was pamphlet No. 979, RBHP.

[45] Ibid., p. 94. Entry, April 4, 1870.

would follow the enfranchisement of the colored people—where was it in the election in Ohio last week?" Hayes did not doubt that the American dream had been realized or that the new citizen would "prove worthy of American citizenship."[46] By 1890, after two decades of hard experience, he had altered his opinion somewhat. Evidently the Fifteenth Amendment was a success in Ohio. It did not necessarily follow, however, that the amendment would work equally well in the South for blacks or that the federal government would insist upon its enforcement.

The Ballot on the National Scene

Hayes spoke just as emphatically in favor of black suffrage when he became President as he had as governor of Ohio. But he had far less success in coercing the recalcitrant South to implement the proposition, for more than talk and righteous indignation were required to move the Southerners. What was needed was a solid North lined up behind a courageous President willing and able to enforce the law in all its vigor. Neither condition prevailed.

Nationally, Hayes was concerned with wiping out the color line in politics, a theme he was to develop in great detail.[47] At the same time, he also wanted to remove the influence of the military in state elections.[48]. What hurt the President most, it seemed, was the way in which Southerners rode roughshod over black rights "the protection of which the people in these states [South Carolina and Louisiana in particular] have been solemnly pledged."[49] However, Hayes

[46] Speech of RBH celebrating the adoption of the Fifteenth Amendment, April 13, 1870, Howard, *Speeches*, p. 102.

[47] *Letters and Messages of Rutherford B. Hayes*, p. 13. Speech on March 5, 1877.

[48] Instructions to the Louisiana Investigation Committee, April 2, 1877, *Letters and Messages of Rutherford B. Hayes*, pp. 20–21.

[49] Hayes, *Diary*, III, 510, entry, November 12, 1878. The many references of Hayes to the racial infidelity of the South on the black problem contrast sharply with the conclusion of Logan, *The Negro in American Life and Thought*, p. 16, who said: "More important is the fact that Hayes was quite complacent about the failure of the South to live up to its part of the

never suggested a remedy for the racial maladies of the South.

One critical hour for Hayes as a racial statesman came in 1879 when the Democrats attached riders to congressional appropriation bills in a concerted and determined attempt (by the South) to repeal every last trace of federal protection of black rights at the polls. The source of the trouble was, at bottom, black rights, but the battle, according to a recent scholar, was fought on the level of congressional versus presidential prerogative.[50] If true, here is an example of how the battle for the protection of civil rights could be swallowed up by larger issues only indirectly related to it. Hayes vetoed seven consecutive money bills.[51] He was determined to maintain the integrity of executive authority as well as the political balance of power. But if the dynamics of race and politics are to be properly understood and appreciated, some attention must be given to the evolution of the Southern policy of President Hayes.

Race and Politics: 1876 and the Southern Policy

How does one account for the difference between the Hayes of 1867 and the Hayes of 1877 on the Southern or black question? In spite of the incompleteness of the record and at the risk of inconclusiveness, attention to some of the forces that played upon the President as he weighed this issue may shed light upon this problem.

The Evolution of a Southern Policy

Guy M. Bryan must now be reintroduced as spokesman (even if unofficial) of the Southern persuasion. As black voters

---

bargain." See *Letters and Messages of Rutherford B. Hayes*, p. 315. Hayes, *Diary*, III, 615, entry, July 21, 1880. Richardson, *Messages*, VII, 494, December 2, 1878.

[50] White, *The Republican Era*, pp. 35–38.

[51] Ibid., pp. 36–38. *Letters and Messages of Rutherford B. Hayes*, pp. 191–95, 180, 182–219. See also Hayes, *Diary*, III, 529–32, 534–35, 543–46, on the riders.

slowly retreated in the face of Southern night riders, Bryan inquired of his former college chum: "Rud, are we done with the Negro? Are you not satisfied by this time that he is not fit to govern himself without the government of the white man? Will the Northern people force the Negro question & social equality upon us with the view to get the exciting question up again for another canvass? Let us have peace for God sake. . . ."[52]

In his reply to Bryan, Hayes suggested that the remedy for the South's illiteracy and racial ills was not the repudiation of democratic government but the education of the ignorant electorate. The South must emulate the North and "*forget to drive* and *learn* to *lead* the ignorant masses around them. . . ."[53] Hayes did not mention race prejudice in his reply to Bryan. He apparently chose to ignore the Southern contention that the black man was disliked solely because of his ignorance and his desperate condition.

When Hayes again threw his hat into the political ring in 1875 as a gubernatorial candidate, Bryan was delighted. He told Hayes that if he took the position that the whites of the North and South were of the same "kith and kin," that the control over blacks must be returned to the South, he would be the nominee of his party for the next presidency, make a great name for himself and be regarded as a benefactor of his country.[54] In his letters, Bryan skillfully developed the theme of reunion between Northern and Southern whites under the necessities of race. Hayes was not unmoved by this political and racial call to arms. He replied to Bryan: "As to Southern affairs 'the let alone' policy seems now to be the true course. . . . The future depends largely on the moderation and good sense of Southern men . . . but I think we are one people at last for all times."[55] Such was the mood of Hayes on the eve of the election of 1876. He had tentatively accepted the

[52] Guy M. Bryan to RBH, December 19, 1874, RBHP (transcribed).
[53] RBH to Guy M. Bryan, January 2, 1875, Hayes, *Diary*, III, 262–63.
[54] Guy M. Bryan to RBH, June 24, 1875, RBHP. See also letter of Bryan to Hayes, January 8, 1875, Hayes, *Diary*, III, 262–63.
[55] RBH to Guy M. Bryan, July 27, 1875, RBHP (transcribed).

Southern position. The Southern exposure had taken effect. Only a similar persuasion of Northern origin was needed to clinch the argument, and that was not long in coming.

When the search for a suitable Republican candidate began, Senator John Sherman of Ohio cast his eyes in the direction of Spiegel Grove, the Hayes residence at Fremont; ". . . considering all things," he told a colleague, "I believe the nomination of Governor Hayes would give us more strength . . . than any other person . . . on the main question: protection for all in equal rights; and the observance of the public faith [Civil Service Reform]; he is as trustworthy as anyone named. . . ."[56] After Hayes received the nomination, Carl Schurz acted as a powerful Northern persuader. He sent Hayes lengthy suggestions for his letter of acceptance. His advice on the Southern question was particularly significant:

> You can make this *your* campaign and relieve it of all the vulnerable points of the party record. You can accomplish this by declaring that the equality of rights without distinction of color according to the Constitutional Amendments must be sacredly maintained by all lawful power of government; but that also Constitutional rights of self-government must be respected and that a policy must be of its existence, not as a nation divided into conquerors and conquered, but as a nation of equal citizens. . . .[57]

Here was an excellent example of studied and calculated political ambivalence. With respect to black rights, how could the laws be enforced while at the same time respecting local self-government? Schurz had firsthand knowledge of the indisposition of the Southerners to give blacks equal rights. His optimism in this regard is unfathomable. Hayes, in the meantime, promised to give the suggestions his "best consideration" and said:

> I now feel like saying something as to the South not essentially different from your suggestions, but I am not decided about it. I don't like the phrase, by reason of its Democratic associations, which you use—local self-government! It seems to me to smack

[56] John Sherman to A. M. Burns, January 21, 1876, RBHP (MSS).
[57] Carl Schurz to RBH, June 21, 1876, RBHP.

of the bowie-knife and revolver. Local self-government has nullified the Fifteenth Amendment in several states, and is in a fair way to nullify the Fourteenth and Thirteenth. But I do favor a policy of reconciliation, based on the observance of all parts of the Constitution—the *new* as well as the old—and, therefore, suppose you and I are substantially agreed on the topic.[58]

One can see from the preceding statements that Hayes knew what the situation was in the South. But a dilemma was soon to be faced. How could reunion, on the one hand, be reconciled with a vigorous enforcement of the amendments relating to the new status of the freedmen, on the other? Would Hayes be a "Moses" of civil liberties for a despised race or a "Joshua" of reunion? While he sincerely wanted and tried to be both, the role of Joshua appealed to him most. The possibilities of significant accomplishment were great since Hayes had committed himself to a single term long before he knew that there would be a disputed election. He would come to the presidency unhampered by the need to mend his personal political fences for the next election.[59]

By July of 1876 Hayes seemed to have been won over to that part of the Bryan position calling for leaving the South to the Redeemers: "You will see in my letter of acceptance," he assured the tireless Texan, ". . . the influence of the feelings which our friendship has tended to foster. It will cost me some support. But it is right. I shall keep cool and no doubt at the end be prepared for either event."[60] Two days later Hayes was slightly more enthusiastic: "You will be almost if not quite satisfied with my letter of acceptance—especially on the Southern situation," he told Bryan.[61] And so, long before anyone could know that there was going to be a disputed election and a so-called "bargain," Hayes had already made up his mind that his course would be one of reconciliation and reunion of Northern and Southern whites. How he would in turn get the Southerners to lay down the "bowie-knife and the re-

58 RBH to Carl Schurz, June 27, 1876, RBHP (transcribed).
59 RBH to Carl Schurz, June 27, 1876, RBHP (transcribed).
60 RBH to Guy M. Bryan, July 8, 1876, ibid.
61 Ibid., July 10, 1876.

volver," was not yet apparent. One thing is certain, the Hayes of 1867 had given way to a different Hayes in 1877.

It should come as no surprise that the letter of acceptance was no altruistic state paper, but a carefully worded sectional formula. In an artful piece of political quality and verbal ingenuity, Hayes picked his way carefully through sectional quicksand as he asked for the South the sympathy of the nation:

> Their first necessity is an intelligent and honest administration of government which will protect all classes of citizens in all their political and private rights. What the South needs most is peace, and peace depends upon the supremacy of the law. There can be no enduring peace if the Constitutional rights of any portion of the people are habitually disregarded. A division of political parties, resting merely upon distinctions of race, or upon sectional lines, is always unfortunate . . . and may be disastrous. Let me assure my countrymen of the Southern states that if I should be charged with the duty of organizing an administration, it will be one which will regard and cherish their truest interests—the interests of the white and of the colored people both, and equally; and which will put forth its best efforts in behalf of a civil policy which will wipe out forever the distinctions between North and South in this country.[62]

Here then was the promise to the South, given openly, long before any thoughts of disputed elections were in the wind. While not going into details, he promised them clean government, implying that carpetbag rule was unclean. Without using the distasteful phrase "local self-government," Hayes implicitly promised that there would be no more federal interference in Southern affairs than there was in Northern affairs.

In spite of the assurances of Hayes's acceptance letter, Schurz was uneasy about the campaign in August of 1876 because the Democrats were saying "Gov. Hayes's administration will be but a continuation of Grant's. . . ."[63] Then with pretended innocence Schurz said: "p. s. some Democrats have ascribed your letter of acceptance, part of it at least, to me. . . ."[64] The

[62] Letter of acceptance, July 18, 1876, Howard, *Speeches*, pp. 159–60.
[63] Carl Schurz to RBH, August 7, 1876, RBHP (transcribed).
[64] Carl Schurz to RBH, August 7, 1876, RBHP (transcribed).

tendency of the Democrats to identify Hayes with Grant might explain, in part, the determination of Hayes to disavow two hallmarks of the Grant Administration: a disposition to keep peace in the South with troops; and corruption in office. In any case, such an approach was ill-omened for the black man. The charge that blacks were unfit for citizenship and office-holding would make it incumbent upon any civil service reformer to acquiesce in any movement to unseat the unfit, blacks included. The real ambivalence in the Hayes position lay in his disapproval of the use of troops while at the same time declaring that the Civil War amendments had to be enforced. One month before the election, Grant's Attorney General informed Hayes of the wholesale nullification of the Fifteenth Amendment by many of the Southern states and by means not excluding murder.[65] Yet, the next day Hayes called on James G. Blaine and found that gentleman's views on the South identical with his own: "By conciliating Southern whites, on the basis of obedience to law and equal rights, he hopes we may divide the Southern whites and so protect the colored people."[66]

So the election of 1876 came with Hayes determined, should he win, not to interfere in Southern affairs in return for Southern obedience to the laws respecting black rights. At the same time, according to his mail, he was made painfully aware of Southern lawlessness. And when he thought that he had lost the election both he and his wife expressed their foremost concern for the "colored people especially . . . ," in the event of a Democratic victory.[67]

Schurz continued to advise Hayes on the black question,[68] but the clearest and best expression of the Republican approach to the blacks and the South after the election of 1876 came from a former Cabinet member of the Grant Administration, Governor J. D. Cox of Ohio. His sentiments summed up essentially what was to become official Southern policy not only

[65] Alphonso Taft to RBH, September 12, 1876, RBHP (MSS).

[66] RBHP (from a transcribed portion of Hayes, *Diary*, October 4, 1876).

[67] Hayes, *Diary*, III, 375–76, entry, November 11, 1876.

[68] Carl Schurz to RBH, December 4, 1876, RBHP (transcribed). Carl Schurz to RBH, December 5, 1875, ibid. Carl Schurz to RBH, January 25, 1877, ibid. RBH to Carl Schurz, January 29, 1877, ibid.

for the Hayes Administration but for all succeeding Republican regimes of the period under study. The plan did not call for *abandonment* but a *moderation* of black political aspiration. Cox wrote a letter to Hayes dated January 31, 1877, setting forth this view at the request of Hayes who, no doubt, was still casting about for a solution to the troublesome and seemingly everlasting black question. His letter is worthy of analysis at some length.

Cox argued that the Republican party had to take responsibility for what many thought was the mess in the South. The stark and naked truth of the matter, he argued, was that the whites of the South, most of whom were Democrats, did not want blacks to be made their political equal. Consequently, they tried to nullify the amendments by state legislation. Black voters were then naturally driven into the Republican party, falling prey to the demagogue and political adventurer from the North seeking to mislead them for political reasons. "Our mistake as a policy was in ignoring this fact," said Cox. But the blacks no longer needed protection in a separate party organization. Such separatism was "now the cause of their greatest danger." Cox reasoned somewhat erroneously that the whites of the South would recognize the political equality of the blacks if this did not threaten to continue the rule of a class with race as its distinguishing characteristic. Continuance of the color line would cause all of the Southern states to take the path of the Mississippi Redeemers of 1877. In that instance black rights would vanish. Cox announced with an air of finality that in the struggle of races, the weaker would go down.

The salvation of blacks, according to Cox, depended upon doing away with political division on the basis of race and color. Cox was thinking about the viability of the Republican party in the South, as well as the welfare of the blacks. He thought it possible to attract to the Republican party "a strong body of the best men representing the capital, the intelligence, the virtue and the revived patriotism of the old population of the South," on the basis of a promise that they would "in honorable and good faith accept and defend the . . . rights of the freedmen." Cox would get these "best men" into the party through the medium of a "carefully scrutinized" federal patronage. He failed to say how he would get blacks into the Democratic party.

What would be the role and place of blacks in this new policy? Cox's grand strategy in this regard was to "moderate the kindled ambition of the colored people to fill places which neither their experience, nor their knowledge of business or of the laws fit them, for. . . ." Black people would simply have to "recognize the fact that the American white people have now a hereditary faculty of self government." Cox was also bitten by the ethnocentric bug which held that the art of self-government was bestowed by God on the Anglo-Saxon alone. Be that as it may, Cox never once suggested that the freedmen *should not* vote. He was simply to be less prominent in office holding and political leadership in the Republican party. Cox seemed to be saying that the blacks were in too much of a hurry to get too far, too soon, and with perhaps too little: "Our fellow citizens of the African descent must recognize the necessity of having patience. . . ." Such was the way to end hostilities, to call a halt to the open political warfare among races in the South, to end an era of revolution: "Such is the picture that I have formed in my own mind of the work . . . your administration may do in the South. . . ."[69] To all this Hayes responded, "On the Southern question your views and mine are so precisely the same that if called on to write down a policy I could adopt your language."[70]

As the disputed election of 1876 neared a solution in favor of the Republicans, Hayes was impatient to play the role of a statesman of reunion. When Schurz urged him to approach national aid to education and internal improvements with caution, Hayes replied: "My anxiety to do something to promote pacification of the South is perhaps in danger of leading me too far." Schurz was afraid that big federal spending might provide more opportunities for corruption. As he saw the situa-

[69] J. D. Cox to RBH, January 31, 1877, RBHP.
[70] RBH to J. D. Cox, February 2, 1877, RBHP.

tion, most legislators could not come within one hundred miles of a railroad without being corrupted. In the meantime Hayes wondered if the healing processes of time would not be better for the South than "injudicious meddling." But he had made up his mind about the future use of troops in the racial and political unrest in the South: "There is to be an end of all that."[71]

On February 18, 1877, Hayes had a conversation with Frederick Douglass. Hayes noted in his diary that blacks approved of his views and that Douglass gave him "many useful hints about the whole subject." Hayes now seemed as much a champion of equal rights as he was a statesman of political and emotional reunion between Northern and Southern whites. "My course," he said in the privacy of his diary, "is a firm assertion and maintenance of the rights of the colored people of the South . . . coupled with a readiness to recognize all Southern people, without regard to past political conduct, who will now go with me heartily and in good faith in support of these principles."[72]

From the time of the letter of acceptance to the inaugural address, the Southern question played a larger role in Hayes's thinking. The inaugural address was much more of a racial document than was the letter of acceptance. He began by saying that the public desired "the permanent pacification of the country." Turning more specifically to the race question, Hayes continued: "With respect to the two distinct races whose peculiar relations to each other have brought upon us the deplorable complications and perplexities which exist in some states . . . ," the problem could be solved only with justice. "I am duty bound," said Hayes, "I fully am determined to protect the rights of all by every Constitutional means at the disposal of my administration. . . ." Then Hayes said exactly what Schurz had advised him to say on the Southern question. The sentence was jerked up from the briny deep of political ambivalence: "And while I am duty bound and fully determined

[71] Carl Schurz to RBH, February 2, 1877, RBHP. RBH to Carl Schurz, February 4, 1877, RBHP (transcribed). Hayes, *Diary*, III, 414, February 9, 1877.

[72] Hayes, *Diary*, III, 417, entry, February 18, 1877.

to protect the rights of all by every Constitutional means . . . I am anxious to use every legitimate influence in favor of honest and efficient local self-government, as the true resources of those states. . . ." Finally, he hoped that everyone would shed party and race prejudice and cooperate in the great work of reunion.[73]

The Southern policy of Hayes, in summary, was first to put an end to the open political warfare between the races in the South. This warfare, in addition to taking a fearful toll in physical violence and intimidation of the blacks, kept open the Civil War breach between Northern and Southern whites. Secondly, Hayes would trust the "best white people" of the South to observe the three amendments relating to black rights. Thirdly, he would build up the economic prosperity of the Southern region by education and liberal internal improvements. Finally, he would provide the South with honest local government. The last point was crucial in its implications. One way Hayes intended to achieve this goal was through the use of the federal patronage, judiciously and responsibly handled. A much more significant implication of the first point was that which called for "the moderating" of the office-holding proclivities of the blacks as succinctly stated by Cox. The leadership of the Republican party in the South was to be put into the hands of the "better class of native Southern whites" who were thought to be purer of soul than the black and white Republicans of 1867. This new native white leadership would be recruited to the party by the skillful use of the federal patronage. Never was it suggested that the black man not vote or leave the party. The new requirement was that he, because of his slavery-bred deficiencies, hand over the reins of political initiative to the superior race. The North and her politicians did not sufficiently consider the possibility that race prejudice was as much responsible for the wrath of the Southern whites against blacks as were the real and imagined deficiencies of the freedmen. How the policy would fare in actual practice remained to be seen.

[73] The Inaugural Address of President Hayes, March 4, 1877, RBHP (a printed pamphlet).

THE RECEPTION OF THE SOUTHERN POLICY

Hayes received many letters expressing an opinion on his Southern policy. More of them were in favor of his policy than were against it. One dominant theme ran through most of them: the division of the black and white vote by the creation of a new Republican party composed partially of old line Whigs of the South who would provide the nucleus of its leadership. Very few, if any, of the letters spoke of abandoning the black man; rather, they dealt with how to protect him. There were also those who saw great danger in the policy and who feared that Hayes had been unduly optimistic in trusting the Southern whites with the protection of black citizenship and in his hope that these whites would join the Republican party.

On the third of April 1877, Hayes directed that federal troops be removed from the State House of Columbia, South Carolina. Seventeen days later the same order was given for Louisiana.[74] As the period of active federal participation in Southern Reconstruction came to an end, Hayes said:

> The result of my plans is to get from those states, their governors, legislatures, press and people pledges that the Thirteenth, Fourteenth, and Fifteenth Amendments shall be faithfully observed; and that the colored people shall have rights to labor, education, and the privilege of citizenship. I am confident this is a good work. Time will tell.[75]

Hayes now thought that he could turn his attention to civil service reform.[76] To one who had shown uneasiness about what looked to some like a surrender of the North to the rebels, Hayes said: "I know how sore a trial this business is to staunch antislavery veterans like you. I expect many to condemn [me]."[77] Hayes could only hope that things would turn out

[74] Instructions of RBH to George W. McCrary, Secretary of War, April 13, 1877, RBHP (transcribed).
[75] Hayes, *Diary*, III, 430.
[76] Ibid.
[77] Hayes, *Diary*, III, 431.

all right. A few months after pulling the troops out of South Carolina and Louisiana, labor troubles elsewhere forced the President to use troops to put down disorder.[78]

Nothing seems to have reconciled blacks to the Hayes Administration as much as the appointment of Frederick Douglass as marshal of the District of Columbia.[79] Hayes himself chose to look upon the appointment of Douglass as symbolic of an intention to upgrade the blacks in the eyes of the nation.[80] Douglass caused quite a stir after a bare month in office when he made a speech in Baltimore on the state of race relations in the District of Columbia. He said that Washington represented "a most disgraceful and scandalous contradiction to the march of civilization as compared with many other parts of the country. On May 18, 1877, the *New York Times* said that Douglass had spoken the truth and that such truth had been spoken about the nation's capital many times before, "but never by a man whose skin was dark colored, and who had been appointed to office in the District."[81] There was an immediate hue and cry for Douglass' removal from office but Hayes refused to bow to these demands.

In early September of 1877, Hayes took a nineteen-day trip into the South, presumably to obtain a personal view of the results of his Southern policy. He visited Ohio, Tennessee, Kentucky, Georgia and Virginia. In spite of much in his mailbag that should have dampened his optimism, he pronounced his policy a success and was jubilant upon his return from the tour. He had been heartily received in the South, if not the Deep South, and he noted triumphantly in his diary:

[78] Ibid., pp. 400, 493. Bennett Milton Rich, *The Presidents and Civil Disorder* (Washington D.C.: Brookings Institution, 1941), pp. 72–86. RBH to Guy Bryan, May 21, 1886, RBHP (transcribed). Telegram of George McCrary, Secretary of War, to General W. S. Hancock, July 27, 1887, RBHP.

[79] Resolutions of the colored citizens of Alabama, April [1877?], RBHP. Colored citizens of Chestertown, Md., March 17, 1877, ibid.; John Hamilton to W. K. Rogers, private secretary to Hayes, March 17, 1877, ibid. Letter of M. Auge, Norristown, Pa., to RBH, March 17, 1877, ibid.

[80] Speech of RBH to A. M. E. Delegation, March 23, 1877, RBHP (transcribed speeches).

[81] Foner, *The Life and Writings of Frederick Douglass*, IV, 102.

"This country is again united! I am very happy to be able to feel that the course taken has turned out so well."[82] Throughout the tour his theme was that of reunion between Northern and Southern whites, universal adherence to the war amendments, and racial harmony. To a Northern audience he called his Southern policy "an experiment" which the failure of the last six years demanded.[83] But when he was in the late enemy territory of Georgia, he swore that his policy was *not* dictated "merely by force of special circumstances," but because he believed it right and just.[84] Hayes tried to convince the whites of the North and the blacks of the South that he had not abandoned the freedmen and that their rights could be protected without federal interference. Turning to the blacks in his Georgia audience, Hayes said:

> And now my colored friends, who have thought, or who have been told that I was turning my back upon the men whom I fought for, now listen. After thinking it over, I believe your rights and interests would be safer if this great mass of intelligent white men were left alone by the general government.

This last phrase brought cheers from the crowd, but whether by white or black was not disclosed.[85] Six months after the commencement of his policy Hayes was convinced that blacks were safer in the South without the protection of the federal bayonets which he had withdrawn.[86] Hayes chose to believe that "the white people of the South have no desire to invade the rights of the colored people. . . ."[87] In his first annual message he defended his removal of the troops from South Carolina

[82] Hayes, *Diary*, III, 443, entry, late September 1877.

[83] Speech of RBH, Friday, August 17, 1877, on the green in front of his uncle Austin Birchard's home, Fayetteville, Vt., RBHP (transcribed speeches).

[84] Address of RBH at Markham House, Atlanta, Ga., September 22, 1877, ibid.

[85] Address of RBH at Markham House, Atlanta, Ga., September 22, 1877, ibid.

[86] Speech at Markham House, Atlanta, Ga., September 22, 1877, RBHP (transcribed speeches).

[87] Speech of RBH at Nashville, Tenn., September 19, 1877, ibid. Speech at War Trace, Tenn., September 20, 1877, ibid. Address at Chattanooga, Tenn., ibid.

and Louisiana as a "much needed measure for the restitution of local self-government and the promotion of national harmony."[88]

The President's heart must surely have leaped for joy when he received a letter from Wade Hampton of South Carolina, reassuring him of local intentions to protect blacks in their rights and to coexist with Republicans. But even here Hampton reported that he was having trouble with dissident members of his own party: "My position here has been a difficult one for besides the opposition to me from political opponents I have had to meet and control that of the extreme men of my own party." If that were not enough to awaken Hayes from his optimistic stupor, a newspaper clipping which Hampton sent him should have done so. The article called Hayes's attention to the "Straight Out Democrat" who wanted no truck with blacks or Republicans, or Southern whites who fraternized with either.[89]

As soon as the midyear elections of 1878 drew near the racial volcanoes erupted. According to a black congressman from South Carolina, the whites were again resorting to violence and intimidation to prevent black political participation. Hayes did nothing but complain in his diary that color was still the hallmark of political division in South Carolina: black Republicans and white Democrats. He wrote: "The South is substantially against us, the vote is light. . . . The people of color took no part . . . the blacks, poor, ignorant, and timid can't stand alone against the whites. The better elements of the South [in whom Hayes had placed so much faith] were not organized. . . ."[90] Only a division of the whites would improve the situation but Hayes had no remedy and seemed reconciled to let nature take its course.[91] Hayes had further cause for dejection when he received a petition from thirty blacks in Mississippi who wanted financial assistance to emigrate to Kansas to escape oppres-

[88] December 3, 1877, Richardson, *Messages*, VII, 459.
[89] Letter of Wade Hampton to RBH, March 25, 1877, RBHP.
[90] Hayes, *Diary*, III, 501–02, entry, November 6, 1878.
[91] Ibid., III, 509, entry, October 5, 1878.

sion.[92] Hayes did nothing but record the sorry situation in the South in his diary.[93]

Post-Mortem on the Southern Policy

Although he was aware of its shortcomings, even after he left the White House Hayes never doubted the underlying wisdom of his Southern policy and that by it he had allayed sectional and racial bitterness in the face of strenuous opposition from both political parties.[94] Contemporaries were more doubtful. A leading radical Republican, W. E. Chandler, felt that Hayes had abandoned the Southern Republican politician and the blacks to the mercy of the Redeemers.[95] Frederick Douglass was grateful to the man who had given him the highest office held by a black in the federal government up to that time, but later accused Hayes of making a virtue out of necessity.[96] Others, reflecting on the past, pronounced the Hayes policy a failure.[97]

Historians have also had their views on the Hayes policy. John W. Burgess said that Hayes's biggest struggle with himself concerned the question of whether he was deserting the black man with his Southern policy.[98] Charles Beard contended that "President Hayes could not strike out boldly had he desired to do so," because he had to deal with a Democratic House for four years and a Democratic Senate for two years.[99] On the other hand there is no evidence to suggest that Hayes showed

[92] Philip Little to RBH, October 13, 1878, RBHP.
[93] Hayes, *Diary*, III, 505, entry, October 26, 1878.
[94] RBH to Guy M. Bryan, February 2, 1882, RBHP (transcribed).
[95] Frederick Douglass to RBH, July 1881, RBHP, Foner (ed.), *The Life and Writings of Frederick Douglass*, IV, 417–18.
[96] W. E. Chandler on the Hayes Policy, December 27, 1877, copy of newspaper clipping in RBH Memorial Library, Fremont, Ohio.
[97] A. M. Middlebrook, Pine Bluff, Ark., to Benjamin Harrison, July 16, 1888, Benjamin Harrison Papers (manuscripts in the Library of Congress), Vol. 34, No. 7268–71. John E. Bryant to Benjamin Harrison [1889], ibid. Vol. 64, No. 15809–18, ibid., No. 14549. George F. Hoar, *Autobiography of Seventy Years*, II, 7, 13–14.
[98] John W. Burgess, *The Administration of President Hayes* (New York: Charles Scribner's Sons, 1916), p. 90.
[99] Charles Beard, *The Presidents in American History*, p. 82.

any inclination to enforce the laws already passed with anything other than verbal vigor.

Rayford Logan has judged President Hayes rather harshly, accusing him of abandoning the blacks, of complacency in the face of the failure of the South to live up to its part of the alleged "bargain" in the Compromise of 1876, and of aiding and abetting the liquidation of blacks from politics by suggesting qualified suffrage based on education.[100] Yet, all but three of the Southern states had fallen to the white Redeemers before Hayes took office. While the net result of the Hayes policy was disfranchisement of the blacks, it was fully ten years after Hayes left office that the Redeemers felt sufficiently strong enough to consummate their victory. The failure of Hayes to enforce the laws in regard to civil rights should not be construed as complacency or apathy on his part. He certainly was concerned about national impotence in this area, however helpless to correct the situation he may have felt. Logan interpreted Hayes's sincere concern for honest and efficient government in the South as an indication of his "approval of the curtailment of the rights of Negroes by the resurgent South." However, Hayes did not suggest education as a means of keeping the blacks out of politics but as the vehicle by which the blacks could ultimately attain and retain full citizenship.

Like most of the Presidents of this period Hayes was either afraid or unwilling to enforce the laws in regard to the civil rights of blacks. His desire for white conciliation and his virtuous penchant for reform made him unduly optimistic about the likelihood of the Southern whites protecting blacks' rights. What Professor Rubin has found to be true of Hayes during his tenure with the philanthropic Slater Education Fund might well apply to his presidency: He was unduly optimistic in the face of the repeated onslaughts of Southern white supremacy which sought relentlessly during this period to push the blacks into political oblivion.[101] On the other hand, his awareness of the lack of

[100] Rayford Logan, *The Negro in American Life and Thought,* pp. 3, 16, 17, 29.

[101] Louis D. Rubin, Jr., *Teach the Freeman: The Correspondence of Rutherford B. Hayes and the Slater Fund for Negro Education, 1881–1887* (Baton Rouge: Louisiana State University Press, 1959), I, xliv.

education among blacks might have dampened his faith in the success of a vigorous enforcement of legislative solutions.

Education and the Solution of the Race Problem

Like so many of his contemporaries, Hayes had an unbounded faith in the efficacy of education to equip the black man to protect his citizenship, to be the indispensable complement of universal suffrage, and to induce the whites of the South to obey the law and the Constitution in regard to the rights of blacks.[102] About a year after he left the presidency Hayes was made chairman of the board of the Slater Fund, a trust set up by a New England philanthropist to further the cause of education for blacks. He devoted the remainder of his life to the education and the "elevation" of the black race. As the Slater trustees saw it, their biggest job was to sell the *cause* of black education to a reluctant South. Hayes insisted that the general agent for the fund be a Southerner and that the education of blacks be done mainly by Southerners.[103] There were no blacks on the Slater Fund board.[104]

Many thought that education in industrial and manual training was best for the freedmen. They were sincerely impressed with the chastening moral and character-building qualities of manual training. And if the blacks lacked many things, according to whites, they needed nothing so badly as they needed character and morality. The Slater Fund, by a judicious distribution of money, encouraged a manual training education for the freedmen. However, Hayes advocated manual training for black and white alike.[105] Apparently Hayes approved of

[102] Hayes, *Diary*, III, 482, 619–21; IV, 272, 467–68.

[103] RBH to J. L. M. Curry, July 15, 1882, Rubin, *Teach the Freeman*, I, 50, ibid. July 25, 1882, I, 46, ibid. July 8, 1882, I, 48, ibid.

[104] RBH to Daniel Coit Gilman, October 10, 1890, *Teach the Freeman*, II, 144–45, 53–55.

[105] Rubin, *Teach the Freeman*, I, 92, 102, 119, 151–52; II, 74–75. Hayes, *Diary*, III, 482; IV, 270, 310, 347, 306, 312. James M. Gregory (colored), professor of Latin, Howard University, to Chief Justice Morrison R. Waite, July 9, 1884, RBHP.

separate but equal educational facilities in the South. In this connection he said to Guy M. Bryan: "I, of course, don't believe in forcing whites and blacks together. But both classes should be fully provided for."[106]

Being an advocate of the cultural improvement of blacks was not without its incidents. Hayes once alluded to the "ignorance, paganism and voodooism" supposedly existing among Southern blacks and drew a sharp rebuke from a resident of Little Rock, Arkansas.[107] Hayes stirred up even more of a hornet's nest when he told students at a Johns Hopkins commencement that the Slater Fund was willing to finance the education of young capable blacks with talent in literature and the arts, but "hitherto their chief and almost only gift has been that of oratory."[108] There were those who came immediately to the defense of black capacity and Hayes was swamped with candidates for free schooling who had aptitude for more than loquacity, including a budding young black scholar at Harvard, W. E. B. Du Bois.[109] Hayes wanted to know from several candidates whether or not their parents were of "full African blood." Hayes wished to see what the blacks could do, unaided by what was called "white blood." One young man replied: "My father nor my mother were of pure African blood. My father was of a gingerbread color while my mother is a bright mulatto and I am also a mulatto."[110] Said Hayes of another candidate: "He is coal black, of true African blood. As we say of Jerseys, 'he can be registered.' "[111] Du Bois explained his genealogy to Hayes: "I omitted stating that I am in blood, about one half or more Negro and the rest French and Dutch."[112] Du Bois's

[106] RBH to Guy M. Bryan, January 2, 1875, Hayes, *Diary*, III, 262–63.
[107] John C. Cherry to RBH, June 7, 1890, Rubin, *Teach the Freeman*, II, 113–17.
[108] November 1, 1890, RBHP (transcribed speeches).
[109] Hugh Brown to RBH, November 3, 1890, Rubin, *Teach the Freeman*, II, 153–55; Brown had two candidates. W. E. B. Du Bois to RBH, November 4, 1890, ibid., II, 158–59. James P. Slade, Superintendent of Schools, East Saint Louis, Ill., to RBH, March 18, 1891, with a candidate in music, ibid., II, 191.
[110] Henry C. Brown to RBH, November 11, 1890, ibid., II, 162.
[111] RBH to A. G. Haygood, October 23, 1877, ibid., I, 218–21.
[112] W. E. B. Du Bois to RBH, April 19, [1890–91?], ibid., II, 192. Harvard Professor N. S. Shaler to RBH, March 2, 1891, ibid., II, 190. Shaler gave Du Bois a good recommendation, including a rundown on his blood make-up.

initial request for funds was refused, whereupon he wrote Hayes a rather strong letter accusing him of bad faith and denouncing the concept of industrial education and theological education for blacks.[113] Eventually, Du Bois was given a stipend of $350 and a loan of $350 more from the Slater Fund to continue his studies in Europe, and when Hayes died in 1893 Du Bois said a good word in his behalf.[114]

Hayes was of the opinion that the educated black would be better prepared to contend for his rights against the whites. He optimistically hoped that if the blacks could be made more acceptable in the Southern Caucasian's sight, short of turning him white, that somehow the whites would relent in their prejudices and give the black man an equal chance. Unfortunately, such was too often not the case. Even so, Hayes hoped that a similar educational transformation would even bring the American Indian closer to assimilation.

Lo, The Poor Indian: His Case, Its Solution

Indian policy from Hayes to Roosevelt was essentially a continuation of what was begun by Grant in 1869, with the exception perhaps that the pace at which the Indian was separated from his land gained momentum and greater efforts were made to civilize him. "You all know who Lo is," the President once jested in a speech. "I mean Lo, the poor Indian."[115]

Hayes held that irrespective of the "character and savage propensities" of the Indians, they deserved the sympathy and justice of the country.[116] He gave the whites a large share of responsibility for the injustices suffered by the Indians.[117]

113 W. E. B. Du Bois to RBH, May 25, 1891, Rubin, *Teach the Freeman*, II, 203–05.

114 W. E. B. Du Bois to RBH, May 25, 1891, Rubin, *Teach the Freeman*, II, 247, 251, 255. W. E. B. Du Bois to Daniel C. Gilman, 1893, ibid., II, 281. Hayes, *Diary*, V, 75–76.

115 Speech of RBH at the Reunion of the 23rd Ohio Veterans, September 1, 1880, RBHP (transcribed speeches).

116 First Annual Message of RBH, December 3, 1877, *Letters and Messages of Rutherford B. Hayes*, p. 94.

117 Hayes, *Diary*, III, 489, entry, July 1, 1878.

On the other hand he praised Custer and remarked that "in case war with the Indians could not be avoided, it should be made short, sharp, and decisive as possible."[118] Still, he believed in the capacity of the Indian for civilization and wanted him educated. This much we owed, according to Hayes, to the "original inhabitants of the land," even though "it may be impossible to raise them fully up to the level of the white population of the United States."[119] Hayes looked forward to "the gradual merging of our Indian population in the great body of American citizenship."[120]

As he prepared to leave the presidency Hayes recommended a four-point program for the Indians. They were to be prepared for citizenship by general and industrial education. In this connection Indian boys and girls were actually educated at the black Hampton Institute during Hayes's Administration.[121] Next, the Indians were to be given land individually. The surplus lands would then be sold and the money used for the benefit of the Indians. Finally, the Indian should be made a full-fledged citizen of the United States.[122] This was essentially the Grant policy and eventually became the highly praised Dawes Act of 1887. But the final racial challenge for President Hayes was yet to come—from Asia.

International Implications of Race: Immigration and Chinese Exclusion

On March 1, 1879, President Hayes vetoed a bill to exclude immigrant Chinese from the United States. This step was not taken in total ignorance of the feelings of the American people. As so often in American history, the public was split on the

[118] Speech of RBH at an anniversary of the Wyoming Battle and Massacre, July 3, 1878, RBHP (transcribed speeches).

[119] Annual Message of RBH, December 6, 1880, *Letters and Messages of Rutherford B. Hayes*, p. 336.

[120] Ibid., p. 340.

[121] Ibid., pp. 279, 339. The success of this initial experiment led to the establishment of a large Indian school at Carlisle, Pa. See letter of W. T. Sherman to Captain R. Pratt, March 5, 1880, RBHP.

[122] Message of RBH to the Senate, on the Ponca Indians, February 1, 1881, *Letters and Messages of Rutherford B. Hayes*, p. 339.

issue. A reading of the President's incoming mail on this subject makes one wonder whether the President vetoed the bill because of his mail or in spite of it. In a certain sense the Chinese question was to the West Coast what the Negro question was to the South. In each instance the racial arguments were of similar pattern and nature. No better illustration of the idea of race at work in political and social thought could be easily obtained than that given by the President's mailbag on the question of the "heathen Chinese," as he was often called in those days.

Those who were in favor of excluding the Chinese advanced a variety of reasons. There were some who wanted Hayes to be against the Chinese because the majority of the people on the West Coast was thought to be against them.[123] Others saw the Chinese as a threat to American labor.[124] But there was a substantial residue of purists whose letters dripped with Sinophobia. One man foresaw an unending flow of Chinese and sounded the alarm: "Their shaved heads are already seen on the peaks of the Rocky Mountains. They look down on the prairies and plains which stretch out to the rising sun."[125] As the Chinese Exclusion Bill neared the executive desk for decision, the letters from the Pacific Slope grew more desperate. One United States senator damned the Chinese roundly: "These people . . . are an indigestible element in our midst, a cold pebble in the public stomach which cannot be digested. . . ."[126]

But there were others who, for a number of reasons, had a good word to say for the Chinese. Employers found their labor cheap

[123] Murray Davis, San Francisco, June 19, 1876, RBHP.

[124] W. J. W. Hubbell to RBH, December 26, 1877, RBHP. Dennis O'Neil, Oakland, Calif., to RBH, March 6, 1878, RBHP. Robert Kirk, San Francisco, to RBH, February 12, 1879, RBHP. John H. Kinkead, governor of Nevada, to RBH, February 28, 1879, RBHP.

[125] W. J. W. Hubbell to RBH, December 26, 1877, and February 26, 1878, RBHP.

[126] Letter and newspaper clipping of George Morrison to Mr. W. K. Rogers (private secretary to Hayes), February 26, 1879, RBHP. Telegram of Aug C. Kennly to RBH, February 27, 1879, for the Astoria, Oregon, Chamber of Commerce, RBHP. Telegram of William Irvin, governor of California, to RBH, February 27, 1879, 9:15 P.M., at the request of the San Francisco Chamber of Commerce, RBHP.

and dependable.[127] Henry Ward Beecher thought that the competition of Chinese labor was a good thing and would check the "progress of socialism among our laboring population. . . ."[128] Even the poet Joaquin Miller came to the defense of the Chinese.[129] To whom would Hayes listen? There were idealists like George William Curtis who felt that passage of the bill would constitute a breach of the national faith.[130]

Hayes was aware of the contents of his mailbag as sampled above. But he was skeptical about the information it contained: "An ocean of facts pours upon us," he complained to the Reverend Mr. Beecher, "alleged facts—facts indicating that this Chinese immigration is in reality a labor invasion. . . . Is there an immigration without wives and mothers?"[131] Skeptical though he may have been, he was leaning in favor of those who saw Chinese immigration as a threat to American labor.

The question may now be asked: Did race play a part in the presidential veto of the Chinese exclusion bill? When the House and Senate passed the bill Hayes had observed:

> I am satisfied the present Chinese labor invasion (It is not in any proper sense immigration. Women and children do not come) is pernicious and should be discouraged. Our experience in dealing with the weaker races—the Negroes and the Indians, for example—is not encouraging. We shall oppress the Chinaman, and their presence will make hoodlums or vagabonds of their oppressors. I therefore would consider with favor suitable measures to discourage the Chinese from coming to our shores.[132]

The President, mindful of the sad experience with the black man and the Indian, saw no cause for optimism regarding America's reception of additional alien races. Again, he seemed

127 A. Schell, Stanislaus County, Knights Ferry, California, to RBH, December 12, 18, 1877, RBHP. James C. G. Kennedy, private promoter of Chinese immigration, to RBH, December 18, 1877, January 15, 1878, RBHP.

128 Henry Ward Beecher to RBH, February 26, 1879.

129 Letter, February 26, 1879, RBHP.

130 Letter, February 22, 1879, RBHP.

131 RBH to Henry Ward Beecher, March 1, 1879, RBHP. This letter was written on the same day that Hayes vetoed the bill.

132 Hayes, *Diary*, III, 522, entry, February 20, 1879.

affected not so much by his own views as by what he thought were the racial sensitivities of the American public. Yet, in this case, the President put the matter of national integrity above the racial consciousness of the public: "I must carefully examine it," he said about the bill. "If it violates the national faith, I must decline to approve it." Three days later he concluded that the Chinese exclusion bill did violate the 1868 Burlingame Treaty of commercial relations with China and he refused to sign it. Among other things, the two countries agreed in the treaty that there would be no restriction on immigration between themselves. He contended that the Chinese had been coming to this country and had complaints lodged against them some twenty years prior to the Burlingame Treaty. Still we negotiated it. Having committed ourselves, Hayes declared, the treaty could not be disregarded.[133] But while defying significant public opinion on the one hand, on the other he made it crystal-clear that he was in sympathy with the movement for Chinese exclusion: "Though we are in sympathy with its purposes," he said, temporarily at least, diplomatic considerations and national honor had to take precedence over matters of race.

Significantly, in the veto message, Hayes carefully pointed out that after ten years of Chinese immigration the Chinese were not melting down in the racial pot: "It may be necessary," he speculated, "in the light of this apparent unassimilableness of the Chinese that this section of the Burlingame Treaty be mutually reconsidered . . . and . . . replaced by more careful methods, securing the Chinese and ourselves against a larger and more rapid infusion of *this foreign race* [italics added] than our system of industry and society can take up and assimilate with ease and safety."[134] Like Theodore Roosevelt who came after him, Hayes was sympathetic with the desire of the Californians to keep out the Chinese. He only criticized the high-handed and arrogant methods of going about this. After all, he reasoned, the Chinese were an ancient, "polite and sensitive people, distinguished by a high sense of national pride." Clearly

[133] Ibid., pp. 522–24, entry, February 23, 1879.
[134] *Letters and Messages of Rutherford B. Hayes*, pp. 159–64.

then, the situation called for more racial diplomacy in obtaining a mutual abrogation of the treaty.

How did the public receive the veto? The President was hailed as a hero, at least in the East. He himself gave the best summation of the public reaction to the veto: "The veto of the anti-Chinese Bill is generally approved east of the Rocky Mountains, and bitterly denounced west of the mountains. I was burned in effigy in one town!"[135] But perhaps one of the best defenses for this veto came from a fourteen-year-old schoolgirl from Plainville, Illinois, who had been given the subject of Chinese exclusion for a theme by her teacher. Most appropriately her essay began: "This is a free country. Its doors are open to all. . . ." In conclusion she said:

> Since writing my essay the President has vetoed the bill before Congress. I am glad to see that he is just, clear headed, far seeing and thinks as I do: that if John Chinaman wants to come here and work for twenty-five cents, and eat our rats and mice besides, why let him come![136]

The veto by no means shut off debate on the Chinese question. Oddly enough there are few surviving anti-Chinese letters in the Hayes Papers denouncing the veto.[137] Hayes made a trip to California in 1880 and stated that domestic difficulties would work out "if the Anglo-Saxon race will stand on that great principle of equal rights to all men. . . ."[138] Chinese exclusion was not destined to reach a successful conclusion until the Arthur Administration.

What final observations can be made about Hayes? He saw blacks and Indians most certainly as "weaker" though not necessarily inferior races. He was definitely conscious of race difference. But still he looked to the eventual integration of blacks and Indians into American life. He did not appear to want to give the same privilege to the Chinese.

[135] Hayes, *Diary*, III, 526, entry, February 28, 1879 [this letter is obviously misdated].

[136] Little Nellie G. Miller to RBH, March 16, 1879, RBHP.

[137] A few such letters came from John Doyle, Philadelphia and Santa Barbara, March 2, 1879, and Reverend John W. Hough, California, June 10, 1879, RBHP.

[138] Speech, September 22, 1880, RBHP (transcribed speeches).

He preferred to leave social equality, a necessary condition for legal race mixing, to time and natural inclination. Since this was a subject to stir the passions, Hayes said that the subject of social equality was better left alone until both races learned to live by the golden rule. Nevertheless, in a rare reference or two, Hayes intimated a dislike of forced integration. He also gave the impression that biologically he preferred to leave racially sundered what God and nature had not put together. Yet there were times when he demonstrated in his thoughts and actions that democracy could ignore the color line.

While Hayes was by no means immune to political motivation, little opportunism can be detected in his basic outlook on race. On the other hand, it is difficult to reconcile the obvious change in his attitude toward the South between the time he was a radical (on black rights) gubernatorial candidate in Ohio in 1867 and the time when his name was prominently mentioned for the presidential nomination. It may be that his changed attitude toward the South represented a sincere disenchantment with Reconstruction.

The idea that Hayes personally abandoned the blacks for Southern support cannot be proved. His big error, if one wishes to call it that, was that he trusted the South to keep its promise to protect black rights, in the absence of federal interference. That there was an explicit agreement to this effect seems improbable, because Hayes had already determined to make this approach long before anyone could possibly have known that the election of 1876 would be disputed. He had become disenchanted with Reconstruction as early as 1875. More than this, a reading of the Hayes correspondence disposes one to believe that at least some of those Southern Whigs were in earnest when they made the proffer of protection for the blacks. What really happened, it appears, was that the better class of whites, the so-called natural leaders of the South, made a promise which was not really within their power to keep. As things turned out, it seems that the promise was made without the consultation or approval of the "red-necked" and unwashed constituency or *its* leaders. Ironically it was the rise of Southern democracy, its roots dug deep into the bedrock of Negrophobia, that constituted the high tide of white supremacy which in the 1890s inundated Whig, Bourbon, and black alike.

As President, the problem of race was ever before Hayes. He had been in the White House only a short time when matters of race threatened to dominate his thinking. For the most part, he led a positive public opinion in favor of blacks and Indians. He tended to follow the people on the matter of the Chinese, in spite of his veto of the Chinese Exclusion Bill. His determination to bring about a reunion between Northern and Southern whites seemed to paralyze his obligation to enforce the laws in the face of an ever recalcitrant South. Hayes was more disposed to use persuasion. It may be that Hayes was impressed by the advice of those who told him that in any contest between the African and the Anglo-Saxon, the African was destined to be defeated. The seeming futility of further efforts may have deterred him from trying to enforce the law in a stubbornly unwilling section. Had not President Grant already tried as much, and failed?

CHAPTER VI

The Racial Attitudes of James A. Garfield (1881), Chester A. Arthur (1881–1885) and Grover Cleveland (1885–1889; 1893–1897)

Between Hayes and Harrison (1877–1889), three Presidents occupied the White House. Garfield's tenure of office was so brief (six months, 1881) that he had little or no chance to show how presidential responsibility would affect his earlier views. For his successor, Chester A. Arthur (1881–1885), there is a notable paucity of printed and manuscript material. Cleveland (1885–1889), had little to say on matters of race. Thus the trio of Presidents can be considered conveniently together.

Garfield

James A. Garfield, the man who succeeded Hayes (in 1881), and whose short presidency was ended by an assassin's bullet, entertained ideas of racial superiority. Using such terms as "Anglo-Saxon liberties" and "Anglo-Saxon mind,"[1] he thought that the American soul was unconsciously affected by the "great deeds of the Anglo-Saxon race, from Agincourt to Bunker Hill."[2]

[1] Argument delivered before the United States Supreme Court, December 1866, in the celebrated Ex Parte Milligan Case, *Great Speeches of James Abram Garfield. . . .* (St. Louis: John Burns, 1881), p. 439. (Hereafter cited as *Great Speeches of Garfield.*)

[2] An oration at the Arlington Cemetery, May 30, 1868, Burke A. Hinsdale, *The Works of James A. Garfield* (Boston: James R. Osgood and Co., 1882, 1883), II, 358. To be hereafter cited as Garfield, *Works.*

He opposed annexation of territory in the tropics on racial grounds. He hoped that a treaty of commercial relations would make the inclusion of the Hawaiian Islands in the American body politic unnecessary. He was wary of any thought of union with Mexico or the islands of the West Indies because

> both . . . are inhabited by people of the Latin races strangely degenerated by their mixture with native races—a population and a territory that I earnestly hope may never be made an integral part of the United States.

If he were given the approval of the entire world plus ten million dollars in gold to annex Cuba, he would refuse to take it. The future of the great Anglo-Saxon makers of civilization lay in the Temperate Zone. The people and the government would be weakened by any flight of the Anglo-Saxon to the tropics.[3]

Garfield spoke of the historic enjoyment of freedom from oppression experienced by the "Anglo-Saxon race."[4] The death of a German-born congressman from Texas provided an occasion to recall "the ancient home, the real fatherland of our race . . . the ancient forests of Germany."[5] During a presidential speech to five hundred Germans assembled in his home town of Mentor, Ohio, his mind naturally recalled the times "when the ruddy, strong, yellow haired, the blue-eyed Saxon came, [and] . . . planted the principle of Teutonic liberty in England."[6]

When the subject of the intermixture of ethnically diverse Caucasians was at issue, Garfield believed in the principle of "hybrid vigor." The conglomerate tendencies of the various races of Europe which made up America were desirable: "Like any other alloy of metals, it makes a stronger result than any of the parts alone. We are better for the mixture."[7] He was not

[3] Speech of James A. Garfield in the House of Representatives, on the Hawaiian Islands, April 6, 1876, Garfield, *Works,* II, 320–21.

[4] When addressing the Ohio Education Association, Cleveland, Ohio, July 11, 1878, Garfield, *Works,* II, 576.

[5] James A. Garfield's memorium on the death of Gustave Schliecher, February 17, 1879, Garfield, *Works,* II, 633.

[6] Speech of James A. Garfield, October 16, 1880, Mentor, Ohio, *Great Speeches of Garfield,* p. 402.

[7] Speech of James A. Garfield, October 16, 1880, Mentor, Ohio, *Great Speeches of Garfield,* p. 403.

equally disposed to extend this hypothesis to the native peoples of Hawaii, Mexico, and the West Indies.

Garfield recognized the reality of race in American life. He recalled the initial dualism of American democracy, the planting of freedom at Plymouth and the seeds of slavery at Jamestown. Slavery had caused the Civil War. Every aspect of the race problem fairly bristled "with new, difficult, and dangerous questions." Like many post-Civil War Northerners of his day he sympathized with the Southerners and the problem of race. The South was a section called upon by the war "to confront the . . . problem of two races, one just relieved from centuries of slavery, and the other a cultivated, brave, proud, imperious race—the two now to be brought together on terms of equality before the law."[8] During the campaign of 1880, Garfield told some 250 assembled blacks that solving the race problem "on the basis of broad justice and equal rights to all" was the most difficult question the nation ever had to face. The presence of the blacks in America presented a tremendous trial of the faith of the American people and the strength of their institutions.[9]

Garfield was not always so disposed to pity the South. Initially he held the usual Midwestern antislavery proclivities. As a young man he debated with himself whether to go to a Southern or an Eastern school. He preferred to go East but then "necessity will sometimes lay its iron hand upon the proudest resolves."[10] He was amazed at the rapidity with which Northerners could be brought to approve of slavery after a trip South and a taste of Southern hospitality. When the war came, Garfield, like many other Northerners, was more concerned about saving the Union than about slavery. Only the exigencies of the war brought about the abolition of slavery. "The black phantom," as he was wont to call the "peculiar institution," was like a

[8] Speech of James A. Garfield in the House of Representatives, "On the Democratic Party," August 4, 1876, Garfield, *Works*, II, 358.

[9] Speech of James A. Garfield on "The Future of the Colored Man," delivered before 250 colored people, October 25, 1880, George P. Edgar, *Gems of the Campaign of 1880: By General Grant and Garfield* (Jersey City, N.J.: Lincoln Associates, 1881), p. 76.

[10] He eventually went to an Eastern school. C. E. Fuller, *Reminiscences of James A. Garfield* (Cincinnati: Stoddard Publishing Co., 1887), pp. 114, 124, 129, 270.

ghost "that would not be laid" to rest.[11] "Slowly," he said about the black man "the nation yielded its wicked and stubborn prejudices against him, till at last blue coats cover more than one hundred thousand swarthy breasts. . . ."[12]

On occasion Garfield was surprisingly frank on matters of race. In a campaign speech to blacks in 1880, disenchantment if not outright impatience with the black man was clearly evident. Slavery had not been abolished for the sake of blacks alone but also "because it was dangerous to the peace and prosperity of the white race and to the stability of the Republic. . . ." He insinuated that the Southerners needed to be pitied more than the ex-slave. He contended that neither the Fourteenth Amendment nor the abolition of slavery solved the race problem. Furthermore, the absence of virtue and intelligence in the black man may have made his freedom a curse rather than a blessing. Garfield was anxious that the black man cease to think of himself as a ward of the federal government. He admonished the ex-slave to stand on his own two feet and pull himself up by his own efforts: "Permit no man to praise you because you are black, nor wrong you because you are black."

Some indication of how Garfield would approach the black problem once he reached the presidency can be obtained from this advice to freedmen:

> All that liberty can do for you is to give you an equal chance, within the limitations of the Constitution, and by the exercise of its proper powers. It is the purpose of the best men of this Continent to give you this equal chance and nothing more.

This was not a particularly heart-warming thought, but had the black man been given an equal chance there would have been less likelihood of his complaining. Garfield was happy that some blacks had been elected to Congress. He let it be known in no uncertain terms that if elected he was not necessarily going to champion the Afro-American's cause or be a

[11] Garfield's speech on the confiscation of rebel property, delivered in the House of Representatives, January 28, 1864, Garfield, *Works*, I, 12.

[12] Speech on calling out the national forces, delivered in the House of Representatives, June 25, 1864, ibid., I, 27–28; oration at Arlington, May 30, 1868, ibid., I, 324.

black "Moses." He would not raise any false hopes in "swarthy breasts," though those bosoms might have been covered with Union blue:

> I will not affect to be anymore your friend than thousands of others. I do not even pretend to be particularly your friend but only your friend with all other just men. On that basis and within those limitations whatever can justly or fairly be done to assure you an equal opportunity it will always be my pleasure to do.

Some might consider it strange that a Republican candidate for President should go out of his way to let the Afro-American know that as President he would not be the black man's "Lord Protector." Others might also think it odd that Garfield would labor to disabuse the black man of the idea that the Civil War was fought for his benefit or for his benefit alone.[13] He had not always felt this way. Just prior to the so-called radical plan of Reconstruction, he rehearsed the entire story of Northern prejudice against the blacks as reflected in the shabby treatment of the black soldier in the Union army. He insisted then that the preservation of the party and the future of the Republic were "inseparably bound up with the rights of the black man" and that justice to all had to be the *sine qua non* of Reconstruction.[14]

Not only was Garfield aware of the presence of blacks in American life, but after the war he verbally committed himself to full equality before the law for the black American. He said: "There ought to be no Pariahs . . . [in America]."[15] However, this noble resolve was chilled by the icy breath of political compromise and choked by "the iron hand of necessity." Although he did not think it went far enough in giving the black man the vote, Garfield approved the Fourteenth Amend-

[13] The preceding paragraphs all relate to Garfield's speech to freedmen, October 25, 1880, Mentor, Ohio, as previously cited in George P. Edgar, *Gems of the Campaign of 1880*, pp. 78–79.

[14] Speech, February 12, 1867, Garfield, *Works*, I, 254. He forgot during this speech that he himself had agreed, against radical wishes, to a compromise on the issue of equal pay for black soldiers on the grounds that the compromise was the best that could be obtained under the circumstances. See Smith, I, 368–69, June 1864.

[15] Garfield's speech of July 4, 1865, Garfield, *Works*, I, 87.

ment because he thought it was the best that could be achieved under the circumstances. Even his insistence upon the right of the blacks to vote was tempered by the phrase "so soon as they [the freedmen] are worthy . . . [and] qualified by intelligence to exercise it."[16]

By 1871, Garfield had begun to back away from the handiwork of so-called Radical Reconstruction. He supported a bill to enforce the equal protection of the laws clause of the Fourteenth Amendment, the KKK Act, but refused to sanction the suspension of habeas corpus and the declaration of martial law. As President Grant struggled with Southern recalcitrance on the race question, Garfield expressed grave doubts about the Fourteenth and Fifteenth Amendments. They gave Congress too much power over the states. Garfield doubted that Congress could punish citizens of the United States for violating state laws. If it were true, he reasoned, the administration of justice under state law would be no more. With reference to the Ku-Klux Klan Act of 1871, Garfield exclaimed: "I give it my cheerful support . . . but when we provide by Congressional enactment to punish *mere* [italics added] violation of a state law, we pass the line of Constitutional authority."[17] Nine years later, when he had accepted the nomination for the presidency, he wrung yet another drop from the bloody shirt, contending that the wounds of the war could never completely heal until every citizen irrespective of color or condition was secure in his "political and civil rights guaranteed by the Constitution and the laws."[18]

In a New York City campaign speech, Garfield praised the

[16] Garfield's speech in the House of Representatives, February 1, 1866, Garfield, *Works*, I, 108. In congressional speeches on the eighth and twelfth of February Garfield said that he was ashamed that manhood suffrage had not been written into the Fourteenth Amendment; ibid., I, 249–54. Garfield believed that once obtained the blacks would not give up their political rights without a struggle. Speech, Orwell, Ohio, August 28, 1868. Garfield, op. cit., I, 397.

[17] *Great Speeches of Garfield*, pp. 207–36. Garfield's speech on the enforcement of the Fourteenth Amendment, delivered in the House of Representatives, April 4, 1871.

[18] Garfield's letter of acceptance of the Republican nomination for the President, July 12, 1880, Mentor, Ohio, Garfield, *Works*, II, 783.

faithfulness of blacks during the war: "We never saw a traitor in a black skin . . . no Union soldier was every betrayed by a black man or woman." Obviously struck with what has since been called "Potomac fever," Garfield vowed to defend the freedom of blacks: "Now that we have made them free, so long as we live, we will stand by these black allies . . . until the sun of liberty, fixed in the firmament of our Constitution, shall shine with equal ray upon every man, black and white, throughout the union."[19] While one might be disposed to pass off these phrases as mere campaign rhetoric, their fervor did last until the inauguration, March 4, 1881.

Almost half of the inaugural address concerned itself with blacks and the problem of the ballot. In the President's opinion the changing of the blacks status from slavery to freedom was the most momentous political change since the writing of the Constitution. To those in the South who were resisting this revolution he said that under our democratic institutions

> there was no middle ground for the Negro race between slavery and equal citizenship. There can be no permanently disfranchised peasantry in the United States. Freedom can never yield its fullness of blessings so long as the law or its administration places the smallest obstacle in the path of any virtuous citizen.[20]

Although he had told the freedmen before the election that they were going to have to stand on their own two feet, he appeared to champion the black cause in his inaugural address. Then he nullified the effectiveness of the entire passage when he said: "So far as my authority lawfully extends they [blacks] shall enjoy the full and equal protection of the Constitution and the laws." This appeared to relieve him of any responsibility for the violation of black rights by local and state officials, which was really the crux of the matter.[21]

Ex-President Hayes provided the prime example of political double talk when he tried to assure his Texan correspondent, Guy Bryan, that he had nothing to fear from Garfield's Southern

[19] August 6, 1880, George P. Edgar, *Gems of the Campaign of 1880*, pp. 46, 51; *Great Speeches of Garfield*, pp. 530–31.
[20] March 4, 1881, Garfield, *Works*, II, 790.
[21] March 4, 1881, Garfield, *Works*, II, 790.

policy: "On the Southern question I am confident of his course. He will be conservative, moderate and liberal!"[22] In any case, Garfield left little doubt about his position on the black man's place. Whether or not he could transcend the "iron law of [political] necessity" and cope with the theory of states' rights sufficiently to enable him to enforce the laws, was another matter.

Race and Politics: Reconstruction and the Ballot

Although his ardor cooled considerably by 1871, initially Garfield was a complete radical on black rights and in 1866 he was impatient because blacks were excluded from President Johnson's plan of Reconstruction. For reasons partly humanitarian he declared: "The spirit of our government demands that there shall be no rigid horizontal strata running across our political society where some classes of citizens may never pass up to the surface." He even contended that black rights could "no longer be left to the caprice of mobs or the contingencies of local legislation."[23] But when the Reconstruction Acts were presented Garfield had "many misgivings" about them. He found them severe.[24] By 1870, he was ready to repudiate Reconstruction almost entirely: "For my part," he declared, "I have never admitted to the doctrine of state suicide. . . . I am glad to know the settled policy of the country has at last condemned it."[25]

One crucial facet of equality before the law concerned the right to vote. In the face of Johnsonian Reconstruction which left the blacks voteless, Garfield, while he was not disposed to give the ballot to ignorant whites or blacks, felt that any

[22] Letter of Rutherford B. Hayes to Guy M. Bryan (Texas, August 13, 1881, RBHP, transcribed).

[23] Garfield's speech on Reconstruction of the Southern states in relation to Johnson's veto of the Freedmen's Bureau Bill, February 1, 1866. Garfield, *Works*, 1, 106–11.

[24] Garfield's speech in the House of Representatives, February 8, 1867, Garfield, *Works*, I, 249, 257; Garfield's speech of February 12, 1867, ibid., I, 252.

[25] Garfield's speech on the bill to readmit Georgia to the Union, June 24, 1870, ibid., I, 263–64.

restrictions should apply equally to all without reference to the color of the skin. But in the absence of such an educational test he suggeted that all men vote irrespective of color: "It may well be questioned whether the Negro does not understand the nature of our institutions better than the equally ignorant foreigner," he remarked.[26] The black man needed the ballot in order to have a say in his own future and to protect himself against the caprice of his late master. Had not blacks helped to save the Union? And would not the South get fifteen more representatives in Congress when the Afro-American was counted as a whole man? Garfield answered these questions in the affirmative. In so doing he had based his plea for black freedom on humanitarian urgency and political necessity. Garfield also contended that voting by black people was no innovation because blacks had voted during the American Revolution.[27]

Like Grant, Garfield was aware of the revolutionary character of mass black suffrage. Both men felt that after the passage of the Fifteenth Amendment the black question would remove itself from "the arena of American politics." Rather prematurely Garfield declared in 1870 that it was time to cut the blacks loose from the national apron strings: "The colored men of this country, having now equal rights before the law must vindicate their own manhood, and prove by their own efforts the wisdom of the policy which has placed their destiny in their own hands."[28] It appeared that as far as blacks were concerned Garfield was preparing to "abandon ship." However, in 1871 he urged enforcement of the representation clause of the Fourteenth Amendment.[29] Ten years later, in his inaugural address, he called attention to the denial of the ballot to blacks in the South and to corrupt local government in that region.

[26] Garfield's speech on suffrage and safety, Ravenna, Ohio, July 4, 1865, ibid., I, 87.

[27] Garfield's speech on suffrage and safety, Ravenna, Ohio, July 4, 1865, Garfield, *Works*, I, 89–93.

[28] Garfield's speech at Mansfield, Ohio, August 27, 1870, Garfield, *Works*, I, 614. On the revolutionary nature of black suffrage see his speech at Hiram College, June 24, 1867, ibid., I, 274.

[29] Garfield's speech on the Fourteenth Amendment and representation, Garfield, *Works*, I, 761–65.

But for a remedy all he could suggest was education, that racial panacea of the Republican era.[30]

Education and the Solution to the Race Problem

Two months before inauguration day a delegation of blacks from several Southern states called on the President-elect at his home town in Mentor, Ohio, and poured out their souls on the problems of black men in the "redeemed" South. Garfield listened. Then he said that all that he had ever spoken or done on the race question was a "matter of profound conviction," but it was inappropriate for him at this time to indicate what he had planned to say or do in his official capacity. The remarks of one of the black speakers drew from Garfield a comment unlikely to give comfort to those who might have hoped that blacks would at last have a champion in the White House. When they observed that in some parts of the South a black majority was being oppressed by a white minority, Garfield leaped into the breach with this question: "Why is it so?" Did the blacks not know that an educated man was really two or three men when pitted against an uneducated one? Then he drove to the heart of the matter:

> . . . No race can reasonably confer and maintain, in the long run, equality that is not upheld by culture and intelligence. Legislation ought to do all it can, [but] in my judgement the education of your race lies at the basis of the final solution of your great question and that cannot be altogether in the hands of the government.[31]

This attitude did not augur well for the blacks under Garfield. At this point he was still under the "halo" of the spirit of the Compromise of 1876. Had not J. D. Cox of Ohio said that in any battle between the races the inferior one was bound to go down? Federal intervention could do nothing to

[30] March 4, 1881, Garfield, *Works*, II, 791.

[31] Garfield's reply to a delegation of colored citizens from South Carolina and other Southern states, January 14, 1881, Mentor, Ohio, Burke A. Hinsdale, *President Garfield and Education* (Boston: James R. Osgood and Co., 1881), pp. 253–56.

prevent a result that was inevitable. The black man would simply have to bide his time until the educational gap had been bridged.

To this formula for racial harmony Garfield also added "time." Yes, "time will bring what mere legislation alone cannot immediately bring in any locality. . . . I have felt for years that . . . [education] was the final solution, the final hope" of the problem. "Gentlemen, that you may take part in this earnest work of building up your race from the foundation into the solidarity of intelligence and industry and strength, and upon those bases at last see all your rights recognized and acknowledged, is my personal wish and hope for your people."[32] Implicit in this position was the idea that when the black man had improved himself society would accept him. This assumption failed to take account of the force of race prejudice.

For a short time Garfield was a trustee of Hampton Institute. According to Smith, his biographer, while Garfield approved of the methods at this school, "the sort of education there given did not appeal to his sympathy very strongly." Garfield was schooled in the liberal arts tradition and "the problem of laying the foundation for the economic self support of a dependent race was something wholly different" from his conception of education. He accused Armstrong of laying undue emphasis on manual training which after all was "incompatible with a very high degree of mental cultivation." Garfield did not think that the "labor feature" was the answer to the need. As he saw it the real problem with blacks was "how best to lead them up from the plane of drudgery to one of some culture and finally of high culture."[33] To more people than Garfield it must have seemed strange that a manual labor education approach would be taken with regard to a people who had known nothing but manual labor for two centuries. Be that as it may, two additional racial minorities briefly engaged Garfield's attention.

[32] Burke A. Hinsdale, *President Garfield and Education*, pp. 253–56.

[33] All of the preceding quotations were cited in Theodore Clarke Smith (ed.), *The Life and Letters of James Abram Garfield* (New Haven: Yale University Press, 1925), II, 802–03.

The Indian and the Chinese

To Garfield the Indian was uncivilized and ignorant. It seemed ridiculous to him that representatives of the government of the United States should "sit in a wigwam and make treaties with a lot of painted and half-naked savages. . . ."[34] He had his doubts about the utility of the peace policy of the Grant Administration for "this wild man of the desert," "that dusky race," and "these gay savages of the western plains."[35] But by 1876 he had become convinced of its wisdom: "I was somewhat in doubt about the wisdom of the peace policy. . . ." Yet, after five years he admitted that many of the "wild, roaming Indians of 1868 are now peacefully employed in taking the final step toward civilization."[36] He also had his doubts about the ability of the Indian to be civilized: "I am not here to say I believe very strongly in the ultimate success of making good citizens of the Indians. . . ."[37]

Garfield's solution to the Indian problem was to stop treating the tribes as nations, to give them a ballot rather than a bullet, and a separate state to themselves. In 1871 he called for the setting up of a territory and then presenting "to all the Indians of the west the alternative of going on in their decline to ultimate extinction, or of joining the movement in the other direction toward civilization. That movement will find its cultivation in the autonomy of a state in which civilized Indians shall be citizens; governing themselves by means of the ballot, and taking into their own hands the direction of their destiny." Since the ballot had been the "salvation" of the black race it could do the same for "such of the Indian race as may be saved from barbarism and extinction." When someone on the House floor questioned the ability of the ballot to cure the

[34] Garfield's speech in the House of Representatives, December 18, 1868, Garfield, *Works,* I, 366–69; in another speech on February 4, 1869, he saw the "ignorant Indian living" hundreds of miles beyond the pale of civilization, ibid.

[35] Speech in the House, February 27, 1869, Garfield, *Works,* I, 375.

[36] Speech in the House, April 20, 1876, Garfield, *Works,* I, 381.

[37] Speech in the House, April 20, 1876, Garfield, *Works,* I, 381.

ills of the Indian, Garfield hastened to add: "I do not believe the wild Indian can use the ballot at the present moment any better than he can use the spelling book. . . ." The ballot and distinct self-government would be the final solution of the Indian problem but the "result would [not] be reached in a day or a year."[38]

Thus far it has been shown that the blacks and Indians were clearly defined racial entities in Garfield's mind. He was also conscious of the racial uniqueness of the Chinese: "The Mongolian race is capable of great personal prowess. . . ." The idea that the Chinese lived off almost nothing, ate unusual foods, and lived in crowded quarters impressed him. Oddly enough, in the matter of assimilation, that is, cultural assimilation, Garfield placed the blacks ahead of the Indian and the Chinese. Of the Chinese he reportedly said:

> . . . They have no assimilation whatever to Caucasian civilization. The Negro assimilates with the Caucasian. He wants all that we want. He adopts our civilization . . . hence we can take him up in the circulation of the body politic and assimilate him—make a man and brother of him, as the phrase goes; but not so in the least degree with the Chinaman.[39]

Since the Chinese were physically closer to the Caucasian in color than the black, it appears that for Garfield, cultural affinity was a more important requirement for successful assimilation than was racial similarity. Garfield was in sympathy with the efforts of Congress and President Hayes to exclude the Chinese.[40]

In summary, Garfield was willing to see the black man and the Indian equally free under the laws to make their way uninhibited in American life. He was unwilling to extend the same privilege to the Chinese. He was conscious of the presence of different races on the American continent and the problems

[38] Speech in the House, January 25, 1871, Garfield, *Works*, I, 377.

[39] Cited in James S. Brisbin, *From the Towpath to the White House: The Early Life and Public Career of James A. Garfield* (Philadelphia: Hubbard Brothers, 1880), pp. 307–08. Brisbin took this information from an interview of Garfield with the Wheeling [W.Va.] *Intelligencer*, December 5, 1877.

[40] George P. Edgar, *Gems of the Campaign of 1880*, p. 39.

as well as the challenges this presented for American life and democratic institutions. He seemed to be in favor of cultural assimilation. In view of the fact that he shied away from annexing Cuba, Hawaii, and other tropical lands for fear of racial degeneration through race mixture, Garfield probably would not have consented to biological racial crossing. He appeared to be quite frank and honest in his opinions but it is possible that political considerations affected his racial thought. It was also possible for him to transcend the color line. Although we shall never know from the preceding discussion of Garfield's views, it seems unlikely that he would have been any more vigorous than R. B. Hayes in intervening in the affairs of Southern states for the protection of the rights of black people. In any case, an assassin's bullet cut him down after four months in office and his Vice-President, Chester A. Arthur, took his place.

Arthur: Black Americans and the International Perspective

Before he came to the presidency, Chester A. Arthur was involved in two civil rights actions concerning blacks. As a young lawyer, in 1852, along with William Evarts, he won for the state of New York the celebrated Lemmon Case, involving the freedom of the slaves of a white Southern couple passing through New York.[41] In 1855, he won a judgment for "Lizzie Jennings," a black woman who, against the law, boarded a Brooklyn streetcar only to be unceremoniously ousted by force.[42]

[41] Burton T. Doyle and Homer H. Swaney, *Lives of James A. Garfield and Chester A. Arthur* . . . (Washington, D.C.: Rufus H. Darby, 1881). The Lemmons were travelers who had their slaves wooed away from them in New York, went to court to regain their property and lost.

[42] George F. Howe, *Chester A. Arthur: A Quarter Century of Machine Politics* (New York: Dodd, Mead and Co., 1934), p. 15; newspaper clipping, November 12, 1928, authored by J. P. Glass, found in the Chester A. Arthur Papers (manuscript in the Library of Congress, Washington, D.C.), Vol. X, No. 2154; Leon Litwack, *North of Slavery*, p. 111. Litwack claims that even though Arthur won the case, the next year a jury refused to convict a company for ejecting a black passenger from his seat in the public car.

As President, he said little about blacks in his annual messages. His personal papers did not survive him, thus leaving a historical hiatus for this period. In his first annual message he came out for national aid to education with special reference to the "illiterate Negro voter." That, apparently, was the last time blacks were mentioned in the annual messages of Chester A. Arthur.[43] When the President died, Frederick Douglass wrote from Paris to some friends in the following manner:

> . . . And while it must be regretted that he [Arthur] has fallen in the midst of his years; there is nothing in his career as President of the U.S. that proved him to have had sympathy with the oppressed colored people of the South.[44]

President Arthur had more to say about Indians than he did about blacks. However, he said nothing new about the Indian. Like his predecessors he wanted the Indian civilized and absorbed "into the mass of our citizens." He asked that they be brought under the pale of American law and given the right to own land. Many of the Indians, Arthur surmised, "recognize the fact that their hunting days are over. . . ."[45] But five days before he left office Arthur threw open the Winnebago, Crow and Creek Indian lands to white settlement: "Thus were these Indians robbed of 500,000 acres granted to them by treaty with the United States," as one historian, Robert McElroy, put it. Upon taking office Cleveland revoked this order and forced the newly arrived whites off the reservations. This act of magnanimity occasioned a premature optimism in the heart of the bedridden Indian crusader, Helen Hunt Jackson, who wrote to Cleveland: "I am dying in the belief that . . . it is your hand that is destined to strike the first steady blow toward lifting the burden of infamy from our country and righting the wrongs of the Indian race."[46]

[43] Richardson, *Messages*, VIII, 58.

[44] Letter of Frederick Douglass to Friends Hayden and Watson, November 19, 1886, Foner, *The Life and Writings of Frederick Douglass*, IV, 444–47.

[45] Richardson, *Messages*, VIII, 54–56, December 6, 1888.

[46] This episode and the accompanying quotations are drawn from Robert McElroy, *Grover Cleveland: The Man and the Statesman: An Authorized Biography* (New York: Harper and Brothers, 1923), I, 221–23, Chap. 9, passim.

President Arthur signed the Chinese Exclusion Bill on May 6, 1882, postponing the immigration of Chinese laborers to America for ten years. The restrictions later became permanent. Just a month before, April 4, 1882, he had vetoed a Chinese Exclusion Bill that had called for the absolute exclusion of the Chinese for twenty years and restrictions on the movements of those already in the country. He felt that the proposed system of "personal registration and passports" for Chinese Americans who were citizens was undemocratic and inimical to the spirit of our institutions. He opposed unrestricted Chinese immigration but unlike the rank and file he thought that Chinese labor had been beneficial to the country, to capitalists and Caucasian workers alike. He was certain that Chinese labor could prove beneficial in the future "without interfering with the labor of our own race. . . ." An unfriendly gesture toward the Chinese might send the rich trade of the Orient elsewhere. For these reasons Arthur would not hastily alienate the Chinese and held out for a ten-year rather than a twenty-year exclusion period.[47]

A rather bizarre reaction to Arthur's veto of the first Chinese Exclusion Bill came from Julia Sand, an apparently semi-invalid spinster from Saratoga, New York, who said to the President in one of more than twenty-five letters: "Your veto of the Chinese bill delighted me. . . . It put me in a very cheerful mood—so cheerful that—what do you think—I sent for a horse and—there being no heathen Chinese around—showed my superiority to race prejudice, by taking a colored fellow being out to drive. He never thanked me though, and probably expected to be rewarded—such is the demoralizing effect of civil rights!"[48] The next month when Arthur signed the bill, Julia was disappointed. "When you vetoed the Chinese Exclusion Bill; the better classes of people throughout the country were delighted. Now you sign it. And what is the difference as it now stands? In quantity less, but in quality just as idiotic and unnecessary as the first. . . . It is contrary to the spirit

[47] President Arthur's veto message on the Chinese Exclusion Bill, April 4, 1882, Richardson, *Messages*, VIII, 113–18.

[48] Julia Sand to Chester A. Arthur, April 15, 1882, Chester A. Arthur Papers (MSS), Vol. 5, No. 107–09, ser. I.

of our institutions and the civilization of the age. The Czar of Russia might well respond to your remonstrance against the persecution of the Jews with an expostulation against your persecution of the Chinese. . . ."[49]

On several other occasions Arthur expressed interest in race relations overseas. He called upon the Russians to suppress "the proscription which the Hebrew race in that country has lately suffered."[50] He felt that the objectives of the International African Association in the Belgian Congo were "philanthropic" and not "permanent political control," and encouraged American participation in the venture.[51] He said that America would not turn her back on Korea, a nation "reaching for a higher civilization. . . ."[52] On the basis of admittedly sketchy surviving evidence then, Arthur during his presidential years was rather indifferent and silent in regard to blacks and Indians. On the other hand, while he signed the Chinese Exclusion Bill of 1882, he did not seem to share the anti-Chinese feelings of some Americans. Would his successor be more active on the racial front?

Cleveland

Grover Cleveland was the lone Democratic President in a predominantly Republican era. Since racial pronouncements of the Democratic party tended to be Negrophobic, Cleveland could logically be expected to follow the party line.

Race and Politics: the Anxious Black and His Vote

It was inevitable that the Republican black man would feel a little uneasy and anxious for his future when a Democrat

[49] Letter of Julia Sand to Chester A. Arthur, May 1882, Chester A. Arthur Papers, Vol. 5, No. 1135, ser. I. In most of her letters Miss Sand kept urging Arthur to be a great President and to transcend what she called the "political dirty work" of the past. Arthur actually paid her a personal visit.

[50] Second Annual Message, December 4, 1882, Richardson, *Messages,* VIII, 127.

[51] Third Annual Message, December 4, 1883, Richardson, *Messages,* VIII, 175–76.

[52] Ibid., p. 174.

reached the White House. Professor Horace S. Merrill goes so far as to say that the black Southerner had no champion in Cleveland's Cabinet and described the two Southern members, Lucius Q. C. Lamar of Mississippi and Augustus H. Garland of Arkansas, as men who "unblinkingly accepted white supremacy." Even so, an examination of Cleveland's correspondence for the period reveals that many contemporaries looked upon the inclusion of Garland in the Cabinet as a move to conciliate blacks and calm their fears. There were those who felt that Garland had given blacks a fair deal when he was Reconstruction governor of Arkansas from 1875 to 1877, and that he had their confidence.

More than a hundred surviving letters expressed concern over black anxiety about the anticipated Democratic Administration. Many voiced the opinion that Garland's appointment as Attorney General would make the black feel that the new Administration was not adverse to his well-being: "I know that you would as Attorney General do more to strengthen Governor Cleveland's Administration by the confidence the Negro race have not only in your sense of justice but in your knowledge of their conditions and needs, than any man he could appoint from any section," said one Arkansas senator.[53] Of course, not

[53] James B. [Duke?], U.S. senator, to Senator Garland, November 15, 1884, Grover Cleveland Papers (manuscript, in the Library of Congress, Washington, D.C.), Vol. 3, No. 441, ser. I (to be hereafter cited as GCP); James G. Tappan, lawyer, Helena, Ark., to Grover Cleveland, November 29, 1884, ibid., Vol. 4, No. 854–57; J. D. Walker, U.S. senator and chairman of the State Democratic Central Committee of Arkansas, to Grover Cleveland, 1884, ibid., Vol. 4, No. 867–71. He was anxious to offset the alleged speeches of James G. Blaine who reportedly was telling the blacks that the world for them was about to end with the coming of a Democratic Administration; A. H. Garland to Colonel Daniel S. Lamont, private secretary to the President-elect, December 29, 1884, explaining how his previous vote for the Blair Education bill was now being used against him, ibid., Vol. 6, No. 1435–37; letter from a Cautius [*sic*] Democrat, ibid., Vol. 3, No. 480; a New York lawyer, John E. [Develin?] to Grover Cleveland, November 19, 1884, GCP, Vol. 3, No. 574; A. S. H. [name illegible] to Grover Cleveland, November 19, 1884, ibid., Vol. 3, No. 577–78; New York lawyer Merret E. Sawyer to Grover Cleveland, November 19, 1884, ibid., Vol. 3, No. 590–93; letter of Mrs. A. W. Curtis, wife of missionary preacher, Beecher, November 20, 1884, ibid., Vol. 3, No. 601–04; W. C. Ramsey, Pennsylvania, to Grover Cleveland, November 26, 1884, ibid., Vol. 4, No. 785–86; H. C. Levins, lawyer, Sedalia, Mo., to Grover Cleveland, November 29, 1884, ibid., Vol. 4, No. 583; a Brooklyn lawyer,

everyone believed such an appointment politically judicious: "But would it be a wise political move to put a Southern man in the law department of the Government? . . ." ran one remark.[54] Another correspondent recommended the local election of postmasters, a woman in the Cabinet, and "if you could see your way clear & the right material in a colored man for your cabinet you would thereby clinch the lip-service of the Democrats . . . and attain the [black] race to the party. . . ."[55]

On the other hand there was talk that the blacks were conspiring to assassinate Cleveland. "The *colored element* is greatly incensed and excited," said an unidentified Washingtonian to General F. J. Porter of New York, who forwarded the letter to Cleveland with the following message: "And I feel it my duty to say to you in confidence and truthfulness. . . . It would be well to look with diligence to the safety of the President-elect. . . ."[56] A former Bostonian, vice-president and one of the founders of the American Social Science Association and disenchanted abolitionist, reported that there was much rejoicing in old Georgetown, the alleged "headquarters of secession," over the election of Cleveland.[57]

Several blacks sent letters to the President-elect. One was anxious lest an educational requirement be attached to the ballot in the South.[58] Another, shortly after moving from North Carolina, complained that he was called a "nigger"

A. C. Augustus Haviland, to Grover Cleveland, November 27, 1884, ibid., Vol. 4, No. 812.

[54] Unidentified newspaper clipping enclosed in a letter from Alexandria, Va., GCP, Vol. 5, ser. I.

[55] R. A. Canby to Grover Cleveland, January 3, 1885, GCP, Vol. 6, No. 1763–64.

[56] Ibid., Vol. 3, No. 507–08, ser. I, letter dated November 17, 1884. Porter was commissioner of police for the city of New York. He apparently took the threats on Cleveland's life seriously and advised that steps be taken for his safety; another writer quoted blacks as saying, ". . . A Guiteau [Garfield's assassin] will be on hand to prevent a Democrat from taking his seat as President. . . ." Ibid., Vol. 3, No. 480.

[57] Carolyn H. Dall, Washington, D.C., to Grover Cleveland, November 18, 1884, GCP, Vol. 3, No. 543–47.

[58] William Hand, Va., to Grover Cleveland, November 20, 1884, GCH, Vol. 3, No. 621–22.

on the streets of Providence, Rhode Island.[59] A black lawyer from Kansas congratulated Cleveland on his victory and expressed confidence that the Democratic party would not abuse the blacks. The intended visit to Cleveland by a committee of black Republicans to ascertain his policy on the race question caused one professional black to write the President-elect. His was a rare kind of letter, for it attacked opportunistic black politicians, "scheming tricky men of our own 'race,'" and accused the Republican party of not appointing "true representative colored men; but persons taken from the curbstone 'scalawag' position, declaring that the Democratic party owed Negro Republicans nothing" and concluding that "the Negro wants to be thrown out upon his own resources and allowed to come by his own exertions."[60]

The epitome of wily political acumen was illustrated in the advice that Congressman Abram S. Hewitt gave Cleveland concerning the virtues of Wormley's Hotel as a place for the President to stay when he arrived in Washington. Besides being a quiet place, Wormley's had

> . . . the great advantage of having been kept by a colored man who for the last thirty years has been a friend of the leading men of the country. He was a Republican but voted the Democratic ticket for the first time in his life to vote for Cleveland. He was known to every colored man in the country; and the fact of your stopping at that house will go very far to allay all apprehensions as to the course of your administration in regard to the Negro race.[61]

Some advice for the inaugural address came from an old antislavery man who felt that the government had done all that it could for the black man and that "the disabilities under which he now suffers, grow out of prejudices with which legislation cannot deal, but which are quite within the reach

[59] Thomas Anthony Fisher to Grover Cleveland, November 25, 1884, GCP, Vol. 4, No. 7522–23.

[60] C. H. J. Taylor, Wyandotte, Kans., to Grover Cleveland, November 28, 1884, GCP, Vol. 4, No. 828–31.

[61] Abram S. Hewitt, House of Representatives, to Grover Cleveland, December 1, 1884, GCP, Vol. 4, No. 880–81. Whether or not Cleveland followed this advice was not determined.

of an enlightened public opinion." Cleveland was told that the Democratic party had a golden opportunity to outstrip the Republicans in the amelioration and ultimate removal of race prejudice against the black man and perhaps win him over. The President was advised to touch upon this subject in his inaugural address and say that "the blacks will be protected in their rights; so far as the federal power extends," and that his sympathies were certainly with a people so long oppressed.[62] That phrase "so far as the federal power extends" was a critical reservation which more than anything else, perhaps, prevented the Presidents from facing the reality of prejudice in the South and the North.

Because it provided the President with a potential rationale for doing nothing about the enforcement of the civil rights of blacks as required by the Fourteenth and Fifteenth Amendments, the correspondence initiated by Cleveland with George T. Curtis, famous jurist and defender of Dred Scott, was significant. The essence of one sixteen-page rambling letter from Curtis was that Congress and the executive could do nothing to enforce the substance of the Fourteenth and Fifteenth Amendments upon individuals. That was a job for the states. And what if the state should refuse to punish persons who denied other people their rights? According to Curtis, such a situation "rests under a deserved reproach. [But] Congress can neither punish nor prevent such acts of individuals."

While Congress had the powers to enforce the Fourteenth Amendment by appropriate legislation, it had not yet passed such laws which, according to Curtis, would "afford a judicial remedy against the [individual] officers of a state which had undertaken to violate one of those prohibitions [of the Fourteenth Amendment]." Since neither Congress nor the Supreme Court had declared for any such legislation, "and until such . . . legislation has been had and been upheld by the Supreme Court, *it is not needful for the executive to carry the construction of the legislative clause further than is above indicated*

[62] William Dorshrimer [?], New York, to Grover Cleveland, December 20, 1884, GCP, Vol. 6, No. 1273–74.

[italics added]." Cleveland was assured that it was natural for the black man to be anxious about the Democratic party and that all the new administration had to do to calm him in the inaugural was "to assert that the Constitution and all its amendments are just as binding upon the executive now, as they ever have been upon any previous incumbent of the executive office . . . ," and that Cleveland had no disposition to treat the amendments as other than binding.[63]

In effect, Curtis urged the President to say to blacks that the laws would be enforced while at the same time assuring Cleveland that neither he nor Congress had any power to enforce the civil rights amendments. This kind of advice, and coming from the distinguished jurist, certainly was not designed to turn Cleveland into a champion of law enforcement in the South or anywhere else where the civil rights were concerned. It was just this kind of constricting interpretation of the Civil War amendments that sent them into suspended animation until the mid-twentieth century. And yet, how can the Presidents of this period be blamed for not enforcing the Civil War amendments when the Supreme Court had ruled in the Slaughterhouse Cases of 1873 and the Civil Rights Cases of 1883 that the Fourteenth Amendment referred to the rights of persons as citizens of the United States and not of the states, and that certain rights could only be redressed under state law?[64]

Inauguration day came at last and sure enough the President appeared to follow the advice of his mailbag. He tried to soothe the anxious blacks with these obviously studied and well-chosen words:

> In the administration of a government pledged to equal and exact justice to all men, there should be not pretext for anxiety touching the protection of the freedmen in their rights, or their

[63] George T. Curtis, New York, to Grover Cleveland, November 15, 1884, GCP, Vol. 4, No. 337–51; George T. Curtis to Grover Cleveland, November 26, 1884, GCP, Vol. 3, No. 780–81; George T. Curtis to Grover Cleveland, December 8, 1884, GCP, Vol. 5, No. 1001–05; George T. Curtis to Grover Cleveland, January 5, 1885, GCP, Vol. 8, No. 1871–72.

[64] Henry Steele Commager, *Documents of American History* (New York: F. S. Crofts and Co., 1938), Document Nos. 292, 204, pp. 86, 71.

security in the enjoyment of their privileges under the Constitution and its amendments.

The President even showed a certain courage on this question when he further stated in regard to blacks:

> All discussion as to their fitness for the place accorded them as American citizens is idle and unprofitable, except as it suggests the necessity for their improvement. The fact that they are citizens entitles them to all the rights due to that relation, and charges them with all its duties, obligations, and responsibilities.[65]

Thus ended the masterful phrases of an inaugural address, well calculated to mollify blacks and their friends. Had they been able to peruse the letters of George T. Curtis, they might have been less at ease. Frederick Douglass was pleased and almost carried away by the President's rhetoric:

> The inaugural address of President Cleveland was all that any friend of liberty and justice could reasonably ask for the freedmen—no better words have dropped from the east portico of the Capitol since the inauguration days of Abraham Lincoln and Gen. Grant. I believe they were sincerely spoken, but whether the President will be able to administer the government in the light of those liberal sentiments is an open question. The one man power in our government is very great, but the power of the party may be greater. The President is not the autocrat but the executive of the nation.[66]

Douglass was not the only black man to approve of the inaugural address. However, it is possible that many of these were maneuvering to obtain crumbs from the "political breadline." For example, one black from Mississippi who was educated in the North praised the inaugural, adding: "I think you should not take up the old Negro office holders and put them in office. . . ."[67]

[65] Cleveland's First Inaugural Address, March 4, 1885, George F. Parker, (ed.), *The Writings and Speeches of Grover Cleveland* (New York: Cassell Publishing Co., 1892), p. 37.

[66] Speech of Frederick Douglass on the return of the Democratic party to power, Washington, D.C., 1885, Foner (ed.), *The Life and Writings of Frederick Douglass*, IV, 417, 413–26.

[67] A. M. Middlebrook, Columbus, Louwdes County, Miss., to Honorable Grover Cleveland, March 27, 1885, GCP, Vol. 24, Nos. 5799–5802.

The Democrats, in spite of their usual anti-black position, were aware of the value of the black vote. One example of this was the remarks of George Hoadly, governor of Ohio. In his opinion the black vote was important to the Democrats. He, too, had advised the President to put a word in the inaugural for the benefit of blacks and felt that the speech had satisfied "men of color throughout the country." Hoadly was confident that he could enlist Cleveland in this drive to salvage black votes because: "I had some conversation with Mr. Cleveland in July, relative to mixed schools, which led me to feel that he would approach the consideration of this question without any prejudice against men of color." Hoadly then made what may have been the first statement to take cognizance of the rising significance of the vote of the Northern blacks in close elections:

> In nearly every Northern state the colored people hold the balance of power between the contending parties. In this state, since 1869, the Republicans have only carried three elections by a majority greater than the colored vote. My own candidacy was the first in which the colored vote was distinctly divided. This was largely brought about by a colored Democratic paper the *Afro-American*, published in Cincinnati . . . edited by Mr. Herbert Clark. Last winter upon my recommendation the General Assembly passed a "civil rights bill" giving the colored people the same rights as the whites in all particulars except in respect to schools and marriage. This year in my annual message I recommended the repeal of the remaining discriminations on account of color, and the House of Representatives has already passed on a bill abolishing separate [*sic*] schools.[68]

This testimony afforded an excellent example of the social revolution in race relations which was going on in the North at the very time the Southerners were stamping out the traces of Reconstruction.

That there was now a Democrat in the White House did

[68] George Hoadly, governor of Ohio, to Daniel Lamont (Cleveland's private secretary), March 25, 1885, GCP, Vol. 24, No. 5845–59. Further investigation of the correspondence between Hoadly and Cleveland might reveal a more positive facet of Cleveland's ideas on race.

not deter the black man from taking his place alongside his white brother in the "political breadline." The turncoat Republican George T. Downing wanted to be Recorder of Deeds for the District of Columbia, a post primarily reserved for blacks and currently held by Frederick Douglass.[69] A New Yorker had to be informed that the post of Liberian minister had already been filled by "Rev. Moses A. Hopkins of North Carolina."[70] On January 5, 1886, the Republican Frederick Douglass resigned his post as Recorder of Deeds after being held over in the position by Cleveland for a year at Douglass' own request.[71]

Without giving any special instructions or admonitions in this relatively critical area, on October 5, 1886, Cleveland relegated to his Southern Attorney General the responsibility for the general supervision of the laws pertaining to the appointments and duties of supervisors and deputies of federal elections.[72] When he was nominated for a second term, one innocuous sentence on blacks graced his letter of acceptance: The government should secure to the colored citizens all their rights

[69] Daniel Lamont to George T. Downing, Newport, R.I., March 4, 1885, GCP (Letter Press Books), Vol. 1, No. 176, ser. IV, subseries A.

[70] Daniel Lamont to Ezra A. Tuttle, Esquire, Temple Court, New York, GCP (Letter Press Books), Vol. 4, No. 414; according to the *National Encyclopedia of American Biography,* XII, 112–13, Hopkins had quite a history: He was born of slave parents in 1846, was the first black to graduate from Auburn Seminary of Theology in New York. He did not learn the alphabet, it was held, until he was twenty. He graduated from black Lincoln University, Pennsylvania, with highest honors in 1874. He died in Monrovia, Liberia, August 3, 1886, and was succeeded by the Kansas lawyer already referred to in this chapter, Charles C. Taylor.

[71] Grover Cleveland to Honorable Fredk. Douglass, January 4, 1886, GCP (Letter Press Books), Vol. 29, No. 35–36, ser. IV, subseries C; Frederick Douglass to Grover Cleveland, January 5, 1886, Foner (ed.), *The Life and Writings of Frederick Douglass,* IV, 428; however, when Cleveland nominated another black man, James C. Matthews of New York, to take the place of the outgoing Douglass, the Senate demurred on the ground that the Recorder of Deeds for the District should be a resident of Washington. Said Cleveland on the matter: "Confessing a desire to cooperate in tendering to our colored fellow-citizens just recognition and the utmost good faith [I] again submit this nomination to the Senate for confirmation." See Richardson, *Messages,* VIII, 531, note to the Senate, December 21, 1886.

[72] Grover Cleveland to Hon. A. H. Garland, October 5, 1886, GCP (Letter Press Books), Vol. 29, No. 84, ser. IV, subseries C.

of citizenship and "their just recognition and encouragement in all things pertaining to that relation."[73]

After having calmed the fears of the blacks in his first inaugural, Cleveland had little more to add on the subject. There were times when he was urged to speak on the Jewish as well as the black question and refused both options. But he showed no hesitation about penning a letter for publication to George William Curtis on civil service reform, for which he was heavily congratulated. The President, it seemed, preferred to speak only upon subjects which were likely to be approved by the whole population, irrespective of section. Occasionally the President endorsed equality before the law but with reference to government discrimination between capital and labor.[74]

Out of office, Cleveland managed a few words on the universal right of suffrage, speaking once about "common brotherhood" and equality before the law in that regard.[75] But in a political speech in Boston a few months before the dawn of a new presidential election year, Cleveland, with obvious reference to a pending federal elections bill, harped on the virtues of reunion of the sections, counseling the "avoidance of unnecessary irritation, and the abandonment of schemes which promise no better result than party supremacy through forced and unnatural suffrage. . . ."[76] The federal elections bill called for strict supervision of voting procedures and was designed to aid blacks in the South. The measure was labeled as a "force bill" by its opponents, which, in a sense, it was in that its purpose was to enforce the Fifteenth Amendment. It is significant that Cleveland termed black suffrage "unnatural." But the issue is beclouded by the fact that even before he came to the presidency Cleveland was a staunch believer in local home rule.[77]

[73] Grover Cleveland's Letter of Acceptance . . . to Patrick Collins et al., September 8, 1888, Albert E. Berg, *Addresses and State Papers of Grover Cleveland* (New York: Sun Dial Classics, 1908), pp. 140–41.

[74] Fourth Annual Message of Grover Cleveland, December 3, 1888, Berg, *Addresses and State Papers of Grover Cleveland*, p. 155.

[75] Speech at Washington's Inaugural Centennial, New York, April 30, 1889, Parker, *The Writings and Speeches of Grover Cleveland*, p. 124.

[76] October 31, 1891, ibid., p. 319.

[77] Cleveland's letter of acceptance of the nomination for governor of New York, to Thomas C. E. Ecclesine, October 7, 1882, Berg, *Addresses and State Papers of Grover Cleveland*, p. 24.

In 1893, in his second inaugural address, Cleveland had even less to say about blacks. He simply noted that equality before the law should be "unimpaired by race or color."[78] As the Southern campaign to hang Jim Crow in albatross fashion around the necks of the blacks in the 1890s rolled along, Cleveland, as far as could be ascertained, said nothing. How he felt about social equality must now be considered.

To be charged with social equality or anything suggesting it during this period was a political kiss of death. Southerners not only refused blacks one iota of social equality but reacted sharply to gestures on the part of others in this direction. Cleveland had to defend himself against the stigma of social equality on a number of occasions. First the Southerners charged that he approved of mixed schools for New York City when he was governor.[79] Cleveland vigorously denied the charge in 1887 and again in 1904 when he said: "Whatever I did I was in favor of maintaining separate colored schools instead of having them mixed."[80] Here Cleveland's position does not coincide with the idea implicit in the testimony of Governor Hoadly of Ohio who said in regard to the black vote:

> Besides, I had some conversation with Mr. Cleveland in January relative to mixed schools; which led me to feel that he could approve the consideration of the question without any prejudice against men of color.[81]

Whatever the ultimate truth of the matter, it is sufficient to note that the President labored mightily to remove any onus from himself in this matter.

Even more revealing was the controversy over the alleged Taylor lunch incident in 1904. This affair began when Congressman Scott of Kansas reportedly started a rumor that Cleveland had invited a black to lunch at the White House while

[78] March 4, 1893, Berg, *Addresses and State Papers of Grover Cleveland*, p. 351.

[79] Nelson J. Waterbury to Grover Cleveland, January 1, 1884, GCP, Vol. 8, No. 1715–16. Waterbury was a New York lawyer, checking on this Southern charge.

[80] Berg, op. cit., p. 432.

[81] Governor Hoadly of Ohio to Daniel Lamont, March 28, 1885, GCP, Vol. 24, No. 545–59.

President. Scott denied that he had made such a statement but not before it was repeated on the floor of the House of Representatives by Congressman Webb of South Carolina. Webb then tried to get Cleveland to verify the matter. Although now out of the White House, Cleveland did not appreciate this insinuation that he had once eaten with a black:

> I have to say this of his [Mr. Scott's] sentiments that a colored man, C. H. J. Taylor, took lunch with me at the White House, that it is a deliberate fabrication out of the whole cloth.

Taylor has already been discussed in this chapter. According to Cleveland he had been an assistant in the office of the city attorney at Kansas City before serving under the President as recorder of deeds for the District of Columbia. "He served in that place with intelligence and efficiency. He has since died. Some people restrain themselves from abusing the dead," said Cleveland. He only found one truthful statement in the entire episode: "He was a black Negro. . . . I am led, however, to doubt his [Scott's] familiarity with his subject when he adds, 'as black as you ever saw.' "[82]

One newspaper reacted to the tone of Cleveland's letter of denial by commenting: "Mr. Cleveland is sarcastic: Sharp reply to Kansas Congressman's Statement. . . ." Webb, however, was most happy with the letter. With it he was able to rebuke blacks before the country. That Cleveland could become so indignant about the charge of dining with a black may have been indicative of the success of the Southern campaign to spread race prejudice. The triumphant Webb gloated: "Mr. Cleveland was a friend of the Negro, but not a fool friend. . . . He never by word or action encouraged the dream of social equality in the breast of the black man . . . [this statement was greeted by great applause from the Democrats in the House of Representatives, reportedly] he was a friend of the colored man but he was also a friend of the Southern white man, sympathized with us in our race problems and race burdens,

[82] Grover Cleveland to Hon. E. Y. Webb, March 1904, Berg, *Addresses and State Papers of Grover Cleveland*, p. 431.

and that, sir," Webb concluded vigorously, "is more than Mr. Roosevelt seemed ever to have done."[83]

Cleveland had to fight off still another charge of social equality. He told Charles Bartlett:

> I have received a number of inquiries similar to yours touching my invitation to Fred Douglass to a wedding reception and signing, while Governor of New York, a bill providing for mixed schools. I do not suppose that Mr. Thomas E. Watson [Georgia] believed or had any reason to believe either of the allegations when he made them. At any rate, they are both utterly and absolutely false. I cannot afford to devote a great deal of time in denying such foolish tales. I shall therefore attempt to cover every phase of the subject once and for all.

He then launched into a final denial of the charges. For the friends of freedom there was little consolation:

> It so happens that I have never in my *official* [italics added] position, either when sleeping or waking, alive or dead, on my head or on my heels, dined, lunched, or supped, or invited to a wedding reception any colored man, woman, or child.

However, there was a redeeming feature in the President's last sentence: "If, however, I had decided to do any of these things, neither the fear of Mr. Watson or anyone else would have prevented me. . . ."[84] On the other hand, Frederick Douglass, according to one historian, "praised the President [Cleveland] for his invitations to State dinners and other *public* [italics added] functions at the White House, something neither Garfield nor Arthur had the courage to do." Douglass went on to say: ". . . I know manliness wherever I find it; and I have found it in President Cleveland. . . . Whatever else he may be, he is not a snob, and he is not a coward."[85] While the evidence here is again inconclusive, the nature of the charges and their authors, plus the indignation and fervor

[83] Newspaper clipping, March 4, 1904, GCP (Scrapbook), Box 18–19 [ca. 1893–1904], ser. 10.

[84] Grover Cleveland to Honorable Charles L. Bartlett, March 14, 1904, Berg, *Addresses and State Papers of Grover Cleveland*, p. 432.

[85] Foner, *The Life and Writings of Frederick Douglass*, IV, 19–20.

with which Cleveland sought to escape the tarbrush of social equality, provide valuable commentary on the racial tenor of the times.

Post-Presidential Views on the Black Race

Like most of his contemporaries Cleveland felt that the education of the blacks would lead "to the proper solution of the race question in the South." At times he seemed to look to the day when the fully educated black would be a complete citizen: "If our colored boys are to exercise in their mature years the right of citizenship, they should be fitted to perform their duties intelligently and thoroughly."[86] Cleveland read Booker T. Washington's famous Atlanta Exposition speech with "intense interest" and said to the black educator: "Your words cannot fail to delight and encourage all who wish well for the race. And if your colored fellow-citizens do not favor your utterances, gather new hope and form new determinations to gain every valuable advantage offered them by their citizenship, it will be strange indeed."[87]

Four years later the ex-President gave Washington a cold, unsympathetic, and unflattering appraisal of the black problem. As he saw it the problem was what to do with

> eight million, who, though free, and invested with all the rights of citizenship, still constitute in the body politic a mass largely affected with ignorance, slothfulness, and a resulting lack of appreciation of the obligations of citizenship.[88]

The validity of this appraisal does not concern us here. That the black man's condition was attributed almost solely

[86] Grover Cleveland to a black man, Is[a?]iah T. Montgomery, January 14, 1891, Parker, *The Writings and Speeches of Grover Cleveland*, pp. 344–45; Cleveland contributed twenty-five dollars to the support of a black school.

[87] Grover Cleveland to Booker T. Washington, October 9, 1895, Allan Nevins, *The Letters of Grover Cleveland, 1850–1908* (New York: Houghton Mifflin Company, 1933) p. 413.

[88] Grover Cleveland to Booker T. Washington, December 3, 1899, Nevins, *The Letters of Grover Cleveland*, p. 521. Cleveland could not put in a fund-raising appearance for Tuskegee but through his good offices "a lady in a Western city" agreed to contribute twenty-five thousand dollars if her offer could be matched.

to his ignorance and allegedly bad character is of more significance. Race prejudice and state and national Jim Crow rulings of the period seemed not to have entered Cleveland's thinking at this point.

Not until 1903 did Cleveland make his "confession of faith" on blacks. At the outset he claimed that he was "a sincere friend of the Negro and a believer in the Booker Washington–Tuskegee" school of thought. Still, his disclosures seemed calculated not so much to praise the black man as to bury him. The occasion was a New York City meeting of the Southern Educational Association. Platform guests included Booker T. Washington, Seth Low of Columbia University, Andrew Carnegie, and Chancellor McCracken of New York University.

"The days of 'Uncle Tom's Cabin' are passed . . . ," reflected Cleveland. The Civil War amendments no more purged the blacks of their "racial and slavery bred imperfections than it changed the color of their skins." Freedom to the contrary, there was still "a grievous amount of ignorance, a sad amount of laziness and thriftlessness" among the freedmen. These were powerful and penetrating racial adjectives to come from an Eastern man. Cleveland's sympathies at this time were clearly with his "kith and kin." He reserved his sympathies for the Caucasian, not for the black brother. Because of the racial deficiencies of blacks "our fellow-countrymen in the Southern and late slave holding states . . . are entitled to our utmost consideration and sympathetic fellowship." They bore the brunt of the black problem.

Enlightened Northern philanthropic support of the industrial education efforts of Booker T. Washington at Tuskegee pointed to the solution of the "vexatious Negro problem at the South." Northern hopes for the black man could only be realized through the blacks themselves and "the sentiment and conduct of the leading and responsible white men of the South. . . ." Twenty-seven years after Hayes, the racial melody of "leave the Negro to the Southern white man" could still seduce Northerners. Even Booker T. Washington was affected by this refrain.

Whether from ignorance, conviction or political necessity, Cleveland was willing to trust the Southern white man with blacks and was very tolerant of Southern racial folkways:

> I do not know how it may be with the other Northern friends of the Negro, but I have faith in the honor and sincerity of the respectable white people of the South in their relations with the Negro and his improvement and well being. They [Southerners] do not believe in the social equality of the race, and they make no false pretense in regard to it. That this does not grow out of hatred for the Negro is very plain.

If not hatred, then what was the basis for the white rejection of blacks as social equals? Cleveland did not elaborate but found "abundant sentiments and abundant behavior among the Southern whites toward the Negro to make us doubt the justice of charging this denial of social equality to prejudice, as we understand the word." Cleveland thought "perhaps it is born of something deeper and more imperious than prejudice as to amount to a radical instinct." Of all the Presidents in this study, only Lincoln, Johnson and Cleveland came close to labeling the sensitivity of the whites to any degree of social proximity to blacks as *instinctive.* Cleveland implied that a feeling was improperly labeled prejudice if it was instinctive. He was impressed with the notion that the South had forgiven the blacks for the "Saturnalia of Reconstruction Days" and the "spoliation of the white men of the South." Irrespective of the nature of Southern prejudice toward blacks, Cleveland was certain of one thing. The North should be tolerant and considerate of the Southern brother who harbors this prejudice and "bear in the heat of the day, and struggle under the weight of the white man's burden."

Cleveland was uncertain about the ultimate destiny of blacks in America. At times there was even a nostalgic hint of the possibility of expatriation: "But whatever may be his ultimate destiny . . . mental and manual education" of the Tuskegee variety would prepare the black man for the "responsibilities" of his place. Cleveland confided both the destiny of the black man and the white man's prejudices into the hands of the Almighty:

"and *if* [italics added] it is within the wise purposes of God, the hardened surface of no untoward sentiment of prejudice can prevent the bursting forth of the blade and plant of the Negro's appointed opportunity into the bright sunlight of a cloudless day."[89]

All of the Presidents of this study, except Lincoln and Johnson, perhaps, spoke of a far distant period when blacks, no longer ignorant, would bask in the sunshine of full citizenship. Like Cleveland, they frequently elected to leave that prejudice, instinctive or otherwise, which made the average Caucasian recoil at the idea of social equality, to time and transcendental powers. This kind of reasoning contained too many *ifs* for black comfort. For example, the black man could look forward to a brighter day *if* he educated and improved himself; *if* God intended for him to remain in America; and *if* the white man's heart was disposed toward kindness to him. Yet who can say that Cleveland had stated the case incorrectly? Could the same thing be said for the Indian?

Cleveland and the Indians

Soon after his election in 1884, Cleveland's attention was drawn to the Indian.[90] He was in office two months when Mrs.

[89] This speech, on which the discussion of the preceding pages is based, may well be considered Cleveland's valedictory on the race question. Found in Berg, *Addresses and State Papers of Grover Cleveland*, pp. 423–25. One of Cleveland's Southern Cabinet members reportedly said of him: "He expressed great sympathy for those of us from the South, who felt that the maintenance of white supremacy in our states was the vital issue. And who might, if the free silver people control the national convention, still feel bound to remain in the party, whatever its declarations, to prevent Negro supremacy." See entry for Friday, April 17, 1896, cited in Festus P. Summers (ed.), *The Cabinet Diary of William L. Wilson, 1893–1896* (Chapel Hill: University of North Carolina Press, 1957), p. 68.

[90] James Codville, Woodstock, Ontario, Canda, to Honorable Grover Cleveland, November 18, 1884, GCP, Vol. 3, No. 535, ser. I. Reverend P. Schwaiger, Lancaster, Pa., to Grover Cleveland [November 20, 1884], GCP, Vol. 3, No. 623–24. Jessie Bolinger to Grover Cleveland, January 31, 1885, GCP, Vol. 8, No. 759–61. Most significantly Bolinger called for the division of Indian lands in severalty as a preliminary step to their civilization. He enclosed an editorial that criticized the Indian policy of the Republicans as one of "starvation tempered by shooting."

Helen Hunt Jackson, literary champion of Indian rights, sent him a copy of her book, A *Century of Dishonor*, which he promised to read at his earliest convenience.[91] When Cleveland revoked ex-President Arthur's order opening thousands of acres of Indian lands to white settlement he became a hero, momentarily.[92] Even Mrs. Jackson thought she saw in Cleveland an Indian "Moses." But while letters poured in to the President, approving his actions, these same letters according to one authority, expressed the belief that the Indian reservation was an obstacle in the path of civilization. Many people, and not necessarily for humanitarian reasons, wanted the Indian absorbed into society. McElroy summed up Cleveland's mail in this manner: "The condition which in the past had made the reservation system measurably effective in guarding Indian lands from white encroachment had passed forever."

Cleveland's Indian commissioner wrote: "It is no longer possible for the United States to keep its citizens out of these Territories. It has been demonstrated that isolation is an impossibility and . . . could never result in the elevation of the Indian." Cleveland later changed his mind on Arthur's order. Apparently public pressure forced him to back away from his heroic stand. In 1886, Congressman Dawes drew up his bill which was based in part upon recommendations of humanitarian groups. The bill gave the Indian citizenship and a farm. But what is often ignored is that the bill allowed all lands not allotted to the Indians to revert to the government to be sold rather cheaply to white settlers, the revenue credited to the

[91] Daniel Lamont (presidential secretary) to Honorable Lyman K. Bass, Colorado Springs, Colo., May 23, 1885 (Letter Book), Vol. 3, ser. IV, subseries A.

[92] Letters of congratulations for his bravery in standing up for the Indians came from James E. Garrettson, M.D., Philadelphia, 1885, GCP (Letter Book), Vol. 3, No. 87, ser. IV, subseries A. Mr. Herbert Welsh, Indian Rights Association, June 27, 1885, ibid., No. 207. George E. Foster, Milford, New Hampshire, October 15, 1885, ibid., Vol. 5, No. 479–80. Cleveland also vetoed a bill which sought to run a railroad through an Indian reservation in northern Montana. While he had approved other such bills, this one, he claimed, did not have the Indians' consent or consultation. See Francis Gottsberger (ed.), *Principles and Purposes of Our Form of Government as Set Forth in the Public Papers of Grover Cleveland* (New York: George G. Peck, 1892), pp. 127–28.

Indians.[93] The unstated implication of the Dawes Act was that it was better and cheaper to try to make the Indian a citizen and farmer *peaceably*, the extra land falling to the white settlers. The Indians were forced to give up all the land they could not physically occupy. The only difference between the various Presidents on this matter was in the degree to which each was willing to see that the Indians would unjustly have their lands taken from them by just means.

Unlike his description of what he thought were the racial deficiencies of blacks, Cleveland found a *diversity* of characteristics among the nonetheless barbaric Indians. Some Indians were "lazy, vicious, and stupid," but others were "industrious, peaceful, and intelligent." Some of them had actually achieved the art of self-government, while others still abounded in the squalor, dependence and the "savagery of their natural state."[94] The diversity of the Indian disposition, progress, and capacity for immediate self-support or improvement was again noted in Cleveland's second annual message. It would be difficult to lead the Indian to civilization while he was still "brooding over unadjusted wrongs." Still the Indian had to be brought within the pale of civilization because "barbarism and civilization cannot live together. It is impossible that such incongruous conditions should coexist on the same soil," thought Cleveland.[95]

Like the black, the Indian was also a part of the white man's burden. "The paths in which they should walk must be clearly marked out for them, and they must be led or guided until they are familiar" with the ways of citizenship, the President told Congress. The white man had to take the red brother by the hand. Cleveland rejected the expedient of extermination for the

[93] McElroy, *Grover Cleveland . . .*, I, 227–28. McElroy saw that battle between the white man and the Indian not as a morality play but a battle of the survival of the fittest.

[94] Cleveland's First Annual Message, December 1885, Parker, *The Writings and Speeches of Grover Cleveland*, pp. 400–09. Cleveland acknowledged resolutions from the Connecticut Indians Rights Association approving his remarks on the Indians. See letter of Daniel Lamont to Mrs. J. C. Kinny, Hartford, Conn., December 15, 1885, GCP (Letter Books), Vol. 6, No. 6, 366, ser. IV, subseries A.

[95] Cleveland's Second Annual Message, December 1886, Parker, *The Writings and Speeches of Grover Cleveland*, pp. 413–15, ibid., p. 423. Fourth Annual Message, December 1888.

Indians.[96] It was significant that he felt that the capacity of the Indian no longer needed demonstration: "It is established. It remains to make the most of it, and when that shall be done the curse will be lifted, the Indian race saved, and the sin of their oppression redeemed."[97] Before and after the Dawes Act that started the Indian on the road to citizenship Cleveland had advocated their civilization and inclusion in the American body politic.[98] His three-pronged approach to the Indian problem called for their civilization, citizenship and ultimate assimilation "with the mass of our population."[99]

As a matter of fact, Cleveland spoke rather freely in support of Indian assimilation, a position not taken in connection with blacks. In the face of protest from the Methodist Church, Cleveland stood by the Administration's policy of exclusive use of English as the medium of instruction in Indian schools supported by the government. The Indian needed English since "all the efforts . . . tend to the ultimate mixture of the Indians with our other people, thus making one community equal in all things which pertain to American citizenship. It will not do to permit these wards of the nation . . . to indulge in their barbarous language because it is easier for them or because it pleases them."[100] While the President's position was a sound one, his approach to Indian culture was cavalier.

During his second term, Cleveland began to have his doubts about the "severalty" clause of the Dawes Act, whereby the

[96] Parker, op. cit., p. 413. Cleveland's First Annual Message, December 1885, ibid., p. 408. The President said: "It is useless to dilate upon wrongs of the Indians and useless to indulge in the heartless belief that, because their wrongs are revenged in their own atrocious manner, therefore they should be exterminated." Cleveland wanted the army to supervise the Indians. See Richardson, *Messages*, VIII, 520. See also Inaugural Address, March 4, 1885, Berg, *Addresses and State Papers of Grover Cleveland*, p. 63.

[97] Fourth Annual Message of Grover Cleveland, December 1888, Parker, *The Writings and Speeches of Grover Cleveland*, p. 42.

[98] Second Inaugural Address of Grover Cleveland, March 4, 1893, Richardson, *Messages*, IX, 392. Grover Cleveland to Hoke Smith, Secretary of the Interior, May 4, 1895, Nevins, *The Letters of Grover Cleveland*, pp. 389–90.

[99] First Annual Message of Grover Cleveland, December 1885, Parker, *The Writings and Speeches of Grover Cleveland*, p. 400.

[100] Grover Cleveland to Reverend James Morrow, D.D., Philadelphia, Pa., March 20, 1888, GCP (Letter Books), Vol. 29, No. 285, ser. IV, subseries C.

Indian was given a farm. "It seems to me that allotments of land in severalty ought to be made with great care and circumspection. . . . If hastily done, before the Indian knows its meaning, while yet he has little or no idea of tilling a farm and no conception of thrift . . . [the giving out of farms might turn out to be simply the exchange] of a reservation life in tribal relation . . . for the pauperism of civilization."[101] The whites were so anxious to get the leftover Indian lands, farms were being doled out to the red man faster than he could adjust to the new relation.

As things turned out, Cleveland's fears about severalty were justified. In his second annual message he complained that the Indians on the farms were deteriorating, idle, not self-supporting, still living communally, some not even knowing where their farms were! He urged that severalty be carried out slowly and with "utmost caution," and thought that the success of the program depended largely upon the intelligence and honesty of the reservation agents.[102] If this were true, then the fate of the Indian hung precariously. For the Indian defined heaven, according to one historian, as "the place where white men lie no more."[103]

International Aspects of Race: Immigration, Assimilation, Nationality

Each President after Hayes felt compelled to take a position on immigration. Opposition to outsiders emphasized the threat to American labor and civilization. Racial objections and considerations were to be found in the anti-immigration dialogue. The President rarely strayed far away from what could be discerned as public opinion on the matter. For example, Cleveland stated in his first inaugural message that the immigration laws should be rigidly enforced to keep out servile competition with

[101] Cleveland's First Annual Message of his second term, December 4, 1893, Richardson, *Messages*, IX, 453.

[102] Cleveland's Second Annual Message, December 3, 1894, ibid., IX, 544.

[103] McElroy, *Grover Cleveland* . . . , I, 220.

American labor as well as customs and habits "repugnant to our civilization."[104]

"In opening our vast domain to alien elements the purpose of our lawgivers was to invite assimilation and not to provide an arena for endless antagonism," declared the President in his second annual message.[105] Cleveland was displeased over the expulsion of naturalized American Armenians by Turkey but took the position that "the right to exclude any or all classes of aliens . . . [was] an attribute of sovereignty."[106]

On March 2, 1897, Cleveland vetoed a bill designed to exclude from the United States any person who could not read and write English or some other language. He called the bill a radical departure from national policy on immigration: "Heretofore we have welcomed all who come to us from other lands except those whose moral or physical condition or history threatened our national welfare and safety [presumably, the Chinese]." Recalling the benefits of the generous policy of American immigration, he attributed much of America's greatness to it and to the successful assimilation of various peoples. To those who thought that the *quality* of the recent immigration was undesirable he said: "The time is quite within recent memory when the same . . . was said of immigrants who, with their descendants are now numbered among our best citizens." A literacy bill was not the answer. Better to admit 100,000 illiterate immigrants than one educated anarchist to stir up the unlettered populace. In view of the disposition during this period to argue that the illiterate black was unfit for citizenship, Cleveland's defense of the uninstructed was rather unexpected:

> The ability to read and write, as required in this bill in and of itself affords, in my opinion, a misleading test of contented industry and supplies unsatisfactory evidence of desirable citizenship or a proper appreciation of the benefits of our institutions.[107]

[104] March 4, 1885, Parker, *The Writings and Speeches of Grover Cleveland*, p. 36. See Cleveland's letter of acceptance, August 18, 1884, ibid., p. 11.

[105] December 6, 1886, Richardson, *Messages*, VIII, 498.

[106] First Annual Message of his second term, December 4, 1893, Richardson, *Messages*, IX, 440–41.

[107] Cleveland's veto message on the Literacy Bill, March 2, 1897, Richardson, *Messages*, IX, 758–60.

In spite of the restrictive Chinese legislation already on the books at this time, the lot of the remaining Mongolians in the Far Western states was not an easy one. In his first annual message, Cleveland reported that "in the Wyoming territory numbers of unoffending Chinamen . . . [were] murdered by a mob. . . ." There was "apprehension lest the bitterness of feeling against the Mongolian race on the Pacific slope" cause similar demonstrations. He proposed that "all of the power of the government . . . be exerted to maintain . . . good faith toward China in the treatment of these men and the inflexible sternness of the law in bringing the wrongdoers to justice. . . ." Cleveland discerned the race element in the opposition to the Chinese: "Race prejudice is the chief factor in originating these disturbances and it exists in a large part of our domain, jeopardizing our domestic peace and the good relations we strive to maintain with China."[108]

Although Cleveland could be very emphatic about protecting those Chinese already here, he was most certainly in favor of restricting any further immigration. When the Senate instructed the President to negotiate a new treaty with China for the total exclusion of Chinese laborers, Cleveland proudly announced that he was one step in front of them on the matter: "The importance of the subject referred to in this resolution has by no means been overlooked by the executive branch. . . . Negotiation . . . was commenced many months ago. . . ."[109] Eight days later Cleveland happily reported that the mission had been accomplished. The Chinese laborers were completely excluded. Cleveland wanted the treaty made public "in view of the public interest which has for a long time been maintained in relation to the question of Chinese immigration."[110]

Cleveland's joy was premature. As things turned out, the Chi-

[108] Cleveland's First Annual Message, December 1885, Gottsberger, *Principles and Purposes of Our Form of Government* . . . , p. 19. Richardson, *Messages*, VIII, 384.

[109] Cleveland's note to the Senate, March 8, 1888, Richardson, *Messages*, VIII, 609.

[110] Cleveland's note to Senate, March 16, 1888, Richardson, *Messages*, VIII, 610. On October 1, 1888, Cleveland accepted a House amendment to the new treaty, designed "to more effectually accomplish . . . the exclusion of Chinese laborers." Ibid., VIII, 630.

nese government was opposed to absolute or permanent exclusion. Seemingly the Chinese ambassador in Washington had overstepped his bounds and his government refused to ratify the treaty, to the annoyance of Cleveland. In a message to the Senate on October 1, 1888, the President repudiated Chinese immigration and announced the experiment of mixing white and yellow a failure:

> The experiment of blending the social habits and mutual race idiosyncrasies of the Chinese laboring classes with those of the great body of the people of the United States has proved by the experience of twenty years and ever since the Burlingame Treaty of 1868, to be in every sense unwise, impolitic, and injurious to both nations.[111]

The President announced that he had labored hard for this latest treaty "to answer the earnest popular demand for the absolute exclusion of Chinese laborers having objects and purposes unlike our own and wholly disconnected with American citizenship."[112] He was willing to pay China an indemnity of $276,619.17 for the violence on the West Coast.[113]

Nationality and religious groups were often designated as races in this period. The persecution of the Jews in Russia in the late nineteenth century did not go unnoticed in the United States. Allegedly the Russians were expelling foreign Jews doing business there. An influential American Jew, Leo Wise, wrote Senator Cox to see if American Jews would be expelled from Russia also. Cox, having many Jews in his district, sent the letter to Cleveland, broadly hinting that the President-elect make a statement to the effect that the Democrats were sympathetic to the plight of the Jews in Eastern Europe.[114]

[111] Cleveland's note to the Senate, October 1, 1888, Richardson, *Messages*, VIII, 631.

[112] Cleveland's note to the Senate, October 1, 1888, Richardson, *Messages*, VIII, 631.

[113] Ibid., VIII, 631, 634. Cleveland reported in his Fourth Annual Message that Congress had voted the money for the indemnity, ibid., VIII, 782. See also a letter of Grover Cleveland to Hon. Geo. F. Edmunds, United States Senate, December 21, 1888, GCP (Letter Book), Vol. 29, ser. IV, subseries C, No. 315–17.

[114] S. S. Cox to Grover Cleveland, December 24, 1884, enclosing a letter of Leo Wise to Hon. S. S. Cox, December 13, 1884, GCP, Vol. 5, Nos. 1152, 1178.

But Cleveland, having previously refused to issue a statement to calm the fears of the anxious black at the time of his election, also refused an official word in behalf of the Jew, at least for the moment. Like most politicians he was cautiously reluctant to express an opinion publicly on controversial subjects. Concerning the propriety of a statement on the Jews, Cleveland said: "I am of the opinion that any statement indicative of my views or feelings upon the subject . . . would be unprofitable." Cleveland could only hope that when his Administration assumed its duties it would "be found abundantly willing and ready to protect the rights of all American citizens in accordance with Democratic faith and precedent."[115]

There was little else said about the Jews until Cleveland left the White House. But even then he was very cautious about berating the Russians on the Jewish problem. Though he deplored Russian anti-Semitism, he felt that America should not forget "that we ourselves have found it impossible to prevent mob violence and murderous assaults upon the Chinese in Wyoming and the Italians in Louisiana. . . ." He could easily have added the blacks in the South to his list. He hoped that the United States would not be asked to take any "violent action" against Russia. In the meantime, the government should speak out "against all false enlightenment that excuses hatred and cruelty toward any race of men. . . ." These sentiments were expressed in a speech at Carnegie Hall and at a time when the blacks in the South might have welcomed some of the sympathy and concern of the American heart now bleeding for the Ashkenazim.[116]

On the occasion of the two hundred fiftieth anniversary of the Jewish sojourn in America, Cleveland praised their achievements and the "unrestricted toleration and equality" they allegedly received in America. Obviously forgetting how sympathetic he

[115] Grover Cleveland to Hon. S. S. Cox, December 29, 1884, GCP, Vol. 6, No. 1420. Daniel Lamont to Mr. Leo Wise, May 7, 1887, thanking him in the President's behalf for a copy of an address entitled "American Israelite," ibid. (Letter Book), Vol. 3, No. 105, ser. IV, subseries A.

[116] Speech made on May 27, 1903, Berg, *Addresses and State Papers of Grover Cleveland*, p. 430.

was earlier to Southern prejudice against blacks, Cleveland declared from his podium at Carnegie Hall:

> I know that human prejudice—especially that growing out of race or religion—is cruel, inveterate and lasting, but wherever in the world prejudice against the Jews still exists, there can be no place for it among the people of the United States. . . .[117]

Cleveland was conscious of the racial affinity between the United States, Britain and Canada.[118] He had nothing but praise for the industrious, frugal and liberty-loving German-Americans who helped us fight the Civil War and who added to the "strength and vigor of American institutions." If they did not find the justice and equality promised them by American institutions they should, counseled Cleveland, "demand from the government which they support—a scrupulous redemption of its pledge."[119] Such emphatic rebukes of race prejudice concerning Germans and Jews would have been even more appreciated by the black man had they been spoken in his behalf.

In summary, it appears that Cleveland had a rather low opinion of the black race, sympathy for the anti-Chinese sentiment of the country, faith in the capacity of the Indian, high praise for Jewish, German, English and Canadian nationalities, and a disposition to see aliens and all minority groups justly treated. He was very much aware of the reality of race and the presence of prejudice among the American people. And while he did not see this prejudice as providing an adequate excuse for injustice, he tended to be rather tolerant of such prejudices in regard to the blacks in the South. He did not speak directly to the question of race mixing but when accused of practicing and advocating social equality he vigorously, if not sarcastically, denied the charges. There was no reason to doubt his sincerity, but that he was affected by considerations of political expedi-

[117] Speech at Carnegie Hall, May 30, 1905, Berg, *Addresses and State Papers of Grover Cleveland*, pp. 440–46.

[118] Cleveland's message to the Senate on an Arbitration Treaty with Britain, January 1, 1897, Richardson, *Messages*, IX, 747. Second Annual Message of Grover Cleveland, December 6, 1886, Ibid., VIII, 500.

[119] Speech to the Semi-Centennial of the German Young Men's Association of Buffalo N.Y., Berg, *Addresses and State Papers of Grover Cleveland*, p. 302.

ency in matters of race seems probable. He could rise above the color line on occasion. He seemed to have played a more active role in regard to Indians and Chinese than he did with blacks. While he was not disposed to lead or influence public opinion on matters of race, he was much more vocal and articulate about the Indians and the Chinese than he was about blacks. His few utterances in regard to the Afro-American were either innocuous or negative in character.

CHAPTER VII

The Racial Attitudes of Benjamin Harrison (1889–1893)

Historians have paid little attention to Benjamin Harrison. Yet two major pieces of legislation designed to better the condition of the freedmen were considered by Congress during his Administration, and according to historian Rayford Logan, both were his recommendations.[1] Unfortunately, Congress defeated the Federal Elections and the Blair Education bills. As a matter of fact, some scholars label the defeat of these bills in 1890 (see page 12) as the racial watershed of the abandonment of the blacks by the Republican party and the nation. That such legislation was presented at the very beginning of the launching of the Southern drive to legally segregate freedmen just thirteen years after another "supposed" abandonment in 1877 seemed not to have bothered these historians. In actual fact Benjamin Harrison, as much as any other President, wrestled mightily with the black question.

[1] Rayford Logan, *The Negro in American Life and Thought: The Nadir, 1877–1901*, pp. 57, 312. The proposed election law would have made false registration, interference with registration by violence, intimidation or bribery a crime, and stealing the ballot box or ballots a felony. The education bill would have given federal assistance for eight years to public school systems of the various states on the basis of the number of the states' illiterates above the age of ten.

Race in Focus: The Black, the Civil War, Prejudice

As was true of all of the Presidents in this book, most of what Harrison had to say on matters of race was uttered in a political context. Like so many political leaders from the Midwest he contended that emancipation was a secondary goal, an incidental, but immortal, result of the Civil War.[2] All of the Presidents considered in here were well aware of the existence of race prejudice in the North. Perhaps this factor caused them to approach matters of race with caution, reluctance and conservatism. Not only the fetters of slavery "but the scarcely less cruel shackles of prejudice which bound every black man in the North have also been unbound" by the Civil War, Harrison said.[3] Some of the Republican political organizations in the North were segregated. Near the end of a speech to the Illinois delegation in 1888 Harrison paused to say a special word to "my friends of the colored organization. . . ."[4] On another occasion he said rather optimistically to an Indiana delegation: "My colored friends . . . all men are now free. You are thrown upon your own resources. The avenues of intelligence and of business success are open to all."[5] Eleven years after Hayes, Harrison also thought "that the race question would cease to divide men by prejudices that should long ago have become extinct."[6]

When talking to three hundred black voters of the Harrison League in Indianapolis in 1888, Harrison declared his sincere respect for the black people of the United States.[7] This speech contained the essence of what he thought about blacks.

[2] Charles Hedges, compiler. *Speeches of Benjamin Harrison and a Complete Collection of His Public Addresses from February, 1888, February, 1892* (New York: United States Book Co., 1892), p. 10. The speech was made March 20, 1888, at Chicago. (Hereafter this source will be cited as Hedges, *Speeches.*)

[3] Speech of Benjamin Harrison to the Illinois Delegation, Indianapolis, July 19, 1888, Hedges, *Speeches,* p. 53.

[4] Speech of Benjamin Harrison to the Illinois Delegation, July 25, 1888, ibid., p. 59.

[5] Speech of Benjamin Harrison, July 26, 1888, ibid., p. 61.

[6] Speech of Benjamin Harrison at Indianapolis, August 6, 1888, ibid., p. 77.

[7] Speech of Benjamin Harrison, June 30, 1888, Hedges, *Speeches,* pp. 33–35.

His initial interest in the black man dated from his youth when he saw escaped slaves being chased across the Ohio River from Kentucky. As a boy at North Bend, Indiana, he happened upon a fugitive slave eating walnuts in his grandfather's orchard. The lad was afraid but "I kept his [the fugitive's] secret," Harrison told the crowd. "Good! Good!" the crowd replied. Harrison thought blacks had made much progress since emancipation—even in Indiana. He recalled "the unfriendly black code" of his state and the old law designed to keep free blacks out. It seemed only yesterday that black people could not testify in Indiana courts against white people, he remarked, and someone shouted, "I know that!" Harrison said, "I have lived to see this unfriendly legislation removed from our statute books and the unfriendly section of our state Constitution repealed . . . the race emancipated and slavery extinct," to which the crowd replied, "A-men to that!" Harrison was happy for these results of the war. He noted that blacks thirsted for education and encouraged them: "It [education] is the open way for the race to that perfect emancipation which will remove remaining prejudices and secure to you in all parts of the land an equal and just participation in the government of the country. It cannot be much longer withholden from you."[8] It would be unfair to the positive spirit of American democracy to cast aside this affirmation of the ultimate inclusion of the black man in American nationality and citizenship as mere political rhetoric, uttered in the heat of a presidential campaign. But it was difficult in those days, as well as now, to separate race from politics.

Race and Politics

When Harrison became a candidate for the presidency, there was plenty of vocal opinion on the subject of blacks in the South. Carpetbaggers, blacks and white Northerners viewed Southern resurgence and entrenchment in the national government, together with the inability of government to protect the

[8] Speeches of Benjamin Harrison to a group of Negroes, June 30, 1888, ibid., pp. 33–35.

rights of blacks in the South, with alarm.[9] Judge Speer, a Georgia-born federal judge from the Southern District of that state, penned a lengthy letter to Harrison concerning blacks, which demonstrated that there were Southerners who wanted them to get equal justice before the law in that region. The judge, who was an independent Democrat, affiliated with the Republicans after the war and consequently lost the good will of his region. He served as a federal judge in Georgia from 1885 until his death in 1918. He thought that the exploiting of the race issue by professional politicians was hampering political democracy in the South. He found the masses of the South dis-

[9] Letter of a Chicago lawyer, Republican, and ex-soldier, then living in Georgia, Ebenezer Wakely, to Benjamin Harrison, 1888, in the Benjamin Harrison Papers (MSS in the Library of Congress, Washington, D.C.), Vol. 30, No. 6182, to be hereafter cited as BHP; Congratulatory Post Card of Henry Hand, Carthagenia, Mercer County, Ohio, to Benjamin Harrison, August 23, 1888, ibid., Vol. 39, No. 8570. The card called for a repeal of all discriminatory laws against blacks in the North as well as the South; Col. George W. Williams, Worcester, Mass., to Benjamin Harrison, 1888, BHP, Vol. 39, No. 8685–86. "Let me entreat you not to send your letter [of acceptance] to the country without some kindly reference to the poor outraged and helpless blacks of the South." D. C. Martin, secretary of the Republican State Committee, Land Office, Gainesville, Fla., to Col. Alexander Lynch, January 8, 1890 (forwarded to Harrison by Lynch), BHP, Vol. 96, No. 21775; New England businessman forced to leave North Carolina, Benjamin F. Pierce, Massachusetts, to Benjamin Harrison, November 28, 1888, BHP, Vol. 49, No. 10713–15. He found that the overriding idea in the South was to "keep the niggers down." Letter of John R. Lynch, black chairman of the Republican State Committee, Jackson, Miss., November 17, 1888, BHP, Vol. 47, No. 10351–59; the black chairman of the Republican Executive Committee of Texas, W. H. McGarver, Carthage, Tex., to Benjamin Harrison, November 17, 1888, ibid., No. 10377–78 accusing the Southerners of using economic pressure to control the blacks; letter of an ex-member of the North Carolina Legislature of 1883, a black, Edward H. Sutton, Baltimore, Md., BHP, Vol. 36, No. 7926, claiming that the Democrats ran his family out of the state. He sent along a little book entitled *Three Times in Jail*, which he had written, but it was not found in these papers; Andrew J. Chambers, New Rome, N.C., August 8, 1888, BHP, Vol. 37, No. 8055–60, asking that a commission be set up to study the condition of the Negro in the United States. Also asking for a commission was the letter of the president of the Colored Man's Industrial League of North Carolina, Andrew J. Chambers (same as above), Durham, N.C., to W. W. Halford, November 8, 1889, BHP, Vol. 90, No. 20411–14. See also the petition of thirty bishops of the African Methodist Church, November 23, 1889, also asking for a commission to be set up to study the progress of the African race in order to "hush the . . . implacable foes who hang upon our flanks as Cosacks [*sic*] upon the Arctic enveloped [the] French from Moscow to the Danube; and deny our just claim to human treatment and civil and political equality upon the ground of our utter worthlessness to the world as an industrial quantity and producing agency . . . ," BHP, Vol. 91, No. 20624–26.

posed to enforce the law but often misled to believe that "federal authority threatened their liberties. . . ." If only the public were given the proper understanding it would be possible to enforce federal laws in the South. Speer attributed lawlessness to a minority. The majority failed to come to the black man's defense because ". . . their sense of justice, and appreciation of wrongs has been simply forestalled by men whose interest it has been to keep up the race issue. . . . The forged race issue, and the fear of Negro domination have terrified the people into support of men and measures otherwise the object of indifference, sometimes of their detestation."

Speer called for the appointment of good district attorneys and marshals, men of fearless character, and asked Harrison "to let it be known that the Department [Attorney General's Office] will regularly, firmly, and unflinchingly, prosecute every intentional violation of the election laws. To let the law breaker, and his political manager know that his prosecution with its cost will certainly follow his crime. Let the voter have the encouraging assurance that a strong, vigilant and just government is at his back. These methods will, inevitably, as it seems to me, settle the Southern problem, a settlement which made by the Southern people themselves will be enduring and perpetual."[10] This concluded one of the most sensible and sincere letters on the Southern question ever to come out of the presidential correspondence. The solution suggested was simple: put men of impeccable character and courage in the Justice Department to enforce the election laws. Send good men to fill these posts in the South, and reassure the Southern masses of the good intentions of the federal government, thereby foiling the petty race politicians of the South who exploit the ignorant masses with their racial shibboleths. He seemed to be pleading for a firmer executive hand from the White House than the Presidents of this period were prepared to give.

[10] United States Judge Emory Speer, Georgia, to Benjamin Harrison, 1888, BHP, Vol. 48, No. 10653–60; see also the friendly letter of an ex-Confederate captain and Republican of North Carolina, O. H. Blocker, to W. A. Guthrie (forwarded to Harrison), November 16, 1888, BHP, Vol. 47, No. 10347–48.

In sharp contrast to Judge Speer, President McIlwaine of Hampden-Sidney College, Virginia, took issue with an alleged remark of Harrison in 1886 concerning the treatment of blacks in the South. In the candid opinion of this learned Virginia minister, the black man, "by the ordinance of nature and God," was inferior and unfit for the place he was seeking in American life.[11] The question of race was inextricably bound up in the politics of this period especially with reference to the South. Every President, sooner or later, had to decide what his approach would be to the racial situation in the South.

The Southern Question: Evolving a Policy

Not only did people mention the conditions of blacks in the South when they wrote the President, but also more specifically, they spoke of the black man as a problem in that region. While the black or the Southern question did not seem to play a large part in the presidential election of 1888, being subordinated to the tariff, Chinese, Irish, and even the Jewish question, the black issue was present and picked up considerable momentum immediately afterward. Many letters came from anxious Southerners who wanted to know what they could expect from the new Administration with regard to the blacks. But even during the presidential campaign, letters full of advice and opinions on the race question poured into the candidate's mailbag.

From Whitelaw Reid of the *New York Tribune* came a query to the President about how best to deal with the black question in his column, for a Southern correspondent had begged him to leave this issue strictly alone, claiming that Harrison wanted it that way. Harrison replied that he had agreed to no such thing: "I feel very strongly upon the question of a free ballot. It is one of the few essential things. I have never failed in any campaign to speak upon it and to insist that the settlement of that question preceded all others in natural order. . . . I would not be willing myself to purchase the Presi-

[11] Reverend Richard McIlwaine, D.D., Prince Edward County, Va., to Benjamin Harrison, November 26, 1888, BHP, Vol. 32, No. 6770–75.

dency for a compact of silence upon this question.[12] Reid agreed.

Presidents of the post-Reconstruction era were interested primarily in the race question where it impinged upon the problem of the ballot. There was no farsighted presidential statesmanship on the black question, no bold advocacy respecting the economic, social and cultural welfare of this racial minority; there was only the approach of the overly cautious politician doing as much as he thought public opinion would allow. Harrison was careful to label his rather frank letter to Reid as "private."

Not until Harrison was actually elected did the search for a politically feasible solution to the Southern question pick up momentum. The old Hayes formula of economic prosperity for the region, of splitting the black vote and bringing about political division in the South on issues other than race, was dusted off.[13] The President was asked to improve the caliber of federal appointments, to enforce the voting laws and to put down violence in the South. Many Southerners, especially Southern Republicans, and Northerners alike expressed to Harrison the general Southern fear of black domination.[14] The theme of

[12] J. Whitelaw Reid to Benjamin Harrison, September 25, 1888, BHP, Vol. 42, No. 9156–58; letter of Benjamin Harrison to J. Whitelaw Reid, September 27, 1888, ibid., No. 9185–87; J. Whitelaw Reid to Benjamin Harrison, October 6, 1888, ibid., No. 9412–14.

[13] G. B. Gowlam, Knoxville, Tenn., to Judge W. D. Kelly, Philadelphia, 1888, BHP, Vol. 46, No. 10122; letter of M. B. Hewson, Marinette, Wis., to Benjamin Harrison, 1888, ibid., Vol. 47, No. 1030–33; Richard Pearson, Asheville, N.C., to Benjamin Harrison, November 12, 1888, ibid., Vol. 46, No. 10206–10.

[14] C. E. Mitchell law offices, Prescott, Nevada County, Ark., to Benjamin Harrison, November 21, 1888, BHP, Vol. 48, No. 10536. He denied that the blacks wanted to dominate, saying that they only wanted equal justice before the law; Robert H. Johnston, a New York businessman doing business in the South, to Benjamin Harrison, 1888, ibid., No. 10643–44. He thought a way was needed whereby the South could ". . . show the North that they are in harmony with them on national issues and at the same time keep the state from *Negro* rule." Francis B. Pardie of R. G. Dunn and Company, manager of the Montgomery, Ala., office, to Benjamin Harrison, 1888, ibid., Vol. 49, No. 10716–17, thanking Harrison for being receptive to advice on the "Southern question" although remaining silent on the matter since the time was not yet ripe. There was a minority in the South with access to the press which was misrepresenting the true views of Southern people. Pardie acknowledged a letter from Harrison. Letter of a Chicago lumberman enclosing a clipping from the *Chicago Tribune*, showing that as late as 1888 blacks were increasingly thought of as a political nuisance in the South. No one wanted to "vote with the darky." The problem

many more letters concerned the formation of a predominantly white man's Republican party in the South as a solution to the charge of black domination. One of the first such suggestions came from a New Orleans manufacturer—who was a newly elected Republican congressman and president of the New Orleans Chamber of Commerce. He wanted to ". . . build up in Louisiana a respectable white man's Republican Party, at the same time giving to the colored man a fair proportion of the patronage, according to his qualifications. I have the confidence and good will of the better classes of the colored element."[15]

---

was how to regulate the black man without abridging his citizenship rights. M. C. Cole, Chicago, to Benjamin Harrison, ibid., No. 10816–17; Henry Booth, Montgomery, Ala., to Benjamin Harrison, December 4, 1888, ibid., Vol. 50, No. 10976–79. Now here was an obviously disenchanted carpetbagger of fourteen years, a native of Iowa, who felt that he had been sent, in the words of Albion Tourgee, on "a fool's errand." White and black Republicans were fighting each other and the ex-master fought them both. Race was the overriding issue. Blacks had been given the unqualified ballot too soon; letter of H. G. [Parsons?], Washington, D.C., to Benjamin Harrison, February 5, 1889, ibid., Vol. 65, No. 15488–89. Harrison asked this man to submit a brief on the black question. He found the blacks in a bad way and a crisis approaching. The black man was unfit for self-government. The only solution was the division of the black vote, an educational test which would put the government in the hands of the white minority in the black belts of the South where the problem was most acute. "The fear of Negro rule haunts us like a grim spectre," complained a Democrat and ex-Confederate, letter of W. R. Campbell to Benjamin Harrison, February 12, 1889, ibid., Vol. 67, No. 15211–17.

[15] H. Dudley Coleman to George Seldon, November 13, 1888, BHP, Vol. 46, No. 10250–51. H. Dudley Coleman to H. H. Hanna, ibid., Vol. 49, No. 10749–51. Both letters were forwarded to Harrison; the President was informed of a Democratic charge that the white Republicans and himself had decided that "the time has come to throw the Negro overboard. . . ." According to this correspondent, white Republicans in the South felt that if the party was going to be viable it needed brains, intelligence and courage enough to manage the political machinery to insure black rights. It was thought that only the whites could provide this leadership. ". . . As long as the Negro dominates the party the whites can be counted upon your fingers, in each county . . . ," concluded the letter of Frederick Speed, Vicksburg, Miss., to Benjamin Harrison, December 8, 1888, enclosing a clipping from the *Clarion Ledger*, Jackson, Miss., November 29, 1888, BHP, Vol. 50, No. 11157–58. The same story, essentially, came from Oxford, Miss. Robert A. Hill to Benjamin Harrison, December 18, 1888, BHP, Vol. 52, No. 11482–84, who said that there were a few blacks capable of holding office and the whites would not object to sharing some patronage with them as was already being done in some Mississippi counties by common consent. He thought, however, that such blacks were in the minority; M. P. Pierce, Washington, D.C., to Benjamin Harrison, December 24, 1888, BHP, Vol. 54, No. 12045–51, enclosing a clipping to show that white Republicans in the South,

There seems little doubt that in the South at least, the black man, as Frederick Douglass once put it, was the ugly duckling of the Republican party. But because the Republicans in that region labored mightily to rub off the taint by relegating the black man to a minor party role was insufficient reason for concluding that the black man was utterly abandoned.

In his reply to Harrison's request for his views on the political picture in the South, Senator W. E. Chandler of New Hampshire revealed no intention to abandon the blacks. To him the issue was whether or not the Fifteenth Amendment would be enforced. He thought that this was also Harrison's position and

---

were in general disrepute and that repression of blacks was justified to keep them out of places they were not qualified to fill; S. J. Wright, Paris, Texas, president of Paris, Choctaw, and Little Rock Railway Company, to Benjamin Harrison, January 18, 1889, BHP, Vol. 60, No. 13573–75, asking for a stronger Republican party but with the white man at the front; J. B. Kinkead, Nashville, Tenn., to Benjamin Harrison, March 4, 1889, BHP, Vol. 69, No. 15890–97, confessed that it was true that a black could not become a member of the Republican club in Nashville, but that the club was trying to elevate and educate the black voter. He said that not the race question but the lust for office and power was the real problem in the South; letter of J. H. Thomason, formerly of the *Birmingham Pilot*, and A. A. Garner, lawyer, to Benjamin Harrison, May 8, 1889, BHP, Vol. 76, No. 17343–44, explaining the rationale for the formation of the "White Republican Protective Tariff League of Alabama." Robert Barber, secretary of the Alabama White Republican Protective Tariff League, Montgomery, to Captain John McCoy, Birmingham (forwarded to Harrison by T. R. Butler), May 14, 1889, BHP, Vol. 76, No. 174. According to this report the league had almost "5000 . . . members . . . all good white men. [This, the man felt, was quite an accomplishment considering that] . . . a new white face had [not] joined our party since our convention in 1867." This man could not understand the furor in the North over this when there were separate political organizations for whites and blacks in that region also; J. Ogden Mawy to E. J. Halford, May 17, 1889, BHP, Vol. 77, No. 17502–05, saying, "*I heard much favorable comments upon the President's attitude towards* the effort to build a white Republican Party in the South." He felt that Harrison was in favor of it; Edwin Dudley, Boston, Mass., to Benjamin Harrison, May 28, 1889, BHP, Vol. 78, No. 17702–18, pronouncing the Republican party dead in South Carolina; David N. Freeman, Atlanta, Ga., to Benjamin Harrison, August 30, 1889, BHP, Vol. 85, No. 19436–39. "The white man must be the basis of any party in this state. . . ." The following letters all asked that the voting laws be enforced in the South to protect black and white Republicans; A. E. Rosenbusch, chairman of the Republican County Committee, Henderson, N.C., to Benjamin Harrison, 1888, BHP, Vol. 49, No. 10745–46; S. Newton Pettis, Pennsylvania, to Benjamin Harrison, November 29, 1888, BHP, Vol. 49, No. 10805–07; John D. Taylor, Congressman from Ohio, to Benjamin Harrison, 1888, BHP, Vol. 49, No. 10867–71; Harrison Reed, ex-governor of Florida, to Benjamin Harrison, December 4, 1888, BHP, Vol. 50, No. 19902–22; former judge B. F. Burnham, Boston, to Benjamin Harrison, February 18, 1889, BHP, Vol. 68, No. 15488–89.

wished it so stated in the coming inaugural address. He brushed aside the charge of "Negro supremacy" as "the great bugbear." Friction between the races was to be expected but "they must live on terms of political equality and the consequences must be patiently borne." Chandler's solution was not the use of troops but the appointment of a strong Attorney General who would "be an actor and not a conservative let-alone-policy man."[16] One Southern congressman thought that Chandler was too radical in his zeal to protect the black vote.[17]

A black lawyer suggested that since the shibboleth of the Southern Democrats was "the ignorant Negro," the solution to the problem would be to pass the Blair Education bill (federal aid to education), give the freedmen five years to learn to read and then put an educational qualification on the suffrage. As a black man he was, he said, taking a very unpopular position but "if this be treason to my race I stand convicted by their ignorance."[18]

Frederick Douglass was not pleased with the whispered tales of a white man's Republican party in the South or the thought that Harrison might give his blessing to such a policy, but he found the President much interested in the subject. As for the "New South," Douglass had little faith in it and urged Harrison to have nothing to do with the movement. He told Harrison that the outcome of the struggle between race and liberty in America depended in large measure upon the way the President and the Republican party exercised their responsibilities: "I reminded the President that for a dozen years or more the party seemed to be paralyzed in the presence of fraud and violence in the South, and that the people had been led to

[16] W. E. Chandler, United States Senate, to Benjamin Harrison, December 22, 1888, BHP, Vol. 52, No. 11663–70.

[17] Sympathetic letter of R. C. Goodrich to Benjamin Harrison, January 29, 1889, BHP, Vol. 63, No. 14258–59.

[18] ". . . My race *must* become educated before they can hope to succeed as a political factor or otherwise. . . . I believe in the New South . . . a new organization of the Republican Party built up with the progressive and enterprising white men in this new South: . . . I would not have you to understand me, by this, that the colored men should not receive appointments as well, for I believe that we are entitled to consideration, but they too ought to possess the same qualifications. . . ." Charles A. Roxborough, Plaquemine, La., to Benjamin Harrison, February 21, 1889, BHP, Vol. 68, No. 15634–41.

expect, from platform and stump, that under this Administration there would be more vigor and courage in enforcing the law." Douglass tried to discourage any deals with the South on the Negro question, for the South he knew was "a South that unblushingly robs; kills and enslaves the Negro; a South in which I have to take my lunch basket because I cannot procure meals at the railway eating station." This kind of South was "not ready to fraternize with the Negro in politics for the Negro's good."[19] Douglass had put his finger on what might well be the conclusion of this book. For with the exception of U. S. Grant, the Presidents of this era all showed a marked lack of vigor and courage in cases where the civil rights of black people were involved.

In 1889, the chairman of the Republican State Central Committee of Georgia in a letter to Harrison painted a rather dismal picture of the party in that state, and accused the editor of the *Atlanta Constitution* of race baiting. The paper allegedly accused the white postmaster in that city of replacing a white man with a black man and putting the black man to work at the same desk with a white lady.[20] The assistant district attorney for the Northern District of Georgia later reported that the controversial postmaster was about to be expelled from the Capital City Club in Atlanta.[21] These incidents show the destructive uses to which the idea of race could be put.

The chairman of the Republican organization in Indiana, L. T. Michener, was also Harrison's campaign manager. He held a conference with fourteen leading black men of Indianapolis, who complained to him about nonrecognition of blacks in that city and petitioned for the protection of their rights in the South. They wondered why "the Administration had

[19] Interview with Frederick Douglass, *Chicago Tribune*, April 27, 1889, BHP (Scrapbooks), Vol. 9, p. 88.

[20] A. E. Buck, Atlanta, Ga., to Benjamin Harrison, 1889, BHP, Vol. 85, No. 19395–99.

[21] E. A. Angier to E. W. Halford [President's private secretary], September 5, 1889, BHP, Vol. 86, No. 19567. The postmaster was General J. R. Lewis, whose wife was accused of "kissing Negro women in her parlor in Macon, Georgia, in 1868. . . ."

not given some representative man of their race in . . . [Indianapolis] a respectable position." They had sent a telegram to the President in regard to the Southern situation and were told only that the telegram had been referred to the Attorney General. They thought this response equivalent to throwing their petition in the wastebasket and threatened to stay at home on election day and "permit the Republican Party to be defeated."

Michener, who reported all this, was very much impressed with the conference, which played a part in causing him to come out in favor of legislation to put down violence in the South. He had talked, he said, to about one hundred white men who felt as he did; many people would be disappointed should the President "fail to take an advance step in his message." Michener urged Republicans to mount an offensive against the Southerners. "An earnest recommendation on the subject . . . will heat the blood of the old fashioned Republicans as it has not been heated in fifteen years; and he will touch the conscience of every good man regardless of party."[22] This was one of the strongest pleas for black protection found in the Harrison papers. Perhaps this kind of plea influenced the President to make a strong plea for protection of voters in his annual message of 1889 and an attempt to pass a Federal Elections bill in 1890.

Unfortunately, the righteous indignation of Michener failed to persist. A letter from E. W. Halford, the President's private secretary, deflated Michener completely, and caused him to say: "There is much truth in your letter concerning the colored question. They [the black delegation] had perfect confidence in the President until they met with what they thought was a chilly reception of the telegram which I mentioned." However, Michener added that there was a white "conservative Republican

[22] Honorable L. T. Michener to E. W. Halford [the President's private secretary was asked to relay these thoughts to the President], October 5, 1889, BHP, Vol. 88, No. 19983–98; the distinguished group of Negroes responsible in part for this moving plea to the President in their behalf included Dr. S. A. Elbert, Hon. J. S. Hinton, Prof. W. D. McCoy, Levi Christy, Rev. J. A. Clay, Rev. Gissell, Rev. Morris Lewis, B. J. W. Carr, R. E. Martin, W. Allison Sweeny, Ben Thornton and Horace Heaton.

element" that felt just as strongly about the lack of protection for blacks in the South as blacks themselves. He then made another significant admission:

> I make it a rule never to introduce this [black] question in talking over the future with the people whom I meet, but nearly every man who visits me, or whom I meet through the state introduces the subject and declares himself to be in favor of legislation which would give the colored men protection, and gives reasons galore for the faith that is in him. I know of but one white man in this state who is of a contrary view. . . . I merely tell you these things in order that you may fully realize the strength of the sentiment which pervades the people of our party.[23]

Although Michener may have overstated the case in recalling he knew only *one* man in his state who was against protection for blacks in the South, this kind of testimony, coming as it does from a leading political figure in the Middle West, should not be lightly dismissed. At the most, it should cause one to exercise caution relative to the theory of wholesale abandonment of blacks by the North. From all indications, racial discontent seems to have been greater than usual during Harrison's Administration: "President Harrison is in a peck of trouble about the color question. He pretends to be at ease but he is not," said one newspaper. Harrison was accused by former Governor Kellogg of Louisiana of alienating Northern and Southern blacks. He allegedly asked the black ex-Senator Blanche K. Bruce of Mississippi to issue a public denial of this.[24] The President did have some thoughts of his own on the black question.

The President on the Question

In his first annual message, Harrison had much to say on the subject of blacks in American life. He began by observing

[23] L. T. Michener to E. W. Halford, October 5, 1889, BHP, Vol. 88, No. 20036–39.

[24] Taken from the *Washington Sunday Herald and Weekly National Intelligencer*, November 10, 1889, BHP (Scrapbooks), Vol. 9, p. 15; see also an undated note from Bruce, BHP, Vol. 94, No. 21407–09.

that it was not the black man's fault that he was in this country. Happily for both races, he was now free. Neither his poverty nor his ignorance was of his own making; these were "our shame not theirs." Harrison was impressed by the progress the blacks had made in acquiring both education and property. "They have as a people showed themselves to be friendly and faithful toward the white race under temptations of tremendous strength." Harrison also expressed respect for the black's Civil War record: "They have their representatives in the national cemeteries, where a grateful government has gathered the ashes of those who died in its defense," he said in a brief resurrection of the bloody shirt.

After raising the fundamental question of the rights of blacks in American life, the President, unlike those before or after him, took the position that the black problem should not be sidestepped. He said: "This generation should courageously face these grave questions, and not leave them as a heritage of woe to the next. The consultation should proceed with candor, calmness, and great patience, upon the lines of justice and humanity, not of prejudice and cruelty. No question in our country can be at rest except upon the firm base of justice and the law." Harrison rejected the popular theme that the Southerners should be allowed to work out the black problem for themselves:

> If it be said that those [Southern] communities must work out this problem for themselves we have a right to ask whether they are at work upon it. Do they suggest any solution? When and under what conditions is the black man to have a ballot? When is he in fact to have those full civil rights which have so long been his in law? When is that equality of influence which our form of government was intended to secure to electors be restored?

Harrison had raised fundamental questions, some of which still await answers today. His talk was plain and relatively uncluttered by political considerations: "The colored man should be protected in all of his relations to the federal government, whether as a litigant, juror, or witness in our courts, as an elector of members of Congress, or as a peaceful traveller upon our interstate railways." This statement reflects the omnipresence of the dual nature of the American federal system as it was then regarded. Harrison implied that violation of intrastate civil liberties was beyond the pale of federal competence. But he seemed also to take an unusually strong position that in everything connected with the federal government there should be no discrimination. A full seven years before the Supreme Court took the opposite position in *Plessy v. Ferguson*, Harrison was contending that there should be no segregation and discrimination in interstate transportation.

He was careful to stay away from anything which might imply that he was usurping state prerogative: "No evil, however deplorable, can justify the assumption either on the part of the Executive or of Congress of powers not granted, but both will be highly blamable if all the powers are not wisely but firmly used to correct these." Congress had the right to control and direct congressional elections, Harrison thought, and urged that body to consider measures to "secure to all our people a free exercise of the right to suffrage and every other civil right under the Constitution and laws of the United States."

A stronger plea for blacks would be difficult to find in this period. Even Theodore Roosevelt did not equal this positive, constructive position toward the protection of black rights in the South in all areas touching the federal relation. These were not the words of political timidity. Neither did they show an inclination, despite campaign charges, to dodge the black question. Nor do they suggest that the titular representative of the Republican party and the nation had any immediate plans for abandoning the blacks or their votes to the Southern white Bourbons.[25]

The Black Vote

If the freedman had not possessed the ballot, the country and its politicians probably would have ignored him. On the other hand, slaves did not have the ballot either, yet they

[25] The preceding several pages of discussion was based upon President Harrison's First Annual Message to Congress, December 3, 1889, Richardson, *Messages*, IX, 55–56.

became a major bone of contention culminating in a national blood bath of catastrophic proportions. Whatever their racial proclivities, Republican politicians could not seem to forget that below Mason and Dixon's line there were potential Republican ballots being cast with increasing infrequency. Given the continuous drive for universal suffrage in American history, it is not impossible that some Americans may have been sincerely discomfited by Southern prostitution of the ballot, the so-called talisman of Greek, Roman, and Anglo-Saxon liberties.

"A free and equal ballot" and its pollution both North and South was one of Harrison's major themes in the campaign of 1888. He noted that the nation was protesting against the mistreatment of the Jews by the Russians and the Irish by the English and asked why a little of that sympathy should not go to the blacks in the South: "Should we not at least in reference to this gigantic and intolerable wrong in our own country, as a party, lift up a stalwart and determined protest against it?"[26] The unfinished business of the Republican party was "to make the constitutional grant of citizenship, the franchise to the colored man of the South, a practical and living reality," he said in Chicago.[27] In view of the strong recommendation he made on this subject in his very first annual message, such sentiments cannot be ignored.

The public was also concerned about the question of the black vote in the South in 1888. In spite of prejudices and discriminations, blacks were voting in the North, as well as *writing letters* to the President. Upon Harrison's nomination, "fifteen thousand colored voters of Kansas," the editor of a black paper, a black congressman from Mississippi and others congratulated the Republican standard-bearer and urged him emphatically, in the words of John R. Lynch, not to fail "to call attention to the criminal suppression of the Republican votes *white* and *colored*, in several of the Southern States [and] take a bold and outspoken position in favor of a rigid enforcement of the Constitution and Laws of the land. . . ."[28]

[26] Hedges, *Speeches*, pp. 10–15. Speech at Detroit, February 22, 1888.
[27] Ibid., pp. 21–22. Speech made in Chicago, March 20, 1888.
[28] C. A. Grinsted, Topeka, Kans., to Benjamin Harrison, June 25, 1888, BHP,

John L. Waller, black editor of a Kansas newspaper, accused James G. Blaine of trying to steer the campaign away from the troublesome black question in favor of the tariff; the editor refused to be bound by this restriction.[29]

In his letter of acceptance, Harrison came out strongly for what he called a pure ballot:

> Our colored people do not ask special legislation in their interest, but only to be made secure in the common rights of American citizenship. They will, however, naturally mistrust the sincerity of those party leaders who appeal to their race for support only in those localities where the suffrage is free and the election result doubtful, and compass their disfranchisement when their votes would be controlling and their choice cannot be coerced.[30]

Vol. 29, No. 6006; Magnus L. Robinson, black editor of the *National Leader*, to Benjamin Harrison, June 28, 1888, BHP, Vol. 29, No. 6372; a white man, James R. Challen, Jacksonville, Fla., to Benjamin Harrison, June 26, 1888, BHP, Vol. 29, No. 6089; John R. Lynch, Miss., to Benjamin Harrison, July 2, 1888, BHP, Vol. 31, No. 6633. Lynch thought that Harrison's speech to blacks in Indianapolis, June 30, 1888, already alluded to in this chapter (pages 243–44), removed all doubt about his concern for the black race; see also W. Calvin Chase of the *Washington Bee*, to Benjamin Harrison, July 9, 1888, BHP, Vol. 33, No. 6960. Chase accused a black man, J. Milton Turner, former minister resident of Liberia, of trying to swing the black vote to Cleveland; on July 16, 1888, "three hundred loyal colored men of Carrollton County, Mo., belong[ing] to the colored Harrison and Morton Club," sent in their support, BHP, Vol. 34, No. 7275; on August 11, 1888, from the Sixth Ward, Harrison and Morton Club of Cincinnati, Ohio, and signed by Robert Harlan, Jr., came these sentiments: "As colored men we thank you for your expressions of friendship toward the race, and renew our assurance of fealty to the cause you so ably represent," BHP, Vol. 37, No. 18174.

29 "I am a colored man. . . . I am one of the Presidential electors at large in Kansas. . . . *I am* for a *protective tariff* for the *highest wages* for American laborers, but I *am not willing* to close my mouth and eyes to the *frauds* committed against the suffrage of nearly a million colored voters in this country. The colored independents will seize upon the words of Mr. Blaine and use them to your harm in your own state. . . . I prefer to take the Republican platform as it is and instead of abandoning any part of it cling for dear life to every principle laid down therein." From the letter of John R. Waller, editor, *American Citizen*, Topeka, Shawnee County, Kans., to Benjamin Harrison, August 14, 1888, BHP, Vol. 38, No. 8315; see also an interview in the *New York Daily Tribune*, Thursday, August 16, 1888, BHP, Vol. 38, No. 8393–99, with one Dr. H. J. Brown, "a leading colored Republican of Baltimore," who claimed that the blacks were going for Harrison. Brown said: "Many colored men have been reading painstakingly enough to read up on social science and the economic questions now agitating the country, and they see the real weakness of free trade. . . ."

30 September 11, 1888, *Public Papers and Addresses of Benjamin Harrison* (Washington: Government Printing Office, 1893), pp. 1–7.

The letter of acceptance brought a ray of hope to the black secretary of the Republican County Central Committee of Hot Springs, Arkansas, a pledge of support from "five thousand colored citizens of New York . . . ," and renewed pleas for the protection of black and white Republicans in the South and the counting of their votes.[31]

The attempted wedding between the issue of a free ballot and the protective tariff was strange, indeed. Harrison contended that if all of the protective tariff Southerners would "throw off old prejudices" and vote for protection they would be strong enough after that to insist that the black vote be counted. Harrison, no less than his Republican predecessors since Hayes, was trying desperately to get the South to take a stand upon a political issue other than race.[32]

Finally, a carpetbagger representative of the Alabama Great Southern Railroad Company described the plight of white Republicans in the South who had to vote with the Democrats in state and local elections and with their own party in national contests in order to escape the taint of association with the "nigger party."[33] Not much has been said about this political

[31] "No one but we who live in *this* God forsaken part of the country [Hot Springs, Ark.] can imagine what we have to undergo to exist. Buldozed-disfranchised [*sic*], assassinated, murdered. In fact treated a good deal worse than when we were slaves, our only hope on earth now is your election." Alonzo Stone to Benjamin Harrison, September 24, 1888, BHP, Vol. 41, No. 9032–33. This letter came from the home state of Cleveland's Southern Attorney General, A. K. Garland; telegram of William Freeman, New York, to Benjamin Harrison, October 25, 1888, BHP, Vol. 45, No. 9836; the mayor of Chicago, John A. Rouchey, to Benjamin Harrison, September 28, 1888, BHP, Vol. 42, No. 9232–33; the chairman of the Republican State Central Committee of Louisiana, P. F. Herwig, New Orleans, October 30, 1888, BHP, Vol. 45, No. 9874–76; letter of James B. Sanford, dealer in "Botanic Blood Balm, the wonderful blood purifier of the age," Atlanta, Ga., [October 1888?], BHP, Vol. 45, No. 9899; J. Medici, of the *Chicago Tribune*, to E. A. Angier, lawyer, Atlanta, Ga., November 17, 1888, BHP, Vol. 47, No. 10388; Henry D. Clay, clerk in the County and Circuit Court of Warrick County, Va., 1888, BHP, Vol. 47, No. 10422–23; Henry G. Thompson to Benjamin Harrison, November 21, 1888, BHP, Vol. 48, No. 10549–50.

[32] Speech of Benjamin Harrison to the Wisconsin and Indiana delegations, October 5, 1888, Hedges, *Speeches*, pp. 162–63.

[33] F. D. Squires, Birmingham, Ala., to Benjamin Harrison, November 19, 1888, BHP, Vol. 47, No. 10449–53; Edward C. Currington, Prince Georges County, Md., to Benjamin Harrison, November 20, 1888, BHP, Vol. 48, No. 10462–63.

schizophrenia in the South. It may well be that the white Republicans in the South, rather than the party leadership in the North, abandoned the blacks first. That the black preferred to be driven to the wall rather than submit to anything less than an equal share in any partnership with white Republicans in the South was to his credit. Meanwhile Republicans in Congress were making the final effort of the century to secure the vote to blacks in the South.

The Federal Elections Bill

In 1888, the former Secretary of the Treasury under Lincoln, Johnson and Chester A. Arthur, Hugh McCulloch of Indiana, looked with misgivings upon black suffrage. For him there could be no political coexistence between the races. The North had expected blacks to die out or be dispersed over the country after the Civil War, but instead the race was increasing, lamented McCulloch. The only way to prevent black domination was for the federal government to continue to refrain "from an interference with local affairs. . . ."[34]

McCulloch to the contrary, pleas for relief continued to be heard,[35] and events suggested that an attempt would yet be made to help blacks. In his inaugural address, Harrison himself wondered how long the issue of race would "continue to hang upon the skirts of progress" in the South. He thought that economic interests could or should transcend racial considerations. He asked for an alliance between Southern protective tariff Whigs and blacks.[36] Meanwhile, Senator W. E. Chandler of New Hampshire was disturbed over the invasion of the North by Southern anti-black sentiment: "It is atrocious that Grady should be vaunting his defiance of the 15th Amendment to the people of Boston, and talking his twaddle from Plymouth

[34] Hugh McCulloch, *Men and Measures of Half a Century* (New York: Charles Scribner's Sons, 1888), pp. 513–16.

[35] Letter of the colored citizens of Springfield, Mass., January 21, 1889, BHP, Vol. 61, No. 13769.

[36] Hedges, *Speeches*, p. 197. Harrison's Inaugural Address, March 4, 1889.

Rock. It all means that the South shall be let alone to suppress the Negro vote."[37]

The Federal Elections bill, recommended by Harrison in his annual message of 1889, came up for consideration in 1890. The bill was designed to give more protection to blacks in federal elections. In his second annual message, Harrison noted that the bill was meeting with resistance: "But it is said that this legislation will revive race animosities, and some have even suggested that when the peaceful methods of fraud are made positively impossible, they may be supplanted by intimidation and violence." Harrison rejected the logic of such arguments. The only thing that might cause animosity, he thought, was "the fact that some electors have been accustomed to exercise the franchise for others as well as themselves. . . . [That kind of anger] ought not to be confessed without shame, and cannot be given any weight in the discussion without dishonor."[38] As for Southern hatred for the law, Harrison said: "No choice is left to me but to enforce with vigor all laws intended to secure to the citizen his constitutional rights." To acquiesce in the prostitution of the ballot by the South was politically unfair to the North. Finally, he thought it unjust to charge him with unfriendliness toward the South when he sought "only to restrain violators of law and personal rights."[39] This was indeed an admirable stand for a free ballot.

Three and a half pages of the third annual message were devoted to the subject of election frauds and the need for legislation.[40] One newspaper commented that Harrison was determined to push the bill through and as a result had become very unpopular in the Senate.[41] The Democratic *New York*

[37] W. E. Chandler to E. A. Angier, federal district attorney in Georgia, December 16, 1889, BHP, Vol. 93, No. 21061. The reference was to Henry Grady, editor of the *Atlanta Constitution.*

[38] Second Annual Message of Benjamin Harrison, December 1, 1890, Richardson, *Messages,* IX, 129. The *Florida Times Union,* March 16, 1890, BHP (Scrapbooks), Vol. 9, p. 88, represented the bill as an attempt of Republicans to keep the Southerners from getting control of the national government.

[39] Ibid., IX, 128–29.

[40] Second Annual Message of Benjamin Harrison, December 1, 1890, Richardson, *Messages,* IX, 208–11. Third Annual Message of Benjamin Harrison, 1891.

[41] *Chicago Herald,* February 2, 1891, newspaper clipping, BHP (Scrapbooks), Vol. 10, p. 71.

World doubted that the bill would ever be heard of again.[42] Meanwhile, John Mercer Langston, a distinguished black leader of the period, was making a grand oration on "The Situation and Demands of the Colored American" to a black Washington audience, in which he called for full equality before the law as promised by the Constitution.[43]

As the election of 1892 neared, more rumors flew. It was charged that Harrison was about to abandon the black voter to a white Republican party in the South, and that he had changed his mind only after being told by Kellogg that such action would alienate Northern and Southern blacks.[44] The *Atlanta Constitution* made capital out of another rumor that Harrison wanted only white businessmen to come to the Republican Convention in 1892 with this bit of racial banter: "President Harrison can't shut out the black brother, he's guine to dat convention."[45]

In his fourth and final annual message Harrison was still asking Congress to secure a free ballot.[46] In his letter of acceptance for his second nomination he deplored fraudulent state elections in the South which shut out the Republicans completely, but despaired of being able to do anything about it. He could only hope that the states would change their laws. He would ask Congress to set up a commission to study the subject of federal appointments and elections.[47]

[42] Newspaper clipping, June 21, 1891, BHP (Scrapbooks), Vol. 13, p. 87.

[43] Langston skipped the subject of a superior race. He denied any desire of the black man to dominate the whites. He left amalgamation in the hands of the Almighty. He brushed aside colonization as irrelevant. As for social equality he was willing to let nature take its course. He denied that the black's past and racial characteristics were sufficient reasons to withhold his rights from him. Finally, the blacks, he thought, had a better constitutional leg to stand upon in this country than did the Indian and the Mongolian. This speech was delivered Tuesday evening, March 24, 1891, at John Wesley A. M. E. Zion Church, Washington, D.C. John Mercer Langston Papers (microfilm, one reel, Howard University Library, Washington, D.C.). The original manuscripts are housed at Fisk University Library, Nashville, Tenn.

[44] Newspaper clipping, August 6, 1891, BHP (Scrapbooks), Vol. 13, p. 186.

[45] Newspaper clipping, February 12, 1892, BHP (Scrapbooks), Vol. 14, p. 76.

[46] December 6, 1892. *The Public Papers and Addresses of Benjamin Harrison, 1889–1893*, p. 156.

[47] Benjamin Harrison's letter of acceptance, September 3, 1892, *Public Papers and Addresses of Benjamin Harrison, 1889–1893*, p. 20.

So it seems that if a positive presidential attitude by itself could have passed the Federal Elections bill, the measure would have passed at this time. It did not do so. Thirteen years later, Senator Hoar, looking back, felt the cause of the elections bill dying was that the Southerners effectively cried "Negro domination." The Republicans were dubious of their ability to pass the bill or enforce it if it were passed, even though a majority of the Senate favored the bill, as Hoar recollected. Hoar claimed that the Republicans backed off when Democratic newspapers North and South bitterly denounced the bill.[48] A similar fate awaited the attempt to wipe out illiteracy among blacks in the South.

The Blair Education Bill

In his letter accepting the Republican nomination in 1888, Harrison called for federal aid to education.[49] Why the bill, designed primarily to eradicate illiteracy among the freedmen of the South, was defeated is not properly the concern of this book. Yet, it is strange that the very remedy which politicians and the country at large had said was the solution to the race problem in the South could not get through Congress. Even the so-called "friends" of the freedmen were against the bill. Such was the case with Albion Tourgee and General S. C. Armstrong of Hampton Institute. Tourgee felt that two-thirds of the money would go to the whites if administered by the South. Armstrong once favored the bill but changed his mind. He thought that the bill gave too much money in too little time. The money might be stolen. It denied the principle of self-help. Education should be left to the South, who had spent thirty-seven million dollars on blacks. Armstrong may have been afraid that federal aid would eclipse private institutions such as his own.[50] But in spite of Armstrong and Tourgee's

[48] George F. Hoar, *Autobiography of Seventy Years*, II, 541–58.
[49] September 11, 1888, *Public Papers . . .*, p. 5.
[50] Albion Tourgee, Mayesville, N.Y., to Benjamin Harrison, December 7, 1888, BHP, Vol. 50, No. 1109–14; S. C. Armstrong to Benjamin Harrison, (1889), BHP, Vol. 90, on the subject; the Women's Christian Temperance

objections, Harrison asked Congress for federal aid to the South in his first annual message of 1889.[51] By 1892, however, Harrison himself had apparently cooled on the subject. While he still favored federal aid to education, he said in his last message to Congress that he was happy to see that many of the "Southern states were advancing their school systems liberally . . . to the great advantage of the children of both races."[52] Clearly, the initial fervor in Harrison's plea for federal aid to education was gone. Neither did the President appear unduly disturbed about the plight of a black politician in Virginia.

John Mercer Langston and Harrison

After the general elections of 1888, John Mercer Langston, a distinguished black lawyer, claimed that he had legitimately won a seat in Congress from Virginia and that white Republicans and Democrats in that state were uniting to unseat him.[53] "Though I be a colored man, when duly accredited upon their vote to such duty and honor; . . . I will not submit to any such thing," said Langston, hoping that Harrison would stand by him.[54] Harrison answered the letter but volunteered no aid. "I notice your statement as to matters in your district," was all he said on the matter.[55] Langston eventually took his seat,

---

Union was for the bill. See Mary A. Hunt to Benjamin Harrison, December 4, 1889, BHP, Vol. 92, No. 20856–57; Flora Adams Darling, December 6, 1889, in favor of the bill, BHP, Vol. 92, No. 20886–88; the secretary of the Connecticut State Board of Education sent in a nine-page letter telling why he was against federal aid to education. See Charles D. Hines, February 12, 1889, BHP, Vol. 67, No. 15240–48. A South Carolinian favored the bill. See W. Walker Russell (1889?), BHP, Vol. 94, No. 21439–40.

[51] December 3, 1889, Richardson, *Messages*, IX, 55.

[52] December 3, 1892, *Public Papers and Addresses of Benjamin Harrison*, p. 2.

[53] He was a graduate of Oberlin College, admitted to the Ohio Bar in 1854, founder and former dean of the Howard University Law School, congressman from Virginia, inspector for the Freedmen's Bureau, and minister to Haiti. See a manuscript biographical letter in John Mercer Langston Papers (microfilm), Howard University Library, Washington, D.C.

[54] John Mercer Langston to Benjamin Harrison, November 10, 1888, BHP, Vol. 46, No. 10156–60.

[55] Benjamin Harrison to John Mercer Langston, November 16, 1888, John Mercer Langston Papers, Letter No. 38.

but not before a number of letters had testified for and against the charge that Langston's adversary, the controversial Mahone, was a white Republican who was trying to make his party respectable by getting whites to join it, while keeping the blacks in the background.[56] But the blacks refused to stay out of sight. They insisted on their share of the federal patronage.

Black Appointments

The Presidents came face to face with race in the matter of federal patronage. Would the distribution of the "spoils of office" be color-blind? There was no lack of racial activity on the "political breadline." But there were charges that President Harrison had "ignored the colored element in the distribution of federal jobs."[57] A Charlestonian, upon hearing a rumor that a black was to be appointed to the Cabinet, con-

[56] The following were against Mahone and in favor of Langston in the controversy: Letter of Republican C. C. Clark, Virginia, to E. B. Elkins, December 7, 1888 (forwarded to Harrison), in BHP, Vol. 50, No. 11107–12; R. H. Kirk, Ft. Monroe, Va., to Benjamin Harrison, December 11, 1888, BHP, Vol. 51, No. 11234–35, accusing Mahone of spending most of the campaign funds furnished him by the party, to defeat Langston! James F. Rinker, M.D., to Benjamin Harrison, January 25, 1889, BHP, Vol. 62, No. 14052–53; a Virginian explained the situation in the Fourth Congressional District thus: "There, race prejudice became dominant in the conflict. Langston, the bolting independent Republican candidate, a colored man, as you know, of superior intelligence, has rendered himself obnoxious to the white electors and many of the colored leaders by his supposed affiliation with the Democracy. . . . drew the color line . . . and as a result received a majority over the . . . regular Republican nominee. . . ." Supported by Mahone. Henry de B. Clay, Newport News, Va., to Benjamin Harrison, February 7, 1889, BHP, Vol. 65, No. 14827–30; the following (out of hundreds) called Mahone a liberal and wanted him in the Cabinet as a friend of blacks; even the black John R. Lynch spoke in his favor. Letter, December 25, 1888, BHP, Vol. 53, No. 11842; Charles Cury [?] to Benjamin Harrison, January 15, 1889, BHP, Vol. 59, No. 13202–06; the black chairman of the Republican County Executive Committee, Birmingham, Ala., spoke for Mahone. J. G. C. Van Auker, to H. M. Blair, U.S. senator, February 2, 1889 (forwarded to Harrison), BHP, Vol. 64, No. 14549–54; S. Basset French, Manchester, Va., to Benjamin Harrison, January 31, 1889, BHP, Vol. 63, No. 14358–61; letter of H. C. Binford, Birmingham, Ala., January 1889, BHP, Vol. 64, No. 14405.

[57] A diplomat in Buenos Aires, J. R. G. Pitkin, to Benjamin Harrison, January 3, 1889, BHP, Vol. 55, No. 12327–28. He had also heard that the "colored" consular post at Santo Domingo would not go to a black this time.

tended that the black man would benefit more by having his vote secured first.[58] A black public school principal from Montezuma, Georgia, commenting upon the same rumor, said: "It is too early for such a step." He would settle for minor positions "for the *col'd* brethren of the party. . . ."[59] A Washington lawyer and another attorney from Columbia, South Carolina, interceded for a recently defeated black politician, Robert Smalls of South Carolina, asking that he be consulted in the distribution of patronage in that state.[60]

An interesting dialogue on race took place between Senator George Frisby Hoar of Massachusetts and George Williams, a black man, relative to the Haitian Mission. This was a "colored" job, but was about to be given to a white man because, as Hoar put it, "it is strange and lamentable, but it is said to be true that the Haytians do not pay the respect to our ministers who are men of their own race that they do to the white representatives of European countries . . . our business interests there have suffered very much from that fact." In the meantime, some other attractive place of service would be substituted for the displaced "representative colored man."[61]

It appears that George Williams was asked to recommend someone for the Haitian appointment. He seems to have wanted the job himself but propriety forbade him from submitting his own name. He failed to propose anyone so Frederick Douglass, a perennial black officeholder, wound up with the job.[62] Wil-

58 W. A. Grant to Benjamin Harrison, January 7, 1889, BHP, Vol. 56, No. 12580–82.

59 L. H. Brown to Benjamin Harrison, February 11, 1889, BHP, Vol. 66, No. 15129–30.

60 W. W. Dudley to Benjamin Harrison, March 12, 1889, BHP, Vol. 70, No. 16073; Samuel W. Melton, Columbia, S.C., to E. W. Halford, April 22, 1889, BHP, Vol. 74, No. 17012–13. In defense of Smalls, this letter said: "I know he has the good wishes of the white people of Beaufort County—not for his politics, but because he is a manly, decent, honest Republican and stands for decency"; Elliot Brayton, Charleston, April 16, 1889, BHP, Vol. 74, No. 1712–13.

61 George F. Hoar to Col. George Williams, Massachusetts, March 23, 1889, BHP, Vol. 72, No. 16435–36.

62 Douglass was appointed by Harrison to head the Haitian Legation. See letter of Frederick Douglass to James G. Blaine, June 25, 1889, Foner (ed.),

liams told the President that America had neglected Haiti.[63]

Black Republicans of Louisiana met in Washington and complained to the President about what they considered the unfair distribution of the federal patronage to the black but loyal friends of the government and party since Reconstruction. They claimed that out of a total of eighteen appointments for their state only two or three had gone to blacks. They also noted that Northern blacks were being discriminated against in the distribution of federal jobs. They also contended that the black vote was crucial in such Northern states as New York, Indiana and Ohio. "Under our form of government numbers is the basis of political power. . . . By what rule of equity is the same denied us? . . . It is unAmerican, unRepublican, and unjust, and can proceed upon only one assumption that of race prejudice." Such behavior, they contended, may have had some justification when the blacks were initially enfranchised, but "a quarter of a century of freedom has enabled the race to secure men of sufficient intelligence, experience and capacity to discharge the duties of citizenship in any position in which they may be called."[64]

A black school teacher from Indianapolis desired a clerk's job in Washington and was described by his white sponsor as a "bright, active, energetic young man who organized a young colored boys voters club during the election."[65] Senator Matt Quay of Pennsylvania recommended a leading black Texas

---

The Life and Writings of Frederick Douglass, IV, 455; and still another letter of Douglass to Blaine, October 14, 1889, ibid., see also letter of Alvey A. Adee, Acting Secretary of State, to Benjamin Harrison, September 17, 1889, in regard to the black Mr. Thompson's (our representative to Haiti) resignation, and the appointment of Frederick Douglass. In addition to being critically ill, Thompson apparently was not earning the respect of the Haitians, BHP, Vol. 87, No. 19698.

[63] George Williams to E. W. Halford, May 7, 1889, BHP, Vol. 76, No. 17334–35; George Williams to Benjamin Harrison, May 7, 1889, ibid., No. 17336–37; Williams to Benjamin Harrison, May 23, 1889, ibid., Vol. 77, No. 17595–97.

[64] April 1, 1889, BHP, Vol. 73, No.16680–82.

[65] Stanton J. Peel, lawyer, to Honorable J. N. Huston, Washington, D.C., April 18, 1889, ibid., Vol. 75, No. 17073. Huston forwarded the letter to Harrison who said that he would give the letter his personal attention. The young black man in question was W. M. Lewis, age twenty-six.

politician, N. W. Cuney, to be the Collector of the Port of Customs at Galveston. Cuney was eventually appointed, but not without some grumbling by the *New York Times:*

> If President Harrison wants to win votes from the white Democrats of Texas he could hardly have set about it in a worse way than by making the appointment of N. Wright Cuney. . . . Cuney is a colored party worker and appears to be more heartily disliked by the Texas Democrats than any other man of his race in the State. He made himself obnoxious to the whites by vigorously denouncing the so-called outrages on blacks and criticizing the State authorities for not protecting the black man from the aggressions of the whites. Democratic newspapers all over the State branded Cuney as a slanderer of the fair name of Texas. . . . Cuney was strongly endorsed by the Republicans of the State . . . and the commission he desired is his.[66]

A black officeholder from the North, a rare thing in this period, complained that the Northern black was being ignored by dispensers of the federal patronage. If the Northern blacks held the balance of power in close elections, why were Southern blacks always rewarded with the plums of office to the exclusion of the black brother in the North? This complaint held that while six major Southern appointments went to blacks, excluding numerous minor ones, none were made in the North except his own, recorder of deeds in the General Land Office of Indiana. Why did Northern congressmen pass over "intelligent, educated, and representative colored citizens" from the North? "It is hardly fair Mr. Secretary, to argue that colored Republicans shall not expect to receive political recognition," the black concluded.[67]

[66] Joseph Bradfield, Washington, D.C., to Benjamin Harrison, enclosing a clipping from the *New York Times,* July 21, 1889. The letter was dated July 22, 1889, BHP, Vol. 83, No. 18850–51.

[67] J. M. Townsend, recorder, General Land Office, Indiana, to E. W. Halford (private secretary to the President), July 31, 1889, BHP, Vol. 83, No. 19058–66. In his letter Townsend included clippings from two colored newspapers, the *Cleveland Gazette* and the *Philadelphia Sentinel,* July 27, 1889. The six major black appointments were listed as follows: Norris Wright Cuney, Collector of the Port at Galveston; General Robert Smalls, Collector of the Port at Beaufort, South Carolina; John R. Lynch, 4th Auditor of the Treasury, Mississippi; John Spellman, Specialist in the Land Office, Mississippi; Mr. Handy, U. S. Registrar or Receiver in Post Office, Alabama.

There seems to have been unusual discontent among racial and national minorities in Indiana in 1889. Harrison was informed that trouble might be brewing for a coming election in Indianapolis. There was some anxiety lest Harrison's own home city go Democratic. ". . . Our Irish friends are seeking recognition with zeal and energy which is characteristic of their race. . . . We need not expect anything from the Germans. The colored people and the laboring men are urgently demanding recognition," said one informant.[68] A set of instructions sent out to party managers in the state of Indiana read thus: "The colored men and the Irish Republicans are not cultivated as much as they should be. They should be sent as delegates to conventions, and recognized in other ways."[69]

The Republican boss in Georgia, while he had not before pressed the President to appoint a black postmaster, now requested that a black man, Madison Davis, be appointed at Athens, Georgia, for the following reason:

> In order to hold our forces and keep all elements solid in support of the Administration a few collected [*sic;* colored?] men will have to be appointed as postmasters. Mr. Davis though classified as a colored man, is in fact as near white as any man can be with colored blood in his veins.[70]

Controversy arose in the government print shop when a black appointment was made in the Federal Bureau of Engraving and Printing. The ultimate disposition of the case is not known, but here was a good illustration of the idea of race at work. A black woman was appointed assistant to the plate printer. According to the senator from Connecticut, J. R. Hawley, who was trying to get the President to act as peacemaker in the affair, the printers were displeased and attempted to make political capital out of the incident: "It seems to me that the colored woman could be assigned to some equally

[68] J. W. Hess to Benjamin Harrison, [n.d.], 1889, BHP, Vol. 75, No. 17202–03.

[69] See memorandum of State Republican Chairman L. T. Michener, October 5, 1889, ibid., Vol. 88, No. 20041–45.

[70] A. E. Buck, Republican Committee Chairman, Atlanta, Ga., to E. W. Halford, January 26, 1890, BHP, Vol. 97, No. 21919–20.

profitable duty. . . . Nobody who is reasonable wants a rub-a-dub discussion of the race question over the case," Hawley advised the President.

The racial "rub" in this case stemmed from the fact that "the Plate Printer and his Assistant [now to be a black woman] work side by side over the small machine all day." Hawley understood that the printers would not object to the black woman working in the "same building where white people are employed in the same room." Hawley wanted the President to know that he himself did not share these personal prejudices against blacks: "I am an old abolitionist and have entertained colored men with bed and board in my own house."[71]

At this point the *Charleston News and Courier* complained about the black post-office appointments: "There is not a black man or colored man in the President's political household. Not one black man or colored man holds a place in the Post Office Department which brings him into contact with the white people in any Northern state from Maine to California. Alas, such appointments have been strictly confined to the Southern states."[72] The *Courier*'s charge substantiates the contention of Northern blacks that they were being slighted in appointments. Blacks would not have been encouraged if they had known that someone had suggested replacing the black Democratic recorder of deeds for the District of Columbia with a white veteran who had lost both feet in the Civil War.[73]

The failure of the Federal Elections bill and the attempted white man's Republican party movement in the South, sanctioned it was though by Harrison, caused the black voters of Ohio to give Harrison a verbal drubbing: "His failure to accord us a decent recognition in the distribution of his official favors is unfair, unjust, and ungrateful. . . . The old game of turkey for the leaders and turkey buzzard for us is played out. . . . Let them win their own victories—if they can—without our help."

71 Senator J. T. Hawley to Benjamin Harrison, February 10, 1890, BHP, Vol. 98, No. 22184–85.

72 Tuesday, April 12, 1891, BHP (Scrapbooks), Vol. 10, p. 109.

73 Benjamin Harrison to James B. Tanner, September, 12, 1889, BHP, Vol. 86, No. 19626; J. B. Cheadle to Benjamin Harrison, September 12, 1889, ibid., No. 19630.

The source of this information reported a black preacher declaring that should he ever again vote for the Republican ticket "may my hand be palsied and my tongue cleave . . . to the roof of my mouth."[74]

The drive of the Northern black for political recognition posed for Harrison a problem with the Southerners, according to the *New York Herald.* Rumor had it that Harrison was thinking about making John Mercer Langston a United States Circuit judge, to which, according to the *Herald,* a prominent North Carolinian allegedly replied: "If Mr. Harrison thinks he will help the Republican cause in Ohio and Indiana by the appointment of a Southern [Langston was really a Northerner] Negro to the bench, he is very much mistaken. . . ."[75] The *Cincinnati Commercial Gazette* explained the state of mind of the Northern black on the patronage issue: "The colored voters would like to see something in the way of official recognition given to someone else besides Fred Douglass, B. K. Bruce, and John R. Lynch."[76] According to the same newspaper Ohio blacks were angry because of 117 employees of the state government, only 2 were black and 1 of these a Democrat. Blacks claimed they were thirty-seven thousand voters strong in Ohio.[77]

John Mercer Langston defended the Republican patronage record in the *Cincinnati Commercial Gazette.* He reported 2393 blacks on the payroll in Washington, drawing a total salary of $1,370,623.98. Sixteen blacks had held diplomatic and consular appointments from Republicans since 1869, while the Democrats had appointed only three, according to Langston. While there were currently only three black congressmen, Langston said that the Republicans had elected fourteen from the South since 1869 while the Democrats had sent none.[78] The

[74] Newspaper clipping from the *Cincinnati Enquirer,* Wednesday, July 1, 1891, BHP (Scrapbooks), Vol. 13, pp. 105–06.

[75] Newspaper clipping, August 16, 1891, ibid., p. 186.

[76] Newspaper clipping, July 16, 1891, BHP (Scrapbooks), Vol. 13, p. 117; newspaper clipping, July 18, 1891, ibid., pp. 124–25.

[77] Undated newspaper clipping [1891], BHP (Scrapbooks), Vol. 13, p. 8.

[78] Newspaper clipping, September 5, 1891, GHP (Scrapbooks), Vol. 13, pp. 60–61.

Afro-American J. M. Townsend, who had himself once complained about lack of recognition for blacks, denied, according to one newspaper, any black dissatisfaction with the Republican party. Now that he had the higher post of recorder of deeds for the District of Columbia he seemed more tolerant of Republicans.[79] Finally, the *New York Sun* reported "the colored wing of the Republican Party of Indianapolis . . . in open revolt against Harrison. . . ."[80] But in 1892, Frederick Douglass was employed to keep black delegates in line for Harrison's nomination and was apparently successful.[81] But blacks were not the only dissatisfied constituents with which Harrison had to contend. He was faced with a small crisis in the House of David.

A *Jew in the Cabinet?*

Jews were equally as interested in political recognition as the blacks and the response of the politicians to the Jewish minority differed little from the reception accorded blacks. When Harrison was first nominated in 1888, the editor of a Jewish paper congratulated him and promised that he would get the thirty thousand Jewish votes from New York City. At the same time the gubernatorial candidate of Indiana, General Hovey, was accused of bigotry with respect to the Jews, "the brothers of Jesus."[82]

On the eve of the election a New York rabbi opened an extensive correspondence with Harrison covering but two subjects, the importance of Jewish votes and the possibility of a Jew in

[79] Clipping from the *Daily Journal,* Friday, September 25, 1891, BHP (Scrapbooks), Vol. 13, p. 116.

[80] Newspaper clipping, June 21, 1891, ibid., p. 90.

[81] Frederick Douglass to Honorable L. T. Michener, June 21, 1892, L. T. Michener Papers, the Library of Congress, Washington, D.C., Box 1.

[82] Benjamin F. Peixotto, editor of the *Menorah, Monthly Magazine of Hebrew Literature and Art,* to Benjamin Harrison, September 12, 1888, BHP, Vol. 40, No. 8803; "Hovey is a dead weight hanging to your neck and he will drown you," Reverend Edward B. M. Browne, L.L.D., rabbi of Mt. Sinai Temple, New York, to Benjamin Harrison, October 5, 1888, BHP, Vol. 43, No. 9369–75.

the Cabinet.[83] Exercising the usual political caution in matters of a controversial nature, Harrison said: "It is impossible for me to discuss now the question which you present for my consideration [that is, a Jew in the Cabinet]." He reminded Browne that he had been nominated without making any promises concerning appointments.[84] But upon Harrison's election, Rabbi Browne saluted him rather piously: "May the God of our common ancestors, Abraham, Isaac and Jacob strengthen you to carry the great burden soon to rest upon your shoulders. . . ." After this Old Testament greeting he quickly turned to a more mundane matter, the subject of "a Hebrew to be a member of your Cabinet. . . ." Browne charged that such a promise had been made to the Jews by Senator Quay of Pennsylvania. Like the blacks, Browne claimed that the Jewish vote could swing elections in doubtful states.

Rabbi Browne also held that the Democrats and Cleveland had done more for the Jews than the Republicans: three United States senators and an ambassador. Had he not told his Jewish public that a vote for Harrison was a vote for a Jew in the Cabinet? And had he not already promised the Cabinet post to an eminent Israelite, Reverend Doctor Wise of Cincinnati, who was about to defect to Cleveland? "There will be another [election] in four years and Jews are long lived as a rule and their memory is very good," said Browne in a veiled threat. However, before he closed he intimated that the Hebrews would "settle for a post below Cabinet rank."[85]

Mr. Peixotto, another Hebrew correspondent, sent the President a book about prominent Jews in America, underlining in "green pencil" the names of those who were instrumental in getting out the Jewish vote. The motive behind this gift was obviously to provide the President with an up-to-date guide in

[83] Reverend Edward B. M. Browne to Benjamin Harrison, October 5, 1888, BHP, Vol. 43, No. 9369–75.

[84] Benjamin Harrison to Reverend Edward B. M. Browne, October 9, 1888, BHP, Vol. 43, No. 9457.

[85] Reverend Edward B. M. Browne to Benjamin Harrison, November 16, 1888, BHP, Vol. 47, No. 10315–22; J. Wolf to Benjamin Harrison, November 16, 1888, extending the congratulations of the Jewish community for Harrison's victory, ibid., No. 10346.

the event a Jew was chosen for the Cabinet.[86] A Vermont state senator sent the President an editorial from a West Coast newspaper which read in part: "Some of our Jewish-American citizens are very much interested in the prospect of one of their numbers entering President Harrison's Cabinet next March. . . ." According to this editorial the most likely candidate was Mr. De Young, "a well-known Jewish Californian, proprietor and editor of the *San Francisco Chronicle* . . . ," and the office in mind was that of Postmaster General. However, this state senator was anxious to discourage the De Young nomination.[87]

Stephen B. Elkins requested that the Jewish Peixotto be appointed to a diplomatic post at Constantinople, replacing Cleveland's Jewish appointee, Oscar Straus.[88] Two days later, Peixotto wrote in his own behalf, accusing Harrison of ignoring faithful party workers.[89] "My friends will not permit me to retire from candidacy for the Turkish Mission," he said in yet another letter.[90] Soon it was evident that both Browne and Peixotto were in competition for the mission at Constantinople. Browne accused Peixotto of paying off a doorman at the White House to prevent him from seeing the President, and complained to Harrison's secretary about allegedly shabby treatment at the White House: "As a 'Christian' gentleman you could not have treated me on my recent visit to the White House with such marked indifference as you manifested toward me unless somebody had *prejudiced you against me. . . .*"[91] A Methodist bishop who did

[86] Peixotto claimed that the Jewish vote was strategic in New York, Wisconsin, Michigan, Indiana, Connecticut and New Jersey. The book was entitled *Hebrew in America*, by Isaac [Markers?] but was not found in the papers. Benjamin Peixotto, New York lawyer, to Benjamin Harrison, November 28, 1889, BHP, Vol. 49, Nos. 10767–68, 10769.

[87] Thomas Harris, state senator, enclosing newspaper clipping to Benjamin Harrison, November 24, 1888, BHP, Vol. 48, No. 10634–36.

[88] S. B. Elkins to Benjamin Harrison, March 23, 1889, BHP, Vol. 72, No. 16428. Elkins became Harrison's Secretary of War in 1891 and a United States senator from West Virginia.

[89] Benjamin Peixotto to Benjamin Harrison, March 25, 1889, BHP, Vol. 72, No. 16486.

[90] Mr. Peixotto to E. W. Halford, April 1, 1889, BHP, Vol. 72, No. 16705.

[91] Reverend Edward B. Browne to E. W. Halford, March 31, 1889, BHP, Vol. 73, No. 16032–33.

not want to be "conspicuous" in his recommendation expressed his preference for a "Christian" at the Turkish Mission.[92] Browne, meanwhile, continued to pressure Harrison for a Jew in the Cabinet and regretted that "the Jew's time for Cabinet office in the Republican Party had not come. . . ."[93]

Elkins called Harrison's attention to the complaint of New York Jews that they had not been recognized "in the way of appointments at your hand. . . ." Elkins argued that the Jews had worked for Harrison during the last election and thought it "nothing more than right, besides, good politics, that they should be fairly rewarded." Peixotto was recommended for Turkey, Simon Wolf for a consularship and a Hebrew lawyer for a judgeship in New Mexico. Elkins found substance in the charge that the Democrats had done more for the children of Israel than had the Republicans.[94] In the end Peixotto did not get the Turkish Mission, to his disappointment. He had hoped to go back to the East as "a full fledged plenipotentiary of my country . . . no longer to be regarded as a mere missionary on behalf of a downtrodden race [but] . . . as you remarked to me 'New York's basket of red apples was already too full. . . .'" The politically hungry Peixotto was ready to settle for almost any office at this point as he again reminded Harrison that it was "the Hebrew vote" that carried the last election.[95] Finally, Rabbi Browne reported that he was anxious to run for Congress but his Hebrew political machine would not support him until a Jew had been recognized by the Administration.[96] But Harrison had perhaps a more pressing problem with which to deal—the erosion of the civil rights of Southern blacks.

[92] John P. Newman of the M. E. Church to E. W. Halford, April 19, 1889, BHP, Vol. 79, No. 17095.

[93] Reverend Edward B. M. Browne to Benjamin Harrison, April 22, 1889, BHP, Vol. 75, No. 17144–47.

[94] S. B. Elkins to Benjamin Harrison, May 16, 1889, BHP, Vol. 76, No. 17460; S. B. Elkins to Benjamin Harrison, December 4, 1889, BHP, Vol. 92, No. 20849–50. Elkins recommended Mr. Louis Sulzbacher for the New Mexico judgeship as a boon to the Jews.

[95] Benjamin Peixotto to Benjamin Harrison, July 9, 1889, BHP, Vol. 82, No. 37–40.

[96] Rabbi Browne to Benjamin Harrison, 1889, BHP, Vol. 87, No. 19878–82.

Civil Equality before the Law

In his campaign for the presidency Harrison claimed that all he was asking of the South was "a manly assertion by each of his individual rights, and a manly concession of equal rights to every other man. . . ."[97] It did not occur to Harrison that this was asking too much. Belief in equality before the law formed a part of his inaugural address as well as his first annual message. In regard to lawlessness in the South, he said: "Surely no one supposes that the present can be accepted as a permanent condition."[98] But the Afro-American League for the advancement of black people's rights did not feel that enough was being done. The league was firmly convinced that the political parties had "ceased consistently to concern themselves with the denial to Afro-Americans of the rights and immunities guaranteed to them by the fundamental law of the land." A copy of these sentiments was sent to the President along with a plea for law enforcement in the South and passage of the Blair Education bill.[99]

A four weeks' tour across the country in 1891 afforded the President plenty of opportunity to speak out against the more violent forms of civil oppression in the South. Yet, most of his forty-odd speeches were completely innocent of any reference to the subject of civil rights. However, he did let fly a few rather impotent remarks concerning his views on race: ". . . While exacting all our own rights let us bravely and generously accord to every other man his equal rights before the law," was the last line of a speech in Atlanta, Georgia, and the crowd cheered.[100] "The supremacy of law is the one supremacy in

[97] Speech at Indianapolis, to the Illinois Delegation, July 19, 1888, Hedges, *Speeches*, pp. 53, 198.

[98] President Harrison's Inaugural Address, March 4, 1889, ibid., p. 198; President Harrison's First Annual Message, December 3, 1889, Richardson, *Messages*, IX, 56–57.

[99] Newspaper clipping sent to Harrison by T. Thomas Fortune, H. C. C. Astwood, et al., of the Afro-American League, January 22, 1890, BHP, Vol. 96, No. 21831–33.

[100] *Our President: From the Atlantic to the Pacific*, 1891 (Kansas City, Mo.: Hudson Kimberg Publishing Co., 1891), pp. 28–29.

this country of ours," brought an ovation from a Memphis, Tennessee, crowd.[101] The President thought it fitting that black soldiers, members of "a race" once denied its citizenship in Illinois, should be guarding the tomb of Lincoln at Springfield.[102]

In the South, the President seemed primarily interested in emphasizing reunion and the return of the former Confederates to national allegiance. A Savannah, Georgia, newspaper called the President's attention to the integrated nature of the crowds that greeted him in the South and the lack of complaints from blacks: ". . . No sad-eyed delegations of sable-hued citizens plucked him [the President] by the gown to pour out a tale of woe . . . ," said the paper rather picturesquely.[103]

On his return to the White House, members of the Virginia State Baptist Convention visited Harrison and implored him to do something about racial violence in the South. The President promised to write them a letter on the subject and he did. The letter showed clearly that he was on the defensive about his civil rights record:

> I have endeavored to uphold the law as the one single admissible rule of conduct for good citizens. I have appealed against race discrimination as to civil rights and immunities, and have asked that law abiding men of all creeds and colors should unite to discourage and suppress lawlessness. Lynchings are a reproach to any community.

On the other hand, the federal nature of our political system made the President feel that his actions had to be limited to mostly verbal thrusts:

> I have not time to explain to you the limitations of federal power further than to say that under the Constitution and laws, I am, in a large measure, wihout the power to interfere for the prevention or punishment of these offences. You will not need be

[101] April 17, 1891, ibid., pp. 38–42; John S. Shriver, *Through the South and West with the President* [Harrison], *April 14th, May 15th,* 1891 (New York: Mail and Express, 1891), p. 12.

[102] *Our President: From the Atlantic to the Pacific,* 1891, pp. 186–90.

[103] Newspaper clipping, *Mirror of Commerce,* May 1, 1891, BHP (Scrapbooks), Vol. 10, p. 73.

> assured that the Department of Justice will let no case pass that is one of the federal jurisdiction without the most strenuous endeavors to bring the guilty persons to punishment.

The letter closed with the promise that the President would give the matter "the most serious consideration and you may be assured that my voice and help will be given to every effort to arouse the conscience of our people and to stimulate efficient efforts to reestablish the supremacy of the courts and public officials as the only proper agency of law enforcement."[104] But nine days later in a speech at Rochester, New York, the President passed up a public opportunity to lend his "voice and help" to the cause. There he spoke mostly about the reunion of the sections, adding perfunctorily that the North demanded from the South only obedience to the Constitution and the laws.[105]

Probably the President felt that the proper place, or at any rate a politically safe place, to discuss racial matters was the annual message to Congress. Lynching, which was increasing in the wake of the elevation of the Southern "poor whites" between 1890 and 1910, received its first presidential notice in Harrison's annual message of December 6, 1892. While Cleveland did not see fit to mention the word "lynching" in the annual messages of his second term, both McKinley and Roosevelt made a special point of calling attention to the subject. President Harrison felt that an aroused public sentiment was needed to sustain law officers against lynch mobs. To underline the seriousness of lynching Harrison noted that the government had just paid the king of Italy $824,000 in connection with the lynching of seven Italians in New Orleans. In 1892, Harrison made what must have been the first plea for a federal antilynching law, a law which was still an unrealized dream more than half a century later:

[104] Benjamin Harrison to Reverend H. H. Mitchell and others of the Virginia State Baptist Convention, May 21, 1892, *The Public Papers and Addresses of Benjamin Harrison, 1889–1893* (Washington: Government Printing Office, 1893), pp. 293–94.

[105] The speech was delivered at the ceremonies of the Soldiers and Sailors Monument, May 30, 1892, Rochester, N.Y., *The Public Papers and Addresses of Benjamin Harrison . . .*, pp. 295–96.

> The frequent lynchings of colored people accused of crime is without the excuse, which has sometimes been urged by mobs for failure to pursue the appointed methods for the punishment of crime. . . . And so far as they [lynchings] can be made the subject of federal jurisdiction the strongest repressive legislation is demanded.[106]

American Indians were not being lynched at this time but they found it increasingly difficult to hold on to their remaining lands.

The Indians

The Dawes Act of 1887 had called for the integration of the Indian into American life. This policy was continued under Harrison. How to "un-Indianize" the Indian was the problem. It was thought in some quarters that the first step was to employ a humane person as Indian commissioner.[107] Such a man, presumably, was T. J. Morgan, the recipient of praises from the *Boston Herald* and the *Congregationalist* for his efforts to put every Indian of school age in school.[108] In his first annual message Harrison voiced agreement with the policy of breaking up the tribal relation and dealing with the Indians as individuals.[109] In all probability Harrison's Indian policy was an amalgam of humanitarian considerations and political pragmatism. The reservations were now surrounded by white settlements and the Indians could no longer be pushed back into the wilderness, Harrison reasoned. If the Indian could not be pushed

[106] Fourth Annual Message of Benjamin Harrison, December 6, 1892, Richardson, *Messages*, IX, 332; see also a weak references to the subject in a speech of September 3, 1892, *The Public Papers and Addresses of Benjamin Harrison* . . . , p. 138, and p. 24, for reference to the Italians; about this time Frederick Douglass allegedly visited Harrison, urging him to speak out against lynching and to ask for antilynching legislation in his annual message, according to Foner, *Life and Writings of Frederick Douglass*, IV, 140.

[107] Memorandum of John D. Long for the Citizens of Massachusetts, to Benjamin Harrison, January 5, 1889, BHP, Vol. 56, No. 12479.

[108] T. J. Morgan, Indian commissioner, to Benjamin Harrison, October 2, 1889, enclosing editorials from the *Boston Herald*, October 6, 1889, and the *Congregationalist*, October 10, 1889, BHP, Vol. 89, Nos. 20215, 20217.

[109] December 3, 1889, Richardson, *Messages*, IX, 45, 48.

back he could be lifted *up* with the aid of a farm for himself and a school for his child and thus become "a self-supporting and responsible citizen."[110] Similar sentiments were expressed in the third and fourth annual messages.[111]

There were disagreements over the proper nature of Indian education and an interfaith squabble regarding Indian supervision during Harrison's Administration. Catholic prelates complained of discrimination in the matter of employment of teachers for the Indian schools. Protestant officials defended themselves by contending that one Catholic female teacher was discharged because "she was determined to marry an Indian," while another Catholic male teacher lost his job for alleged nocturnal visits to the room of a female teacher while her roommate was absent.[112]

Whatever the humanitarian impulses that initially prompted the program of "civilization" for the Indians, it is impossible to ignore the rapidity with which the so-called "surplus" Indian lands were given to the whites during Harrison's Administration.

[110] Ibid.

[111] Ibid., December 9, 1891, p. 201; ibid., December 6, 1892, p. 326.

[112] One man who did not think the Indian capable of absorbing the same high-school education given to whites was Senator P. B. Plumb. See his letter to Secretary of Interior, John Noble, August 30, 1889, BHP, Vol. 85, No. 19449–52. See also his letter to Honorable Herbert Welsh, Pennsylvania, January 26, 1890, BHP, Vol. 97, No. 21924–27; Commissioner Morgan may have been humane but he still had a touch of the "white man's burden" in him: Of the Indian he said, "We ask them to recognize that we are the better race; that our God is the true God; that our civilization is the better; that our manners and customs are superior. . . ." See the newspaper clipping from the *Independent*, 1892, carrying Commissioner Morgan's speech entitled, "Our Indian Fellow-Citizens," BHP, Vol. 11, pp. 116–18. See the following letters for the Catholic question: Bishop John Ireland to Benjamin Harrison, August 19, 1889, BHP, Vol. 84, No. 19259–60; Cardinal L. Gibbons to Benjamin Harrison, August 27, 1889, BHP, Vol. 84, No. 19367–68; vice-director of the Bureau of Catholic Indian Missions, George L. Williard, to Benjamin Harrison, August 27, 1889, BHP, Vol. 74, No. 19386–89; letter of Benjamin Harrison to Bishop John Ireland, September [n.d.], denying discrimination, BHP, Vol. 88, No. 19960–67; Indian Commissioner T. J. Morgan to the Secretary of the Interior, November 26, 1889, BHP, Vol. 91, No. 20691–703, explaining the reasons for two of the dismissals in question; T. J. Morgan to Benjamin Harrison, December 18, 1889, BHP, Vol. 93, No. 21113–14; T. J. Morgan to E. W. Halford, BHP, Vol. 93, Nos. 21225–26, 21227–33; letter from the Indian Rights Association, December 21, 1889, BHP, Vol. 93, No. 21237–39; BHP, Vol. 94, No. 21293; BHP, Vol. 95, No. 21502–12.

There never seemed to be any question of the power or right of the government to sell to the whites all of the land not used by the Indians, after the latter had been given farms. Harrison was concerned only that justice be done and the Indian fairly compensated.[113]

Senator Plumb of Kansas and Senator John T. Morgan of Alabama were in favor of opening up the Cherokee strip in the Oklahoma Territory to white settlement.[114] The Indians were not living on this land, but had leased it to white cattlemen for grazing purposes. In his third annual message Harrison advocated that the Five Civilized Tribes be made citizens and given representation in Congress.[115] But the white hunger for the Indian lands in Oklahoma was growing. The annual message of the Cherokee Indian Chief Mayes to the Cherokee people reflected the fear. Other communications from whites in the Indian territory asked that the land be opened up, and that the credit for this go to the Republicans rather than to the Democrats. Other correspondents charged that Chief Mayes and the ruling class in the territory were not Indians at all but white men with only a token quantity of Indian "blood" in them.[116] At this point Harrison was accused of proposing to force the cattlemen out of the Cherokee strip in order to coerce the Indians to sell the land for forty-nine cents an acre for white settlement.[117]

[113] *The Public Papers and Addresses of Benjamin Harrison . . .*, pp. 157, 160, for the President's messages on the Sioux, Sac and Fox, and Chippewa Indians.

[114] Senator S. B. Plumb to Benjamin Harrison, December 15 [1889?], BHP, Vol. 93, No. 21051–52; John T. Morgan, Alabama, to Benjamin Harrison, June 11, 1889, BHP, Vol. 79, No. 17983–18006. This was a letter of twenty-three pages. Among other things Morgan was in favor of statehood for the Cherokee nation: "These Indians are as well fitted for statehood as some of the states now in the Union. . . ."

[115] December 4, 1891, Richardson, *Messages*, IX, 202.

[116] Lucius Fairchild, Cherokee commissioner, to the Secretary of the Interior, November 14, 1889, BHP, Vol. 90, No. 201489–92; John J. Dille, Indian territory, to E. W. Halford, October 10, 1889, BHP, Vol. 88, No. 20082–84; G. Sayre, Cherokee commissioner, Tahleguah, Indian territory, to Benjamin Harrison, November 26, 1889, BHP, Vol. 91, No. 20709–15.

[117] I. C. Parker, U.S. judge, Fort Smith, Ark., to Benjamin Harrison, February 8, 1890, enclosing newspaper clipping of the rumor in the *Post Dispatch*, February 7, 1890, BHP, Vol. 98, No. 22171–73. See also No. 2206–07.

In the meantime, the task of separating the Indian from his land progressed speedily. Harrison proudly announced in his third annual message: "Since March 4, 1889, about 23,000,000 acres have been separated from Indian reservations and added to the public domain for the use of those who desire to secure free homes under our beneficent laws." Harrison did not appear to feel that any wrong had been done the Indian in the transfer. He said: "It is also gratifying to be able to feel, as we may, that the work has proceeded upon lines of justice toward the Indian. . . . [He] may now, if he will, secure to himself the good influence of a settled habitation. . . ."[118]

Yet one cannot help but think that the Indian paid a huge price in land for "the good influence of a settled habitation." It would appear that the white man benefited much more from the transaction than the Indian. But Harrison, at least in his official expressions, did not see it that way. The Indian should have been grateful that while he was being relieved of his "surplus" land for a specific compensation, he was gaining the dubious boon of civilization, "the fruits of industry and the security of citizenship." According to Harrison, "the good work of reducing the larger Indians Reservations by allotments in severalty to the Indians and the cession of the remaining lands to the United States for disposition under the Homestead law has been prosecuted during the year with energy and success. . . . In September, I was able to open to settlement in the territory of Oklahoma 900,000 acres of land, all of which was taken up by settlers in a single day." Obviously pleased with himself, Harrison proceeded to apologize to Congress for having been unable to make even more Indian land available: "It was a source of great regret that I was not able to open at the same time the surplus lands of the Cheyenne and Arapahoe Reservations, amounting to about 3,000,000 acres . . . deserving and impatient settlers are waiting to occupy these lands. . . ." An insufficient appropriation by Congress was holding up the purchase of this acreage. The President asked for a "special ap-

[118] December 9, 1891, Richardson, *Messages*, IX, 203.

propriation" so that the settlers could have their homesteads by early spring.[119]

Harrison also reported that he had hoped to get his hands on over 900,000 additional acres of the Cherokee strip but the Indians there refused the price of $1.25 an acre which he thought was ". . . fair and adequate . . . and should have been accepted by the Indians."[120] The President did veto one bill designed to shave off land from the Uncompahgre Reservation when he learned that the whites were only after the mineral deposits thought to exist there.[121]

In view of the preceding testimony, however incomplete, it is difficult to avoid the inference that the Dawes Act benefited the white settlers who would not be denied in their hunger for land, more than it did the Indians. Whatever the motivations behind the act, the net result was a drastic shrinkage of Indian acreage. On the other hand, it is equally difficult to doubt the sincerity of those, including Harrison, who hoped that the Indian would become a civilized citizen in the American sense of the word and integrated into American life. For instance, Harrison was in favor of absorbing the reservation schools into the public systems of the states and Territories in which they were located. He appeared to have none of the usual qualms or reservations accompanying this subject when applied to the blacks. "There is a great advantage, I think," said Harrison, "in bringing the Indian children into mixed schools. This process will be gradual. . . ."[122] Harrison approved of the project of taking Indians into the army and thought this would improve race relations between red and white.[123] He also had to deal with yellow and white relations.

119 Third Annual Message, December 9, 1891, Richardson, *Messages*, IX, 202.

120 Ibid., IX, 203.

121 Veto message on a bill to change the boundaries of the Uncompahgre Reservation, June 17, 1890, Richardson, *Messages*, IX, 87.

122 Harrison's Third Annual Message, December 9, 1891, Richardson, *Messages*, IX, 201. See his Fourth Annual Message, December 6, 1892, ibid., IX, 326.

123 Ibid., IX, 196.

Benjamin Harrison and the Chinese

In the presidential campaign of 1888, Harrison's position on the yellow question caused as much anxiety, if not more, as his position on the black question. When Republican politicians began searching for suitable presidential timber, some of them were tempted to view Harrison as a liability on the Pacific Coast because of his alleged record on the Chinese. As a senator, Harrison had initially voted against the Chinese Exclusion bill though he later fell in line with it. "Thus far this is the only substantial objection I have heard against him, and [the] only one likely to injure him," said S. B. Elkins to the chairman of the Indiana Republican State Committee, L. T. Michener.[124]

[124] S. B. Elkins to L. T. Michener, Indianapolis, Ind., March 3, 1888, BHP, Vol. 28, No. 5814; P. T. Heath to L. T. Michener, March 3, 1888, BHP, Vol. 28, No. 5815–16; George N. Steele, Washington, to Benjamin Harrison, June 12 [1888?], BHP, Vol. 29, No. 5937. The following letters all inquired of or made excuses for Harrison's initial pro-Chinese stance and urged him to make a statement to the effect that his *present* view of the question was now changed. John F. Swift, San Francisco, to George B. Williams, March 15, 1888, BHP, Vol. 28, No. 5830; John H. Mitchell, United States senator from Oregon, to Benjamin Harrison, March 17, 1888, BHP, Vol. 28, No. 5835–37; R. E. [Lord?], California, to Benjamin Harrison, June 25, BHP, Vol. 29, No. 6021. A newspaper clipping accused Harrison of believing that ". . . this is a country not only intended for the white and black sons of Ham, Shem, and Japhet, but also for the yellow sons of Adam as well." See William Armstrong, New York, to Benjamin Harrison [1888], enclosing said newspaper clipping, BHP, Vol. 31, No. 6395–97; letter and newspaper clippings of William W. Goodrich to Benjamin Harrison, June 26, 1888, BHP, Vol. 30, No. 6125–26. See also Nos. 6171, 6224–26, 6289–90, 6242–43, 6248, 6298, for more anti-Chinese statements; William Steward to Benjamin Harrison, June 26, 1888, BHP, Vol. 31, No. 1446–48; R. R. Wright, principal of Ware High School, Augusta, Ga., to Benjamin Harrison, June 30, 1888, BHP, Vol. 31, No. 6035–36. He was a delegate to the Chicago Convention. Letter from Spikenard, Jackson County, Oreg., July 2, 1888, BHP, Vol. 31, No. 6046–48. The following letters begged Harrison to put an anti-Chinese thought in his letter of acceptance for the benefit of the Californians: George Steele, Chicago congressman, to Benjamin Harrison [1888?], BHP, Vol. 32, No. 6815–17. W. H. Dimond, chairman of the Republican State Central Committee, San Francisco, Calif., to Benjamin Harrison, July 6, 1888, BHP, Vol. 32, No. 6838–39. R. I. Eaton, Portland, Oreg., to Benjamin Harrison, July 7, 1888, BHP, Vol. 32, No. 6887. Eaton said in part: "The people, especially the laboring classes of the Coast are very sensitive on the subject of Chinese immigration, and it requires very

Harrison was not oblivious to the pressure to commit himself on the Chinese question once he had received the nomination. "I cannot in any private letter anticipate what I shall say in my formal letter of acceptance but I do not believe the people of the Pacific Coast will be disappointed at what I shall say on the Chinese question," Harrison told one Californian.[125] One anti-Chinese politician requested Harrison to by all means make a distinction between his opposition to undesirable European immigration and Chinese immigration. The Chinese were to be excluded not because of lack of honesty, virtue, or industry but on the specific ground of race dissimilarity.[126]

Sometime in July or August there appeared in the newspapers a letter that Harrison wrote to a Missouri preacher in February of 1888, explaining his metamorphosis on the Chinese question. He had opposed the first Chinese Exclusion bill because he thought it would violate the Burlingame Treaty with China, and also because he thought exclusion un-American, "and it was a little hard for me to let go of the old idea that this was the free home of all comers," he confessed. But he did "let go,"

---

little to inflame their passions or to excite their prejudices against anyone favoring such immigration." The Oregon senator, John H. Mitchell, to Benjamin Harrison, July 7, 1888, BHP, Vol. 33, Nos. 7165, 7184, "You get him, to have a paragraph in his letter of acceptance about the prohibiting of the Italian labor or pauper, Emigrants, coming to the U.S. and depriving our depressed Irish citizens that come to America from oppressed Ireland." W. D. Reinhart, St. Louis, Mo., July 18, 1888, BHP, Vol. 34, No. 7353–61; letter of John H. Buel, Michigan, to Benjamin Harrison, July 17, 1888, BHP, Vol. 34, No. 7293–95; letter of Smith Gildersleeve to Benjamin Harrison, August 2, 1888, BHP, Vol. 36, No. 7909; letter of Judge John D. Works, San Francisco, August 2, 1888, BHP, Vol. 36, No. 7934–35; Y. W. Witter [?], pastor, First Presbyterian Church, Virginia City, Nev., to Benjamin Harrison, August 16, 1888, BHP, Vol. 38, No. 8398; Senator George Edmunds [?] to Benjamin Harrison, September 11, 1888, BHP, Vol. 40, No. 8743–48; "One of the greatest curses of this country is the influence of the Chinese. They are a menace to the World," said Robert Kirk, Alameda, Calif., to Benjamin Harrison, August 20, 1888, BHP, Vol. 39, No. 8473–75; letter of W. H. Miller, Dunbar, Nebr., to Benjamin Harrison, [1888?], BHP, Vol. 44, No. 9576.

[125] Benjamin Harrison to George [Osgoodby?] Pomona, Calif., July 14, 1888, BHP, Vol. 34, No. 7190-A.

[126] John F. Swift, San Francisco, the Pacific Club, to L. T. Michener, July 16, 1888, BHP, Vol. 34, No. 72840–87. See the *Dictionary of American Biography* for Swift's anti-Chinese affiliations.

and apparently for reasons of political expediency: "I think there has been a very general change of sentiment on that subject since. . . . We do not need to ask anybody to come to this country now, as we formerly did, and I think we have a right to preserve our own institutions by exercising a fair election as to who shall come here." Harrison had now made up his mind that the time had come to close the door to the Mongolian forever. What is significant here is not the merit of the argument but the alteration of Harrison's attitude on the subject in response to a politically powerful and exploitable public sentiment.[127]

When the time came for Harrison to write his letter of acceptance he appeared to follow the advice of those who had urged him to include an anti-Chinese paragraph for the benefit of voters on the West Coast. Though he may have simply been stating an independent judgment, it seems indisputable that he was much affected by the anti-Chinese breeze that swept across the Rocky Mountains from the West. His letter of acceptance seemed to court the prejudices of the people more openly than did his earlier letter to the Missouri preacher. What he had told the preacher privately he now restated publicly. Some restriction upon immigration had become necessary. The time to close the door to all but "proper immigration . . ." was at hand. According to Harrison the earlier impetus for immigration was due to the fact that "the pioneer wanted a neighbor with more friendly instincts than the Indian." Here was a rather novel reason for immigration. The letter of acceptance differed significantly from his earlier remarks to the preacher in that the race factor was added to the standard demands for exclusion of paupers and criminals. Harrison's affliction with the presidential virus caused him to say deliriously, as it were:

> We are also clearly under a duty to defend our civilization by excluding alien races whose ultimate assimilation with our people

[127] A newspaper clipping of a letter by Benjamin Harrison to Reverend J. B. Brandt, February 29, 1888, from the *St. Louis Globe Democrat,* sent in by John F. Swift, BHP, Vol. 34, No. 7326–29; see speech, August 15, 1888, Hedges, *Speeches,* p. 89.

is neither possible nor desirable. The family has been the nucleus of our best immigration, and the home, the most potent assimilating force in our civilization.

Harrison felt that these objections to Chinese immigration were "distinctive and conclusive . . . generally accepted . . . entirely beyond argument."[128] In a skillfully contrived sentence of his inaugural address he rather subtly let it be known that he was not adverse to shutting out *other* undesirables: "There are men of all races, even the best, whose coming is necessarily a burden upon our public revenues or a threat to social order. These shall be identified and excluded."[129] In his first annual message Harrison lamented the failure of the anti-Chinese treaty under Cleveland, pledged his continued devotion to total exclusion but cautioned the country not to mistreat Chinese aliens who were legitimately on our shores.[130]

In summary, Benjamin Harrison was conscious of race and race prejudice in American life, North and South. He was rather lenient in his assessment of the status, hopes, and aspirations of blacks and Indians, but apparently had second thoughts about adding the Mongolian to the melting pot. In the sources examined for this book, Harrison did not express himself on the subject of race mixing. While he appeared sincere, political opportunism seemed clearly reflected in his shifting stance on the Chinese question. He could not ignore matters of race. His strong recommendation of the unsuccessful Federal Elections and aid to education bills reflected a genuine effort to reopen the attack upon the smoldering race problem, a step unique among Presidents after the Compromise of 1876.

Harrison spoke vigorously, positively, strongly and clearly on the race problem, in his annual messages. He called for a more

128 Benjamin Harrison's letter of acceptance, September 11, 1888, Hedges, *Speeches*, pp. 111–13.

129 March 4, 1889, Hedges, *Speeches*, p. 199.

130 December 3, 1889, Richardson, *Messages*, IX, 34; for further complications and difficulties with the Chinese, see Harrison's speeches for December 9, 1891, Richardson, *Messages*, IX, 186–88; December 6, 1892, ibid., IX, 330; see Third Annual Message, December 9, 1891, for his alarm over the possibility of a large Jewish immigration from Russian persecutions. He spoke well of the Jews but was against a sudden influx. See Richardson, *Messages*, IX, 188.

complete inclusion of blacks in American life. What was more unique was the comparative absence of the usual political hedging in his racial dialogue—except on the Chinese. However, Harrison did not always take full advantage of opportunities outside of official channels to influence public opinion. Further investigation might show that in his strong advocacy, by annual messages, of the Blair Education bill, the Federal Elections bill, and antilynching legislation, Harrison exerted greater leadership in matters of race, no matter how unsuccessful, than any of the post-Reconstruction Presidents, not excluding Theodore Roosevelt.

CHAPTER VIII

The Racial Attitudes of William McKinley (1897–1901)

President William McKinley, no less than his predecessors, showed an interest in efforts to improve the quality of American citizenship. He, too, found it politically expedient to take a stand against the "too ignorant and the too vicious; and all those who make war upon our institutions."[1]

The International Aspects of Race

Almost immediately after taking office in 1897, McKinley had to contend with an outbreak of violence against foreign nationals which threatened to have international repercussions. His solution was to call the attention of Congress to the lynching of three Italians in Hahnville, Louisiana, and ask for six thousand dollars for the heirs of the dead men.[2] As far as can be ascertained, families of lynched blacks received no reparations. Toward the end of his term the Chinese issue reappeared.

[1] Richardson, *Messages*, X, 15 (1897).

[2] May 1897, ibid. In the First Annual Message of his second term, December 6, 1900, McKinley reported the additional lynching of a Mexican citizen in California, August 1895, another one in La Salle County, Texas, October 5, 1895, and still more lynchings of Italians in Louisiana, ibid., X, 233–36. Murphy J. Foster, Baton Rouge, La., to Honorable John Hay, July 25, 1899, relative to the lynching of an Italian in Tallulah, La. William McKinley Papers (manuscript in the Library of Congress, Washington, D.C.), Vol. 35, No. 6777, hereafter to be cited as WMP.

Acting Secretary of State Alvey A. Adee wanted the Secretary of War to tell him whether the Chinese Exclusion bill was considered to apply to conquered Puerto Rico and the Philippine Islands. Adee, who looked upon the exclusion law as a temporary expedient, was opposed to such a step. To him the Chinese were essential to the labor and trade of the Philippines.[3] McKinley, however, attributed the recent antiforeign demonstrations in China to "the character of the Chinese races, and the traditions of their government." To him they were "a primitive people. . . ."[4]

The Spanish-American War turned the attention of many other observers toward racial considerations. The Thanksgiving Day sermon of the Reverend Charles Parkhurst of the Madison Square Presbyterian Church took the country to task for its victory over the Spanish. What had we done except conquer "a people ten times our inferior in brute force, military genius, and personal fibre"? The idea that American expansion was justified because "a virile race cannot exist within a limited area" was all "rot" to this preacher, who was of the opinion that America still had many unsolved problems at home and should "not go tramping around the globe to find something to do. . . . There is not today respect enough for the authority of the general government to secure to the Negro the rights that belong to him as a citizen, although such rights were nominally conferred upon him a third of a century ago. . . ." Also the "great undigested masses of foreign stuff [coming] here . . ." alarmed the preacher and he failed to see the logic of shutting out the Chinese while sending "cards of invitation to the Maylays [Filipinos]."[5]

Racial yeast was at work when Andrew Carnegie told the President: "I have ventured to say that in supreme crises the racial element will be found the most potent and . . . will con-

[3] Alvey A. Adee to the Secretary of War, August 4, 1899, WMP, Vol. 35, No. 6900–02.

[4] William McKinley's Fourth Annual Message, December 3, 1900, Richardson, *Messages*, X, 192.

[5] Newspaper clipping of a Thanksgiving Day sermon by the Reverend Doctor Charles H. Parkhurst, Madison Square Presbyterian Church, 1898. The article was sent to McKinley by Andrew Carnegie. WMP, Vol. 21, No. 4220.

trol action." In the shadow of the Spanish-American crisis Carnegie urged a rapprochement of the "English-speaking race." His estimate was that Europe looked upon Britain as an intruder whose only "secure and permanent home is with her own race." In this connection he sent McKinley a penciled memorandum of a talk between himself and the Prince of Wales relative to closer relations between the great "English-speaking race." This document was labeled "strictly confidential *please destroy.*" The prince reportedly said with reference to Carnegie's suggestion of a racial entente, "*Yes I like that*—I like that." In Carnegie's opinion, "with Britain standing by us you have nothing to fear from European action [in taking on the Spanish]."[6]

Carnegie thought that an editorial from the *London Spectator* supported his contentions: "English sympathy," it asserted, "is with our own flesh and blood. . . . America is on the whole fighting for a just cause." These words were penciled in red, probably indicating the importance Carnegie attached to them. A little later the *Spectator* came close to outright racial arrogance, bidding the United States to conduct herself as befitted a member of the Anglo-Saxon race: "We shall require from our own flesh and blood a standard of rectitude and faith and fair fighting which we should not demand from any other nation. . . ." The *Spectator* did not want to hear of a Spanish cruiser being blown up in New York Harbor, but was unsurprised when the *Maine* was blown up in Havana. Such an act "was only one more proof of what Southern races will do when they grow mad with injured pride and the black spirit of revenge. . . ."[7]

When the shooting started, the revolutionary junta in Hong Kong assured the Filipinos that America would secure their independence, their faith, and the rights of the different races. This rebel communiqué concluded very enthusiastically, "Hurrah for liberty and right! Hurrah for the great Republic of the

[6] Andrew Carnegie to William McKinley, April 27, 1898. WMP, Vol. 13, No. 2527–30.

[7] Newspaper clipping from the *Spectator*, April 23, 1898, WMP, Vol. 13, No. 2531–32, ser. I.

United States of North America! Hurrah for President McKinley and Rear Admiral Dewey."[8] This festive mood was not destined to endure. Next month the *London Spectator* predicted that America would never give the Philippines back to Spain and went on to observe that the United States could govern the islands with the help of black troops "immune" to yellow fever. The *Spectator* saw no difficulty in using black troops to hold Puerto Rico, the Philippines and Hawaii because:

> The prejudice of color, fierce as it is in the states, would not operate against a colonial army. More especially if that army is a good one. The bravery of the trained Negro is never questioned. He is accustomed not only to obey, but to respect white officers. . . .[9]

In short, America could use black troops to help her control the tropics and thus turn a domestic source of weakness into an instrument of empire!

McKinley informed Admiral Dewey that he wanted to avoid conflict with the revolutionary Aguinaldo. He also made it clear that he desired undisputed American possession of the islands. How he hoped to accomplish both these things is difficult to understand. If only the Filipinos would lie still and let McKinley take up the white man's burden, "the insurgents," he hoped, "will come to see our benevolent purpose and recognize that before we can give their people good government our sovereignty must be complete and unquestioned. . . . We accepted the Philippines from high duty in the interests of the inhabitants and for humanity and civilization. Our sacrifices were with this high motive. We want to improve the condition of the inhabitants, securing their peace, liberty and the pursuit of their highest good."[10]

[8] April 1898, WMP, Vol. 13, No. 2596–14.

[9] May 10, 1898. The Providence Sunday *Journal* contained the above excerpts from the *Spectator*, WMP, Vol. 15, No. 2858.

[10] January 8, 1899. The memorandum of the President was sent through Alger and Long, Secretaries of War and Navy, to Otis and Dewey. WMP, Vol. 23, No. 4563. "This war . . . will bring also burdens, but the American people never shirk a responsibility. . . ." Speech of McKinley in Cedar Rapids, Iowa, October 11, 1898. See *Speeches and Addresses of William*

David Starr Jordan of Leland Stanford University was critical of America's role in the islands. He found some immigrants concerned about the effect of Philippine annexation on the labor market.[11] Jacob C. Schurman, head of the President's Commission to the Philippines and president of Cornell University, advised the President in a top secret document to try being nice to the Filipinos while making it clear that force would be used if necessary. He thought the knowledge that McKinley stood ready to send more troops would have a good "moral effect" on the islanders.[12]

Some Americans could not resist the temptation to make a racial evaluation of the Filipinos. General Harrison Gray Otis told the *New York Times* he found a "fair degree of intelligence among them." Still he would not give them self-government because they did not have the proper "appreciation of republican liberty and self government" as Americans understood those terms.[13] In another place Otis confessed that the Filipinos fought not like the Indians but like civilized people. Although he left no doubt that he thought them inferior to the whites, he boasted of his impartiality in regard to their fighting qualities: "You see," he said, "I am disposed to give the devil his due, and if the devil happens to be a Filipino it makes no difference."[14] According to Admiral Dewey, however, the Filipinos were "far superior in their intelligence and more capable of self-

---

McKinley: From March 1, 1897 to May 30, 1900 (New York: Doubleday and McClure Co., 1900), pp. 87, 110, passim. "President McKinley was a conscientious Methodist, and he fully believed that in the Philippines the White man's burden was laid upon the United States," wrote the historian James Ford Rhodes, *The McKinley and Roosevelt Administrations, 1897–1909* (New York: Macmillan Co., 1922), p. 187.

11 " 'You going to keep the Philippines?' " an Italian reportedly asked Jordan one day. " 'You let them fellows come here, work seven cents a day, you never get another Republican vote from me, never, never, never.' " Then Jordan concluded, "Nor will there be another vote from me. . . . David Starr Jordan to Lyman Abbott, May 11, 1891, WMP, Vol. 30, No. 5930–32.

12 J. C. Schurman to the Secretary of State, June 3, 1899, WMP, Vol. 32, No. 6212–15.

13 Harrison Gray Otis to William McKinley, July 13, 1899, enclosing newspaper clipping, WMP, Vol. 34, No. 6682–83.

14 The second article of Otis came from the *New York Journal*, July 9, 1899, ibid., No. 6684.

government than the natives of Cuba, and I am familiar with both races."[15] Taking the opposite side was the Negrophobic historian James Ford Rhodes, who said that soldiers and officers of the American army were never "more mistaken than when they called the Filipinos 'Niggers,' as in all essentials the Filipinos stood far in advance of the American Negro."[16]

He may not have accepted the racial implications, but President McKinley believed in social Darwinism so far as economics and industry were concerned: "In this age of keen rivalry among nations for mastery in commerce, the doctrine of evolution and the rule of the survival of the fittest must be as inexorable in their operation as they are positive in the results they bring about." McKinley seemed eager to take on the responsibilities of the white man's burden abroad. "If we accept them," he said concerning the Filipinos, "in a spirit worthy of our race and our traditions, a great opportunity comes with them."[17]

The President was rather optimistic about the Filipino mental potential and recommended some degree of self-government for them according to their capacity: "The Filipinos are a race quick to learn and to profit by knowledge. . . ." Whatever his motives, McKinley took the idea of a white man's burden in the Philippines very seriously. Said he: "I have called the Filipinos 'the wards of the nation.' Our obligation as guardian was not lightly assumed."[18]

McKinley felt about Cuba much as he did about the Philippines.[19] Also, he never suggested full self-government for the Puerto Ricans. He would give them local control until they learned the art of self-government. He advocated education and told Congress that changes in Puerto Rico should not be too

[15] Cited in James Ford Rhodes, *The McKinley and Roosevelt Administrations*, p. 188.

[16] Cited in James Ford Rhodes, *The McKinley and Roosevelt Administrations*, p. 194.

[17] Message to Congress, December 5, 1899, Richardson, *Messages*, X, 143, 172.

[18] December 3, 1900, Richardson, *Messages*, X, 121–22, 222.

[19] Ibid., X, 64, 67. December 18, 1897, ibid., X, 38.

abrupt, so "that the history and racial peculiarities of the inhabitants . . . be given due weight."[20]

Race, Politics and McKinley

While international aspects of race loomed large during the McKinley era, domestic racial matters were never out of sight.

McKinley, the Blacks and the South

In a speech at the Metropolitan Opera House in New York in 1889, McKinley came out for equality before the law for blacks: "Our black allies must neither be deserted nor forsaken. And every right secured them by the Constitution must be as surely given to them as though God had put upon their faces the color of the Anglo-Saxon race." McKinley believed that participation in the Civil War had earned the blacks that right.[21]

Unlike Theodore Roosevelt, who could not attack lynching without also making extended comments on the horrors of rape, McKinley put the matter simply in his first inaugural: "Lynchings must not be tolerated in a great and civilized country like the United States. . . . Equality of rights must prevail. . . ."[22] As governor of Ohio in 1896, he made a ringing declaration against lynching in that state. He praised three men who had lost their lives in preventing a lynching. He urged the General Assembly "to use all the power at its command to frown upon

[20] Richardson, *Messages,* X, 144, passim. One scholar contended that race had something to do with the hesitancy on the part of some Americans on the question of Cuban annexation and the apparent enthusiasm for the Teller Resolution preserving Cuban independence: "There was a general repugnance to the idea of admitting to the Union an alien and subordinate people, Roman Catholic in faith, with a large admixture of Negro blood." Margaret Leech, *In the Days of McKinley* (New York: Harper and Brothers, 1959), p. 188.

[21] May 30, 1889, J. S. Ogilvie (ed.), *Life and Speeches of William McKinley* (New York: Ogilvie Publishing Co., 1896), p. 9.

[22] March 4, 1897, *Speeches and Addresses of William McKinley: From March 1, 1897 to May 30, 1900* (New York: Doubleday and McClure Co., 1900), p. 196.

and stamp out this spirit of lawlessness. . . . Lynchings must not be tolerated in Ohio."[23]

The few firsthand expressions of McKinley on the subject of the black American had a sincere ring about them. He once told a black Kentuckian: "I assure you that I sympathize with you in your aspirations for vour race, and I join with you in the hope that the race problem will soon cease to cause any political or social misunderstanding."[24] After an allegedly non-political trip to Georgia, McKinley had to defend himself against the charge that he had studiously ignored black Republicans while on his trip. "I am sure no colored Republicans who met me would circulate such a report. . . . The story is absurd. I met colored men everywhere," said McKinley in rebuttal.[25]

During the presidential campaign of 1896, McKinley congratulated black riflemen of Cleveland for the progress their race had made since emancipation: "You have done better, you have advanced more rapidly than it was believed possible at that time."[26] When he was but a prospective candidate for the presidential nomination, McKinley had denied that he was not in sympathy with the black Republicans in their struggle for equal rights and recognition; that he was more concerned with tariff protection than with "colored" protection; and that he favored the formation of a white man's Republican party in the South.[27] When he could not attend a black exposition, McKinley sent these remarks to a black Texan: "It is as true in regard to a race as it is in regard to individuals—their destiny is

[23] Murat Halstead, *Life and Distinguished Services of William McKinley Our Martyr President* ([Chicago]: Memorial Association, 1901), pp. 163–64, for McKinley's message to the General Assembly of Ohio, January 1896.

[24] William McKinley, governor of Ohio, to Mr. E. J. Harden, Lexington, Ky., July 11, 1894, WMP, Vol. 1, No. 58a.

[25] William McKinley to Reverend I. Dawson, Eutaw, Ala., April 15, 1895, WMP (Letter Book), Vol. 87, No. 109, ser. II. See letter of William McKinley to Col. J. P. Hanson, Macon, Ga., February 27, 1895, ibid., No. 90.

[26] Cited in Murat Halstead, *Life and Distinguished Services of William McKinley* . . . , pp. 457–58.

[27] William McKinley to the state chairman of the Republican party in Georgia, A. E. Buck, Atlanta, Ga., January 8, 1896 (enclosing a letter of McKinley to Honorable Walter H. Johnson, Atlanta, defending himself against the anti-black charges discussed above, WMP (Letter Book), Vol. 87, Nos. 218, 191, ser. III.

largely in their own hands; and it is intensely gratifying to observe the spirit of self help among the colored race."[28] He urged black college students to continue to push themselves up by their own efforts.[29] He praised Frederick Douglass for aiding the advancement of "his race."[30]

In 1899, McKinley privately declared himself on the black question with a ringing statement supporting American nationality for black people:

> I am now and always have been in favor of fair and impartial treatment of my colored fellow-citizens—recognizing them as I do as being an integral part of the citizenship of the Republic, entitled to the protection of its laws and the enjoyment of its privileges without discrimination.[31]

A report from Chicago indicated that blacks there were dissatisfied with McKinley's Administration. Rumor had it that black volunteer units of the Spanish-American War were going to be discharged, to the displeasure of some blacks. A Chicago black expressed his sentiment to John Green, a black employee in the Postal Stamp Agency in Washington:

> Our people feel that while the President cannot under the Constitution intervene with federal authority to prevent outrages upon our people in the South, he can at least use the influence of his great office by saying some word of condemnation against wholesome lawlessness and crime. He [McKinley] and Mark Hanna were there in Georgia, in the vicinity of the spot where

[28] William McKinley to Mr. Edward Banks, Houston, Texas, July 1, 1896, WMP (Letter Book), Vol. 88, No. 35, ser. II. When he could not attend the national convention of the National Negro Business League, McKinley sent his "best wishes for the advancement and prosperity of your race." See letter of William McKinley to Principal Booker T. Washington, August 22, 1901, ibid., Vol. 172, No. 383, ser. II.

[29] McKinley's speeches to Negroes at Tuskegee, December 16, 1898, and at Georgia A.&M. for blacks, December 18, 1898, *Speeches and Addresses of William McKinley* . . . (New York: Doubleday and McClure Co., 1900), pp. 168–69, 178.

[30] This remark was made in connection with his inability to attend an unveiling of a monument to the late Frederick Douglass. William McKinley to Mr. F. E. Kittredge, Albion, N.Y., April 3, 1899, WMP (Letter Book), Vol. 90, No. 387.

[31] William McKinley to Dr. C. C. Stewart, June 12, 1899, WMP (Letter Book), Vol. 87, No. 132, ser. II.

nine colored men were shot by a mob, and uttered no word of condemnation against these murderers and usurpers of law.

It is significant that this segment of black opinion accepted the idea that the President was constitutionally unable to intervene and prevent violence in the South. Green's informant was fresh from commencement exercises at Wilberforce College for blacks in Ohio. There he met leading blacks from the South who were waiting to see what the President would say in his annual message about racial oppression in the South. In the event that he did not take a stand on the race question, the blacks would stump the South against him.

How was this reportedly growing alienation of blacks to be checked? According to Green's confidant, let the Administration and its friends establish contact with the black masses and pay less attention to the professional politicians. In addition: "Let the President be the President of the whole, and act as he would if Indians were killing Negroes; or if the Negroes of the South were treating the whites as the whites of the South are treating the Negroes. . . . I have told you the truth as I see it . . . ," said Ransome, in conclusion.[32]

Officeholder Green sent the President a copy of his reply to the dissident Ransome. He was slightly obsequious when he wrote the President: "Please don't consider me obstrusive: for you know, I love you, and wish to see your future crowned with success." In his note to the President, Green tried to impeach the integrity of Ransome's contention that blacks did not wish to see all of the black troops mustered out of the service: "So far as my information goes, the war in the Philippines is exceedingly unpopular amongst all colored people without regard to conditions." Green then offered to mount the political stump for the black vote in the North, provided he could get a "general railroad pass."[33]

[32] R. C. Ransome, Chicago, to John B. Green, Washington, June 27, 1899, WMP, Vol. 33, No. 6484–86. A document in the McKinley Papers from the Adjutant General's office, July 13, 1899, showed that every black volunteer unit had been mustered out of the service, ibid., Vol. 34, No. 6711.

[33] John B. Green, U. S. Postal Stamp Agency, to William McKinley, June 29, 1899, WMP, Vol. 33, No. 6495.

As things turned out, McKinley was concerned enough about the issue of black troops to discuss it with the Secretary of War, Elihu Root, who responded in the following manner:

> About the colored regiments: I am embarrassed by the fact that as I am informed, while the colored troops have always fought well, the colored officers in the volunteer regiments raised for the Spanish War were failures. I am told that they have not the faculty of commanding; or of enforcing discipline, and are not respected by their troops as are white officers. I am inclined to think that unless we are prepared to appoint colored men as line officers it is easier for us to stop at the beginning than it would be in the middle. As to all this of course I am a novice. . . .

Rather than raise a black regiment with white officers and risk alienating blacks, Root felt it a wiser course not to raise one at all. On the other hand he was in favor of raising a national Cuban army as a means of draining off Cuban troublemakers.[34] McKinley remained unconvinced by Root's reasoning against the establishment of a black regiment, that is, the inability of the blacks to produce good officers. To Root he said:

> I note what you say about the colored regiment. This subject is always one of difficulty. But I feel very much inclined to organize a colored regiment, making the field officers (white) all regulars, and the line officers all colored. It does seem to me that if we exercise the same care in the selection of the line officers for the colored regiment that we have and are exercising with the line officers of the white regiments, we can secure a fine lot of soldiers.

McKinley then suggested a number of black officeholders and leaders, including the president of Wilberforce University, who might help in recruiting as line officers "the very best types of their race." McKinley seemed to feel that if black soldiers had been found who fought well, there just might be some around who could lead satisfactorily. Racially, this may well have been McKinley's finest hour:

[34] Elihu Root to William McKinley, August 17, 1899, WMP, Vol. 36, No. 7057–58.

> The colored regiments fight magnificently, and I see that those in the Philippines have already shown the same splendid fighting qualities that were evidenced in Cuba. The regiment will be picked men, and the colored leaders should be made to feel and understand it. If they do, they will be put upon their mettle, as a result of which we will have a set of officers who can demonstrate their fitness to command.[35]

"The Southern Delegations," said McKinley's chief patronage dispenser, "are among the most interesting features of the beginning of a Republican administration." The political bread-line was a rather colorful spectacle: "Black men who want official recognition that will enable them to shine among the leaders of their race; red men with landed interests to protect. . . . All these people gather in Washington . . . in pursuit of their ambitions."[36]

As has been noted before, in no area did the Presidents have to face up to matters of race as they did in connection with the federal patronage. The problem became more complicated after Reconstruction when the Republican party in many Southern states such as Georgia became almost wholly black and the white Republican leaders had to "respect their [blacks'] wishes in the appointment of postmasters and other federal officers," in order to maintain their leadership.[37] So long as blacks could vote in the South the black politician could not be entirely ignored. Recognition of this fact probably helped to trigger the drive of the Southern Democrats to rid themselves of the black vote in an otherwise white political establishment.

During McKinley's first year in office Blanche K. Bruce, J. C. Napier and John C. Clemmons, all black men, were recommended for political office. McKinley himself wanted to make Bruce register of the Treasury, provided Mark Hanna ap-

[35] William McKinley to Elihu Root, August 19, 1899, WMP, Vol. 36, No. 7080–81.

[36] Joseph Little Bristow, *Fraud and Politics at the Turn of the Century* (New York: Expose Press, 1952), p. 71.

[37] Ibid., p. 74.

proved.[38] Napier's sponsor described him as a man of high character and argued that since a black man from Tennessee had never been named for a national position, this appointment would help to snare the black vote in that state.[39] As things turned out for "Mr. John C. Clemmons, the worthy colored Republican" from El Paso, Texas, the only available job was "that of laborer in the Post Office Department."[40] P. B. F. Pinchback, the former lieutenant governor of Louisiana, was in the competition for Recorder of Deeds in the District of Columbia.[41]

An excellent example of the operation of the idea of race at this time was afforded by the application of George H. Jackson of New Haven, Connecticut, for a consular appointment. In behalf of the President, J. A. Porter, his private secretary, asked the Secretary of State to find something for Jackson who was described as

> a very worthy and well educated colored citizen whose petition is numerously indorsed by influential men throughout Connecticut, including the entire delegation from the state Congress. For this reason the President is inclined to believe that if the suitable opportunity occurs, it would be well for Mr. Jackson to receive some appointment *proper for a colored man to hold* [italics added].[42]

Just what kind of position Porter or McKinley thought "proper for a colored man to hold" remains undetermined. However, the incident suggests that the concept of "the black

[38] William McKinley to Mark Hanna, November 24, 1897, WMP (Letter Book), Vol. 90, No. 65, ser. II.

[39] John Addison Porter (private secretary to the President) to L. G. Gage, Secretary of the Treasury, May 8, 1897, in which Porter quotes a portion of a letter to the President from H. Clay Evans, Commissioner of Pensions, in support of Napier, WMP (Letter Book), Vol. 92, No. 49.

[40] J. Addison Porter to Honorable James Gary, Postmaster General, June 16, 1897. J. Porter to John C. Clemmons, June 16, 1897. J. Porter to John C. Clemmons, June 28, 1897, WMP (Letter Book), Vol. 94, No. 241.

[41] J. A. Porter to Honorable P. B. F. Pinchback, June 9, 1897, WMP (Letter Book), Vol. 93, No. 324.

[42] J. A. Porter to John Sherman, Secretary of State, June 28, 1897, WMP (Letter Book), Vol. 94, No. 283, ser. II.

man's place" was not unique to the Southern side of Mason and Dixon's line.

Blanche K. Bruce, former United States senator from Mississippi, successful aspirant for register of the Treasury, thanked the President for the appointment of a black man, John C. Devereaux, as Collector of the Port of Customs at Savannah, Georgia, and for placing John C. Dany in a position in Wilmington, North Carolina:

> They are both excellent appointments and will be gratefully received by the colored people of this country. Your Administration is less than one year old, and yet you have done more for this class of our fellow-citizens than any of your distinguished predecessors. God bless you, Mr. President.[43]

Coming from a major black politician whose tenure of service spanned the Reconstruction and post-Reconstruction years, this was a strong endorsement of the appointment record of William McKinley. This kind of courtship of blacks, coming six years after the defeat of the Federal Elections bill, makes one want to question again the theory of black abandonment by the Republican party. It may be significant to note in this connection that Theodore Roosevelt was later to lament McKinley's generosity in giving top appointments to blacks in Georgia. On the other hand, Bruce's enthusiasm for McKinley may have been due to the fact that he had personally received an office from the President's hand.

McKinley's appointment record notwithstanding, many blacks were still discontented. A staunch presidential defender, John P. Green, tried desperately to calm the fears of one such dissatisfied black faction. During the Spanish-American War he told the president of the Colored Voters' League of Pittsburgh, Pennsylvania, "it would be in bad taste for any body of men to meet in convention to make themselves felt and demand full recognition and representation within the Republican Party." Green's praise for McKinley knew no bounds. He was optimistic about the black man's relation to the federal government: "We colored

[43] B. K. Bruce to William McKinley, February 10, 1898, WMP, Vol. 11, No. 2124.

Americans, from a national point of view, are being better treated now and more fully recognized under the present administration, both in civil office and in the army, than ever before in the history of this nation. I would therefore most earnestly advise you to postpone this convention to another time." Green sent a copy of his letter to the President, signing it rather fittingly, "Yours to command, John P. Green."[44]

Wallace A. Gaines of Kentucky was recommended for patronage in this manner: "He was my most trusted Lieutenant among the Negroes in the campaigning for delegates and electoral votes and is the recognized Negro leader of Kentucky and one of the coming leaders of his race in the South."[45]

At McKinley's request, another black officeholder, Judson Lyons, Treasury Department, vigorously tried to convince disgruntled blacks from Missouri to "stay in the party, else you may be lost." Lyons contended that six million dollars was paid annually to black officeholders, representing "the high water mark of our political journey and this President McKinley has done in a very large measure, notwithstanding he has been tied down by the Civil Service law. . . ." Most authoritatively and not without a trace of pomposity, Lyons told the blacks of Missouri: "Your letter . . . to the President has been handed to me, and owing to the great amount of work he has to do, I will endeavor to relieve him of that much by replying to it myself."[46] But McKinley was no more effective than his predecessors in protecting blacks in their right to vote in the South.

The Black Vote

Like most Republicans, McKinley was in favor of the black vote. In 1879 he opposed an attempt by the Democrats to

[44] John P. Green to John M. Clark, president of the Colored Voters' League, 1898, WMP, Vol. 15, No. 2906.

[45] Sam J. Roberts to William McKinley, August 2, 1898, ibid., Vol. 16, No. 3184, ibid., No. 3233.

[46] Judson Lyons to Albert W. Washington, August 21, 1899, WMP, Vol. 36, No. 7100–02. See also letter of George Cortelyou, one of the President's secretaries, to Judson Lyons, August 21, 1899, ibid., No. 7099.

repeal the federal election laws,[47] and in 1885 called for the enforcement of the clause in the Fourteenth Amendment that reduced representation in states where citizens were denied the right to vote.[48] As a congressman, McKinley had said about the Federal Elections bill of 1890: "The consciences of the American people will not be permitted to slumber until this great Constitutional right—the equality of suffrage, the equality of opportunity, freedom of political action and thought—shall not be the mere cold formalities of Constitutional enactment as now, but a living birthright which the poorest and humblest citizen, white or black . . . may confidently enjoy. . . ." McKinley's list of rights was much broader than the typical Republican position on this issue in that he employed the use of a term that had not yet gained much currency as far as racial dialogue on the black man was concerned: "the equality of opportunity."[49]

Still, McKinley showed the usual timidity on things racial when political contingencies were involved. He said to Mark Hanna: "In regard to the question you write about [the black vote], I don't think it is wise to commit me. We can never give our consent to a practice which disfranchises any of our fellow-citizens. I believe that the time is coming when the injustice will be corrected by the people of the South themselves." From Jefferson onward, the vain hope had been entertained that eventually the Southerners would voluntarily make things racially right. McKinley shared this traditional faith. "In the meantime," McKinley went on to add, "we cannot

[47] Speech of William McKinley in the House of Representatives, April 18, 1879, R. L. Paget (ed.), *McKinley's Masterpieces: Selections from the Public Addresses in and out of Congress of William McKinley* (Boston: Joseph Knight Co., 1896), pp. 86–87.

[48] Campaign speech at Ironton, Ohio, October 1, 1885, Joseph P. Smith, compiler, *Speeches and Addresses of William McKinley* (New York: D. Appleton and Co., 1893), pp. 165–80, 171–72. See also McKinley's speech on October 5, 1889, Cleveland, Ohio, J. S. Ogilvie (ed.), *Life and Speeches of William McKinley*, pp. 51–52.

[49] Speech of William McKinley in the House of Representatives, July 2, 1890, Joseph P. Smith, *Speeches and Addresses of William McKinley*, pp. 456–58.

abate our insistence upon the exercise of constitutional rights."[50]

From his sickbed in Bordeaux, France, Albion Tourgee, long-time racial champion of justice for the blacks, detected the rising tide of Negrophobia that was about to inundate the South in the 1890s. He wrote to McKinley: "A revival of that most dangerous and horrible feature of American life, a display of race antagonism at the South compels me to express to you my sincerest sympathy and keenest apprehension." He confessed that he had once entertained the hope that Christianity and the sense of liberty and justice inherent in the American mind would be sufficient to solve the race problem short of the blood and violence that had marked the travail of liberty in Western Europe. But now he was very pessimistic. It seemed to him that the sun of racial justice had set forever in the United States. "But that soothing theory [of peaceful solution] I have long since abandoned. I believe that the United States would just as readily approve the massacre of the colored race throughout her borders; as France would approve by the verdict of her masses, the slaughter of the Jews."

In the eyes of Tourgee, America had truly reached, in 1896, some kind of nadir in the history of race relations: "The pulpit is silent; the press regards such manifestations as those in North and South Carolina only with a sort of vague disfavor." Tourgee had once hoped that the bravery of the blacks in the Spanish-American War coupled with "the known disinclination of the white people . . . to military service in time of peace . . ." would have opened the way for black regiments, manned by black officers, to serve in America's overseas possessions: "But now, I fear it is useless to hope for any legislation which may open the door, even the least, to the colored man, who has again been placed under the heel of race prejudice in the United States." How different was Tourgee's gloomy testimony when contrasted with the optimistic ravings of Blanche K. Bruce and the two petty black politicians, Green and Lyons!

As had most of the Presidents of the period, Tourgee con-

[50] William McKinley to Mark Hanna, Thomasville, Ga., February 26, 1895, WMP (Letter Book), Vol. 87, No. 89, ser. II.

fessed that the more he studied the race question the more baffled he became as to how to handle it. He had once tried leaning on the Everlasting Arms by asking the blacks to declare an annual day of prayer in their churches for the purpose of petitioning the Almighty for racial justice. The blacks ignored his suggestion but Tourgee thought they might be more amenable if the same suggestion came from the President. There was nothing more to hope for but divine intervention, since the race problem was beyond remedy by any human means: "It has so cankered the political and moral sentiment of the American people, that no organized resistance to it is possible. It seems to be one of those questions which only God can handle." Finally, Tourgee saw a connection between the race question and the ultimate destiny of American liberty: "I cannot doubt that the American Republic may pay the price of its own injustice, by finding in the race problem the end of its liberties and the destruction of its original character."

What had cast this shadow of pessimism across the racial horizon for Tourgee? His pessimism was apparently triggered by the legal disfranchisement of blacks in North Carolina,[51] the state where Tourgee himself had gone on what he called "a fool's errand" some twenty or more years earlier to wrestle with the race problem. Now he was trembling for McKinley. He trembled more for the future of his country and the fate of liberty.[52]

And so, as the nineteenth century drew to a close, McKinley was aware of the worsening condition of blacks at the polls, although prosperous enough at the patronage table. However, once shut off from the polls, the lever by means of which blacks had been demanding and receiving patronage would fail to operate and black office holding would slowly die like grapes on a severed vine. There is no evidence that McKinley planned

[51] Charles Emory Smith, Postmaster General, to William McKinley, May 17, 1899, enclosing an article on the subject of Negro disfranchisement in North Carolina, appearing in the *Philadelphia Press,* WMP, Vol. 31, No. 5996–97.

[52] Albion Tourgee to William McKinley, November 23, 1898, WMP, Vol. 21, No. 4150–51. Tourgee's letter was a classic statement on the race question and its implications for American democracy. Also this letter was excellent testimony on the frustration if not disenchantment of a racial liberal.

to do anything about this situation, although one could hardly say that he was *unconcerned* about it.

In conclusion, McKinley was no rabid racist. His attitude toward blacks seemed positive. On the other hand, there is no denying that he did feel that American [white] civilization was superior and carried with it superior obligations toward Asian peoples. Though by no means unconscious of race, the President expressed little if any race prejudice toward blacks. There seem to be no expressions by the President on the subject of race mixing. Yet he did demonstrate that he could, in his racial thought, transcend the color line. He seemed sincere in what he said in matters of race, but he was governed chiefly by political necessity. His patronage record for blacks seems extremely generous and deserves further investigation. While vociferous on the Filipino question, and in private strongly in favor of blacks, McKinley was uninclined to dwell publicly on matters of race.

CHAPTER IX

Theodore Roosevelt (1901–1909) and the Matter of Race: Basic Approach

Theodore Roosevelt had more scholarly knowledge of and interest in the subject of race than any of his predecessors who were considered in this book. Much of what he had to say in a theoretical way about race was said *after* he left the presidency.

The Idea of Race: The Darwinian Perspective

Like the average American, Roosevelt was aware of racial and ethnic differences in men. At age fourteen, on a trip overseas, according to his diary, he witnessed "a row between an arab and a black man. . . ."[1] He recalled how he had spent the most "amusing and interesting hour" of his young life watching a Moslem procession in Cairo, Egypt. He saw "all sorts of men and beasts . . . continually passing. Various races of men could be recognized, such as the white, black, Egyptian and Eastern whites, Arab or Syrian. . . . Also a beautiful white Circassian lady inmate of some rich man's harem. . . ."[2] Many

[1] Theodore Roosevelt, *Theodore Roosevelt's Diaries of His Boyhood and Youth* (New York: Charles Scribner's Sons, 1928), p. 277. He made this entry in his diary on November 28, 1872.

[2] Ibid., entry for December 7, 1872, Cairo, Egypt, p. 289.

years later, as governor of New York, he spoke of the diversity, in "race origin," of the people of that state.[3]

Though guilty of using the word *race* loosely on occasion, Roosevelt did not have the same reverence for the terms *Aryan, Anglo-Saxon,* and *Teutonic* as did the "racists" of his day. He thought it "absurd" to use the term *Anglo-Saxon* to mean anything except "the dominant race in England between the first and eleventh centuries." He surmised that "all our terminology in race questions [was] usually employed incorrectly."[4] The average American carried in his blood "the strains of many different racial stocks."[5] Roosevelt wrote to a friend how happy he was to discover that an Italian author he was reading recognized the relationship between race and language and classified *Aryan* as a linguistic and not a biological term.[6] He dissociated the American from the Anglo-Saxon branch of the Caucasian race: "We are not the same as any old-world race, we are a new race. . . ." In a slightly Anglophobic manner he intimated that there were only a few select Englishmen he cared to have as his guests: "The average Englishman is not a being which I find congenial or with whom I can associate. I wish him well; but I wish him well at a good distance from me. . . ."[7]

[3] State of New York, *Public Papers of Theodore Roosevelt, Governor, 1899* (Albany: Brandow Printing Co., 1899, 1900), I, 247.

[4] Theodore Roosevelt, *Letters,* selected and edited by Elting E. Morison, (Cambridge: Harvard University Press, 1951–54), III, 76. (Hereafter to be cited as Roosevelt, *Letters.*) Roosevelt referred to the Dutch and the British as "the two races." See letter of Theodore Roosevelt to Earl Grey, London, England, November 22, 1902, Theodore Roosevelt Papers (Personal Letter Books in the Library of Congress, Washington, D.C.), Box 144, Bk. No. 7, p. 180. [Hereafter this source will be cited as TRP (PL).] Roosevelt spoke of French, New England, Virginia and Tennessee blood as if these were racial entities. See Theodore Roosevelt, *The Winning of the West* (New Knickerbocker edition, New York: G. P. Putnam's Sons, 1889, 1891, 1896, 1917), 4 vols., passim.

[5] Roosevelt to Lady Gregory, County Calway, Ireland, June 8, 1903, TRP (PL), Box 145, Bk. No. 10, pp. 69–70.

[6] Roosevelt to Benjamin Wheeler, president of the University of California, May 11, 1904, TRP (PL), Box 147, Bk. No. 17, p. 180.

[7] Roosevelt to F. R. Dunne (Mr. Dooley), December 3, 1904, TRP (PL), Box 149, Bk. No. 22, pp. 215–19. Those select Englishmen with whom he would break bread were John Morley, James Bryce, Saint Loe Strachey, and Cecil Spring-Rice.

In his lectures at Oxford in 1910, Roosevelt ridiculed the generation of fifty years before which regarded the Teuton and Aryan "with reverential admiration, as if the words denoted not merely something definite but something ethnologically sacred."[8] Students of race had found not the "slightest connection between kinship in blood and kinship in tongue." There was no certainty that the ancestors of the Teutons ever spoke Aryan at all. The high-level societies and civilizations of the world have rarely been the result of the efforts of one race, but the consequency of a variety of racial types and social cultures, Roosevelt concluded.[9] He took one author to task for trying to attribute "everything good to Aryans and Teutons," including Dante and the Apostle Paul.[10]

Evolution was a part of Roosevelt's racial frame of reference, and he accepted "the fundamental truth of evolution" as necessary for "sound scientific thought. . . ."[11] He found a striking analogy between the "changes, the development and the extinction of [animal] species . . . ," and man and his institutions.[12] Just as one could trace the rise and fall of members in the animal kingdom, the same could be done for human societies, races, and nations. A belief in social Darwinism was implicit in these remakrs. As with animals so, too, with men in history: "A new form may result from the specialization of a long existing, and hitherto very slowly changing, generalized or nonspecialized form; as for instance occurs when a barbaric race from a variety of causes suddenly develops a more complex cultivation and civilization."[13] From such an

[8] Theodore Roosevelt, *The Works of Theodore Roosevelt* (National Edition, New York: Charles Scribner's Sons, 1926), XII, 40. (Hereafter this source will be cited as Roosevelt, *Works*.)

[9] Roosevelt, *Works*, XII, 40.

[10] Ibid., XII, 109. In 1911 Roosevelt reviewed Stewart Houston Chamberlain's book, *The Foundations of the 19th Century*, for *Outlook Magazine*.

[11] Ibid., XII, 108, from a lecture entitled "Biological Analogies in History."

[12] Ibid., XII, 30–31, 55.

[13] Roosevelt, *Works*, XII, 36. In one discussion about the relation between man and the brute Roosevelt saw more similarity between the highest monkey and the African Bushman "than between the same monkey and the herring or eft [a newt]. . . ." See letter of Roosevelt to John Burroughs, August 1, 1903, TRP (PL), Box 145, Bk. No. 11, pp. 168–69.

assumption, Roosevelt went on to make all of his judgments of race.

He realized the danger involved in taking "the leap of faith" from animals to men, but such analogies fascinated him and he made them, nevertheless. With men no less than animals, he concluded, those who reached the top of the ethnological heap did so because of superior strength. Inversely, weakness could cause one to lose his place. There was nothing eternal or fixed about position on the racial totem pole. The flexibility of Roosevelt's racial views may have been due to his rather keen realization of the evolutionary nature and impermanence of racial position.

White Superiority in Race and Civilization

Taking his cue from evolution in the animal phyla, Roosevelt arrived at the conclusion that the Caucasian was superior to all other people in race and civilization. In *The Winning of the West*, he unblushingly awarded the prize of superiority in race and culture to the white-skinned, English-speaking Anglo-Saxon.[14] He was impressed with the rise and spread of civilized man over the earth, his advances in the conquest of nature, and his achievements in the arts and sciences between 1492 and 1910. Who was responsible for this progress, almost unparalleled in human history? "One race, the so-called white race, or . . . more accurately, the group of peoples living in Europe, who undoubtedly have kinship of blood, who profess the Christian religion, and trace back their culture to Greece and Rome." Earlier, he had said that civilization could be attributed not to one but a variety of racial types. Perhaps he was speaking of a variety of white types. Who could blame him for being impressed with the fact that "peoples of European blood [held] dominion over all America and Australia and the Islands of the

[14] Roosevelt, *The Winning of the West*, I. See his Chapter One entitled significantly, "The English Speaking Peoples." He was thirty-one years of age when this book was first published.

sea, over most of Africa and the major half of Asia"?[15] He did not expect political control over these territories to be as lasting as the ethical and cultural aspects of that conquest.

In a burst of ethnocentric adoration of Western civilization, Roosevelt credited "substantially all of the World's achievements worth remembering [since 1492] . . . to the people of European descent." He was generous in sharing the glory equally among his white compeers and did not limit the applause for carrying the torch of civilization to any one branch of the Caucasian racial tree. Beginning with the Iberian peoples of Portugal and Spain, almost every nation of Europe had sought and found a place in the movement of expansion, according to Roosevelt. Even so, he thought that the moment of greatness had arrived for the modern progeny of the hoary Anglo-Saxon: "For the last three centuries, the great phenomenon of mankind has been the growth of the English speaking peoples and their spread over the world's waste spaces," he told an English audience.[16] He attributed the urban inclinations of the white race at the end of the nineteenth century to the characteristic tendency of the "highly civilized races" to dwell in cities.[17]

When he awarded the prize for the best civilization to the Caucasian, Roosevelt made one significant exception—Japan. The rise of Japan and her approximation "of the characteristics that have given power and leadership to the West . . . [was for Roosevelt] a phenomenon unexemplified in history."[18] The racially flexible Roosevelt admitted the Japanese to the charmed circle of "civilized nations." The fact that a people beyond the pale of Western "blood and culture" could accomplish such a feat duly impressed him.

[15] Roosevelt, *Works,* XII, 48–49.
[16] Roosevelt, *Works,* XII, 50.
[17] Ibid., XII, 223. These remarks were made in 1895 in the course of Roosevelt's review of Albert Shaw's *Municipal Government in Great Britain* for *Outlook Magazine.*
[18] Ibid., XII, 49.

THE IMPERMANENCE OF WHITE SUPERIORITY

Roosevelt told the white race not to forget that its supremacy was very recent and by no means immutable. Had not "the attitude of the Asian and African, of Hun and Mongol, Turk, Tartar; Arab and Moor . . . been that of successful aggression against Europe" only a scant thousand years prior to 1492? Had it not taken more than a century after the voyages of Columbus "before mastery in war began to pass from the Asiatic to the European"?[19] Roosevelt had unusual historical acuity and no mean knowledge of that discipline. His view of history was not ethnocentric, though some of his conclusions could be so labeled. He said Western scholars did not always appreciate the proper significance of the Mongol invasions of the thirteenth century. This ignorance he attributed in part "to the natural tendency among men of Western Europe to think of history as only European history and of European history as only the History of Latin and Teutonic Europe." This was the kind of ignorance that caused some people, upon the defeat of Russia by Japan in 1905, to make "such comically absurd remarks . . . as the one that for the first time since Salamis Asia had conquered Europe . . . [when] as a matter of fact, the recent military supremacy of the white European race is a matter of only some three centuries."[20] For Roosevelt the real key to history and civilization was not race but power.

In 1894, Roosevelt had an opportunity to consider the future of the white race when he reviewed for a magazine, a book by Charles Pearson of England and Australia. The best chapter, for Roosevelt, was one titled "The Unchangeable Limits of the Higher Races." He agreed with Pearson's thesis that the white race could live only in the Temperate Zone and could never hope to displace the tropical peoples, but he took issue with some

[19] Roosevelt, *Works,* XII, 49.

[20] Jeremiah Curtin, *The Mongols: A History* (with a Foreword by Theodore Roosevelt) (Boston: Little, Brown and Co., 1907), pp. x–xi. The preceding thoughts on the Mongols were drawn from Roosevelt's foreword to this book. For more in praise of the Mongols see Roosevelt to Mr. J. J. Jusserand, Paris, France, July 11, 1905, TRP (PL), Box 150, Bk. No. 26, pp. 317–19.

of Pearson's other ideas. Pearson felt that when finally freed from European domination the black, red, and yellow races would then challenge the industrial and military supremacy of the whites. The whites would be unable to respond psychologically to this challenge because of the mere shock of having to recognize the equality of the colored peoples. The Chinese would in time dominate Asia, including Asiatic Russia. Roosevelt did not share these views. The Chinese were militarily incompetent, unlike the Tartars, and in spite of numerical superiority Chinese troops "would be formidable only under a European leader." Roosevelt also predicted that once the British left India that subcontinent would sink into insignificance.

The idea of a future military challenge from the African was too remote a possibility to warrant serious speculation. "By that time the descendants of the Negro may be as intellectual as the Athenian," said Roosevelt, apparently not believing that the alleged inferiority of the blacks was permanent. While he agreed that "the Negroid peoples, the so-called Hamitic and Bastard Semitic races of Eastern and Middle Africa [were] formidable fighters," they were no match for the white man of the Temperate Zone. Even in 1894 Roosevelt expected Africa and Asia to shake off Western imperialism ultimately. But even so, in the event a challenge should arise from other races, the whites had a duty to face it like men, for the phenomenon would signify "that this particular nation . . . has itself become civilized in the process and we shall simply be dealing with another civilized nation of non-Aryan blood." While Roosevelt probably did not relish the thought that those of "non-Aryan blood" might one day rise, he did not believe, as did the more rabid racists of his day, that only the whites could achieve civilization.

For all his racial reasonableness, Roosevelt detested the Chinese. He praised the United States and Australia for having the "clear instinct of race selfishness, [which] saw the race foe and kept out the dangerous alien," and for preserving the choice spots of the Temperate Zone for white occupancy. Those two countries recognized that the presence of the Chinese was "ruinous to the white race," and future civilization would be grateful to them for this foresight. Roosevelt was glad to see the Russians holding back the Chinese in Asia. He chided the English aristocracy for depositing the African in the Temperate Zone.[21]

The White Man's Burden and the Great Rule of Righteousness

No less than his contemporaries, Roosevelt was of the opinion that contemporary white supremacy in race and civilization imposed heavy duties and responsibilities in regard to the inferior alien races of the globe. He boasted of the long centuries of preparation for self-government that allegedly lay behind the Anglo-Saxon:

> It is no light task for a nation to achieve the temperamental qualities without which the institutions of free government are but an empty mockery. . . . What has taken us thirty generations to achieve we cannot expect another race to accomplish out of hand, especially when a large portion of that race start very far behind the point which our ancestors had reached even thirty generations ago. . . .

Roosevelt took this approach in regard to the Filipinos and told Congress that "patience and strength, forbearance and steadfast resolution . . ." had to be exercised in regard to the Filipinos. "Our aim is high . . . to make them fit for self-government. . . ." He doubted that history would be able to produce "a single instance in which a masterful race such as ours . . ." had shown such "disinterested zeal" for the progress of an alien people.[22]

Roosevelt was impatient with the Southerner who refused self-government to the black American while demanding it "for

[21] The discussion in the five preceding paragraphs is based on Roosevelt's review of Charles Pearson's book, *National Life and Character: A Forecast* (1894). This review, originally appearing in *Outlook Magazine,* was found in Roosevelt, *Works,* XIII, 208–09, 211–13, 222.

[22] First Annual Message of Theodore Roosevelt, December 3, 1901, Richardson, *Messages,* X, 437.

brown men who live somewhere else." The kind of American public opinion that demanded that the "rights of the Filipinos, the Puerto Ricans and other kindred peoples" be maintained, becomes "a mere curse" to the dependent people "if it persists in refusing to look at the facts as they are, and to demand that which is not only impossible but highly undesirable." Roosevelt seemed to be saying that even if the Filipinos *were* capable of self-government, it would be *undesirable* to give it to them.[23] Besides, it might take "a century" to get the Filipinos to stand alone like the Cubans.[24] Furthermore Roosevelt thought America was doing for the Filipinos in ten years something that represented "far more than ten thousand years in our own race history."[25]

Roosevelt showed his impatience with those who waxed sentimental on the Philippine question when he said to Bishop Potter: "I do not care a rap for the ordinary anti-imperialist creature. . . ."[26] He was also impatient with intellectuals who wanted to give up the islands: "It is to my mind the mark of a lazy, careless, ignorant, or timid man to advocate the easy talk of abandoning our duty towards less advanced races by insisting upon the obvious untruth that they should be treated as, for instance, the Swiss or Norwegians, or men of Vermont or Iowa can and must be treated."[27] He told the great poet laureate of imperialism, Rudyard Kipling, that he had trouble dealing with "the fools who seem to think that any group of pirates and head-hunters needs nothing but independence in order that it may be turned forthwith into a darkhued New England town meeting."[28]

[23] Theodore Roosevelt to the Earl of Cromer, Cairo, Egypt, May 23, 1905, TRP (PL), Box 150, Bk. No. 25, pp. 286–87.

[24] Theodore Roosevelt to Bishop C. H. Brent, Manila, May 19, 1905, ibid., pp. 241–42.

[25] Theodore Roosevelt to Earl Grey, April 1, 1902, ibid., Box 143, Bk. No. 4, p. 33.

[26] Theodore Roosevelt to Right Reverend Bishop B. C. Potter, January 2, 1902, ibid., Box 143, Bk. No. 3, p. 15.

[27] Theodore Roosevelt to Mr. Archibald R. Colquhoun, London, England, April 15, 1904, TRP (PL), Box 147, Bk. No. 16, pp. 440–41.

[28] Theodore Roosevelt to Rudyard Kipling, November 1, 1904, ibid., Box 149, Bk. No. 21, pp. 94–95. Also in this letter Roosevelt referred to Bogotá and Panama as "corrupt and Pithecoid communities."

In his English lectures of 1910, Roosevelt elaborated upon the duties that bore heavily upon the shoulders of the Caucasian. The greatest problem of the modern nation was that of its complicated relations "with the alien races. . . ." How were Americans and Europeans to deal with this variety of peoples, some of whom possessed "a more ancient civilization than [their] own," while others had just come out of the barbaric stage? Roosevelt was certain that the way to solve the problem was *not* by "the sentimentality of the stay at home people. . . ." Neither was the raw brutality of the men . . . at home or on the Frontier who exploited the alien races on the basis that might makes right, the proper way to discharge the white man's burden.

In the long run, Roosevelt theorized, there could be no real justification for one race controlling or managing another "unless the management and control are exercised in the interest and for the benefit of that other race." England and America were doing just that. Roosevelt now discussed his rule for dealing with alien races. As a working practice he may have developed this rule during the Spanish-American War of 1898, if not earlier. In any case, he always tried to follow it closely in matters of race: "As regards every race everywhere, at home, abroad, we cannot afford to deviate from the *great rule of righteousness* [italics added] which bids us to treat every man on his worth as a man."

The great rule was a two-edged sword. A member of an alien race should not be shown any favoritism. No, indeed! He should be made to hew to the line as much as the whites. Nor should he be allowed to "cumber the ground," that is, to stand in the way of civilization as the Indians had done. On the other hand, whenever a member of one of the alien races "acts in such a way which would entitle him to respect and reward if he were one of our own stock he is just as entitled to that respect and reward . . . even though that other stock produces a much smaller proportion of men of this type than does our own." He quickly added that "this has nothing to do with social intermingling, with what is called social equality." He meant only that "elementary justice" should be accorded every man and woman who earned rewards that accrued from "thrift, sobriety, self-control, respect for the rights of others, and . . . the intelligence to work to a given end. To more than such treatment no man is entitled, and less than such treatment no man should receive."[29] Such was Roosevelt's formula for dealing with inferior peoples. Although it was handed down from the mountain of white supremacy, in many ways it was an admirable doctrine. Still, it was difficult to understand how any personal approach to race relations could exclude social equality. This omission weakened Roosevelt's racial formula considerably, especially with respect to blacks.

The Inferiority of Blacks

In Roosevelt's hierarchy of race the black man was inferior. "I entirely agree with you that as a race, and in the mass, the [blacks] are altogether inferior to the whites," he wrote in 1901 to the author Owen Wister.[30] For Roosevelt, intellectual development was very important in social evolution. "A perfectly stupid race can never rise to a very high place. The Negro, for instance, has been kept down as much by lack of intellectual development as by anything else."[31] Commenting further to Owen Wister, he said: "The Negro and the white man as shown by their skulls, are closely akin, and taken together, differ widely from the round skulled Mongolian. . . . But admitting all that can be truthfully said against the Negro, it also remains true that a great deal that is untrue is said against him; and more is untruthfully said in favor of the white man who lives beside and upon him." Nevertheless, Roosevelt saw the American black as a fledgling, unable to stand alone: "I do not believe that the average

[29] Roosevelt, *Works,* XII, 57–58, for materials used in the preceding five paragraphs.

[30] Theodore Roosevelt to Owen Wister, Roosevelt, *Letters,* V, 226.

[31] These remarks were made in the course of a review of a book by Benjamin Kidd. Roosevelt, *Works,* XIII, 24. See also *North American Review,* 61:94–107 (July 1895).

Negro in the United States is as yet in any way fit to take care of himself and others as the average white man—for if he were, there would be no Negro race problem."[32]

The President agreed with a British colonial administrator, Sir William Johnston, who thought that the black man tended to regress in his native land. To Roosevelt, the success of the Haitian revolution was a "curse." Although the revolution was justified it delayed emancipation elsewhere and, more seriously, cut Haiti off completely "from all white leadership," depriving her of "an element naturally fit for uplifting leadership." This was the reason, as Roosevelt saw it, why Haiti was the most backward country in the West Indies.[33]

The Afro-American was not dismissed entirely as a possible racial rival as far as time and numbers were concerned. In his reflections upon slavery and the black man in his treatise on the westward movement, Roosevelt said: "The Negro, unlike so many of the inferior races, does not dwindle away in the presence of the white man. He holds his own."[34] The black man was a good *breeder* and Roosevelt was not one to ignore the significance of that! He said he was thankful that the suppression of the slave trade and the Civil War had ended this potential black threat to the white race in the United States.

The Reality of Race Difference: Barriers of Race and Culture

By now it should be apparent that Roosevelt was much concerned with race difference. He was no less cognizant of cultural diversity. In spite of his rather flexible racial frame of reference, he also thought in terms of a line beyond which an alien race could not venture. The Anglo-Saxon racial citadel predicated on a dislike of amalgamation, was to be held inviolate. While Roosevelt's wall of race and culture did not reach the height of that erected by many of his contemporaries,

[32] Roosevelt, *Letters,* V, 226.
[33] Roosevelt, *Works,* XII, 218.
[34] Roosevelt, *The Winning of the West,* II, 44.

he, as they, had his own racial inner sanctum. And the prospect of Asiatics and blacks entering therein was not pleasing to him. While he tended to praise national more than "racial unity," Roosevelt contended that when "we come to race differences as fundamental as those which divide from one another the half dozen great ethnic divisions of mankind . . . differences of nationality, speech and creed [sank] into littleness."[35]

Race Consciousness and the Yellow Peril

Two groups whose ethnic differences were of such consequence as to militate against race mixing, were the Chinese and the Japanese. They were viewed by Roosevelt as a potential racial threat to the Caucasian. He believed in assimilation, but not in the biological form. His was an assimilation of feeling: "In this country our own safety lies in a general assimilation—general cordial feeling without regard to difference of creed or of race origin, when in short we treat every man of his own worth as a man," he said in a speech on Catholicism in 1900.[36]

Roosevelt preferred to see the Hawaiian Islands remain primarily a haven for white men.

> Hawaii whether it wills or not shall, so far as in my power lies, be kept for the small, white land-owners, and we shall discourage by every method the race suicide which would be encouraged by the planters in their insistence upon bringing every kind of Asiatic to help them make fortunes for a moment and insure the extinguishment of their blood in the future.[37]

Concerning the Persians, Roosevelt said: "Their thoughts are not our thoughts. . . . I am not sure of the reason—it is not merely that they are an oriental people, or a non-Aryan race. The Finns and Hungarians, although of course much mixed with our blood, are perhaps less akin to us by race . . .

[35] Roosevelt, *Works,* XII, 41. Roosevelt said these things in his Oxford lectures of 1910, where one finds the clear statement of his racial credo.

[36] Theodore Roosevelt, governor of New York, to Frank Travis, [n.d.] 1900, Roosevelt, *Letters,* II, 1349.

[37] Theodore Roosevelt to Honorable James Wilson, Secretary of Agriculture, February 3, 1903, TRP (PL), Box 144, Bk. No. 8, p. 208.

than the Persians." The non-Aryan and non-Christian Japanese were in many ways closer to the white man than were the Slavs, Roosevelt thought. He was fascinated with the changes that took place when a portion of the Slavs in the Balkans adopted different "creeds and cults," namely, Moslem faith and civilization.[38]

No better illustration of the alienation of races because of cultural differences was afforded than by the Japanese, according to Roosevelt. "No other book I have read on Japan has given me so vivid a picture of the real conditions of this strange alien civilization," said Roosevelt after reading Lafcadio Hearn's *Japan.* While Japanese civilization was admittedly high, "the people who make it up have ideals as alien to ours on some points . . ." as were the beliefs of post-Homeric Greece.[39] Some articles on Japan sent by a friend brought forth the following significant remarks about the people from the land of the rising sun:

> As for their having a yellow skin, if we go back two thousand years we will find that to the Greeks and the Romans the most dreaded and yet in a sense the most despised barbarian was the white-skinned, blue-eyed and red or yellow haired barbarian of the North—the men from whom you and I in a large part derive our blood. It would not seem possible to the Greek or Roman of that day that this Northern Barbarian should ever become part of the civilized world—his equal in civilization. The racial differences seemed too great.

Roosevelt went on to add that personally and officially he admired the Japanese as a "wonderful and civilized people" who "are entitled to stand on an absolute equality with all other peoples of the civilized world." Of course, there were undesirable Japanese as there were also undesirable Americans.

[38] Theodore Roosevelt to Cecil Spring-Rice, London, England, January 18, 1904, TRP (PL), Box 147, Bk. No. 15, pp. 52–54. See also letter of Theodore Roosevelt to Cecil Spring-Rice, March 19, 1904, ibid., Box 147, Bk. No. 16, pp. 224–27.

[39] Theodore Roosevelt to Mr. Grant Lafarge, February 11, 1905, TRP (PL), Box 150, Bk. No. 24, p. 74. Roosevelt was returning a book on the Japanese.

But he would simply apply the great rule. He would brook no discrimination against the Japanese. "I should," he said:

> hang my head with shame if I were capable of discrimination against a Japanese General or Admiral, statesman, philanthropist or artist, because he and I had different shades of skin; just as I would hang my head with shame if I were capable of thus discriminating against some man with black hair and black eyes, because I have brown hair and blue eyes.[40]

In spite of his admiration for the Japanese, Roosevelt called for the immediate annexation of Hawaii in 1896, mainly to control Asiatic immigration there. Already, he complained about, "the influx of population [there consisted] . . . not of white Americans but of low caste laborers drawn from the yellow races."[41] Roosevelt called the failure of annexation "a crime against the United States . . . a crime against white civilization."

The Japanese ambassador, a Japanese baron, and Roosevelt agreed, in private conversation, that the Japanese should have hegemony in the Yellow Sea since the Americans enjoyed that same privilege in the Caribbean. In these talks the Japanese ambassador resented any insinuation by the West that the Japanese would become dangerously conceited should they defeat the Russians in a possible future struggle. According to Roosevelt: "They then proceeded evidently with much feeling against the talk about the yellow terror, explaining that . . . they had had to dread the yellow [terror] of the Mongolians as much as Europe itself . . . their aspirations were in every way to become part of the circle of civilized mankind, a place to which they were entitled by over two thousand years of civilization of their own, they did not see why they should be classed as barbarians." Roosevelt was obviously impressed with this face-to-face racial encounter: "I told them that I entirely agreed with them, that without question some of my own ancestors in the tenth century had been part of the white terror of the Northmen, a terror to which we now look back

[40] Theodore Roosevelt to Dr. D. B. Schneder, June 19, 1905, TRP (PL), Box 150, Bk. No. 26, pp. 136–37. Schneder had just returned from Japan.
[41] Theodore Roosevelt, "On the Issues of 1896," *Century Magazine*, 51:71 (November 1895).

with romantic satisfaction." There was much, he thought, the whites could learn from the Japanese who, in turn, could learn from the whites "the idea of the proper way of treating womanhood." Roosevelt was simply fascinated by the Japanese: "The Japs interest me and I like them. I am perfectly aware that if they win out [over the Russians?] it may possibly mean a struggle between them and us in the future; but I hope not and believe not."

For some time, Roosevelt favored the Japanese over the Russians, in spite of the differences in race, civilization and culture. "I am not much affected by the statement that the Japanese are of an utterly different race from ourselves and that the Russians are of the same race. While there were some people of a very low standard from whom nothing could be expected, Roosevelt observed that the longer he lived the more he felt that there were some races widely different from each other, "which nevertheless, stand about on an equality in the proportions of bad and good which they contain. . . ." Roosevelt did not expect Japanese morality to be any better than that displayed at Berlin, Vienna, St. Petersburg, Paris, London or Washington. Roosevelt closed this long epistle on race with this admonition to his correspondent: "Be very careful that no one else gets a chance to see this."[42]

Japanese interest in the Red Cross convinced Roosevelt that they were humane, not cruel, and so "we need concern ourselves little about the 'yellow peril.'"[43] Roosevelt did not share the British opinion that the Russians would defeat Japan in a war and then threaten Europe. He thought that the Japanese would win, and he approved of their winning. "The Japs have played our game because they have played the game of civilized mankind. People talk of the 'yellow peril' and speak of the Mongol

[42] Theodore Roosevelt to Cecil Spring-Rice, June 13, 1903, TRP (PL), Box 147, Bk. No. 17, pp. 495–502. This letter concerned the subject of Roosevelt's long talk with the Japanese minister to the United States, Takahira, and Baron Kaneko, a Japanese Harvard graduate. Roosevelt put the Turks in the white race physiologically, but found them culturally foreign and "a curse to Europe."

[43] Roosevelt to George Kennan, American Consulate, Yokohama, Japan, June 2, 1904, ibid., p. 368.

invasion of Europe, why, descendants of those very Mongols are serving under the banners of Russia . . . not Japan. We may be of general service, if Japan wins out, in preventing interference to rob her of the fruits of her victory."[44] When actually faced with the reality of the rise of Japanese power, Roosevelt would back away from the strong pro-Japanese position taken here.

One reason for Roosevelt's second thoughts on the Japanese was his suspicion that the Japanese themselves were prejudiced against the whites: "I have no doubt that they include all white men as being people . . . whom, as a whole, they dislike and whose past arrogance they resent; and doubtless they believe their own yellow civilization to be better. . . ." Though favoring Japan over Russia, Roosevelt wanted to transfer Ambassador George Meyer from Rome to St. Petersburg to keep an eye on both antagonists. "Japan is an oriental nation," he said, "and the individual standard of truthfulness in Japan is low. No one can tell her future attitude. We must therefore play our hand alone. . . ."[45] Roosevelt distrusted the Russians more, but more than any other factor at this time the idea of race prevented him from embracing the Japanese completely. "But I wish I were certain that the Japanese down at bottom did not lump Russians, English, Americans, Germans, all of us, simply as white devils, inferior to themselves not only in what they regard as the essentials of civilization, but in courage and forethought, and to be treated politely only so long as would enable the Japanese to take advantage of our various national jealousies, and beat us in turn." Two American military attachés stationed with the Japanese army gave Roosevelt this impression. These men allegedly reported that the Japanese were particularly antagonistic toward Americans because they thought that the United States had thwarted their hopes in Hawaii and the Philippines.

The information from the attachés apparently carried great

[44] Roosevelt to John Hay, Secretary of State, July 28, TRP (PL), Box 148, Bk. No. 18, p. 311.

[45] Theodore Roosevelt to George V. L. Meyer, American ambassador to Italy, December 26, 1904, TRP (PL), Box 149, Bk. No. 23, pp. 6–8.

weight with Roosevelt and helped him to go sour on the Japanese. The alleged attitude of the Japanese Roosevelt called "a latent feeling that I had not in the least expected. . . ." What caused the friction between America and Japan seems to have been the clash of imperialistic ambitions. Race apparently did not originate the problem although it certainly did accentuate it. For some time Roosevelt was very tolerant of the anti-white attitude of the Japanese. He felt there was some justification for it. As he saw it, up until about 1894 the foreign nations used to treat the Japanese with utter contempt: "And I think Springy," said Roosevelt to Spring-Rice, "you and I will both admit that our traveling countrymen, not to speak of the inhabitants of Continental Europe, are not always ingratiating in their manners toward races whom they regard as their inferiors."

Roosevelt could well understand the elation of the Japanese after winning major victories over the Russians. He asked his friend, Spring-Rice, to imagine what would happen had England or America been "lorded over by one yellow race for a long term of years . . ." and then won some victories over another yellow race. He hoped that this dislike of all things white by the Japanese was "only a passing phase," but if it were not, the West would simply have to "trust in the Lord and keep our powder dry and our eyes open."[46] What is interesting about this exchange between Roosevelt and Spring-Rice so far as this book is concerned is not so much the international relationships, intriguing though they are, but the racial matrix in which the President discussed them.

As the end of the conflict between Russia and Japan drew near, Roosevelt's references to the Japanese were increasingly characterized by ambivalence, a mixture of admiration tempered by fear. He thought the Japanese were wonderful people and that in twelve years the Western nations would dread her more than they did any other nation. Yet, Roosevelt was not worried.

[46] Theodore Roosevelt to Cecil Spring-Rice, December 24, 1904, TRP (PL), Box 149, Bk. No. 23, pp. 42–52. The preceding four paragraphs were based on this extremely lengthy letter. Additional evidence of Roosevelt's fear of the Japanese is found in his letter to William Howard Taft, February 9, 1905, ibid., Box 150, Bk. No. 24, p. 49. See also his letter to Sir George Otto Trevelyan, May 13, 1905, ibid., Box 150, Bk. No. 26, p. 174.

He would treat the Japanese justly, courteously and generously, while building and keeping our navy "at the highest possible point of efficiency." To do otherwise would be to court disaster.[47]

Race and the Russo-Japanese War

Although he eventually became a mediator in the Russo-Japanese War, Roosevelt was by no means a *disinterested* spectator. At first he secretly rejoiced with every Japanese victory over the Slav. "You must not breathe it to anybody," he cautioned his son to whom he was about to divulge some information from a friend on the fighting prowess of the Japanese:

> "The Japanese are the most dashing fighters in the world. The Anglo-Saxon or Slav may be courageous, but when they get into a hot place they count the cost and consider the chances of getting out again. The Jap goes in to return no more forever, and such an end is his wish."[48]

Then the President slowly began to realize that victory for Japan would represent a new and "formidable power in the Orient. . . ." And should she succeed in reorganizing China, the result would be a real shifting of the balance of power "as far as the white races are concerned." In his opinion Japan was destined to become a great civilized power, but he could not be indifferent to the racial and cultural gap which separated her from the Occident. Oddly enough the *cultural* differences seemed paramount with Roosevelt at this time. "I don't mean that the mere race taken by itself would cause such a tremendous difference. I have met Japanese, and even Chinese, educated in our ways, who in all their emotions and ways of thought were well nigh identical with us. But the weight of their own ancestral civilization will press upon them and prevent their ever coming into exactly our mould. However, this is mere speculation." He also felt that Russia and Japan would exhaust them-

[47] Theodore Roosevelt to Cecil Spring-Rice, June 16, 1905, TRP (PL), Bk. No. 26, pp. 60–64.

[48] Theodore Roosevelt to his son, Theodore Roosevelt, Junior, February 10, 1904, TRP (PL), Box 147, Bk. No. 15, pp. 335–36. Roosevelt to Theodore Roosevelt, Junior, March 5, 1904, ibid., pp. 96–97.

selves in the course of the war and conclude peace. In that happy event there would not be either "a yellow peril or a Slav peril." He was still willing to recognize the Japanese as a world power, should they win the war.[49]

Roosevelt tried to get the two countries to make peace.[50] His earlier willingness to see a Japanese triumph had vanished. "I should be sorry to see Russia driven out of East Asia, and driven out she surely will be if the war goes on," he told the United States ambassador to England, Whitelaw Reid.[51] Roosevelt told his friend Henry Cabot Lodge that the Kaiser intended to urge Russia to sue for peace before all was lost and wanted Roosevelt to make overtures to the Japanese. "I do not desire to be asked to squeeze out of Japan favorable terms to Russia," said the President. Nevertheless, he did send a memorandum to that effect.

Roosevelt was struggling mightily with himself about his position on the Japanese question. He tried desperately to maintain the great rule. He reasoned that even if the Japanese did get a "big head" toward the whites after defeating Russia, "they cannot behave worse than the State of California is now behaving toward the Japanese." He could not understand how the West Coast could insult Chinese and Japanese and still expect to benefit from Oriental markets. He could not understand the indifference on the Pacific Slope to the need for a strong navy in the face of proven Japanese military and fighting capabilities.[52]

To Russia's charge that she was fighting the battle of the white race, Roosevelt replied that Russia had treated members of the white race even worse than she had treated Japan. How-

[49] Theodore Roosevelt to Cecil Spring-Rice, March 19, 1904, TRP (PL), Box 147, Bk. No. 16, pp. 224–27.

[50] Theodore Roosevelt to Andrew D. White, June 1, 1905, ibid., Box 150, Bk. No. 25, p. 383. See also a memorandum of the State Department of the American ambassador in St. Petersburg, Mr. Meyer, asking the czar to sue for peace before he lost everything. Ibid., June 5, 1905, pp. 431–32.

[51] Theodore Roosevelt to Honorable Whitelaw Reid, June 5, 1905, TRP (PL), pp. 450–51.

[52] Theodore Roosevelt to Henry Cabot Lodge, June 5, 1905, TRP (PL), Box 150, Bk. No. 25, pp. 443–49.

ever, he hated to see the destruction of Russia as "an Eastern Asiatic power. . . . It is best that she should be left face to face with Japan so that each may have a moderative action on the other," he said to Lodge.[53] For this reason he did not want to see Russia humiliated. It is difficult at this point to escape the conclusion that Roosevelt appeared to be working against the imperial aspirations of Japan because he did not want to see Russia driven off the Pacific coast of Asia by a power alien in race and civilization. "I shall do my best to persuade Japan to be moderate. I have already pointed out to them that Eastern Siberia is of no value to them . . . ," said Roosevelt to his ambassador.[54]

Roosevelt's personal correspondence of 1902–1905 suggests that he frequently thought about the racial consequences of the Japanese rise to power and was worried about a possible yellow peril to the white race. Roosevelt did not want to see the crushing of a white, though Slavic, Russia by a powerful but alien and yellow Japan.[55] The President, who both admired and feared the Japanese, was caught between these two conflicting opinions. However, he had an Oriental problem much closer at home.

The Japanese in California

The racial intemperance of California embarrassed the Oriental diplomacy of the President. This was especially true since he held the Japanese in such high esteem, despite his racial

[53] Theodore Roosevelt to Henry Cabot Lodge, June 16, 1905, TRP (PL), Bk. No. 26, pp. 96–115. Roosevelt had presented Japanese peace proposals to the Russian ambassador, who mentioned the race issue.

[54] Roosevelt to George V. L. Meyer, American ambassador to Russia, June 19, 1905, TRP (PL), Box 150, Bk. No. 26, pp. 117–20.

[55] The only monograph on the role of Roosevelt in this war discounted the idea of an underlying race issue and says: "It was not a color conflict . . . ," but a purely commercial and later a political one. Dennett took three chapters to counter the arguments of Roosevelt's critics who contended that although they had won most of the victories, the Japanese did not get enough at the peace table, while the Russians felt that they themselves had absconded with the lion's share of the booty. See Tyler Dennett, *Roosevelt and the Russo-Japanese War: A Critical Study of American Policy in Eastern Asia in 1902–1905* (New York: Doubleday, Page and Co., 1925), pp. 328, 281–87.

reservations. "You cannot feel as badly as I do over such actions as that by the idiots of the California Legislature," he said to the American ambassador at Yokohama. Nevertheless he admitted the right of California to prevent the admission of Japanese workers on the grounds that the "frugality, abstemiousness, and clannishness [of the Japanese] make them formidable to our laboring class." These charges against the Japanese were strange. They were too thrifty and too temperate in food and drink. These characteristics were much praised when found among whites. Roosevelt recalled that since foreigners were forbidden to own land in Japan, the right of the California courts to refuse naturalization of Japanese should be accepted by them. "I am powerless," said the President, although he wished that the Californians would not insult foreign powers and "yet decline to make ready for war."[56] The historian James Ford Rhodes astutely observed that "the opposition to the immigration of the Japanese was not on account of their inferiority as being of the yellow race but on account of their superiority. . . . It was fortunate that in the presidential chair was a man of a culture who appreciated the Japanese civilization and at the same time was a true American full of sympathy for the West and who understood the views of the Californians."[57] Superior characteristics might not be enough to prevent rejection of an ethnic minority should the dominant group decide to utilize the prerogatives of their numerical superiority.

"I am utterly disgusted at the manifestations which have begun to appear on the Pacific Slope in favor of excluding the Japanese exactly as the Chinese are excluded," Roosevelt complained to Lodge.[58] Over a year and a half later, he explained to Edward Grey of England that the source of the friction with

[56] Theodore Roosevelt to George Kennan, American ambassador, Yokohama, Japan, May 6, 1905, TRP (PL), Box 150, Bk. No. 25, pp. 95–97. See also Theodore Roosevelt to Honorable William H. Moody, Attorney General, Boston, July 15, 1905, ibid., Bk. No. 26, p. 384. See also Theodore Roosevelt to Honorable Lloyd C. Grissom, American diplomat in Japan, July 15, 1905, ibid., pp. 385–86.

[57] Rhodes, *The McKinley and Roosevelt Administrations, 1897–1909*, pp. 370–77.

[58] Theodore Roosevelt to Henry Cabot Lodge, May 15, 1905, TRP (PL), Box 150, Bk. No. 25, pp. 190–93.

Japan was the "labor question, itself one phase of the race question."[59] He was more explicit on the subject with another Englishman, John Saint Loe Strachey. Concerning restriction of Japanese immigration, Roosevelt said he had to recognize the facts, one of which "was the great fact of race," a factor which "so many sentimentalists tend[ed] to forget."[60] To still another Englishman, Arthur Balfour, he wrote that the "practical problem of statesmanship . . ." in the Japanese crisis was how to keep on good terms with them, while at the same time "keeping the white man in America and Australia out of home contact with them."[61]

That the Japanese situation in America was a race question standing by itself was not immediately apparent to Roosevelt: "I did not clearly see this at the outset." But gradually he saw the light: "It was merely a recognition of the fact that in the present stage of social development of the two peoples . . . it is not only undesirable but impossible that there should be racial intermingling and the effect is sure to bring disaster."[62] Roosevelt wondered how the country could assimilate, en masse, a people with whom Americans had little cultural and racial affinity, without inciting race conflict.

The position of Roosevelt on Japanese immigration in California presented both an interesting puzzle and a splendid example of the embarrassing position into which the mental reservation against racial intermingling could get one. According to his great rule a man should be treated according to his worth. On that basis he had admitted the Japanese to the society of civilized nations. Yet, he denied them entrance to his racial inner sanctum, that is, social intermingling, and rejected mass Japanese immigration not because "either nation is inferior to the other . . . [but] because they are different.[63] Visible differ-

[59] Roosevelt, *Letters,* V, 528, 612. December 18, 1906.

[60] Ibid., V, 532.

[61] Roosevelt, *Letters,* VI, 963. December 18, 1906.

[62] Ibid., VI, 1503–04. See also his letter to Senator Philander C. Knox, February 8, 1909, passim.

[63] Roosevelt, *Letters,* VI, 1415. See also Theodore Roosevelt, *An Autobiography* (New York: Macmillan Co., 1913), pp. 411–15.

ences of race and culture made it impossible for him to forget that the Japanese were one of the "alien races." His great rule of righteousness lost its potency upon encountering the greater rule of race consciousness.

Race Mixing

If Roosevelt was adverse to the mixing of whites with the Japanese, a race which he thought culturally and mentally equal to the Caucasian, the chance of his extending this right to blacks was slim indeed. He preferred to avoid the subject of social equality between whites and blacks, and rarely, if ever, let the words fall from his lips. During a discussion of the voting right section of the Fourteenth Amendment, however, he wrote to Grenville Dodge: "I wish to emphasize that we are not fighting for social equality, and that we do not believe in miscegenation; but that we do believe in equality of opportunity, in equality before the law."[64] Here was an all too common racial platform upon which whites of the North and the South could join with a minimum of discomfort.

Roosevelt had given thought to the scientific aspects of race crossing. In past centuries there had existed a persistent, though by no means exclusive, belief that race mixing would destroy one or both races involved. Now, with Mendelian discoveries as yet imperfectly understood, Roosevelt believed that when "two divergent and persistent human types" such as white and black were crossed, neither the white nor the black type persisted in the mulatto offspring in any degree of purity. Only if the mulatto continued to breed to either the white or the black type exclusively would one of the types reappear in pure form in succeeding generations, thus eliminating one ancestral root.[65]

Five years before he died, Roosevelt went to Brazil and was shocked at the degree of race mixing and the attitude of the old Iberians toward mixing with blacks and Indians: "The difference

[64] Theodore Roosevelt to General Grenville Dodge, November 14, 1904, TRP (PL), Box 148, Bk. No. 21, pp. 421–22.

[65] Theodore Roosevelt to Henry F. Osborn, 1908, Roosevelt, *Letters*, VI, 1436.

between the United States and Brazil is the tendency of Brazil to absorb." He gaped and marveled that in Brazil "any Negro or mulatto who shows himself fit is without question given the place to which his abilities entitle him." He saw blacks laboring side by side with the white working class in all walks of life and "apparently nobody had any idea of discriminating against them in any office or business relationship because of their color." Even for the cosmopolitan Roosevelt, this was a sight to behold. He noted that "in the lower ranks intermarriages are the most numerous, especially between the Negroes and the most numerous immigrant races of Europe." He carefully emphasized that the blacks were not marrying into the upper classes, noting that "the great majority of the men and women of high social position in Rio are of unmixed blood . . . [and] the great majority of the political leaders are pure whites. . . ."

Race mixing in Brazil was not going to create a mongrel race, Roosevelt thought, because the black was disappearing through absorption. Brazil was making him a white man! Roosevelt did not comment on how he felt this related to the problem in the United States. He would only say that the ideas of the two countries regarding the treatment of blacks were wholly different: "The best men in the United States, not wholly among the whites, but among the blacks also, believe in the complete separation of the races so far as marriage is concerned." Again his great rule could not stand the test. Roosevelt was casting his lot with "the best men."[66]

On the other hand, Roosevelt did not seem averse to mixing English-speaking genes with those of the aborigines. He always appeared more disposed to rejoice when *Indians* rather than blacks mixed with the whites. After a visit to a Sioux Indian reservation in 1892, he pronounced the half-breed superior to the pure Indian and decided that even a worthless white man was a better mate for an educated or partly educated Indian woman than "a good blanket Indian of her own race." Roosevelt also observed that white and red racial combinations came out better

[66] Theodore Roosevelt, "Brazil and the Negro," *Outlook*, 106:409–10 (February 26, 1914).

than black and white: "The mixed bloods who are part Indian and part white, have an enormous advantage over the mixed bloods of Negro and white ancestry, in that they have comparatively little race prejudice to combat." He noted that many leading citizens of the West had Indian blood in their veins. But it was the *lack* of prejudice against "halfbreeds or quarterbreeds living among whites . . ." that impressed him most. This fact had been borne out on his ranch "where a sharp line of distinction is drawn invariably against mulattoes or Negroes."[67]

Roosevelt seemed delighted because the English on the frontier refused to intermarry with Indian women while the French had no such scruples. He stated in his epic on the West that the English "were trammelled by the queer pride which makes a man of English stock unwilling to make a red-skinned woman his wife, though anxious enough to make her his concubine."[68] However, when he reached the presidency he told Congress that "the Indian should be treated as an individual—like a white man. . . . The marriage laws of the Indians should be made the same as those of the whites."[69] He felt that the process should be gradual, but he betrayed no apparent apprehension about the "mixing of bloods." In his third annual message he said: "In dealing with the Indians our aim should be their ultimate absorption into the body of our people."

One could well ask, if the Indian, why not the Japanese, or the black? Was it because in the mixture of red and white the white type tended to persist? He explained it this way: "In portions of the Indian Territory the very mixture of blood has gone on at the same time with progress in wealth and education so that there are plenty of men with varying degrees of purity of Indian blood who are absolutely indistinguishable in point of *social, political* and *economic* ability from their white associ-

[67] Theodore Roosevelt, *Report of Honorable Theodore Roosevelt, Made to the United States Civil Service Commission Upon a Visit to Certain Indian Reservations and Indian Schools in South Dakota, Nebraska and Kansas* (Philadelphia: Indian Rights Association, 1893), passim, pamphlet found in Library of Congress.

[68] Roosevelt, *The Winning of the West,* I, 33.

[69] First Annual Message, 1901, Roosevelt, *Works,* XV, 13.

ates."[70] Roosevelt was also impressed with the fact that the people of Oklahoma bragged about their Indian blood and were not ashamed of it. This might explain his approval of red and white mixing. When he reflected upon his experiences with men of Indian blood in his regiment in 1898 he said: "They behaved exactly like the whites, and their careers since have been exactly like the white man's."[71] So stood Roosevelt on race mixing. He was willing to open his racial inner sanctum for the Indian but he slammed the door shut in the face of the Japanese and the African. Of course the Indian, as the occupant of the land desired by the white man, was a different matter.

The Indian

While Roosevelt gave his blessing to Indian-white intermarriage, he was not equally generous toward the red man in other respects. For example, he defended the "winning of the West" on the ground that nothing should have been allowed to stand in the way of civilization—not even the Indian. "The most ultimately righteous of all wars," the young and strenuous Roosevelt once said, "is a war with savages." Had the whites been repulsed, civilization would have been obliterated, he felt. On the other hand, he could not excuse the whites completely for their behavior in the Indian wars: "A sad and evil feature of such warfare [was] that the whites, the representatives of civilization, speedily [sank] almost to the level of their barbarous foes in point of hideous brutality."[72] Nevertheless, the clash between the Indian and the white man was inevitable and the results justified: "It is nonsense to talk about our having driven most of these Indians out of their lands. They did not own the land at all *in the white sense* [italics added], they merely occupied it as the white buffalo hunter did. . . ."[73]

Roosevelt disliked seeing the Indians "at ease in Zion," living off the income from lands leased to white cattlemen for grazing.

[70] Third Annual Message, Roosevelt, *Works,* XV, 163.
[71] Roosevelt, *Letters,* VI, 1434–35.
[72] Roosevelt, *The Winning of the West,* II, 56–58.
[73] Roosevelt, *Report . . . to Civil Service . . . ,* 1893, pp. 18–19.

He wanted to see them work.[74] "I earnestly wish to see every Indian reach the status where he will vote and be in every respect on the entire equality with the white citizens," Roosevelt said to an Indian who had gained the right to vote.[75] He never spoke so clearly and unequivocally in regard to blacks—except on the subject of the great rule.

In spite of all the stern talk in regard to Indians, Roosevelt could be very patient with them. When Chief Joseph came to Washington uninvited, Roosevelt directed the Secretary of the Interior to pay the old chief's way back home because: "He is a great old Indian, a really noteworthy man, and I want to show him consideration this time."[76] In response to the gift of a buffalo robe from a Sioux chief, Roosevelt said: "When the scenes painted on the robe took place, you were a wild Indian. . . . Now you are the Chief Justice."[77]

The President took eight pages to soothe Chief No Shirt of the Umatilla tribe, Pendleton, Oregon. The chief had traveled all the way to Washington to see the President in the face of instructions to send his complaints in writing, and was now obliged to return home without seeing Roosevelt. The President professed that he wanted "to be as much a father to the red people as to the white . . . ," and chided the Chief for acting "like a headstrong child. . . . It is not a good example to set to your people." No Shirt was under the impression that the government had promised every Indian twenty-five dollars annually. He believed that he was supposed to live as he pleased for twenty-five years and then make a new treaty with the government. Roosevelt patiently tried to clear up these misconceptions. No Shirt was anxious to arrange his grazing leases so that he would get two payments instead of one and was quoted by

[74] Theodore Roosevelt to the Secretary of the Interior, January 30, 1902, TRP (PL), Box 143, Bk. No. 3, p. 104. The letter had reference to the Indians of Standing Rock.

[75] Theodore Roosevelt to Ben Brave, Ogcome, South Dakota, February 2, 1904, TRP (PL), Box 147, Bk. No. 15, p. 207.

[76] Theodore Roosevelt to the Secretary of the Interior, March 8, 1904, TRP (PL), Box 147, Bk. No. 16, p. 107.

[77] Theodore Roosevelt to Mr. James W. Foley, Bismarck, N.D., enclosing the letter to Chief Justice John Grass, October 31, 1904, TRP (PL), Box 149, Bk. No. 21, p. 77.

Roosevelt as saying: "'I have to have my money to make my living . . . and of course I want my money whenever I need it.'"[78] The Indian may have been of a different race but he was already on the scene. Newcomers from overseas had to be let in to the United States and here race reared its head.

Race and Immigration

At first there seemed to be no racial basis to Roosevelt's immigration policy. As President he asserted: "We need every honest and efficient immigrant fitted to become an American citizen. . . ." However, he would exclude anarchists, the morally unsavory, and the economically and educationally incompetent.[79] He tried to apply his great rule to immigration in his annual public message to Congress in 1905, while privately negotiating for the exclusion of Asiatics. Publicly he took the position that there should be no discrimination against anyone wanting to come to this country except on the ground of his

> mental and social quality. . . . We cannot afford to pay heed to whether he is of one creed or another, of one nation or another. We cannot afford to consider whether he is Catholic or Protestant, Jew or Gentile; whether he is Englishman or Irishman, French or German, Japanese, Italian, Scandinavian, Slav, or Magyar. What we should desire to find out is the individual quality of the individual man.[80]

A few years earlier, in 1901, Roosevelt had called for the continued exclusion of Chinese laborers on the grounds that such immigration was a threat to American labor.[81] Though he rejected the Chinese as a group, he could apply his great rule to them individually. For example, he interceded for a Chinese mother trying to get support from her English husband for their child. Roosevelt described her as "an exceptionally fine character. . . . I know her. . . . She is one of the best women there

[78] Chief No Shirt to Theodore Roosevelt, May 18, 1905, TRP (PL), Box 150, Bk. No. 25, pp. 204–11.
[79] First Annual Message, Richardson, *Messages,* X, 427.
[80] Ibid., XI, 1166.
[81] Richardson, *Messages,* X, 426. First Annual Message, December 3, 1901.

are."[82] In response to complaints of alleged misconduct toward the Chinese Secretary of Legation, Roosevelt said: "I should also like the strictest orders issued to the inspectors that no kind of insolence against Chinese gentlemen will be permitted." Roosevelt was against Chinese coolies but he would tolerate no discourtesy to Chinese manufacturers, bankers, students and travelers.[83] He instructed his Acting Secretary of State to issue a directive to American diplomats in China to be courteous to all Chinese eligible to come to the United States.[84] "I am trying in every way to make things easy for the Chinese here," he told his American minister at Peking.[85] So far, it seems that Roosevelt was willing, to some extent, to accept any racial group that proved its fitness by surviving and competing successfully. On the other hand he wanted to make certain that *his* race would survive and remain the best competitor.

Race Suicide

Since Roosevelt did not believe that the superior position of the white race was permanently fixed, he was almost fanatically concerned with race preservation and the prevention of race suicide. In 1895, he said that the "ability to fight well and breed well . . ." were among the essential qualities of social efficiency.[86] In 1902 he said:

> The man or woman who deliberately avoids marriage and has a heart so cold as to know no passion and a brain so shallow and

[82] Theodore Roosevelt to John Hay, Secretary of State, March 1, 1904, TRP (PL), Box 147, Bk. No. 16, p. 62. See also letter of Theodore Roosevelt to Honorable George B. Cortelyou, Secretary of Commerce and Labor, ibid., p. 64.

[83] Theodore Roosevelt to Honorable V. H. Metcalf, Secretary of Commerce and Labor, May 16, 1905, TRP (PL), Box 150, Bk. No. 25, p. 88. Roosevelt to Metcalf, June 12, 1905, ibid., pp. 495–97. It appears that the secretary of the Chinese legation was mistaken for an ordinary coolie, was treated roughly and almost sent back to China, ibid., pp. 70–71, 91, 94.

[84] Theodore Roosevelt, to Honorable V. H. Metcalf, Secretary of Commerce and Labor, May 16, 1905, TRP (PL), Box 150, Bk. No. 26, pp. 194–98.

[85] Theodore Roosevelt to W. W. Rockhill, May 18, 1905, ibid., Bk. No. 25, pp. 232–33.

[86] Roosevelt, *Works*, XIII, 240. He was reviewing Benjamin Kidd's book, *Social Evolution*.

selfish as to dislike having children, is in effect a criminal against the race and should be an object of contemptuous abhorrence by all healthy people.[87]

A little later Roosevelt wrote to author Hamlin Garland on the same race suicide theme: "But you are all worried about big families. . . . A race whose men will not work and will not fight ought to die out, and unless it will . . . it generally does. And of course if the women flinch from breeding the deserved death of the race takes [place] even quicker. I have a high regard and veneration for the woman who is the mother of my children. . . ." Roosevelt felt that the "woman who flinched from childbirth" stood on a par "with the soldier who drops his rifle and runs in battle."[88] In his annual message of 1904, Roosevelt charged that a race which did not have plenty of strong healthy children was decadent.[89] He told the English historian, Trevelyan: "The diminishing birthrate among our people is an . . . ugly thing. In New England, for instance, the old native stock is not quite holding its own."[90]

Roosevelt was concerned about the tendency, as he saw it, of well-to-do families to die out, resulting in the "elimination of the fittest." He thought he had here identified "the greatest problem in civilization."[91] Roosevelt reviewed Octavia Charles Beale's *Racial Decay* in 1911. He heartily approved of the Australian author's thesis that the decline of the birth rate in France, Britain, Australia, and New Zealand was due in part to what Roosevelt called "the capital sin; the cardinal sin against the race and against civilization—wilful sterility in marriage. . . ." At its present rate of decline, Roosevelt predicted that the birth rate in Australia would be stationary by 1950: "If this is so, them the men who rally to the battle cry of

[87] Theodore Roosevelt to Mrs. Bessie Van Vorst, Philadelphia, October 18, 1902, TRP (PL), Box 144, Bk. No. 7, pp. 441–43. An article in *Everybody's Magazine* on "The Woman Who Toils," brought forth this short dissertation by Roosevelt on race suicide.

[88] Theodore Roosevelt, to Hamlin Garland, West Salem, Wis., July 19, 1903, TRP (PL), Box 145, Bk. No. 11, p. 6.

[89] December 6, 1904. Richardson, *Messages*, X, 811.

[90] Theodore Roosevelt to George Otto Trevelyan, March 9, 1905, TRP (PL), Box 150, Bk. No. 24, pp. 306–13.

[91] Roosevelt, *Letters*, V, 637.

'a white Australia' [Roosevelt was one of them] have indeed ground for anxiety as they think of the teeming myriads, steadily increasing north of them in Asia." Roosevelt thought the book was very poor stylistically but racially he recommended it to "every sincere patriot" in Australia, England, the United States and Canada.[92]

The possible decline of the white race and, more specifically, the English-speaking people, was a specter that haunted Roosevelt. He feared that the white race would become soft and allow itself to be pushed out of first place. Convinced that America was also being visited with the immoral plague of "wilful sterility," any marriage with less than four children brought Roosevelt little comfort. White people in some quarters of America, particularly New England, did not sufficiently appreciate the fact that "it was the warfare of the cradle" more than anything else "which gave the English-speaking peoples their preponderant and dominating position in Europe." As Roosevelt saw it, if the English and French continued to neglect their family duties "the future of the white race will rest in the hands of the Germans and the Slavs." Five years before he died, Roosevelt again attacked the practice of begetting less than four children per family and charged that the Puritan conscience of New England was "so atrophied, so diseased and warped" that it could not recognize the great truth "that the fundamental and unpardonable crime against the race [was] the crime of race suicide."[93] In Roosevelt's opinion the men—and women—who kept the cradle occupied would also rule the world.

In conclusion, Roosevelt's racial frame of reference recognized the white as the superior race and the yellow and black as alien and inferior. Although he had great respect for the yellow Japanese, he feared the Asiatics as racial rivals. In Roosevelt's opinion white superiority was not inherent or self-evident but an earned position of power that could be lost should the race fail to praise the Lord and keep its powder dry. The alien and inferior races were the white man's burden. This burden could

[92] Roosevelt, *Works*, XII, 184, 186.
[93] Roosevelt, *Works*, XIII, 187–89, 191, 202.

best be handled by adhering to the Rooseveltian great rule of righteousness, which was to treat every man as an individual according to his worth as a man. However, the great rule seemed unable to dissolve his basic repugnance for those unlike himself, and in consequence, he usually objected to racial intermixture. The red Indian was a notable exception. Finally, while Roosevelt considered other races inferior as general groupings, armed with his great rule, he could sometimes ascend to great heights of racial justice in dealing with individual persons and special situations.

CHAPTER X

Theodore Roosevelt and the Black American

The problem of the blacks in America was as troublesome for Theodore Roosevelt as it had been for Abraham Lincoln forty or so years earlier. If the African slave of antebellum days had been a "troublesome property," the freedmen of the post-Civil War era proved equally irksome. Paul Buck was correct when he said: "The Negro problem ye have with ye always." And it seems that not even Roosevelt's great rule could change that.

The Great Rule of Righteousness: Solution to the Race Problem

As governor of New York in 1889, Roosevelt had begun to consider the problem of "doing justice to and getting good results from the colored race. . . ." Even then he was at his wit's end to know what to do. He invited Booker T. Washington, Paul Lawrence Dunbar, and a black Harvard graduate, William Lewis, to come and discuss the black question with him.[1] In spite of the terrible problem presented by the presence of blacks on this continent, Roosevelt was certain of one thing. Discussing the situation with Albion Tourgee, he declared that the black man was here to stay and could neither be killed nor driven

[1] Roosevelt, *Letters*, II, 1364–65. "Paul Lawrence Dunbar is a man for whom I have high regard on account of his literary ability," said Roosevelt in a letter to the Secretary of the Interior, October 1, 1901, TRP (PL), Box 142, Bk. No. IA. See also the letter of Theodore Roosevelt to Honorable John Wise, New York, September 20, 1901, ibid., p. 3.

away. "The only wise and honorable and Christian thing to do is to treat every black man and every white man strictly on his merits as a man, giving him no more and no less than he shows himself worthy to have."[2] As long as he was President he would follow this great rule of righteousness, this merit system of race relations. For the most part he did this in all things except race mingling or social equality—the great exception to the great rule.

History may yet record that Roosevelt had more conferences at the White House on the race question than any other President. Lyman Abbott, editor of the *Outlook*, and Silas McBee, editor of the *Churchman*, were both invited to the White House to talk about "the question of the colored race." Roosevelt's personal letter books are full of similar invitations to come in and talk it over.[3] In restating his great rule to Brander Matthews, Roosevelt remained convinced that we had to "treat the individual Negro just as we treat the individual white man . . . give him a fair chance . . . a square deal; punish or penalize him as we would a white man if he falls short or goes wrong . . . encourage him if he goes right."[4] Not even the Catholic or labor question harried the President as did the black question.

Southern recalcitrance on matters of race made the problem even more difficult for the President. More than any of his predecessors in the White House, Theodore Roosevelt recognized that a major stumbling block in the road of race relations was the unbending determination of the South. He was more disposed than others to give the white South a lion's share of the blame for the eternal racial confusion in that region. He might not dare to do so publicly, but privately he excoriated the Southern country gentlemen, alluding to them as "grown-up and often vicious children" on the color question.[5]

[2] Roosevelt, *Letters*, III, 190–91.

[3] Theodore Roosevelt to Dr. Lyman Abbott, November 21, 1902, TRP (PL), Box 144, Bk. No. 7, pp. 177–78. See another letter of Roosevelt to Abbott, ibid., p. 7. Theodore Roosevelt to Mr. Silas McBee, New York, January 15, 1903, TRP (PL), Box 144, Bk. No. 8, p. 74.

[4] Theodore Roosevelt to Brander Matthews, Narragansett, R.I., July 11, 1903, TRP (PL), Box 145, Bk. No. 10, p. 413.

[5] Theodore Roosevelt to Lyman Abbott, July 18, 1903, TRP (PL), Box 145, Bk. No. 11, p. 1. Theodore Roosevelt to Lyman Abbott, October 29, 1903, ibid., Box 146, Bk. No. 13, pp. 182–84.

Unlike his predecessors, Roosevelt did not believe that education, at least "the scholastic kind," was the panacea for problems of race. He was extremely dubious about the utility of education in the state of Mississippi, the home of Vardaman, "that unspeakable creature."[6] Race relations in the South puzzled the President greatly. Southern resistance to his application of his great rule of righteousness upset him.[7] For he knew that the Southern question was, at bottom, a race question. He chastised Ray Stannard Baker in 1908 for thinking that the political struggle in the South was merely a social conflict between the few and the many. The conflict was, for Roosevelt, "an expression of a fundamental fact far deeper than that. . . . The fact of race, the conflict between race and race, which with the average man goes immeasurably further down than any conflict between the few and the many."[8]

After the election of 1904, Roosevelt was no nearer a solution of the race problem than he was when he inherited the job from McKinley three years earlier. He vowed to the historian James Ford Rhodes that he would meet the problem in the spirit of Abraham Lincoln. He agreed with Rhodes that Reconstruction as it actually occurred had been a mistake. On the other hand he did not agree that no one in the South wanted to re-establish slavery after the war. Roosevelt informed Rhodes and the president of Massachusetts Institute of Technology, Henry Pritchett, that in the South there was a "partially successful movement to bring back slavery,"[9] under the form of peonage, in at least three states. He chided Rhodes for failing to see that the North could have been justified in being bitter toward the South for breaking up the Union in 1861. While he

[6] Theodore Roosevelt to Charles A. Gardiner, November 18, 1903, ibid., Box 146, Bk. No. 13, p. 365.

[7] Theodore Roosevelt to Carl Schurz, December 24, 1903, Roosevelt, *Letters*, III, 679–80.

[8] Roosevelt, *Letters*, VI, 1048.

[9] Roosevelt, *Letters*, IV, 1049–51. Roosevelt's authority for his opinions on slavery was one of his political appointees, Judge Jones of Alabama. See also Theodore Roosevelt to Lyman Abbott, June 22, 1904, TRP (PL), Box 145, Bk. No. 10, pp. 235–37. Theodore Roosevelt to Judge Jones, August 31, 1903, TRP (PL), Box 146, Bk. No. 12, pp. 55–56. Theodore Roosevelt to Henry Pritchett, December 14, 1904, TRP (PL), Box 149, Bk. No. 22, pp. 359–70. Roosevelt, *Letters*, IV, 1067. Pritchett wanted the South to be left alone.

could not as a public man say this for fear of "embitter[ing] the people," Roosevelt thought Rhodes labored under no such handicap and should not have absolved the South of its share of the blame.[10] Roosevelt entertained another theory in regard to race matters which tended sometimes to nullify the thrust of his great rule.

On Attempting the Impossible in Matters of Race

Although Roosevelt found the black problem troublesome, he did not believe in attempting the impossible in matters of race. He objected, as a matter of principle, to what he called "unrealizable ideals." In 1911, he told a group of student preachers, "Don't preach the impossible."[11] In matters of race some things were thought impossible. For example, Reconstruction convinced Roosevelt that federal legislation in itself could not solve the black problem. Instead, the black man's hope lay "in the constant workings of those often unseen forces of the national life which are greater than legislation."[12] As he once told a labor meeting, nothing promoted mental dishonesty and moral insincerity more "than the habit of either promising the impossible, or of demanding the performance of the impossible."[13] Roosevelt never departed significantly from this position, which played no little part in his demonstration of presidential paralysis when he came to matters of race.

An insinuation that the government was derelict in its duty to enforce the Fourteenth Amendment in the South caused Roosevelt to snap back: "The cause of the violators is not helped by any claim that they have been ingenious enough to escape punishment, and that the government, in any one of its branches, or in all of them, lacks the will, the strength or the

[10] Theodore Roosevelt to James Ford Rhodes, February 20, 1905, TRP (PL), Box 150, Bk. No. 24, pp. 152–53; Roosevelt, *Letters*, IV, 1125.

[11] From an address entitled "Realizable Ideals," Roosevelt, *Works*, XIX, 627.

[12] Ibid., XIII, 162. Letter to William Lewis, Roosevelt, *Letters*, II, 1364–65.

[13] State of New York, *Public Papers of Theodore Roosevelt, Governor*, 1899 (Albany: Brandow Printing Co., 1899, 1900), I, 262–63. This speech was made September 3, 1901. See also Richardson, *Messages*, X, 423.

ingenuity to mete out the proper reward." Roosevelt acted like a doctor who, though he could diagnose the disease, refused to write the prescription: "In my position," he wailed, "I have seen nothing that could be gained by my saying anything in public on these [race] subjects at the present time, and I write to you for your own private information."[14] Roosevelt did not feel in a position to be a racial statesman, not in public at any rate. It was the duty of the moralist and reformer "to denounce this wrong doing. . . ."[15]

According to Roosevelt, the nature of the American presidency was not conducive to the championship of unpopular causes. He told an English historian that the American executive office tended to put a premium upon a man's staying out of trouble rather than upon the accomplishment of results.[16] Perhaps this is why the President shied away from any public crusade for racial adjustment. He was almost always cautious in the extreme. Once while thinking about what to put into a speech he said: "Off hand I would suggest that the race question be treated simply incidentally by an allusion to show that I have set the same standard for black man and for white. . . ."[17] He regretted the presence of a civil rights plank in the Republican platform of 1904 because "it is always a mistake to put in any plank which the party does not mean to insist on . . . where a wrong cannot be remedied it is not worth-while to sputter about it."[18]

The President was really looking for more overt support from the public: "The thing that astounds me," he said to Lyman Abbott in regard to lawlessness in the South, "is the queer doughfaced indifference with which the North submits to this

[14] Theodore Roosevelt to Charles A. Gardiner, New York, November 18, 1903, TRP (PL), Box 146, Bk. No. 13, pp. 365–66.

[15] Theodore Roosevelt to Carl Schurz, December 24, 1903, ibid., Bk. No. 14, pp. 261–67. Roosevelt, *Letters,* III, 680.

[16] Theodore Roosevelt to George Otto Trevelyan, May 28, 1904, TRP (PL), Box 146, Bk. No. 17, pp. 342–44.

[17] Theodore Roosevelt to Elihu Root, June 2, 1904, ibid., Box 147, Bk. No. 17, pp. 385–90.

[18] Theodore Roosevelt to Honorable John C. Rose, June 28, 1904, ibid., Box 148, Bk. No. 18, p. 146.

matter."[19] The President was not leading. He was waiting to be led. He attacked what he saw as the "hypocrisy" of Southerners such as John Sharp Williams of Mississippi who, according to Roosevelt, denounced our adventure in the Philippines as a violation of the Declaration of Independence when his own state negated that document in regard to blacks. Roosevelt found Williams "peculiarly repulsive" and thought if Williams "would lead a movement to give the colored people of his own district but a fraction of the rights" enjoyed by the Filipinos, the race problem in the South would be well on the road to solution.[20]

Roosevelt was conscious of the disproportionate political power wielded by the South because of the neutralized black vote but was insufficiently moved thereby to crusade against it. Actually he did not oppose disfranchisement of the ignorant, but he did not want to see this done on the basis of color. After taking the South to task in a letter to Lyman Abbott, he was immediately seized with another attack of presidential caution: "Now I am well aware that there are plenty of things which are wrong, which nevertheless it may be impossible at the moment to change, and that in such cases [it is necessary] to take facts as they are, to make the best of a bad business. But if the issue is forced upon me, I shall certainly not hesitate to meet it. . . ." Then, apparently realizing the political liability involved should his statement be made public, Roosevelt said to Abbott: "I have written you thus frankly in the midst of a political campaign, where I have nothing to gain and everything to lose by any agitation of the race question." However much the combative cave man in foreign affairs, on the race question the President tiptoed and carried no stick whatsoever. "You will have noticed that in my speech of acceptance I did not touch upon this [race] matter at all. If I can avoid touching upon it and retain my self-respect, I shall do so; but I have not the slightest question as to what the rights of the

[19] Theodore Roosevelt to Lyman Abbott, July 26, 1904, TRP (PL), Box 148, Bk. No. 18, pp. 307–10.
[20] Ibid.

matter is, or as to what should be done if it were possible."[21] Political realism brought the President, in this case, to the very brink of moral bankruptcy.

As he worked on his letter of acceptance, Roosevelt decided against saying anything directly about the Fourteenth Amendment. But not to do so at least indirectly would make it appear that he was "dodging the whole question." So he tentatively decided to bring up the subject diplomatically by stating that "the colored people should be treated here" in America as the ex-Confederate Luke Wright, was treating the islanders in his administration of the Philippines.[22] The President thought this devious approach a master stroke of political adroitness: "You will notice that by this I do not promise any legislative or executive action by the Federal Government, and I hold up a Democrat and an ex-Confederate as a man upon whose actions we should model ours." Roosevelt did not interpret this political scheming as an indication of any shallow commitment to the cause of racial justice on his part: "I feel too deeply on this subject to be willing to make it an issue for partisan advantage." Any open discussion of the black question would impede the progress of those who were, according to Roosevelt, "honestly working for the solution of the color problem in the South."[23] Roosevelt also informed Booker T. Washington of this grand strategy.[24] Yet it seems likely that Roosevelt was motivated chiefly by the desire not to upset the political odds in his favor by raising the "impossible" issue of race.

When his acceptance letter appeared, the President was forthright about every subject except race. He covered the tariff, capital and labor, the gold standard, better treatment of the Jews in Romania, Armenians in Turkey, Americans in China,

[21] Theodore Roosevelt to Lyman Abbott, July 26, 1904, TRP (PL), Box 148, Bk. No. 18, pp. 307–10. Theodore Roosevelt to Honorable John Lowndes McLaurin, Bennettville, S.C., July 1, 1904, ibid., p. 175. Theodore Roosevelt to W. A. White, Emporia, Kans., February 15, 1904, ibid., Box 147, Bk. No. 15, pp. 363–64.

[22] Theodore Roosevelt to Lyman Abbott, August 18, 1904, ibid., Box 148, Bk. No. 19, pp. 90–91.

[23] Theodore Roosevelt to John Byrne, August 31, 1904, TRP (PL), Box 148, Bk. No. 19, pp. 141–42.

[24] Theodore Roosevelt to Booker T. Washington, ibid., p. 19.

and the Filipinos. And then, just as he had told his correspondents he would do, Roosevelt very casually referred to the race problem in America with an analogy to the Philippines.[25] If on this occasion the President showed little moral courage, few political realists would deny that he demonstrated political sagacity.

As he studied campaign strategy for the 1904 election Roosevelt said: "If I am to be blamed by anyone for any failure in my duty, active or passive, toward the South, it must be for failure to take action as regards the nullification of the Fourteenth and Fifteenth Amendments in the South." The United States Supreme Court to the contrary, Roosevelt believed that he had an obligation to enforce the Civil War amendments and frankly admitted his failure to do so. Some of his predecessors thought that they lacked power to interfere in Southern affairs, the amendments to the contrary notwithstanding. But while Roosevelt realized that he should have enforced the law he hastened to defend his admitted inaction on the racial front: "I do not think it would have been wise policy from the national standpoint, nor yet from the standpoint of the colored people themselves, for me to take such action."[26]

Roosevelt liked to think that his attitude on the "colored question" was modeled on that of the moderate Abraham Lincoln and not upon the more radical ways of Sumner, Garrison, or Wendell Phillips. He still found every possible course on racial matters "beset with difficulties." Two things stood in his way: the pathological race and sectional hatred of Southern whites, "and the entire inability of immense masses of Southern blacks to meet any test which requires both intelligence and moral vigor. . . ." The President had hit upon a neglected element in the race questions of the period, the inability of blacks of the South to sustain any indigenous movement of their own for their rights. What the President may have been inferring was this: If blacks had been able

[25] Theodore Roosevelt to Honorable J. G. Cannon, chairman of the Republican National Committee, September 12, 1904, ibid., pp. 307–46.

[26] Theodore Roosevelt to Henry E. Taft, New York, September 12, 1904, TRP (PL), Box 148, Bk. No. 19, pp. 377–78.

to mount a drive with some degree of success, he, Roosevelt, provided public opinion was at his back, would have been more willing to give his blessing and support to the cause. He was afraid to try and then have the trial fail.

So long as blacks lacked sufficient "intelligence and moral vigor" Roosevelt could not "take an impossible position" on the black question. But even more than the ignorance of the blacks, and the Negrophobia of Southern whites, Roosevelt lamented "the indifference of the great masses of people [in the North] to whom the wrongdoing in the South is a matter afar off and of little immediate consequence, and who are impatient of any attempt to make things better in any way."[27] The President certainly had his troubles, but he seemed sincere in his anxiety and concern about the problem of race. Recognition of this fact contributes more to an understanding of the policy deficiencies of the period than does the usual calcified conclusion that the nation and the Republicans callously abandoned the black man after 1877, or 1884, or 1900.

Like Abraham Lincoln, Roosevelt found himself being accused of being both too liberal and too conservative on the race question. *Collier's Weekly* thought him too liberal in the South while praising his negative attitude toward the Filipinos.[28] Carl Schurz and the *New York Evening Post* liked his attitude on the blacks but opposed his Philippine policies.[29]

While he would not lift a finger to enforce the Civil War amendments, Roosevelt refused to agree with a suggestion from James Ford Rhodes and the president of Massachusetts Institute of Technology that the Fifteenth Amendment be repealed. Fortunately for blacks, the Republicans could not forget that potential votes for their party were being kept away from the polls in the South. For Roosevelt it was out of the

[27] The two preceding paragraphs are based on a letter of Theodore Roosevelt to John Byrne, September 14, 1904, TRP (PL), Box 148, Bk. No. 19, pp. 413–15. See also Theodore Roosevelt to Francis Leupp, September 19, 1904, ibid., p. 481.

[28] Theodore Roosevelt to Mr. P. F. Collier, September 26, 1904, TRP (PL), Box 148, Bk. No. 20, p. 110.

[29] Theodore Roosevelt to his son Kermit Roosevelt, October 26, 1904, ibid., Box 149, Bk. No. 21, pp. 5–10.

question that there could be permanent acquiescence in the North to the suppression of the black vote which on national issues made one vote cast in Mississippi equal to four white votes in Illinois. But no matter how angry he became with the Southerners, the President steadfastly refused to attempt the impossible. When he heard about a move by a group of Western congressmen to push for enforcement of the Fourteenth Amendment, he disapproved of the step and did what he could to see it aborted. He did not think it expedient to make "a bad situation worse by either a hopeless or a foolish effort to make it better. I have refused," he openly confessed,

> to entertain any project of the kind advocated by Senator Platt, by Senator Crumpacker, and others, because as is so often the case in politics I am confronted, not with the question of doing what is ideally right (which would of course be at once to reduce the representation in those states . . .) but of doing what is mostly expedient and practical although not ideally right; that is, to decline to start an agitation from which, as far as I can now see, no good will come.[30]

While the President did not wish to be heard in public on the black question, while he sought to thwart any congressional efforts to provide a political remedy for blacks, and while the presidential arm of civil restitution remained inert, he remained hopeful of the power of public opinion. He wanted to use it, not as a means of getting the North to take action against the South, but as a means of persuading the South to mend its ways. He scolded the editor of *The Review of Reviews* for saying a kind word about Vardaman of Mississippi and urged him to take a stand against "elementary wrongdoing" in the South.[31]

Sometime in 1904 Roosevelt invited Edward A. Alderman,

[30] Theodore Roosevelt to Mr. Ernest Hamlin Abbott, December 16, 1904, TRP (PL), Box 149, Bk. No. 22, pp. 355–58. Theodore Roosevelt to Henry Pritchett, Massachusetts Institute of Technology, December 14, 1904, TRP (PL), Box 149, Bk. No. 22, pp. 359–70. See also Ray Stannard Baker, *Following the Color Line*, where Baker, too, pleaded that the "agitation for the repeal of the Fifteenth Amendment . . ." be resisted.

[31] Theodore Roosevelt to Dr. Albert Shaw, editor, *The Review of Reviews*, October 7, 1903, TRP (PL), Box 146, Bk. No. 12, p. 456.

president of the University of Virginia; Judge Thomas Jones of Alabama; Silas McBee, editor of the *Churchman*; Lyman Abbott; and Nicholas Murray Butler to spend the night with him and discuss the black question. He was preparing for a Lincoln's Day speech and was undecided as to whether he should mention the race question and if so, how. When Butler offered a way to slip a black reference into the speech, Roosevelt was grateful: "You have given me a great suggestion. I must take as my text Lincoln's 'with malice toward none, with charity toward all' statement and his other statement that he 'had not willingly planted a thorn in the breast of any man.' "[32] Booker T. Washington, who had become one of the President's political advisors, was asked by Roosevelt to comment on a draft of the speech.[33]

Roosevelt also was being urged to say something in behalf of people in the Congo, the Jews in Russia, the Manchurians in Asia, and the Americans in Turkey. He took the same attitude in regard to these matters that he took on the race question generally. He would not attempt the impossible and would speak only if he were certain that public opinion was at his back. According to Roosevelt, "the business of an active politician is not to complain of defects which cannot be changed but to do the best he can in spite of them."[34] However, he was tempted to launch a crusade against the Turks provided the American people would sustain him. But he doubted the wisdom of such a crusade when he had "plenty of evils to fight here at home, evils connected with race prejudice, especially against the Negro. . . ."[35]

As he had done in 1904, Roosevelt again objected to the inclusion of a plank in the Republican platform of 1908 calling for the reduction of Southern representation for refusal to let

[32] Theodore Roosevelt to Dr. N. M. Butler, 1904, TRP (PL), Box 149, Bk. No. 22, pp. 412–13.

[33] Theodore Roosevelt to Booker T. Washington, December 28, 1904, ibid., Bk. No. 23, p. 38.

[34] Theodore Roosevelt to Cecil Spring-Rice, TRP (PL), Box 150, Bk. No. 26, pp. 493–500. Theodore Roosevelt to Brooks Adams, July 18, 1903, ibid., Box 145, Bk. No. 11, p. 4.

[35] Theodore Roosevelt to George Otto Trevelyan, May 13, 1905, Box 150, Bk. No. 25, pp. 172–78.

the blacks vote.[36] Neither would he encourage Senator Lodge to push another Federal Elections bill. Roosevelt thought that some parts of the South would become another Haiti if the ballot was given to blacks without qualification. As for the great majority of them in the South, Roosevelt concluded that they were unfit for suffrage.[37] He was prepared to wait for the South to see the wisdom of giving qualified blacks political expression.[38]

In Roosevelt's opinion, the salvation of blacks lay in the adoption of his great rule of righteousness and Booker T. Washington's program of industrial education.[39] The black man should walk softly in the political arena, stay away entirely from things social, train himself industrially for useful work, make friends with the "best white men of the South," and concentrate upon his duties as well as his rights. Of course all of this was contingent upon the hope that the whites would endorse and live by his great rule.[40] Roosevelt had no use for loudmouthed black agitators. He admired Booker T. Washington because he "was not led away, as the educated Negro so often is led away into the pursuit of fantastic visions."[41] Perhaps Baker was correct in 1908 when he wrote that blacks had been forced to "concede the futility of trying to progress by political action and legislation."[42]

Roosevelt's timidity about attempting the impossible in racial matters neutralized the effectiveness of his great rule of righteousness. What, then, was the origin of this great rule, this merit system of race relations that guided Roosevelt? The concept may have developed out of Roosevelt's Spanish-American War experiences. The performance of black troops in this war seemed to have had an ameliorating effect upon Roosevelt just as the Civil War exploits of the black soldier had melted a few of the iron bars of race prejudice earlier. He stated

[36] Roosevelt, *Letters,* VI, 919.
[37] Ibid., VIII, 1132.
[38] Roosevelt, *Works,* XVII, 305.
[39] Roosevelt, *Letters,* II, 1109. Roosevelt, *Works,* XII, 220–21.
[40] Roosevelt, *Works,* XI, 275. Ibid., XVII, 303.
[41] Ibid. Roosevelt, *Letters,* II, 364–65.
[42] Ray Stannard Baker, *Following the Color Line,* p. 272.

that although his regiment was laden with Southerners of strong color prejudice, his men accepted the black troops, even to the extent of a willingness "to drink out of the same canteen with them."[43] Even though he once tried to show that the white soldier was superior to the black trooper, Roosevelt bestowed great praise upon the black men who fought in the Spanish-American War. However, he thought white noncommissioned officers showed more initiative in matters of command than their black counterparts.[44]

On June 4, 1903, Roosevelt observed in Springfield, Illinois: "It is a good thing that the guard around . . . [Lincoln's] tomb . . . should be composed of colored soldiers. It was my good fortune at Santiago to serve beside colored troops. A man who is good enough to shed his blood for his country is good enough to be given a square deal afterwards. More than that no man is entitled to, and less than no man shall have. . . ."[45] Four years later at the Arlington National Cemetery Roosevelt said that any war well fought taught a lesson in real democracy which was needed in our civic life. When a soldier sees that his buddy can stand up under fire and do his part, then differences of wealth, occupation and place of birth all pale into insignificance.[46] Already we have seen that when Roosevelt gave his Oxford lectures in 1910 he presented his great rule of righteousness as a formula for dealing with alien races. During his presidency he had actually tried to apply the great rule to blacks except in matters he deemed undesirable, impossible or inexpedient. He forgot the great rule in the instance of Oriental immigration. But in the last analysis the great rule was a tremendous weapon in Roosevelt's racial arsenal. The merit system of race relations gave a certain dynamic, optimistic, and positive character to Roosevelt's approach to the problem of the blacks in America, even in the narrowly political context in which most Presidents viewed race.

[43] Roosevelt, *Works,* XI, 92–94.

[44] Fellow army officers and others chastised Roosevelt for these strictures upon the quality of the Negro soldier. Roosevelt, *Letters,* II, 1305–06, 1351.

[45] Theodore Roosevelt, *Addresses and Presidential Messages of Theodore Roosevelt,* 1902–1904 (New York: G. P. Putnam's Sons, 1904), p. 224.

[46] Roosevelt, *Works,* XI, 341–42.

Race and Politics

Armed with his great rule of righteousness, Roosevelt insisted that blacks should be allowed at least the minimal rights of citizenship. He was definitely out of sympathy with the tide of Negrophobia then sweeping the South that, in his own words, "aimed at depriving all colored men, good and bad, intelligent and degraded alike," of elementary political and civil equality. His declared position on the matter was an admirable one: "If ninety-five percent of the blacks were unfit to hold office . . . rule those ninety-five out, but not the other five percent simply because of the color of their skins."[47] However, it was difficult to maintain the complete objectivity in the racially sensitive area of rape and lynching.

Roosevelt's Approach to Lynching

Roosevelt was keenly aware of the role that race played in the lynching of blacks. While governor of New York, he had chosen to bring up this subject at the unveiling of a monument in honor of Frederick Douglass at Rochester, New York, though it might be questioned whether this was the best of occasions for a discussion of lynching. Much less does it seem the proper time or place for a dissertation on the horrors of rape, but this was exactly what Roosevelt provided his audience. After a few introductory platitudes, he declared: "This worst enemy of the colored race is the colored man who commits some hideous wrong, especially if that be the worst of all crimes, rape; and the worst enemy of the white race is the white man who avenges that crime by another crime [lynching] equally infamous." If it were in his power

[47] Roosevelt, *Letters,* III, 681. Theodore Roosevelt to Oswald Garrison Villard, July 25, 1903, TRP (PL), Box 145, Bk. No. 11, pp. 95–96. Theodore Roosevelt to Lyman Abbott, July 26, 1904, ibid., Box 148, Bk. No. 18, pp. 307–10; ibid., Box 148, Bk. No. 18, p. 465.

he would render the country a great service by calling for swift and speedy punishment of the twin crimes of rape and lynching. He urged blacks to make war on the vicious and disorderly elements in their own race. Returning to the horrors of rape he asserted that "every scoundrel who commits rape, or some similar infamy, and every body of men who usurp the power of the law . . . by committing deeds which would make a red Indian blush with shame, prove that they are unworthy of citizenship."[48]

The President's strictures against lynchings and mob violence were thus reduced in forcefulness by his constant emphasis on the infamous character of rape by blacks. All of his future antilynching speeches followed the same pattern as the one cited above. When a reporter and personal friend witnessed a lynching in South Carolina, Roosevelt felt obliged to reassure Booker T. Washington that the reporter had taken no direct part in the proceedings.[49] After reaching the White House, Roosevelt was slow to castigate lynching publicly. He refused the request of a bishop that he denounce violence in the Pennsylvania coal fields, saying rather indelicately to the churchman: "I think it would be a little like denouncing the prevalence of vice in the tenderloin district of New York City. There is not half so much reason for denouncing it as for making a similar public utterance about the recent lynchings in the South." Roosevelt preferred to hold his fire because one thing a President or any public official had to learn "is not to jeopardize one's power for doing the good that is possible by efforts to correct evils over which no one has control and with which one is only himself generally concerned."[50]

While cautious about his own antilynching statements, Roose-

[48] State of New York, *Public Papers of Theodore Roosevelt, Governor*, pp. 332–35. This speech was made on June 10, 1899. Two days before this he commuted the ten-year sentence of a white man accused of attempted rape. Ibid., p. 235.

[49] Theodore Roosevelt to the reporter discussed above, George R. Koester, November 8, 1901, TRP (PL), Box 142, Bk. No. 2, p. 117. Theodore Roosevelt to Booker T. Washington, November 9, 1901, ibid., Bk. No. 3, p. 179.

[50] Theodore Roosevelt to Bishop Ethlebert Talbot, South Bethlehem, Pa., October 29, 1902, TRP (PL), Box 144, Bk. No. 7, p. 78.

velt encouraged and commended those who did speak out against that "dastardly practice." He said to one writer, "I think that in your last story on lynching you have done better missionary work than in almost any other of your stories that I know. . . ."[51] Through Attorney General Knox, the President tried to find a job for a Southern law-enforcement officer who had saved a black from a lynch mob and was promptly turned out of office at the next election.[52] "We are now passing through an era of lawlessness in this country. Lynching has become very common, and where the victims are colored men it takes the inhuman aspect of putting to death by torture—usually burning alive . . . ," Roosevelt remarked to the Attorney General.[53]

When the President decided to make a public statement on lynching he wanted to be sure that it came at the right time and the right place. At first he was inclined to use the official channel of the annual message. As usual, he did not want to make a frontal assault on the problem but preferred to approach the subject indirectly by tying in lynching with whatever he had to say on labor troubles.[54] Judge Jones of Alabama could hardly have been encouraged by Roosevelt's lukewarmness and hesitation in response to his request that the President come out against lynching:

> As about lynching, when the chance comes, I am going to speak as strongly as I know how . . . but I certainly shall not say anything of a sectional character. In all probability I shall distinctly state that what I say is based upon incidents which have occurred in the north as well as in the south, the east as well as in the west.[55]

[51] Theodore Roosevelt to Octave Thanet, February 7, 1903, ibid., Bk. No. 8. The magazine was *Cosmopolitan*.

[52] Letter of P. E. Knox, March 10, 1903, ibid., Box 145, Bk. No. 9, p. 27.

[53] Theodore Roosevelt to P. E. Knox, July 24, 1903, TRP (PL), Box 145, Bk. No. 11, p. 81.

[54] Theodore Roosevelt to Rollo Ogden, July 29, 1903, TRP (PL), Box 145, Bk. No. 11, p. 120.

[55] Theodore Roosevelt to Judge Thomas G. Jones, July 30, 1903, ibid., pp. 150–51.

The President's long awaited attack upon lynching in the South came in August of 1903, in the form of a letter of congratulations to a *Northern* governor, Durbin of Indiana, for the thwarting of lynchings in that state. Almost half of the letter to Governor Durbin dealt with the horrors of rape and the necessity for swift trial and conviction of rapists and murderers. In Roosevelt's opinion the crime of rape was so terrible that the rapist had forefeited "the right to any kind of sympathy whatsoever." Such a statement on the part of the President was certainly not calculated to foster moderation in the heart of the lyncher. More than that, when President spoke on rape he seemed to have only blacks in mind; the rapist, he said, did more harm to his race "than any white man can possibly do them." The President seemed more concerned with the effect of the lynchings on the white man and his children than he was about the black lynch victim: "There are certain hideous sights which when once seen can never be wholly erased from the mental retina. . . ." After concerning himself with rape, the President then disclosed to Durbin that three-fourths of the recent lynchings had not been for rape at all but for murder or lesser crimes. He asked that all criminals be punished without regard to race, creed or color. Finally, he noted that when blacks were involved, "the mob seems to lay most weight not on the crime but on the color of the criminal."[56]

In spite of the oblique way in which the President approached the question of lynching in the South, he still drew applause. He thanked the editor of the *New York Evening Post* for a favorable editorial and for being one of those who had convinced him that "now was the time to speak" instead of waiting for the annual message to Congress.[57] He accepted congratulations from Silas McBee and boasted of his strategy of avoiding a charge of sectionalism by writing his strictures on

[56] Roosevelt, *Addresses and Presidential Messages of Theodore Roosevelt*, pp. 277, 280–81. Letter of Theodore Roosevelt to Honorable Winfield Durbin, governor of Indiana, August 6, 1903, TRP (PL), Box 145, Bk. No. 11, pp. 239–43.

[57] Theodore Roosevelt to Rollo Ogden, August 11, 1903, TRP (PL), Box 145, Bk. No. 11, p. 330.

lynching to a *Northern* governor.[58] However, according to a friendly United States marshal in Atlanta, Georgia, Roosevelt did not fool many persons in the racially sensitive South.[59]

After the Durbin letter the President continued to encourage those who spoke out against lynching. His own attacks on that crime continued to be accompanied by condemnation of rape. Apparently he feared that an unqualified attack upon lynching might be construed by some as an approval of rape. He had nothing but contempt for those blacks who would not lift a finger, as he put it, in the apprehension of a fellow criminal.[60]

After he left the presidency, Roosevelt continued to devote half of his antilynching speeches to a condemnation of the black rapist, calling the problem a national rather than a Southern one. He came dangerously close to justifying lynchings in rape cases when he said in 1911: "In the many cases in which the lynching is not for rape there is literally not the slightest excuse of any kind or sort that can be advanced for it." Pennsylvania received Roosevelt's congratulations for apprehending, convicting, and sending a black rapist to prison in five days. He only regretted that the state did not have the death penalty for rape, a crime "graver" than murder. When a man is put to death for rape one need not have the slightest sympathy for him because such a man was outside the pale of humanity, as Roosevelt saw it. Such sentiments seemed strange, appearing in an article designed to deter the lyncher. Stranger still that an editorial on lynching should call for a more stringent law against rape while failing to call for equally swift punishment for lynchers.[61]

[58] Theodore Roosevelt to Silas McBee, editor of the *Churchman*, August 12, 1903, ibid., p. 342.

[59] Theodore Roosevelt to Walter H. Johnson, September 18, 1903, ibid., Box 146, Bk. No. 12, p. 264.

[60] Roosevelt, *Works*, XV, 351–52. For further light on lynching see Box 144, Bk. No. 22; Box 148, Bk. No. 19; Box 146, Bk. No. 12, of TRP (PL).

[61] Theodore Roosevelt, "Lynching and the Miscarriage of Justice," *Outlook*, 99:706–07 (November 1911). As a Progressive party candidate in 1912, Roosevelt accused the Democrats of brutality toward the blacks and the Republican party of hypocrisy in championing black rights in the South while doing nothing at home in the North, where lynchings and race riots still took place. Roosevelt, *Works*, XVII, 300–04.

In 1906 Roosevelt, acting in his capacity of commander in chief, with one stroke of the pen discharged from the service about 160 black soldiers who had allegedly shot up the town of Brownsville, Texas, and killed a white man. Six of the soldiers were Medal of Honor winners and thirteen had citations of merit for bravery in the Spanish-American War. Although it seems unlikely that he would have applied the same remedy to white troops in similar circumstances, Roosevelt insisted that race had nothing to do with this rather severe punishment. He was angered, he said, by the fact that no black would come forward to tell who did the shooting. He had previously stated that he had nothing but contempt for blacks who would not lift a finger to help apprehend one of their own criminals. According to one biographer, Henry Pringle, there were grave doubts as to the guilt of the men even though a Senate committee supported the President. James Ford Rhodes, while upholding Roosevelt, implied that the action might have been a little despotic.[62] To date the issue of the guilt of the soldiers remains unsettled.[63] Meanwhile, the problem of the complexion of the Republican party in the South flared up.

From Black to Lily-White Republicanism

Although he reversed himself in the election of 1912, as President, Roosevelt resisted earlier attempts to establish "lily-white" Republicanism in the South. He poured cold water on one such attempt in Alabama.[64] In February of 1904, he asked that Louisiana not send a lily-white delegation to the Republican Convention. He also continued his plea that Southerners give those few blacks who "by character and in-

[62] James Ford Rhodes, *The McKinley and Roosevelt Administrations*, pp. 338–41. Henry F. Pringle, *Theodore Roosevelt: A Biography* (Harcourt, Brace and Co., 1931), pp. 458–64. Letter of Theodore Roosevelt to Lyman Abbott, 1908, Roosevelt, *Letters*, VI, 1026.

[63] James Tinsley, "Roosevelt, Foraker, and the Brownsville Affray," *Journal of Negro History*, 41:63 (January 1956). Tinsley did not think that race was a significant factor in Roosevelt's actions.

[64] Theodore Roosevelt to General Grenville Dodge, November 12, 1903, TRP (PL), Box 146, Bk. No. 13, p. 327. It seems that Dallas B. Smith of Opelika, Ala., became a liability to the party by his lily-white leanings.

telligence show themselves entitled to such favor, a chance." He had to assure the Southerners that "there shall be nothing like Negro domination." Still, Louisiana sent a white delegation. Once more Southern whites had rejected his great rule. Apparently the lily-white Republicans disapproved of Roosevelt's position on the race question.[65]

Even though he rejected lily-white Republicanism in early 1904, Roosevelt, like Hayes and the compromisers of 1877, believed that the blacks should not play a prominent role in Southern politics. By June of 1904 he was trying to show Booker T. Washington that "the safety of the colored man in Louisiana is to have a white man's party which shall be responsible and honest, in which the colored man shall have representation but in which he shall not be the dominant force—a party in which, as is now the case in the federal service under me, he shall hold a percentage of the offices, but in which a majority of the offices shall be given to white men of high character who will protect the Negro before the law." Roosevelt was certain that Washington felt the same way he did in that matter. To attempt black domination in Louisiana, "even if it were in the interest of the Negro would be attempting the impossible," he explained to Washington.[66] But then the President had a change of heart. Some days later he told Washington that his recent letter in which he appeared to defend the idea of a white man's party "has gone out of date." The Republican National Committee had just refused to seat the lily-white delegation from Louisiana and Roosevelt was not above tacking with the political winds. However, he still betrayed some remorse over the failure of lily-whiteism in Louisiana that year. "Politically," he told Washington, "I think this may be of momentary advantage. I wish I were as sure that it was a good thing for white and black men in Louisiana."[67] He did not say so, but Roosevelt was thinking about

[65] Roosevelt, *Letters*, IV, 739. See the *Charlotte, North Carolina Observer*, March 16, 1904, Grover Cleveland Papers (Scrapbooks), Box 10–19, ser. 10.

[66] Theodore Roosevelt to Booker T. Washington, June 8, 1904, Roosevelt, *Letters*, IV, 825–26.

[67] Theodore Roosevelt to Booker T. Washington, June 17, 1904, TRP (PL), Box 148, pp. 25, 23. The President told the chairman of the Republican

the fact that rejection of the lily-white contingent meant Louisiana's delegation would be primarily black and not representative of the best people in the community, the white people, without whose support neither Washington nor Roosevelt believed the Southern black could survive. When Roosevelt stood at Armageddon battling for the Lord in 1912, the all-black Republican contingents from the Deep South were refused seats in the Progressive Convention with his approval, on the grounds that they were not representative of their constituent communities.[68] Whatever the problems of party, the area of jobs was an excellent place to apply the great rule.

Race and the Federal Patronage

When Roosevelt was associated with the Civil Service Commission in 1894, he was very proud of the complaint of the Mississippian who said that under the methods of the civil service "white men and men of color [were] treated with exact partiality." Although he had not yet enunciated his great rule, he liked the merit system of examinations in the civil service which gave "capable colored men . . . an even chance with honest and capable white."[69] Color discrimination had been reported but Roosevelt said that there was no law on the books providing for investigation of such charges. He recommended enactment of such a law.[70] However, he told the Justice Department in 1908 concerning the Interstate Commerce Commission: "While there is nothing in the law which forbids separate accommodations, these accommodations must be equal." He was speaking about the practices of a Southern

National Committee that he was sorry that the lily-white delegation had been turned down, but thought it was to be expected "as they were so foolish as to let themselves be tainted with the lily-white business."

[68] Theodore Roosevelt, "Progressivism and the Colored Man," *Outlook*, 101:909–14 (August 1912). See also *The Negro Question: Attitude of the Progressive Party Toward the Colored Race* . . . (New York: Mail and Express Job Print, Stoddard Sutherland Press, 1912).

[69] Roosevelt, *Letters*, I, 381.

[70] Ibid., I, 357.

railroad.[71] In this case the President showed no anxiety to break with the *status quo*. But he was still ahead of Southern practice in that he wanted to make the separate accommodations equal in substance.

Even the most limited application of his great rule to federal patronage brought down Southern anathema upon the head of Roosevelt. Such was the case following his appointment of a black man, Doctor William Crum, to be Collector of the Port of Customs at Charleston, South Carolina, in 1902. Apparently the impression was abroad that he would make no black appointments in the South at all. He was "pained" by this evidence of Negrophobia. Did the South not know that he appointed only men of the highest character and intelligence to office North and South, "whether white or black"? The President then uttered some of the finest words in the history of positive and democratic racial thought. He told Southerner R. G. Rhett that while he would try to pay attention to local sentiment, in the matter of appointments he could not

> consent to take the position that the door of hope—the door of opportunity is to be shut upon any man no matter how worthy, purely upon the grounds of race or color.

Even though he believed the majority of the blacks in the South were unfit to hold office, Roosevelt would still reward and encourage those who he felt endeavored to prepare themselves to be good citizens. To act otherwise would be wrong, according to his great rule.[72] In terms of race this was one of Roosevelt's best moments. To be sure, the preceding remarks were private, but they were sent into the heart of the Southland at the very apogee of the concerted efforts by that region to drive the blacks to the wall.

The President was deeply disturbed about Southern unreasonableness on matters of race. He remained bewildered by Southern

[71] Ibid., VI, 488.

[72] Theodore Roosevelt to R. G. Rhett, Charleston, S.C., November 10, 1902, TRP (PL), Box 144, Bk. No. 7, pp. 162–64. The letter is also found in Roosevelt, *Addresses and Presidential Messages of Theodore Roosevelt . . .*, pp. 267–69.

attacks upon him. Had he not, he argued, given the four top positions in South Carolina to white men, including the son of a Confederate soldier? Had Crum been charged with unfitness? No. Roosevelt surmised that he had been charged with no "other offense save his color. . . ."[73] In fact, the mayor of Charleston objected to the Crum appointment mainly because he was black. The mayor said that South Carolina, since Reconstruction, had sworn never again to submit to black rule. Crum's nomination was labeled as an "insult to the white blood." Roosevelt gave the same reply to the mayor that he had given to R. G. Rhett.[74]

After his strong letter in defense of the merit system of race relations, Roosevelt became uneasy. He was still uncertain as to how he would fare in case of adverse popular opinion: "What I shall do about Dr. Crum's case I do not know at present," he told Lyman Abbott.[75] He appeared to weaken in the face of Southern displeasure, and wondered if Crum could not be switched to a lesser post.[76] Senator Frye of Maine reported that some of Crum's friends had suggested that he withdraw his name "for the good of the colored race." In the end, Roosevelt withstood the pressure. "If he [Crum] on his own initiation takes such action I might accede to his request, but most certainly I shall not ask him to do it."[77] On March 4, 1903, Roosevelt informed Booker T. Washington that Crum's name would be on its way to the Senate the next day.[78] Thanks to Southern roadblocks, the Senate failed to act before it adjourned and Roosevelt, just as he had promised Booker T. Washington, appointed Crum anyway. He told the latter, "Ad-

[73] Theodore Roosevelt to R. G. Rhett, Charleston, S.C., November 10, 1902, TRP (PL), Box 144, Bk. No. 7, pp. 162–64. The letter is also found in Roosevelt, *Addresses and Presidential Messages of Theodore Roosevelt . . .*, pp. 267–69.

[74] Theodore Roosevelt to Honorable J. Adger Smith, mayor of Charleston, S.C., November 26, 1902, TRP (PL), Box 144, Bk. No. 7, pp. 203–06.

[75] Theodore Roosevelt to Lyman Abbott, December 5, 1902, ibid., p. 275.

[76] Theodore Roosevelt to John G. Capers, Charleston, S.C., December 19, 1902, TRP (PL), Box 144, Bk. No. 7, p. 275.

[77] Theodore Roosevelt to Walter P. Frye, February 14, 1903, TRP (PL), Box 144, Bk. No. 8, p. 308.

[78] Theodore Roosevelt to Booker T. Washington, March 4, 1903, TRP (PL), Box 144, Bk. No. 8, p. 463.

minister your office not only with probity and efficiency but with such tact and judgement that no just cause of complaint can be found against you."[79]

In spite of his pleadings with several senators, the month of March rolled by and found Crum still unconfirmed.[80] More than that, he had not been paid his salary! Roosevelt then instructed the Attorney General to look into the matter.[81] On the eve of the new year, 1905, Crum's nomination was still in committee. Roosevelt accused Senator "Pitchfork" Ben Tillman of South Carolina of filibustering on the appointment.[82] In the end Crum was confirmed, but irrespective of the outcome, the incident afforded an excellent illustration of the idea of race at work in politics.

In 1903, Roosevelt wrote the editor of a Georgia newspaper that his application of the great rule to federal patronage had nothing to do with "social equality" or "Negro domination."[83] He had tried to help the black cause by appointing white Southerners who believed in "the propriety of the national government doing what it can to secure elementary civil rights to the blacks."[84] Roosevelt took pride in his racial appointment record. One achievement pleased him especially; he alleged that he was the first President to appoint "colored men to responsible positions in the North. . . ." To those who claimed that he had not appointed as many blacks to Southern offices as previous post-Civil War Presidents had done, Roosevelt answered: "I could not give the exact number of Negro appointments that I have made in the South; but I have decreased the total

[79] Theodore Roosevelt to Dr. William Crum, Collector of Customs, Charleston, S.C., March 26, 1903, TRP (PL), Box 145, Bk. No. 9, p. 244.

[80] Theodore Roosevelt to Honorable J. H. Gallinger, United States senator from New Hampshire, March 9, 1904, TRP (PL), Box 147, Bk. No. 15, p. 120. Theodore Roosevelt to N. Waldrich, April 16, 1904, TRP (PL), Box 147, Bk. No. 16, p. 446.

[81] Theodore Roosevelt to his Attorney General, May 2, 1904, TRP (PL), Box 147, Bk. No. 17, p. 88.

[82] Theodore Roosevelt to Honorable J. H. Gallinger, December 31, 1904, TRP (PL), Box 149, Bk. No. 23, p. 80. See also John Hope Franklin, *From Slavery to Freedom* (New York: Alfred A. Knopf, 1948), p. 427.

[83] Roosevelt, *Addresses and Presidential Messages . . .*, p. 271.

[84] Theodore Roosevelt to Elihu Root, 1906, Roosevelt, *Letters*, V, 368.

number of appointees, and I think I have immeasurably raised their character."[85] He soon found that in Mississippi, blacks with character were not enough.

Mississippi Appointments

The President had anxious moments about Mississippi.[86] He reappointed a black postmistress in Indianola who had been named initially by McKinley, and she was promptly driven out of town. Roosevelt was stunned because the "best white people" of this Mississippi hamlet did not lift a finger to save her. His first reaction was to close the post office.

An editorial from a Mississippi paper praised the President for clearing up an allegedly rotten system of federal patronage in the South, including a supposedly notorious "Negro, Jim Hill." Roosevelt was proud to be complimented and sent a copy of the editorial to some of his friends. One sentence read:

> There are very few Negroes holding federal office in this state, and all of these, without a single exception of which we are aware, were appointed originally by one of the President's predecessors in office.

The editor expressed gratitude for this state of affairs and contended that Roosevelt was being abused by men who were ignorant of the real situation; he did not care about "Mr. Roosevelt's private views on sociological questions."[87] Unconsciously perhaps, by drying up the patronage, Roosevelt helped the Southern campaign to grind the blacks into the dust. But the Southerners were still unsatisfied. They would stop at nothing less than total exclusion of blacks from the political arena. To his credit, the President refused to give in without a struggle.

[85] Theodore Roosevelt to Lyman Abbott, 1908, Roosevelt, *Letters*, VI, 121.

[86] Theodore Roosevelt to Booker T. Washington, December 27, 1901, TRP (PL), Box 143, Bk. No. 5, p. 138.

[87] Theodore Roosevelt to Mr. Silas McBee, December 17, 1904, TRP (PL), Box 149, Bk. No. 22, pp. 300–09. He also sent copies to James Ford Rhodes and Henry Pritchett. Roosevelt distributed a similar editorial from the Montgomery, Ala., *Evening Times*, December 5, 1903, reprinted in part in a letter to Carl Schurz, January 2, 1904, TRP (PL), Box 149, Bk. No. 22, pp. 359–70.

Georgia Appointments

The President also had troubles in Georgia. Here was an especially difficult case because he believed that there were a number of excellent black men already in office in that state "whom excellent white men, otherwise inclined to go with us, will not tolerate, simply because of their color." The three best offices in Georgia reportedly were held by blacks appointed during the McKinley era. He would not have done that, said Roosevelt. As a matter of wisdom and for the good of both races he would not have given more than one of the three top places to blacks. However, as he explained to Nicholas Murray Butler,

> to refuse to reappoint or continue in office a good servant simply because he is colored is an entirely different thing. Yet it is wholly impossible to make this distinction clear to most thoroughly good men in Georgia.

The President soon discovered that many prospective white Republicans refused to sit in convention with blacks. As a result, "the Party [in Georgia] is practically a black man's party," a most unstable compound at the polls, the blacks being unable to hold their own against the whites unassisted. The problem seemed insoluble but Roosevelt would not agree to bar blacks from conventions or to withhold reappointment merely because they were black.[88] But he did replace an apparently unfit black man at Athens, Georgia. On the other hand he successfully resisted pressures to remove the black Collector of the Port at Savannah and send him to Haiti. At first he had hesitated to make this appointment. But when letters came from Georgia objecting to the man solely because of his color, "I signed the nomination paper," said the Presi-

[88] Theodore Roosevelt to Nicholas Murray Butler, Columbia University, February 4, 1902, TRP (PL), Box 143, Bk. No. 3, pp. 194–95. Theodore Roosevelt to R. G. Rhett, November 10, 1902, ibid., Box 144, Bk. No. 7, pp. 162–64.

dent.[89] The principle of the great rule had triumphed in Georgia.

Texas, Louisiana and New York

The story in Texas differs little from that in the states already discussed. Booker T. Washington's advice was sought in Texas and Louisiana politics also. Roosevelt explained the political situation to Elihu Root thus:

> The Texas lily-white Republicans have recently denounced me because of my policy in filling the offices with Negroes. The fact that in Texas I have not appointed one single Negro; that every appointment has been a white man and that in that state I have happened to be able to make my appointments almost exclusively of Republicans, is not allowed to interfere with their view of the situation.

Roosevelt referred to the situation discussed above as "the usual sweet reasonableness . . ." of the South.[90] In Louisiana Roosevelt found it difficult to secure good men who were at the same time personally influential, in spite of Booker T. Washington's help.[91]

From the standpoint of public policy, Roosevelt thought it would be a good idea to give Charley Anderson, black, a good appointment in New York: "I want to appoint a colored man to a conspicuous position in my own state." Anderson could be made Collector of Internal Revenue, provided another spot could be found for the only Jew presently holding federal

[89] See three letters of Theodore Roosevelt to Colonel Alexander Lawton, February 19, March 1, and May 1, 1902, TRP (PL), Box 143, Bk. No. 3, pp. 267, 314, and Bk. No. 4, p. 218.

[90] Theodore Roosevelt to Elihu Root, Secretary of State, October 3, 1903, TRP (PL), Box 146, Bk. No. 12, p. 39. For additional evidence of Negroes in Texas politics see letter of Theodore Roosevelt to R. B. Hawley, October 31, 1901, TRP (PL), Box 142, Bk. No. 2, p. 42. Theodore Roosevelt to Booker Washington, April 4, 1902, ibid., Box 143, Bk. No. 4, pp. 45–46. Theodore Roosevelt to Honorable Walker T. Burns, Houston, Tex., April 15, 1902, ibid., Box 143, Bk. No. 4, p. 85, and Box 144, Bk. No. 6.

[91] Theodore Roosevelt to M. A. Hanna, 1902, TRP (PL), Box 143, Bk. No. 3, p. 119. See also ibid., Box 143, Bk. No. 4, pp. 54, 170–71, Box 143, Bk. No. 3, p. 435.

office in New York.[92] Five thousand miles further west, in Hawaii, the president also wished for more political integration: "I want to if possible to get an alliance between the best type of pure white and the best type of Kanaka, and have the combination govern on the straight American principle," he said.[93]

A Southern Policy

After the preceding survey of the trials and tribulations of the President with federal appointments in the South, can it be said that he possessed a Southern policy? Certain patterns are discernible. To begin with, the Southern policy was grounded upon his slowly evolving great rule of righteousness. Roosevelt was determined to raise the *quality* of black officeholders in the South, even if it meant reducing the quantity, which it did. He found this a very difficult job.

In a number of respects Roosevelt's approach to the South resembled that of President Hayes. He first concluded that the Republican party in the South consisted of a "set of black and white scallawags, with a few commonplace decent men . . ." who did nothing but wrangle among themselves; making no effort to gain the popular support or confidence of the community, it had fallen into disrepute. These unscrupulous men were interested only in the federal patronage and sending corrupt delegations to the National Convention. With high-caliber white and black appointments, Roosevelt tried to build a "respectable" Republican party in the South, a party established on the basis of the great rule of merit, a party that would be effective not only nationally but also at the local and state levels, a party that would have the respect of the grass-roots communities.[94] Roosevelt knew that his efforts

[92] Theodore Roosevelt to Honorable T. C. Platt, December 22, 1904, ibid., Box 149, Bk. No. 22, p. 454. Theodore Roosevelt to Honorable G. N. Bliss, New York, February 2, 1905, ibid., Bk. No. 23, p. 480.

[93] Theodore Roosevelt to Honorable George Carter, Honolulu, Hawaii, 1902, TRP (PL), Box 143, Bk. No. 3, p. 131.

[94] Theodore Roosevelt to Henry Cabot Lodge, October 11, 1901, TRP (PL), Box 142, Bk. No. 1A, pp. 289–99.

to purge the party would get him into trouble with Mark Hanna whom he accused of securing the appointment of "very bad Negroes to office during McKinley's administration in order to keep the black delegations solid. . . ."[95] The Southerners, by repudiating the Republicans on the basis of color, and by boycotting them, had been successful in bringing Southern Republicanism into disrepute.

Roosevelt claimed that Booker T. Washington was in sympathy with his policies in the South. He said that both he and Washington believed that those few men of color and impeccable character "especially Crum, would be cordially received as officials by the white men of the communities. . . . We were both taken in by the protestations of the better class of whites that they did not object to an occasional colored man in office, provided he was an upright, decent and efficient man. But when the stress came the decent whites . . . truckled to the baser portions of the communities. . . ."[96] The President had now discovered one of the dilemmas of all of his predecessors, the insincerity of so many white Southerners who told the North that they were not really opposed to blacks but only against ignorance, stupidity, incompetence, and corruption which the blacks allegedly represented. In the final analysis they always lined up against any black as a black, whether he be stupid or intellectually alert.

One significant aspect of Roosevelt's Southern policy was his appointment of Northern blacks to office in the North. He claimed to have appointed a larger number of them than Southern blacks. One noteworthy instance was his appointment of a black graduate of Harvard, Henry Lewis, as Assistant United States District Attorney in the state of Massachusetts.[97] But then the hardest test of his great rule was still to come.

[95] Theodore Roosevelt to Lyman Abbott, November 5, 1903, ibid., Box 144, Bk. No. 13, pp. 248–49.

[96] Theodore Roosevelt to Carl Schurz, January 2, 1904, TRP (PL), Box 146, Bk. No. 14, pp. 371–74. Letter to James Ford Rhodes, December 15, 1904, ibid., Box 149, Bk. No. 22, pp. 372–73. Letter to Henry Prichard, December 14, 1904, ibid., pp. 359–70.

[97] Theodore Roosevelt to United States District Judge Thomas G. Jones, July 30, 1903, Montgomery, Ala., TRP (PL), Box 145, Bk. No. 11, p. 150.

Social Aspects

The crucial test for Roosevelt's great rule of righteousness lay in the area of social equality. Although he scorned race mixing, he did not exclude other types of social intercourse. A letter of 1900—written but never mailed—provides an interesting summary of his social outlook in matters of race. After declaring his fidelity to the great rule, Roosevelt said:

> My children sit in the same school with colored children. I strive my best to secure to colored men an exact equality of right with their white neighbors. I have had them eat at my table and sleep in my house.[98]

In 1893, the future President reported to his sister Anna that his two sons used to slide downhill with other small boys, "most of them colored."[99] In 1900 he supported a bill to "secure equal educational rights to colored children" in the state of New York.[100] "Can you not come on here and spend the night with me?" Roosevelt asked a black man.[101]

No discussion of this kind would be complete without mentioning the celebrated Booker T. Washington dinner with Roosevelt in the White House on October 18, 1901. Perhaps there was no better example of the increasing racial intolerance and recalcitrance in the South at the turn of the century than the racial storm that broke in the Southern press after this integrated meal; "even in the North there was a division of opinion in regard to the propriety of the act," testifies one source.[102] James Ford Rhodes implied that the dinner was improper in the sense that after it the blacks looked upon Roosevelt as a savior, expecting him to give them social equality as Lincoln had given

[98] Roosevelt, *Letters,* II, 1306.

[99] Theodore Roosevelt to his sister Anna, January 9, 1893, *Letters from Theodore Roosevelt to Anna Roosevelt Cowles, 1870–1918* (New York: Charles Scribner's Sons, 1924), p. 124.

[100] The State of New York, *Public Papers of Theodore Roosevelt, Governor . . .,* I, 96–97.

[101] Roosevelt, *Letters,* II, 1365.

[102] Joseph B. Bishop, *Theodore Roosevelt and His Times: As Shown in His Own Letters* (New York: Charles Scribner's Sons, 1920), I, 165–70.

them political freedom. Roosevelt should have considered, thought Rhodes, the effect that the incident would have on the white people of the South.

Rhodes reported the reaction of one white man from Tuskegee, Alabama, to the dinner: "Now when I meet the man who has done all this [that is, eat at the White House] I can't call him Booker like I would call an ordinary nigger, but by thunder! I can't call a nigger mister, so I just say professor!" Another Southerner would have approved of a stag dinner, "but to invite him to the table with ladies—that is what no Southerner can brook!"[103] Henry Cabot Lodge was disappointed in the granitelike nature of the Southern racial heart shown by this instance. In a consoling thought Lodge said: "Everyone here . . . is with you heart and soul on the Booker Washington matter. . . . I am always hoping that they [the South] will learn and broaden, and then comes a thing like this. . . . But they surely will learn and we must go on hoping."[104]

The President was dumfounded by the intensity of the racial venom of some Southerners: "I really felt melancholy for the South at the way the Southerners behaved in the matter," he told one friend.[105] To another friend he said:

> I suppose you have been amused at finding that our innocent dinner to Booker T. Washington has not only become a national but an international affair. It never entered my head that any human being would so much as comment upon it; for it seemed entirely obvious and natural to show Booker Washington a little ordinary courtesy as I was consulting and advising with him on public policies of real importance.[106]

[103] Cited in James Ford Rhodes, *The McKinley and Roosevelt Administrations . . .* , pp. 227–30.

[104] Henry Cabot Lodge to Theodore Roosevelt, October 19, 1901, Henry Cabot Lodge (ed.), *Selections from the Correspondence of Theodore Roosevelt and Henry Cabot Lodge,* 1884–1918 (New York: Charles Scribner's Sons, 1925), I, 508.

[105] Theodore Roosevelt to J. B. Bishop, *Commercial Advertiser,* October 21, 1901, TRP (PL), Box 142, Bk. No. 1A, p. 407. Letter to Honorable Lucius M. Littquer, Gloversville, N.Y., October 24, 1901, ibid., pp. 411–12. James Ford Rhodes, *The McKinley and Roosevelt Administrations,* p. 230.

[106] Theodore Roosevelt to Mr. Phillip B. Stewart, October 25, 1901, TRP (PL), Box 142, Bk. No. 1A, p. 416. See two letters of Roosevelt to Washington, preparatory to the dinner, ibid., Bk. No. 1B, Bk. No. 1A, p. 55.

Roosevelt struggled to maintain his moral integrity against the reaction of "the idiot or vicious Bourbon element of the South. I shall have him [Washington] to dine just as often as I please. . . ."[107] Roosevelt confessed to Albion Tourgee that it seemed perfectly natural for him to invite Washington "and the very fact that I felt a moment's qualm on inviting him because of his color made me ashamed of myself and made me hasten to send the invitation."[108] However, "he did not again invite a Negro to dine at the White House."[109] In this instance, public opinion had struck a mortal blow to his great rule of righteousness. The comical aspect of the incident was not lost on Finley Peter Dunne. Roosevelt had to tell him relative to an anticipated visit to the White House: "First, you need *not* black your face . . . come on to Washington and dine with me. . . ."[110] Not only did the Southerners object to the black man coming to dinner but also to "colored officials coming to my receptions," Roosevelt told his son.[111] A Maryland senator even made up some campaign buttons showing Booker T. Washington and Roosevelt at dinner, and used them to his advantage.[112] Under these circumstances, Roosevelt found it odd that no one objected when he held a reception at the White House for clergymen and their wives and daughters six months later, two blacks being a part of the group.[113]

The Flexible Roosevelt

And so in spite of a racial theory that placed the Caucasian ahead of all racial competitors, Roosevelt's great rule of right-

[107] Theodore Roosevelt to General Curtis Guild, Jr., Boston, October 28, 1901, TRP (PL), Box 142, Bk. No. 3, p. 449.

[108] Roosevelt, *Letters,* III, 190.

[109] Ibid. See editor's note on bottom of page 181.

[110] Theodore Roosevelt to Finley Peter Dunne, November 1901, TRP (PL), Box 142, Bk. No. 2, p. 168.

[111] Theodore Roosevelt to his son, Theodore Roosevelt, Jr., October 31, 1903, ibid., Box 146, Bk. No. 13, p. 199.

[112] Theodore Roosevelt to Lyman Abbott, October 29, 1903, ibid., Box 146, Bk. No. 13, pp. 182–84.

[113] Roosevelt, *Letters,* III, 1638–39.

eousness, his merit approach to race relations, allowed him to view matters of race positively and flexibly. He was very articulate on matters of race and was ever preoccupied with the question of the position of the white man on the racial ladder. Yet, he would not champion the enforcement of the Fourteenth and Fifteenth amendments. He thought that intermarriage between whites and blacks was undesirable. He was reluctant to sanction any biological connection between the whites and the Japanese. Rather incongruously, perhaps, he looked with favor upon the racial intermixture of whites and Indians. His great rule allowed him to transcend the color line with great facility. He was sincere in his beliefs but subordinated them largely to public and political pressure. The problem of race was ever before him, and he wrestled mightily with the issue. While he conducted a vigorous private correspondence in the black man's favor and on occasion made admirable attempts to encourage a positive public opinion, President Roosevelt was very hesitant about exerting strong executive leadership in matters of race.

CHAPTER XI

The Racial Attitudes of American Presidents: Conclusions and Reflections

Conclusions in history are as strong as the evidence upon which they rest. This book is certainly no exception to the rule. On the assumption that ideas count in history, and following Sidney Hook in the belief that we are morally responsible for the historical consequences to which ideas lead, some final impressions are here recorded.

It should be said at the outset that the Presidents from Abraham Lincoln to Theodore Roosevelt concerned themselves very little with the mental and physical characteristics of race. On the contrary, they tended to express incidental racial opinions closely related to the social and political contexts in which the various problems of race arose. In the main, these Presidents did not dwell overmuch upon the question of black inferiority. On the other hand, they clearly assumed the superiority of their own racial group.

All ten Presidents, with the possible exception of Chester A. Arthur for whom there is insufficient evidence, were race conscious, which is to say that the concept of race seems to have been a well-defined element in their thinking. The Presidents could not escape the matter of race. Many of them admitted during this period that the Negro question, or the Southern question, as they called it interchangeably, was one of their greatest difficulties. Eight of the ten Presidents—Lincoln, Johnson, Grant, Hayes, Harrison, McKinley, Roosevelt and to a lesser degree, Cleveland—played rather significant though not always decisive roles in race relations during their terms of office. Few, if any, of them were willing to exploit the full potentialities of the presidential office in the interest of racial statesmanship.

Obviously the Presidents of the United States must play a role of some kind in race relations. They can enforce the laws and they can provide additional moral leadership. The Presidents of this period, and the postwar Republican party, were faced with what appeared to be a *fait accompli*. They were faced with the reality that the South, by methods sometimes open to question, was steadily wiping away black voting majorities. With the exception, perhaps, of a brief optimism on the part of Hayes, the Presidents were very pessimistic about their ability to do anything about the situation in the South. They felt helpless. Suggestions poured into the White House via the mails. The Presidents feared to move, it being impossible to know the right move to make. And yet one gets the feeling that they did not fear so much to move as they dreaded making a move that would fail. They seemed convinced that force, which, after all, had already been tried, would do more harm than good and would in all probability end in failure. Politicians hate to fail, and these men were politicians. They were most unwilling to be quoted publicly on racial matters, except through the safe and acceptable medium of the annual message, where they sometimes strongly, sometimes innocuously, took up the issue of the suppression of the ballot with its accompanying physical violence. But as this book has demonstrated, even the annual messages and letters of acceptance were carefully contrived political formulas designed to appeal to all sections and peoples of the country without thereby completely alienating any one of them.

As a matter of fact, the confusions, the hesitations, the ambivalences, and the caution exhibited by the Presidents in matters of race become intelligible and understandable only when viewed in the context of sectional politics. Indeed, one is tempted to conclude that the bane of the race question as it concerned blacks was the ever-increasing tendency to treat it politically rather than morally. In fact, one must be impressed by the regularity with which the Presidents judged the black question to be at root a matter of politics. With the exception of education, the Presidents did not take up economic or social aspects of the race question, except perhaps to deny the relevance of social equality to the race problem. Privately, some of them, especially Roosevelt, could on occasion work up tremendous righteous indignation about the black man's plight and Southern recalcitrance. But in attacking the problem of race, the Presidents, as Lincoln said about General McClellan, had the "slows."

If the Presidents of this period are judged only on their expressed intentions in matters of race, they make a good showing. When measured by actual accomplishment, with one or two notable exceptions, their record is one of stark failure to enforce the federal laws involving matters of race, and an extreme reluctance to champion an unreserved racial equality in the full spirit of American democracy. When it came to a choice between vigorous action or inaction in matters of race the Presidents were paralyzed. With the exception of Grant, the Presidents of the era showed a marked lack of vigor and courage in matters of law enforcement. Grant knew that only the use of force could carry the day and at last even he despaired of its use. Even though it can be argued that certain crucial rulings of the United States Supreme Court literally pulled the legal rug out from under the blacks, when it came to law enforcement on the national level in matters of race, the executive arm was palsied. Does this mean that the Presidents of the period abandoned the blacks? It does not. Almost all of those concerned sensed the fact that there was something strangely un-American about it all, those "goings on" in the South. As far as could be ascertained they never did look upon the Southern situation as permanent or desirable—even if they did appear to acquiesce reluctantly in the face of a *fait accompli,* the racial *coup d'état* of the Redeemers.

Almost all of the Presidents were aware of race prejudices in the North. Nevertheless, they still thought of the black problem as primarily a Southern one. They probably felt this way because most of the nation's blacks were in the Southern region, traditionally the home of the "peculiar institution." The Presidents rarely talked about removing prejudice anywhere. They seemed content to let people keep their prejudice as long as the blacks were accorded the elementary rights of citizenship.

An attempt was made in this book to determine the extent to which Myrdal's thesis that the core of the black problem in America inhered in the white population's fear of amalgamation. Five of the Presidents, Lincoln, Hayes, Johnson, Garfield, and Theodore Roosevelt, were against the biological mixing of the races. The study failed to uncover any statement on this subject from Grant, Arthur, Cleveland, Harrison, or McKinley. However, on one occasion Grant publicly disclaimed any intention to champion the cause of social equality for blacks. In the final balance, therefore, presidential attitudes between 1865 and 1908 would appear to support rather than to contravene the Myrdal thesis.

All of the Presidents demonstrated at some time or other that they could ignore the color line. Indeed, their words and actions bear witness that democratic principles were capable of breaking through the race barrier even though subsequently to be impaled upon the white picket fence of social nonacceptance. With the exception of Andrew Johnson, there seems no reason to doubt that the expressed beliefs of these men rested upon sincere conviction rather than shallow opportunism, though no President of the era was entirely free from the latter characteristic.

Did these Presidents lead public opinion on matters of race? Omitting Arthur and Garfield for lack of evidence, it seems that four of them, Johnson, Hayes, Harrison, and Roosevelt, made attempts to lead public opinion, while the remaining four, Lincoln, Grant, Cleveland, and McKinley, did not. Although Lincoln made no attempt to lead public opinion on the matter of race, he occasionally took the initiative on the issue of slavery. Andrew Johnson led public opinion both negatively and positively. On the one hand he tried to persuade Southerners to give the blacks their basic rights—even the right to vote. But on the other hand, he later used the prestige of his office to turn Southerners against the blacks. President Grant did very little leading, although he made a splendid personal statement in connection with the ratification of the Fifteenth Amendment. Grant also made strong pleas for the blacks in several of his annual messages. President Cleveland seemed to sympathize with Southern prejudices. Harrison could have led in this area much more than he did. McKinley seemed to speak more convincingly on the subject in private than he did publicly. Roosevelt did a little leading and some following but he appeared more prone to follow than to lead in this touchy matter of race.

Contrary to what one might expect, the personal ideas of the Presidents on matters of race appear to have influenced their actions less than what they thought were the views of the majority of American people on the subject. While this observation may seem oversimple, it leads to the important conclusion that if these particular Presidents had felt that the American public was deeply and truly in favor of racial equality, they would have acted very differently. Expressions of racial thought in this period were sharply split between negative and positive, including the private presidential mail. What particular sources and kinds of public opinion most influenced the Presidents is a topic which should richly reward the trained investigator.

Even in the late nineteenth century the idea of race exerted a significant effect upon America's international relations. Of course, there was much less concern in those days over Old World opinion of American treatment of its minorities, though that aspect was never entirely absent. It was immigration that brought the country face to face with race in international focus. Chinese, Japanese, Italians, Jews, Irishmen and other such group descriptive terms held racial significance for the Presidents as well as for many of the people. The Presidents seem never to have doubted that blacks, like these other groups, were American citizens who should and somehow would eventually enjoy the full blessings of American democracy. But they did not seem equally disposed to dream this same dream for Orientals, perhaps because substantial immigration was a real possibility from Asia rather than from Africa. As a matter of fact, when it came to the question of the biological acceptability of racial minorities, "lo, the poor Indian" led all the rest. As the aboriginal inhabitants lost their hunting grounds to white despoilers, many of the Presidents expressed a surprising willingness to see red men assimilated into American life, without the usual reservations against intermarriage and social equality which were applied to blacks and less often to Orientals.

A final observation, though perhaps not a historical assertion, remains to be made. Recent historical literature has concluded that the black man and his cause were abandoned by the Republican party after Reconstruction and many dates have been given for the "farewell to the bloody shirt." Such representation, while not wholly false, tends to obscure the complexity of this problem, and does the Presidents less than justice. To be sure, Republican politicians North and South came increasingly to doubt the political utility, capacity, and sagacity of the black Republican of the South. There were rumors here and there of attempts to establish "white men's parties" in the South, one actually being formed in Alabama during Harrison's Administration.

Probably more significant than their attitude toward blacks as such was the preoccupation of Republicans with the subject of rehabilitating the party in the South and making it more respectable. Most of the Southern white Republicans beat a hasty retreat from the party after Reconstruction, leaving it almost wholly black. Those who yet remained swore to the Presidents that the only way to make the party viable in the South was to find ways of getting more whites into it. Black members were not to be pushed out of the party, discouraged or abandoned. But it was felt that the whites should *lead*. The conscious shift in policy called for blacks to be less prominent in Southern party *leadership*, not membership, than had been the case prior to 1877. For the next thirty years, in consequence, while solutions to the problems of an effective party in the South were being discussed but never settled, the black man, in the main, continued in the Republican party. However, he became increasingly impotent politically, due to the success of the efforts of the "militant South" to drive him away from the ballot box and office holding.

The Republican party continued to support, or at least recognize, the blacks in the South and to listen to protests of the Northern black wing of the party that they were being discriminated against in favor of the black brother in the South. The dissatisfaction of the black Northern wing was especially evident during Harrison's Administration. And it does appear that as Southern proscription of the blacks steadily advanced, the number of Republican appointments to Southern blacks diminished. But although this patronage did decrease, it was never halted. Indeed, Roosevelt, two months after McKinley's death in 1901, and not without misgivings, announced that the three most important federal appointments in Georgia were held by blacks placed there by his predecessor, William McKinley.

"Farewell to the bloody shirt" did not necessarily mean deserting the blacks. Rather did it mean something like this: let us not needlessly antagonize the South any more; let us get Northern and Southern whites on good speaking terms; let us pay attention to Southern white sensitivities as much as we can without sacrificing our principles, in the hope that we can entice respectable whites into the party; at the same time let us coax them ever so gently to accept and support the exercise of at least the elementary rights of citizenship by the blacks. In the presidential mail of the era, the ambivalent themes of genuine *dislike* of and equally sincere *concern* for blacks dominate, showing mixed motives, extreme perplexity, and outright confusion over this problem.

The study of the racial ideas of American Presidents, making full use of the presidential correspondence preserved by the Library of Congress and other depositories, constitutes an insufficiently understood facet of American intellectual and social history. Few subjects could be more timely, from either a domestic or a diplomatic viewpoint. It is to be hoped that in the future, professional historians will give to this important subject and its allied themes the kind of detailed study which it has awaited vainly for so many years.

Bibliography

Unpublished Manuscript Materials

The Papers of Chester A. Arthur, Washington, D.C.: Library of Congress.

The Papers of Grover Cleveland, Washington, D.C.: Library of Congress.

The Papers of U. S. Grant, Washington, D.C.: Library of Congress.

The Papers of Benjamin Harrison, Washington, D.C.: Library of Congress.

The Papers of Rutherford B. Hayes, Fremont, Ohio: Rutherford B. Hayes Memorial Library.

The Papers of Andrew Johnson, Microfilm, Washington, D.C.: Library of Congress.

The Papers of John Mercer Langston, Microfilm, Washington, D.C.: Howard University Library.

The Robert Todd Lincoln Collections of the Papers of Abraham Lincoln, Washington, D.C.: Library of Congress.

The Papers of William McKinley, Washington, D.C.: Library of Congress.

The Papers of Louis T. Michener, Washington, D.C.: Library of Congress.

The Papers of Theodore Roosevelt, Washington, D.C.: Library of Congress.

Published Autobiographies, Memoirs, Speeches and Writings

Angle, Paul (ed.), *Created Equal? The Complete Lincoln-Douglas Debates.* Chicago: University of Chicago Press, 1958.

Basler, Roy (ed.), *Collected Works of Abraham Lincoln.* 8 vols. New Brunswick: Rutgers University Press, 1953.

Beale, Howard K. (ed.), *The Diary of Gideon Welles: Secretary of the Navy Under Lincoln and Johnson.* 3 vols. New York: W. W. Norton and Company, 1960.

Berg, Albert E. (ed.), *Addresses and State Papers of Grover Cleveland.* New York: Sun Dial Classics, 1908.

Chittenden, L. E. (comp.), *Abraham Lincoln's Speeches.* New York: Dodd, Mead and Company, 1895.

Cleveland, Grover, *Public Papers . . . 1883.* Albany: Argus Company Printers, 1883.

Cramer, Jessie Grant, *Letters of Ulysses S. Grant to His Father and Youngest Sister, 1857–1878.* New York: G. P. Putnam's Sons, 1912.

Curtin, Jeremiah, *The Mongols: A History* (with a Foreword by Theodore Roosevelt). Boston: Little, Brown and Company, 1907.

Curtis, Edward S., *The North American Indian* (Foreword by Theodore Roosevelt). 20 vols. Cambridge: Harvard University Press, 1907.

Dennett, Tyler (ed.), *Lincoln and the Civil War: In the Diaries and Letters of John Hay.* New York: Dodd, Mead and Company, 1939.

Dodge, Grenville, *Personal Recollections of President Abraham Lincoln, General Ulysses S. Grant and General William T. Sherman.* Council Bluffs, Iowa: Monarch Printing Company, 1914.

Eaton, John, *Grant, Lincoln and the Freedmen: Reminiscences of the Civil War with Special Reference to the War for the Contraband Freedmen of the Mississippi Valley. . . .* New York: Longmans, Green and Company, 1907.

Edgar, George P., *Gems of the Campaign of 1880: By General Grant and Garfield.* Jersey City, N.J.: Lincoln Associates, 1881.

Foraker, Joseph Benson, *Notes of a Busy Life.* 2 vols. Cincinnati: Stewart and Kidd Company, 1916.

Fuller, C. E., *Reminiscences of James A. Garfield. . . .* Cincinnati: Stoddard Publishing Company, 1887.

Gilder, Richard Watson, *Grover Cleveland: A Record of Friendship.* New York: Century Company, 1909.

Gottsberger, Francis, *Principles and Purposes of Our Form of Government as Set Forth in the Public Papers of Grover Cleveland.* New York: George G. Peck, 1892.

Grant, Jessie Root, *In the Days of My Father, General Grant.* New York: Harper and Brothers, 1925.

Grant, U. S., *Personal Memoirs of U. S. Grant.* 2 vols. New York: C. L. Webster Company, 1885–1886.

Great Speeches of James Abram Garfield! St. Louis: John Burns, 1881.

Hayes, R. B., *Letters and Messages of Rutherford B. Hayes.* Washington, D.C.: [no publisher], 1881.

——, *Inaugural Address of the Governor of Ohio to the General Assembly, January 13, 1868.* Columbus: L. D. Myers and Brothers, State Printers, 1868.

——, *Inaugural Address of Governor R. B. Hayes to the Assembly of Ohio, January 10, 1876.* Columbus: Nevins and Myers, State Printers, 1876.

Hedges, Charles (comp.), *Speeches of Benjamin Harrison and a Complete Collection of His Public Addresses from February, 1888, February, 1892.* New York: United States Book Company, 1892.

Hinsdale, Burke A. (ed.), *The Works of James A. Garfield.* 2 vols. Boston: James R. Osgood and Company, 1882, 1883.

Hoar, George F., *Autobiography of Seventy Years.* 2 vols. New York: Charles Scribner's Sons, 1903.

Johnson, Andrew, *The Constitutionality and Rightfulness of Secession.* Made in the Senate of the United States, December 18, 19, 1860. [No place of publication, no publisher, no date.]

——, *Speech of Honorable Andrew Johnson of Tennessee on The War for the Union.* Delivered in the Senate of the United States, July 27, 1861. Washington, D.C.: Congressional Globe Office, 1861.

——, *Speech of Honorable Andrew Johnson of Tennessee on The State of the Union.* Delivered in the Senate of the United

States, February 5th and 6th, 1861. Washington, D.C.: Congessional Globe Office, 1861.

Lodge, Henry Cabot (ed.), *Selections from the Correspondence of Theodore Roosevelt and Henry Cabot Lodge, 1884–1918.* 2 vols. New York: Charles Scribner's Sons, 1925.

McClure, J. B. (ed.), *Abraham Lincoln's Speeches Complete. . . .* Chicago: Rhodes and McClure Publishing Company, 1891.

McCulloch, Hugh, *Men and Measures of Half a Century.* New York: Charles Scribner's Sons, 1888.

McKinley, William, *Speeches and Addresses of William McKinley: From March 1, 1897, to May 30, 1900.* New York: Doubleday and McClure Company, 1900.

Moore, Frank, *Speeches of Andrew Johnson.* Boston: Little, Brown and Company, 1865.

Nevins, Allan (ed.), *The Letters of Grover Cleveland, 1850–1908.* New York: Houghton Mifflin Company, 1933.

Nicolay, John G., and John Hay (eds.), *Abraham Lincoln's Complete Works Comprising His Speeches, Letters, State Papers and Miscellaneous Writings.* New York: Century Company, 1894.

Our President: From the Atlantic to the Pacific, 1891. Kansas City, Mo.: Hudson Kimberg Publishing Company, 1891.

Paget, R. L. (ed.), *McKinley's Masterpieces: Selections from the Public Addresses in and out of Congress of William McKinley.* Boston: Joseph Knight Company, 1896.

Parker, George F. (ed.), *The Writings and Speeches of Grover Cleveland.* New York: Cassell Publishing Company, 1892.

The Public Papers and Addresses of Benjamin Harrison, 1889–1893. Washington, D.C.: Government Printing Office, 1893.

Randall, James G., and Theodore C. Pease (eds.), *The Diary of Orville Hickman Browning, 1850–1864.* Vols. XX, XXII of the *Collections* of the Illinois State Historical Library, Lincoln Series, II. Springfield: Illinois State Historical Library, 1927.

Richardson, James Daniel (comp.), *A Compilation of the Messages and Papers of the Presidents, 1789–1897.* 10 vols. Washington, D.C.: Government Printing Office, 1896–1900.

Roosevelt, Theodore, *The Negro Question: Attitude of the Progressive Party Toward the Colored Race. . . .* New York: Mail and Express Job Print, Stoddard Sutherland Press, 1912.

——, *Theodore Roosevelt's Diaries of His Boyhood and Youth.* New York: Charles Scribner's Sons, 1928.

——, *An Autobiography*. New York: Macmillan Company, 1913.

——, *Report . . . Made to the United States Civil Service Commission Upon a Visit to Certain Indian Reservations and Indian Schools in South Dakota, Nebraska and Kansas*. Philadelphia: Indian Rights Association, 1893.

——, *Addresses and President Messages of Theodore Roosevelt, 1902–1904*. New York: G. P. Putnam's Sons, 1904.

——, *The Works of Theodore Roosevelt* (National Edition). 20 vols. New York: Charles Scribner's Sons, 1926.

——, *Letters* (selected and edited by Elting E. Morison). 8 vols. Cambridge: Harvard University Press, 1951–1954.

——, *The Winning of the West* (New Knickerbocker Edition). 4 vols. New York: G. P. Putnam's Sons, 1889, 1891, 1896, 1917.

Rubin, Louis D. Jr. (ed.), *Teach the Freeman: The Correspondence of Rutherford B. Hayes and the Slater Fund for Negro Education, 1881–1887*. 2 vols. Baton Rouge: Louisiana State University Press, 1959.

Shriver, John S., *Through the South and West with the President* [Harrison] *April 14th, May 15th, 1891*. New York: Mail and Express, 1891.

Speech of Governor Andrew Johnson on the Restoration of State Government. Delivered at the meeting held in the Hall of the House of Representatives, Thursday evening, January 21, 1864, to take initial steps to restore civil government in Tennessee. Nashville: *Dispatch* Printing Company, 1864.

Speeches and Addresses of William McKinley. New York: D. Appleton and Company, 1893.

Speeches and Addresses of William McKinley, March 1, 1897–May 30, 1900. New York: Doubleday and McClure Company, 1900.

Speeches and Letters of Abraham Lincoln, 1832–1865. New York: E. P. Dutton and Company, 1907.

State of New York, *Public Papers of Theodore Roosevelt, Governor, 1899*. 2 vols. Albany: Brandow Printing Company, 1899, 1900.

Summers, Festus P., *The Cabinet Diary of William L. Wilson, 1893–1896*. Chapel Hill: University of North Carolina Press, 1957.

Swinging Round the Circle or Andy's Trip to the West. Petroleum V. Nasby (ed.). New York: American News Company, 1866.

William, Charles (ed.), *Diary and Letters of Rutherford B. Hayes*. 5 vols. Columbus: Ohio State Archaeological and Historical Society, 1925, 1926.

Young, John Russell, *Around the World with General Grant. . . .* 2 vols. New York: American News Company, 1879.

Primary Source Materials on Race

Abolition Is National Death: Of the Attempt to Equalize the Races the Destruction of Society. New York: Van Evrie Horton and Company, 1868.

Adams, Charles Francis, "The Doctrine of Equality and the Race Problem," Vol. 4 of *Great Debates in American History,* ed. Marian Miller. New York: Current History Publishers, 1913.

Baker, Ray Stannard, *Following the Color Line: An Account of Negro Citizenship in the American Democracy.* New York: Doubleday, Page and Company, 1908.

Browne, P. A., *The Classification of Mankind by the Hair and Wool of Their Heads, with an Answer to Dr. Prichard's Assertion that the Covering on the Head of the Negro is Hair, Properly so Termed and not Wool.* Philadelphia: A. Hunt, 1850.

Bruce, Phillip Alexander, *The Plantation Negro as a Freedman: Observations of His Character, Condition and Prospects in Virginia.* New York: G. P. Putnam's Sons, 1889.

Bryce, James, *The American Commonwealth.* 2 vols. New York: The Macmillan Company, 1888.

Burmeister, Karl Hermann, *The Black Man: The Comparative Anatomy and Psychology of the African Negro.* Translated by Julian Freidlander and Robert Tomes. New York: W. C. Bryant and Company, 1853.

Campbell, John, *Negro Mania.* Philadelphia: Campbell and Power, 1851.

Carnegie, Andrew, *The Negro in America.* An address delivered before the Philosophical Institution of Edinburgh. Cheyney, Pa.: Committee of Twelve, 1907.

Douglass, Frederick, *U. S. Grant and the Colored People: His Wise, Just, Practical and Effective Friendship Thoroughly Vindicated by Incontestable Facts in His Record from 1862 to 1872.* Washington, D.C.: [no publisher], 1872. Copy in the Rutherford B. Hayes Memorial Library, Fremont, Ohio.

Estlin, J. B., *A Brief Notice of American Slavery and the Abolitionist Movement.* London: Leeds Anti-Slavery Association, William Tweedie, 1846, 1853.

Fisk, General Clinton B., *Plain Counsels for Freedmen in Sixteen Brief Lectures*. Boston: American Tract Society, 1866.

Gilman, Daniel, "A Study in Black and White: An Address at the Opening of the Armstrong Slater Trade School Building," *Occasional Papers*. No. 10, Baltimore: Trustees of the John F. Slater Fund, 1897.

Hall, G. Stanley, "A Few Results of Recent Scientific Study of the Negro in America," Massachusetts Historical Society *Proceedings*, 2nd Series, 19:95–107, 1905.

Jacobs, C. W., *The Free Negro Question in Maryland*. Baltimore: John W. Wood, Printer, 1859.

Johnston, Sir Harry, *Views and Reviews: From the Outlook of an Anthropologist*. London: William and Newgate, 1912.

Macaulay, Thomas Babington, *Critical, Historical and Miscellaneous Essays*. Vols. 5–6. New York: Hurd and Houghton, 1875.

Morgan, Thomas Jefferson, *The Negro in America and the Ideal American Republic*. Philadelphia: American Baptist Publication Society, 1898.

M. S., *The Adamic Race: Reply to Ariel, Drs. Young and Blackie on the Negro*. New York: Russell Brothers Publishers, 1868.

Ratze, Friedrich, *The History of Mankind*. 3 vols. Translated by F. S. Butler. New York: Macmillan and Company, 1896.

St. John, Oliver Star, *Moses or the Man Who Supposes Himself to Be Moses, No Moses at All* [satire of Andrew Johnson]. New York: American News Company, 1866.

Virey, Julian, *The Natural History of the Negro Race*. Translated by J. H. Guenbault. Charleston, S.C.: D. Dowling, 1837.

Von Bort, P. H., *General Grant and the Jews*. New York: National News Company, 1868.

War of the Rebellion: Official Records of the Union and Confederate Armies. Washington, D.C.: Government Printing Office, 1889.

Monographic Literature on Race

Benedict, Ruth, *Race, Science and Politics*. New York: Modern Age Books, 1940.

Buck, Paul H., *The Road to Reunion, 1865–1900*. Boston: Little, Brown and Company, 1937, 1938.

Bunche, Ralph, "Conceptions and Ideologies of the Negro Problem." New York: Schomburg Collection, New York Public Library. (Typewritten.)

Conant, Melvin, *Race Issues on the World Scene: A Report on the Conference on Race Relations in a World Perspective.* Honolulu: University of Hawaii Press, 1955.

Cornish, Dudley Taylor, *The Sable Arm: Negro Troops in the Union Army, 1861–1865.* New York: Longmans, Green and Company, 1956.

Curti, Merle, *The Growth of American Thought* (2nd edition). New York: Harper and Brothers, 1951.

Dennett, Tyler, *Roosevelt and the Russo-Japanese War: A Critical Study on American Policy in Eastern Asia in 1902–1905*, New York: Doubleday, Page and Company, 1925.

DeSantis, Vincent P., *Republicans Face the Southern Question—The New Departure Years, 1877–1897.* Johns Hopkins University Studies in History and Political Science, ser. 47, No. 1. Baltimore: Johns Hopkins Press, 1959.

Donald, David, *Lincoln Reconsidered: Essays on the Civil War Era.* New York: Alfred A. Knopf, 1956.

Eaton, Clement, *Freedom of Thought in the Old South.* Durham, N.C.: Duke University Press, 1940.

Franklin, John Hope, *From Slavery to Freedom.* New York: Alfred A. Knopf, 1948.

Frazier, E. Franklin, *Race and Cultural Contacts in the Modern World.* Durham: Duke University Press, 1940.

Handlin, Oscar, *Race and Nationality in American Life* (revised edition). Boston: Little, Brown and Company, 1957.

Harris, Norman Dwight, *History of Negro Slavery in Illinois and the Slavery Agitation in that State.* Chicago: University of Chicago Press, 1904.

Hart, A. B., *Slavery and Abolition*, Vol. 16 of *The American Nation: A History.* Edited by A. B. Hart. 28 vols. New York: Harper and Brothers, 1906.

Hesseltine, William B., *Lincoln's Plan of Reconstruction.* Confederate Centennial Studies. Edited by William Stanley Houle. Tuscaloosa, Ala.: Confederate Publishing Company, 1960.

Hirshon, Stanley Philip, "Farewell to the Bloody Shirt: Northern Republicans and the Southern Negro, 1877–1893." Ph.D. dissertation, Columbia University, 1959.

Hofstadter, Richard, *The American Political Tradition and the Men Who Made It.* New York: Alfred A. Knopf, 1948.

——, *Social Darwinism in American Thought, 1860–1915.* Philadelphia: University of Pennsylvania Press, 1944.

Johnson, Gurion B., "A History of Racial Ideologies in the United States with Reference to the Negro." 2 vols. New York: Schomburg Collection, New York Public Library. (Typewritten.)

Lind, Andrew (ed.), *Race Relations in World Perspective: Papers Read at the Conference on Race Relations in World Perspective.* Honolulu: University of Hawaii Press, 1955.

Linton, Ralph, *The Science of Man in World Crisis.* New York: Columbia University Press, 1945.

Litwack, Leon F., *North of Slavery: The Negro in the Free States, 1790–1860.* Chicago: University of Chicago Press, 1961.

Logan, Rayford, *The Negro in American Life and Thought: The Nadir, 1877–1901.* New York: Dial Press, 1954.

Myrdal, Gunnar, *An American Dilemma: The Negro Problem and Modern Democracy.* 2 vols. New York: Harper and Brothers, 1944.

Parker, Arthur C., *The Life of General Ely S. Parker, Last Grand Sachem of the Iroquois and General Grant's Military Secretary.* Buffalo Historical Society, New York: Baker, Jones, Hausauer, Inc., 1919.

Quarles, Benjamin, *The Negro in the Civil War.* Boston: Little, Brown and Company, 1953.

Rhodes, James Ford, *A History of the United States from the Compromise of 1850.* 7 vols. New York: Macmillan and Company, 1906.

Rushmore, Elsie Mitchell, *The Indian Policy During Grant's Administration.* New York: Marion Press, 1914.

Simkins, Francis B., *The South Old and New: A History.* New York: Alfred Knopf, 1947.

Stanton, William R., *The Leopard's Spots: Scientific Attitudes Toward Race in America, 1815–1859.* Chicago: University of Chicago Press, 1960.

Tannenbaum, Frank, *Slave and Citizen: The Negro in the Americas.* New York: Vintage Books, 1946, 1963.

Ten Broek, Jacobus, *The Anti-Slavery Origins of the Fourteenth Amendment.* Berkeley: University of California Press, 1951.

Thorpe, Francis (ed.), *The Federal and State Constitutions, Colonial Charters, and Other Organic Laws. . . .* 7 vols. Washington, D.C.: Government Printing Office, 1909.

Turner, Edward R., *The Negro in Pennsylvania: Slavery, Servitude, Freedom, 1639–1869.* Washington, D.C.: American Historical Association, 1912.

United Nations Educational, Scientific and Cultural Organization, *The Race Question in Modern Science.* UNESCO, New York: Whiteside and William Morrow, 1956.

——, *The Race Question in Modern Science: The Race Concept.* Paris: UNESCO, 1952.

——, *The Race Question and Modern Thought:* Buddhism and the Race Question. Paris: UNESCO, 1948.

White, Leonard D., *The Republican Era: 1869–1901: A Study in Administrative History.* New York: Macmillan Company, 1958.

Wolf, Hazel, *On Freedom's Altar: The Martyr Complex in the Abolitionist Movement.* Madison: University of Wisconsin Press, 1957.

Woodward, C. Vann, *Reunion and Reaction: The Compromise of 1877 and the End of Reconstruction.* Boston: Little, Brown and Company, 1951.

Biographies and General Monographic Literature

Badeau, Adam, *A Military History of U. S. Grant from April 1861 to 1865.* 3 vols. New York: Appleton and Company, 1881.

Barnard, Harry, *Rutherford B. Hayes and His America.* New York: Bobbs-Merrill Company, 1954.

Beale, Howard K., *The Critical Year: A Study of Andrew Johnson and Reconstruction.* New York: Frederick Ungar Publishing Company, 1930, 1958.

——, *Theodore Roosevelt and the Rise of America to World Power.* Baltimore: Johns Hopkins Press, 1956.

Beard, Charles A., *The Presidents in American History.* New York: Julian Messner, 1935.

Bishop, Joseph B., *Theodore Roosevelt and His Times: As Shown in His Own Letters.* 2 vols. New York: Charles Scribner's Sons, 1920.

Brisbin, James S., *From the Towpath to the White House: The Early Life and Public Career of James A. Garfield.* Philadelphia: Hubbard Brothers, 1880.

Bristow, Joseph Little, *Fraud and Politics at the Turn of the Century.* New York: Expose Press, 1952.

Burgess, John W., *The Administration of President Hayes* (The Lapwell Lectures, Delivered at Kenyon College). New York: Charles Scribner's Sons, 1916.

Doyle, Burton T., and Homer H. Swaney, *Lives of James A. Garfield and Chester A. Arthur.* Washington, D.C.: Rufus H. Darby Printer and Publisher, 1881.

Foner, Phillip S. (ed.), *The Life and Writings of Frederick Douglass.* 4 vols. New York: International Publishers, 1950–1955.

Foster, Lillian, *Andrew Johnson, President of the United States: His Life and Speeches.* New York: Richardson and Company, 1866.

Halstead, Murat, *Life and Distinguished Services of William McKinley Our Martyr President.* [Chicago]: Memorial Association, 1901.

Hinsdale, B. A., *President Garfield and Education.* Hiram College Memorial. Boston: James R. Osgood and Company, 1881.

Howard, James Quay, *The Life, Public Services and Selected Speeches of Rutherford B. Hayes.* Cincinnati: R. Clark and Company, 1876.

Howe, George F., *Chester A. Arthur: A Quarter Century of Machine Politics.* New York: Dodd, Mead and Company, 1934.

Howland, Edward, *Grant as a Soldier and Statesman: Being a Succinct War History of his Military and Civil Career.* Hartford: Burr, 1868.

Laski, Harold, *The American Presidency: An Interpretation.* New York: Harper and Brothers, 1940.

Leech, Margaret, *In the Days of McKinley.* New York: Harper and Brothers, 1959.

Lewis, Lloyd, *Captain Sam Grant.* Boston: Little, Brown and Company, 1950.

Lomask, Milton, *Andrew Johnson: President on Trial.* New York: Farrar, Straus and Cudahy, 1960.

Longaker, Richard P., *The Presidency and Individual Liberties.* Ithaca, N.Y.: Cornell University Press, 1961.

McCarthy, Charles H. Allen, *Lincoln's Plan of Reconstruction.* New York: McClure, Phillips and Company, 1901.

McElroy, Robert, *Grover Cleveland: The Man and the Statesman: An Authorized Biography.* 2 vols. New York: Harper and Brothers, 1923.

McKitrick, Eric L., *Andrew Johnson and Reconstruction.* Chicago: University of Chicago Press, 1960.

McPherson, Edward, *The Political History of the United States of America During the Period of Reconstruction. . . .* Washington, D.C.: Solomons and Chapman, 1880.

Mannheim, Karl, *Ideology and Utopia: An Introduction to the Sociology of Knowledge.* New York: Harcourt, Brace and Company, 1936.

Merrill, Horace Samuel, *Bourbon Leader: Grover Cleveland and the Democratic Party.* Boston: Little, Brown and Company, 1957.

Milton, George Fort, *The Uses of Presidential Power, 1789–1943.* Boston: Little, Brown and Company, 1944.

Ogilvie, J. S. (ed.), *Life and Speeches of William McKinley. . . .* New York: Ogilvie Publishing Company, 1896.

Pollard, James E., *The Presidents and the Press.* New York: Macmillan Company, 1947.

Porter, Horace, *Campaigning with Grant.* New York: Century Company, 1897.

Pringle, Henry F., *Theodore Roosevelt: A Biography.* New York: Harcourt, Brace and Company, 1931.

Quarles, Arthur Benjamin, *Lincoln and the Negro.* New York: Oxford University Press, 1962.

Randall, J. G., and Richard N. Current, *Last Full Measure.* New York: Dodd, Mead and Company, 1955.

Rhodes, James Ford, *The McKinley and Roosevelt Administrations, 1897–1909.* New York: Macmillan Company, 1922.

Rich, Bennett Milton, *The Presidents and Civil Disorder.* Washington, D.C.: Brookings Institution, 1941.

Savage, John, *The Life and Public Services of Andrew Johnson . . . including his State Papers, Speeches . . . Addresses. . . .* New York: Darby, 1865.

Sawyer, John J., *Life of Andrew Johnson.* Greenville: Eastern Tennessee Publishing Company, 1901.

Sievers, Harry Joseph, *Benjamin Harrison: Hoosier Warrior Through the Civil War Years, 1833–1865.* New York: University Publishers, Inc., 1952.

Smith, Theodore Clarke (ed.), *The Life and Letters of James Abram Garfield.* 2 vols. New Haven: Yale University Press, 1925.

Stoddard, William, *The Lives of Presidents Rutherford B. Hayes, James Abram Garfield and Chester Alan Arthur.* New York: Frederick A. Stokes and Brother, 1889.

Periodical Literature

Arendt, Hannah, "Race Thinkers Before Racism," *The Review of Politics,* 6:36–73, January 1944.

Armstrong, S. C., "Work and Duty in the East," *The American Missionary,* 26:378–80, December 1882.

Ashley, W. H., "Education of the Mexican," Journal of the *Proceedings* and Addresses of the National Education Association, 6–15, 1886.

Ashmore, Harry, "The Durable Issue," *The American Scholar,* 30:555–58, Autumn 1961.

Atkinson, W. Y., "The Atlanta Exposition," *North American Review,* 161:305–93, October 1895.

Baldwin, S. L., "The Education of the Mongolian 'Chinese,'" Journal of the *Proceedings* and Addresses of the National Education Association, 211–31, 1886.

Barrows, Isabel C. (ed.), *The First Mohonk Conference on the Negro Question: Held at Lake Mohonk, Ulster County, New York, June 4, 5, 6, 1890.* Boston: George H. Ellis, Printer, 1890.

Bartholomew, W. H., "Educational Work Among the Colored Race," Journal of the *Proceedings* and Addresses of the National Education Association, 229–31, 1886.

Berthoff, Rowland T., "Southern Attitudes Toward Immigration, 1865–1914," *Journal of Southern History,* 17:328–62, August 1951.

Blumentritte, Ferdinand, "Race Questions in the Philippine Islands," *Popular Science Monthly,* 55:472–80, August 1899.

Blyden, Edward W., "The African Problem," *North American Review,* 161:327–99, September 1895.

Boas, Franz, "Human Faculty Determined by Race," American Association for the Advancement of Science, *Proceedings,* 43: 301–27, 1894.

Brademas, John, "An Apology for Politics," *The American Scholar,* 30:559–62, Autumn 1961.

Broughton, Willis, "The Negro's Place in History," *Arena,* 16:612–21, September 1896.

Bryce, James, "Thoughts on the Negro Problem," *North American Review,* 153:641–60, December 1891.

Carter, Hugh, "Reappraising Our Immigration Policy," *Annals* of the American Academy of Political and Social Science, 261:185–92, March 1949.

Clarke, James B., "The Negro and the Immigrant in the Americas: An International Aspect of the Color Problem," *Annals* of the American Academy of Political and Social Science, 49:32–37, September 1913.

"Consistency and Inconsistency in Intergroup Relations," *Journal of Social Issues,* 5:1, 1949.

Count, Earl, "The Evolution of the Race Idea in Modern Western Culture During the Period of Pre-Darwinian Nineteenth Century," *Transactions,* New York Academy of Sciences, 8:139–65, January 1946.

Cravath, E. M., "The Higher Education of the Negro," *American Missionary,* 26:370–72, December 1882.

Culp, D. W., "The Past and Future of the American Negro," *Arena,* 17:789–92, April 1897.

Curry, J. M., "The Negro Question," *Popular Science Monthly,* 55:177–85, June 1899.

Davies, Wallace, "The Problem of Race Relations in the Grand Army of the Republic," *Journal of Southern History,* 13:355–72, August 1947.

Dawes, H. L., "Have We Failed with the Indians?" *Atlantic Monthly,* 84:280–85, July–December 1899.

Fairchild, Henry Pratt, "Public Opinion on Immigration," *Annals* of the American Academy of Political and Social Science, 262:185–92, March 1949.

Green, John C., "The American Debate on the Negro's Place in Nature," 1780–1815, *Journal of the History of Ideas,* 15:384–96, 1954.

———, "Some Early Speculations on the Origin of Human Races, *American Anthropologist,* 56:31–41, February 1954.

Gunby, A. A., "General Statement on the [Race] Problem," Journal of the *Proceedings* and Addresses of the National Education Association, 254–66, 1890.

Harvey, Charles M., "The Louisiana Exposition in World Perspective," *Atlantic Monthly,* 84:549–57, October 1899.

Hass, Theodore, "The Legal Aspects of Indian Affairs from 1887 to 1957," *Annals* of the American Academy of Political and Social Science, 311:12–28, May 1957.

Hunt, J. A., "On the Negro's Place in Nature," *Anthropological Review*, 2:15–16, November 1863.

Johnson, Gurion B., "Southern Paternalism Towards Negroes After Emancipation," *1865–1914 Journal of Southern History*, 23:483–509, November 1957.

McCurly, W. S., "Impossibility of Race Amalgamation," *Arena*, 21:446–55, April 1899.

McNickle, D'arcy, "Indian and European Relations from Discovery Down to 1887," *Annals* of the American Academy of Political and Social Science, 311:12–28, May 1957.

Masuoko, J., and R. Yokely, "Essential Structural Requisites in Race Relations," *Social Forces*, 33:30–55, October 1954.

"Race Issue in the South: Press Comment," *Public Opinion*, 8:302–65, January 1890.

"Race Problem: Editorials of the Speech of Senator Ingalls of Kansas on the Butler Emigration Bill," *Public Opinion*, 8:397–400, February 1890.

Reade, J., "Intermingling of Races," *Popular Science Monthly*, 30:336–41, January 1887.

Reuter, Edward B., "Race Theory," *Journal of Sociology*, 50:452–561, May 1945.

Richter, Melvin, "A Debate on Race: The Tocqueville-Gobineau Correspondence," *Commentary*, 25:151–60, January 1958.

Riddleberger, Patrick W., "The Radicals: Abandonment of the Negro During Reconstruction," *Journal of Negro History*, 45: 88–102, April 1960.

Ripley, William Z., "Race, Progress and Immigration," *Annals* of the American Academy of Political and Social Science, 34: 130–38, July–December 1909.

Roosevelt, Theodore [Book Review of Charles Pearson's *National Life and Character: A Forecast*], Sewanee Review, 2:353–76, May 1894.

——, "Brazil and the Negro," *Outlook*, 106:409–11, February 1914.

——, "Lynching and the Miscarriage of Justice," *Outlook*, 99:706–07, November 1911.

——, "Progressivism and the Colored Man," *Outlook*, 101:909–14, August 1912.

Ross, A. H., "The Indians," *American Missionary*, 26:377–88, December 1882.

Royce, Josiah, "Race Questions and Prejudices," *International Journal of Ethics*, 16:265–88, April 1906.

Royer, Madame Clemence, "The Mental Faculties of Monkeys," *Popular Science Monthly*, 30:17–24, November 1886.

Ruffner, W. H., "The Co-Education of the White and Colored Races," *Scribner's Monthly*, 8:86–90, May 1864.

Saveth, Edward N., "Race and Nationalism in American Historiography," *Political Science Quarterly*, 54:421–41, 1939.

Schafer, Boyd C., "Men Are More Alike," *American Historical Review*, 57:593–612, April 1962.

Scheiner, Seth M., "President Theodore Roosevelt and the Negro, 1901–1908," *Journal of Negro History*, 47:169–82, July 1962.

Scheips, Paul J., "Lincoln and the Chiriqui Colonization Project," *Journal of Negro History*, 37:418–53, October 1952.

Shaler, Nathaniel S., "Scientific Aspects of the Negro," *Public Opinion*, 18:147, February 1895.

Shannon, Fred, "The Federal Government and the Negro Soldier, 1861–1865," *Journal of Negro History*, 11:563–83, October 1926.

Snowden, Frank M., Jr., "The Negro in Ancient Greece," *American Anthropologist*, 50:31–41, 1948.

Taylor, Joseph, "The Restriction of European Immigration and the Concept of Race," *South Atlantic Quarterly*, 50:25–37, January 1951.

Tinsley, James A., "Roosevelt, Foraker, and the Brownsville Affray," *Journal of Negro History*, 41:43–65, January 1956.

Wesley, Charles, "The Concept of Negro Inferiority in American Thought," *Journal of Negro History*, 25:540–60, October 1940.

Dictionaries, Encyclopedias, and General Reference Works

Commager, Henry Steele (ed.), *Documents of American History*. New York: F. S. Crofts and Company, 1938.

Craigie, William A., and James R. Hulbert, A *Dictionary of American English on Historical Principles*. 4 vols. Chicago: University of Chicago Press, 1902.

Harris, Abraham, and Sterling Spero, "The Negro Problem," *Encyclopedia of the Social Sciences*, XI, 335–36. New York: Macmillan Company, 1933.

Lippmann, Walter, *Public Opinion.* New York: Harcourt, Brace and Company, 1922.

MacCoby, Eleanor E., et al., *Readings in Social Psychology.* 2nd edition. New York: Henry Holt and Company, 1958.

Mathews, Mitford M., *A Dictionary of Americanisms on Historical Principles.* 2 vols. Chicago: University of Chicago Press, 1957.

Murry, James A. H., *A New English Dictionary on Historical Principles.* 10 vols. Oxford: Clarendon Press, 1914.

Ogburn, William, and Meyer Nimkoff, *Sociology.* Boston: Houghton Mifflin and Company, 1950.

Work, Monroe N., *A Bibliography of the Negro in Africa and America.* New York: H. W. Wilson Company, 1928.

Personal Library of Rutherford B. Hayes, Hayes Memorial Library, Fremont, Ohio

The Black Question

Baskervill, William M., and W. M. Beckner, *Shall the Negro Be Educated or Suppressed? A Symposium on Dr. Haygood's Reply to Senator Eutis's Paper on Race Antagonism.* Nashville: Open Letter Club, 1889.

Blair, Francis Preston, *The Destiny of the Races of This Continent: An Address Delivered Before the Mercantile Library.* New York: Buell and Blanchard, Printers, 1859.

"Education of the Freedmen—1882–1893," Organizations and *Proceedings* of the Trustees of the John Slater Fund, Inc.

Hartzell, J. C., "The Negro Exodus," *Methodist Quarterly Review,* 31, October 1879. [A reprint.]

Haygood, Atticus Greene, *Our Brother in Black, His Freedom and His Future.* New York: Phillips and Hunt, 1881.

———, *Pleas for Progress.* Nashville: Publishing House of the Methodist Episcopal Church South, 1889.

Morris, Charles S., "The Nation and the Negro," *The* [Cleveland] *Plain Dealer,* January 16, 1891.

Negro Problem: Decision by the Court of Public Opinion, 1878. [An account of a discussion held at the Colored Lincoln University, Chester County, Pennsylvania.]

Nells, William Cooper, *The Colored Patriots of the American Revolution, with Sketches of Several Distinguished Colored Persons: To Which Is Added a Brief Survey of the Conditions and Prospects of Colored Americans.* Boston: R. F. Wallcutt, 1885.

Open Letter Club, *A Reply to Senator Eutis's Letter on Race Antagonism.* [A reprint from *The Forum.* No date of publication.]

Stetson, George Rockford, *The Southern Negro as He Is.* Boston: Press of G. H. Ellis, 1877.

Whipple, Henry Benjamin, *Sermon Preached Before the Society for the Promotion of Church Work Among the Colored People.* Baltimore: Press of Frederick A. Hahzscage, 1877.

Williams, George Washington, *History of the Negro Race in America from 1619 to 1880. Negroes as Slaves, as Soldiers, and as Citizens; Together with a Preliminary Consideration of the Unity of the Human Family. . . .* 2 vols. New York: G. P. Putnam's Sons, 1883.

The Chinese Question

Becker, Samuel E. W., *Humors of a Congressional Investigating Committee: A Review of the Report of the Joint Special Committee to Investigate Chinese Immigration.* Washington, D.C.: [no publisher], 1877.

Boalt, John H., *The Chinese Question: A Paper Read Before the Berkley Club. . . . August, 1877.* San Francisco: [no publisher], 1877.

Gibson, Otis, *The Chinese in America.* Cincinnati: Hitchcock and Walden, 1877.

Layres, Augustus, *Facts Upon the Other Side of the Chinese Question: With a Memorial to the President of the United States from Representative Chinamen in America.* [No place of publication, no publisher], 1876.

Meade, Edwin R., *The Chinese Question: A Paper Read at the Annual Meeting of the Social Science Association of America.* New York: Arthur and Bonnell, 1877.

Sawtelle, Mrs. Mary P., . . . *The Foul, Contagious Disease. A Phase of the Chinese Question. How Chinese Women Are*

Infusing a Poison Into the Anglo-Saxon Blood. [A reprint of an article taken from the *Medico Literary Journal.*] 1:[no pages], November 1878.

Six Chinese Companies, *Memorial of the Six Chinese Companies: An Address to the Senate and House of Representatives of the United States.* Testimony of California's Leading Citizens Before the Joint Special Congressional Committee. San Francisco: [no publisher], 1887.

Speer, William, *The Oldest and the Newest Empire: China and the United States.* Philadelphia: Parmalee and Company, 1870.

Star, J. B., *The Coming Struggle: Or What the People of the Pacific Coast Think of the Coolie Invasion.* San Francisco: Bacon and Company, 1873.

U. S. Circuit Court, 9th Circuit, . . . *Rights of Chinese. Opinions of Honorable Lorenzo Sawyer . . . and Honorable Ogden Hoffman.* California: [no publisher], 1880.

Index

·7